5 ♥ Alice IN THE COUNTRY OF Hearts

Volume 5

Created by
QuinRose X Soumei Hoshino

HAMBURG // LONDON // LOS ANGELES // TOKYO

Alice in the Country of Hearts Volume 5
Created by QuinRose X Soumei Hoshino

Translation - Beni Axia Conrad
English Adaptation - Lianne Sentar
Copy Editor - Hope Donovan
Retouch and Lettering - Star Print Brokers
Production Artist - Rui Kyo
Graphic Designer - Al-Insan Lashley

Editor - Cindy Suzuki
Print Production Manager - Lucas Rivera
Managing Editor - Vy Nguyen
Senior Designer - Louis Csontos
Art Director - Al-Insan Lashley
Director of Sales and Manufacturing - Allyson De Simone
Associate Publisher - Marco F. Pavia
President and C.O.O. - John Parker
C.E.O. and Chief Creative Officer - Stu Levy

A **TOKYOPOP** Manga

TOKYOPOP and 🙂 are trademarks or registered trademarks of TOKYOPOP Inc.

TOKYOPOP Inc.
5900 Wilshire Blvd. Suite 2000
Los Angeles, CA 90036

E-mail: info@TOKYOPOP.com
Come visit us online at www.TOKYOPOP.com

ISBN: 978-1-4278-3147-7

First TOKYOPOP printing: November 2010
10 9 8 7 6 5 4 3 2 1
Printed in the USA

Alice in the Country of Hearts

ハートの国のアリス

~ Wonderful Wonder World ~

5

QuinRose × Soumei Hoshino

ハートの国のアリス
~ Wonderful Wonder World ~

5

CONTENTS

♥25 Dance Lesson

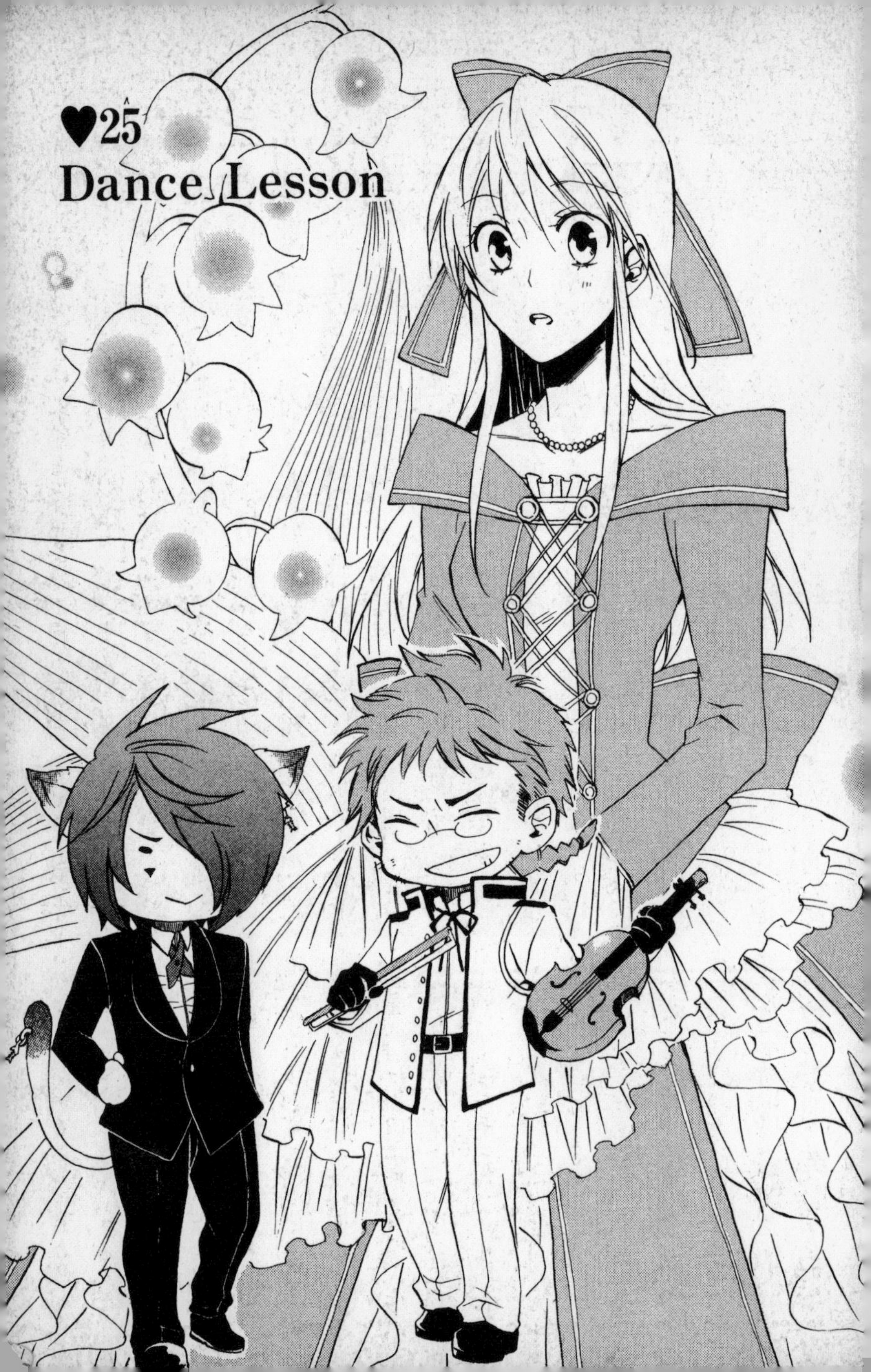

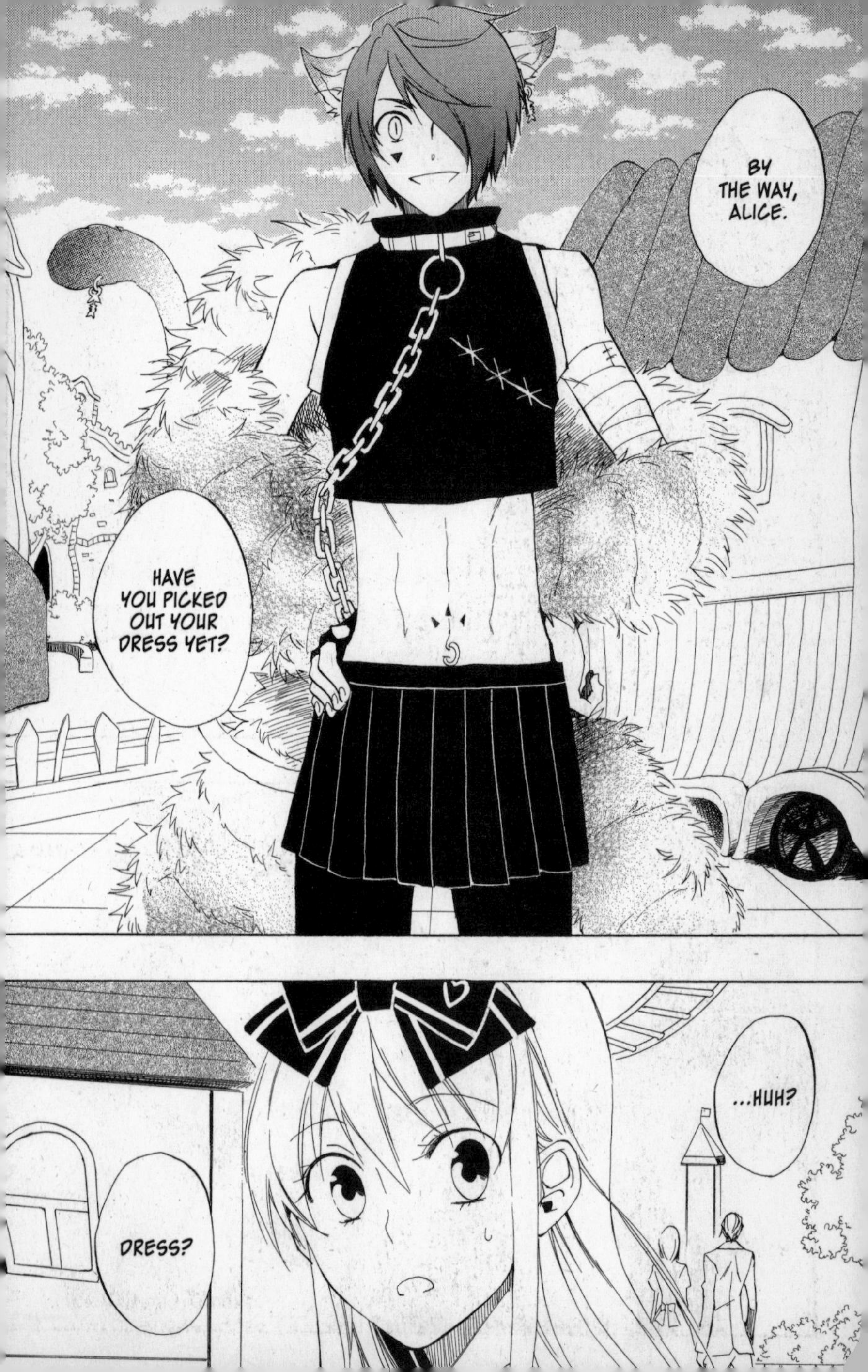
BY THE WAY, ALICE.
HAVE YOU PICKED OUT YOUR DRESS YET?
...HUH?
DRESS?

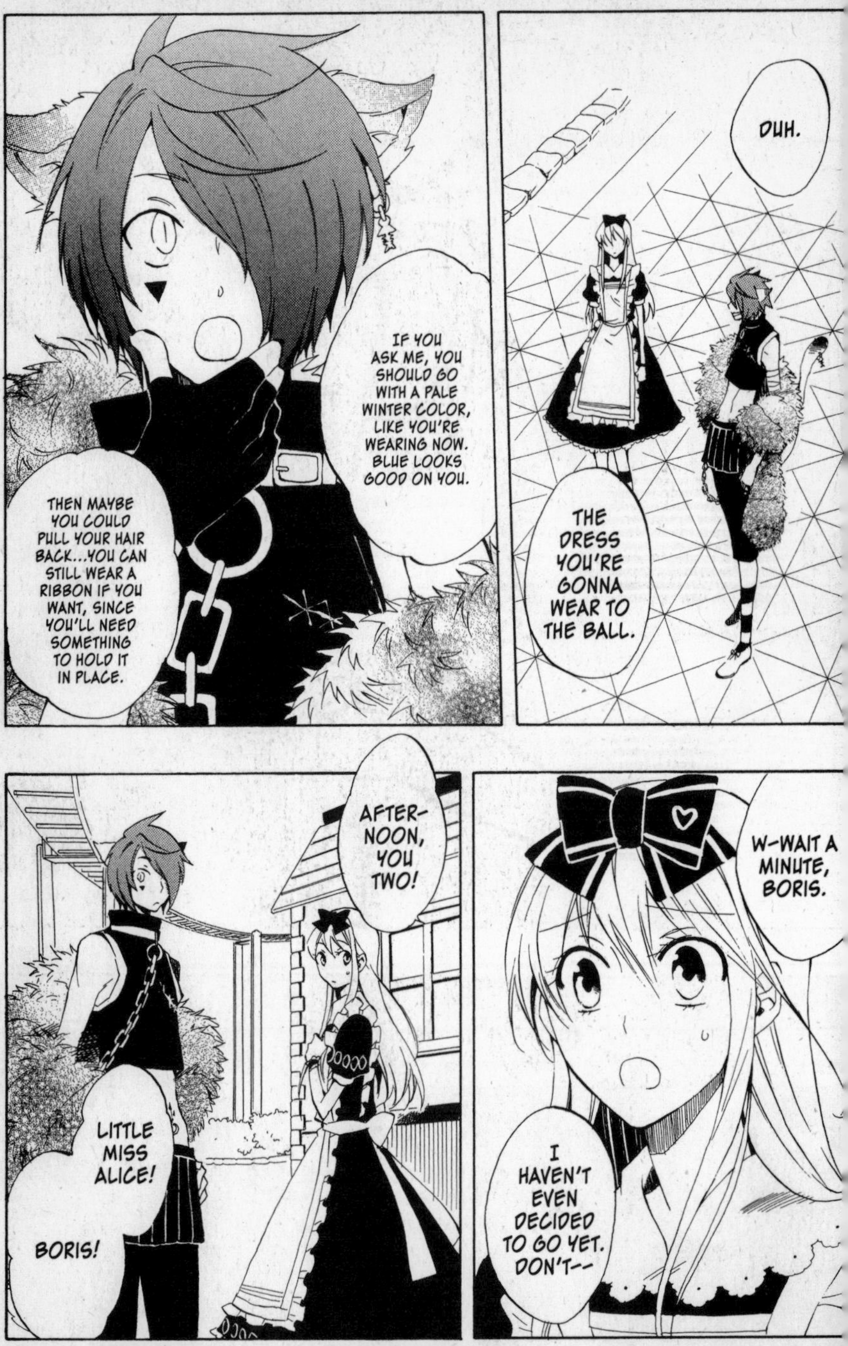
DUH.
THE DRESS YOU'RE GONNA WEAR TO THE BALL.
IF YOU ASK ME, YOU SHOULD GO WITH A PALE WINTER COLOR, LIKE YOU'RE WEARING NOW. BLUE LOOKS GOOD ON YOU.
THEN MAYBE YOU COULD PULL YOUR HAIR BACK...YOU CAN STILL WEAR A RIBBON IF YOU WANT, SINCE YOU'LL NEED SOMETHING TO HOLD IT IN PLACE.
W-WAIT A MINUTE, BORIS.
I HAVEN'T EVEN DECIDED TO GO YET. DON'T--
AFTER-NOON, YOU TWO!
LITTLE MISS ALICE!
BORIS!

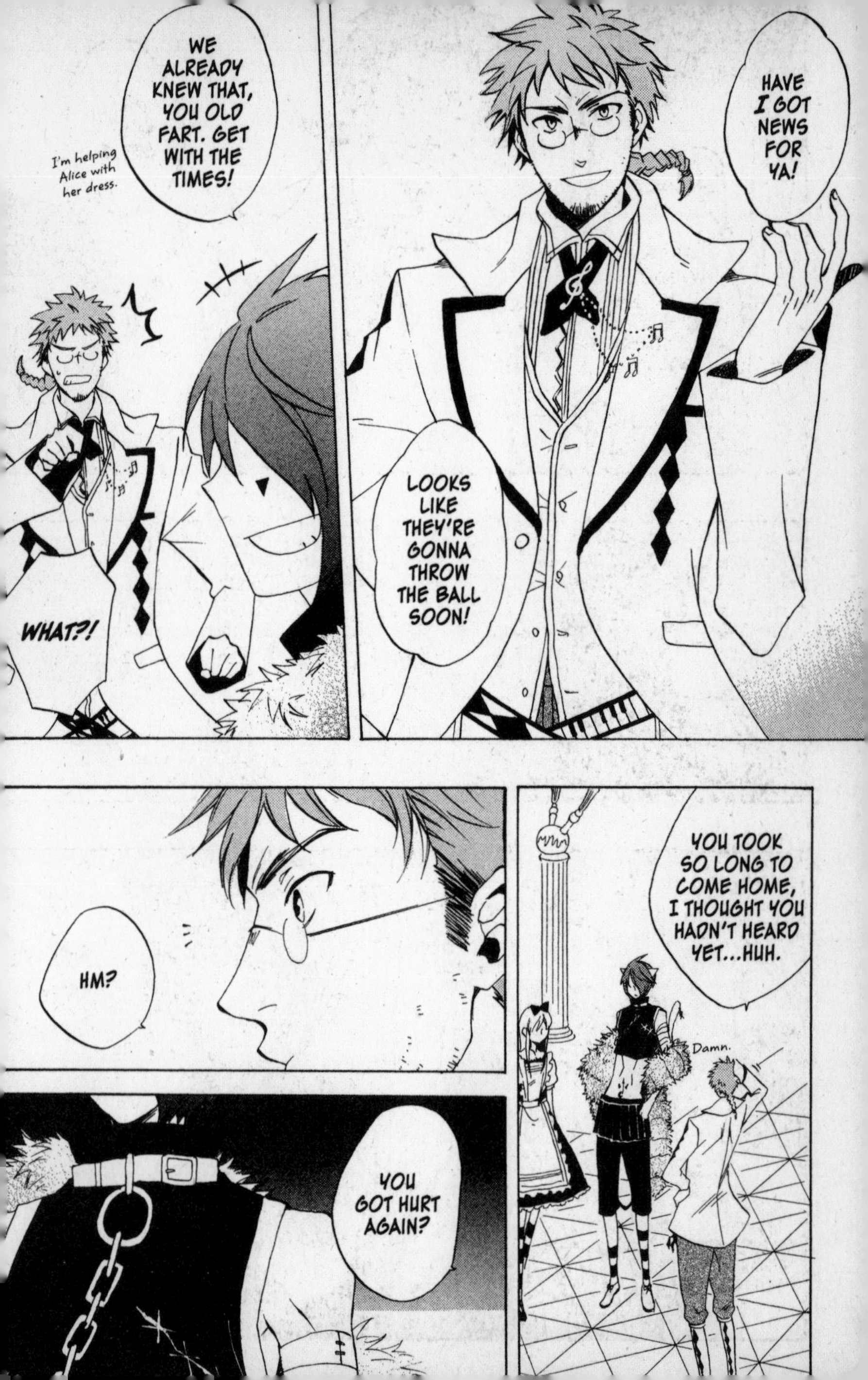
HAVE I GOT NEWS FOR YA!
LOOKS LIKE THEY'RE GONNA THROW THE BALL SOON!
WE ALREADY KNEW THAT, YOU OLD FART. GET WITH THE TIMES!
I'm helping Alice with her dress.
WHAT?!
YOU TOOK SO LONG TO COME HOME, I THOUGHT YOU HADN'T HEARD YET...HUH.
Damn.
HM?
YOU GOT HURT AGAIN?

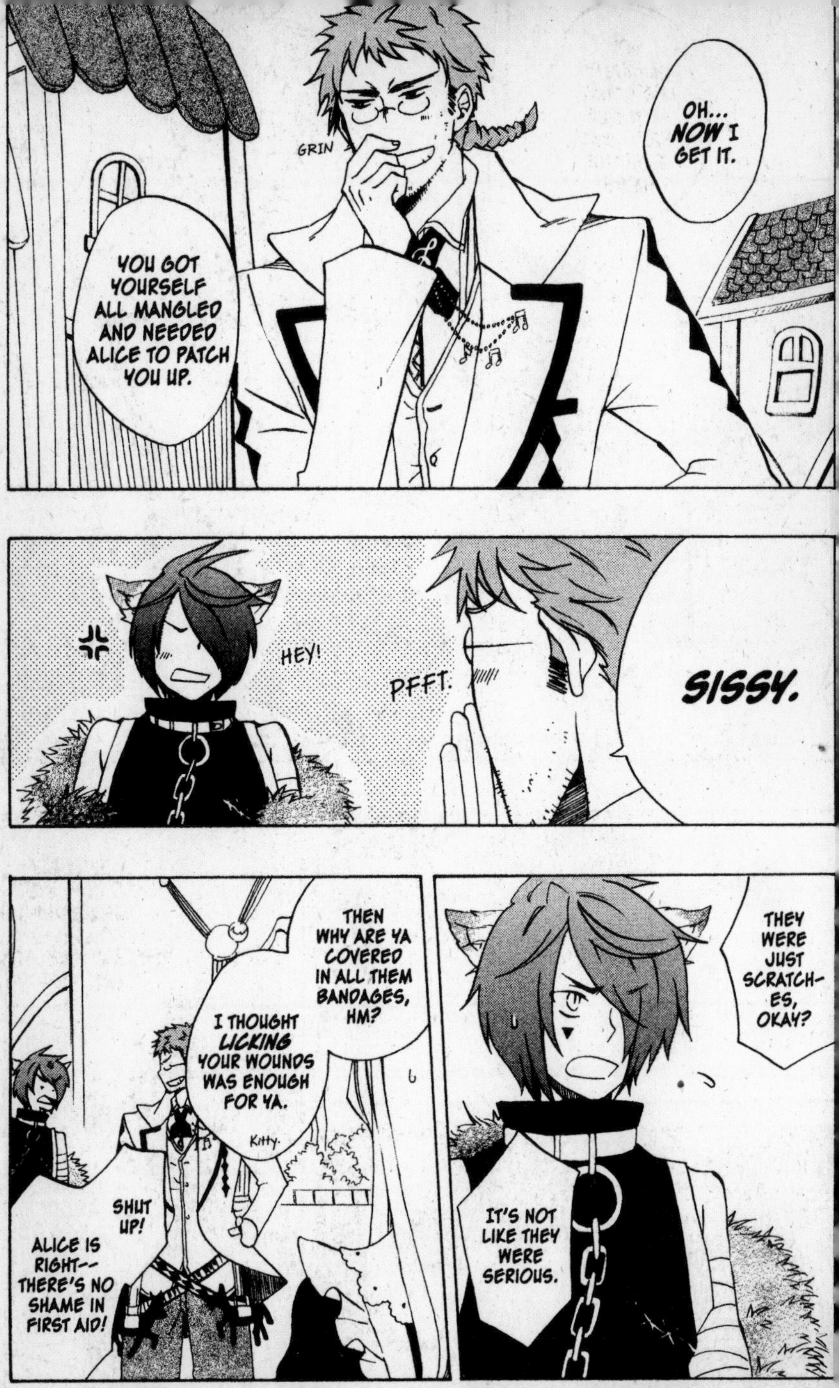
OH... *NOW* I GET IT.
GRIN
YOU GOT YOURSELF ALL MANGLED AND NEEDED ALICE TO PATCH YOU UP.
SISSY.
PFFT.
HEY!
THEY WERE JUST SCRATCH-ES, OKAY?
IT'S NOT LIKE THEY WERE SERIOUS.
THEN WHY ARE YA COVERED IN ALL THEM BANDAGES, HM?
I THOUGHT *LICKING* YOUR WOUNDS WAS ENOUGH FOR YA.
Kitty.
SHUT UP!
ALICE IS RIGHT-- THERE'S NO SHAME IN FIRST AID!

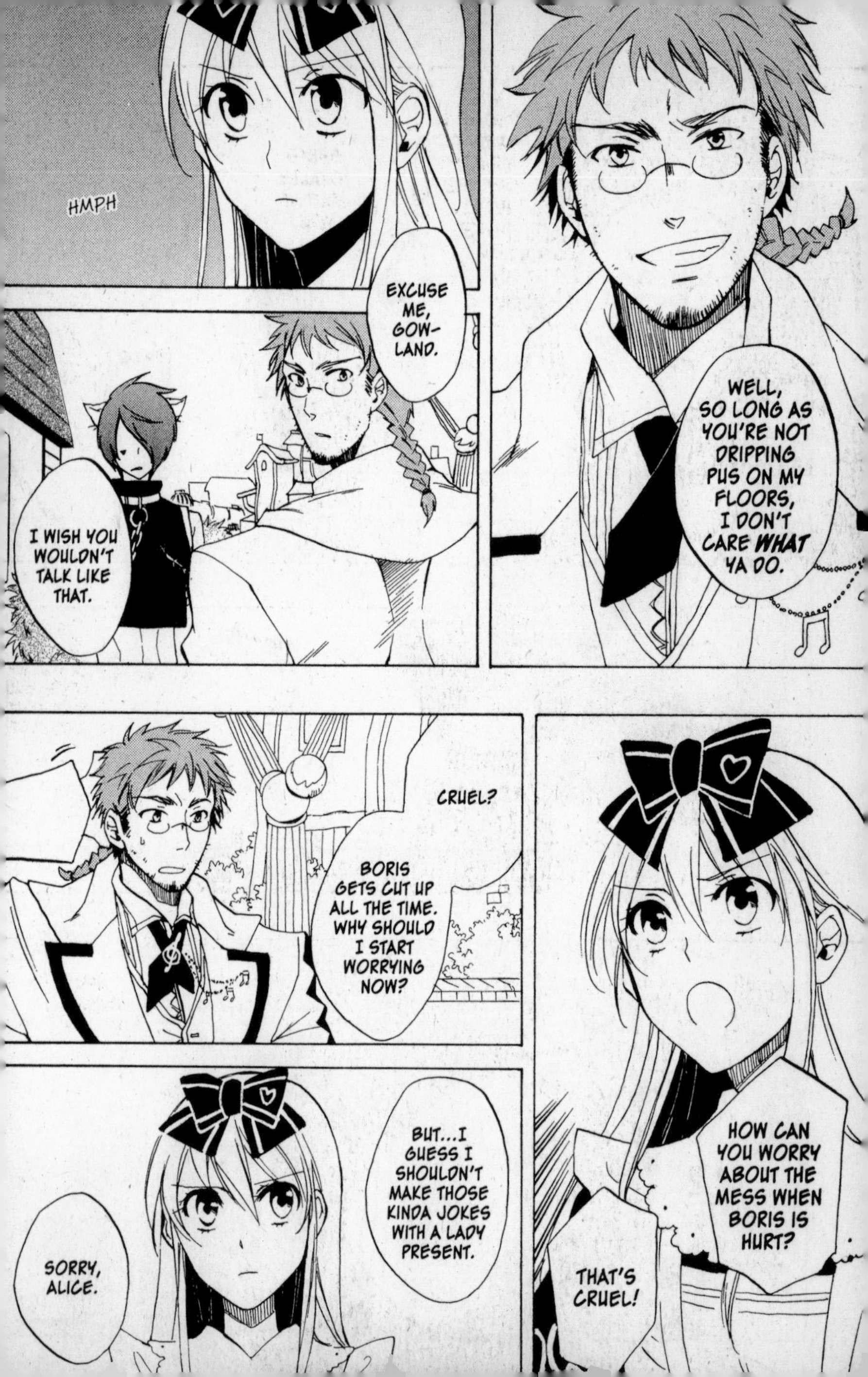
WELL, SO LONG AS YOU'RE NOT DRIPPING PUS ON MY FLOORS, I DON'T CARE *WHAT* YA DO.
HMPH
EXCUSE ME, GOW-LAND.
I WISH YOU WOULDN'T TALK LIKE THAT.
HOW CAN YOU WORRY ABOUT THE MESS WHEN BORIS IS HURT?
THAT'S CRUEL!
CRUEL?
BORIS GETS CUT UP ALL THE TIME. WHY SHOULD I START WORRYING NOW?
BUT...I GUESS I SHOULDN'T MAKE THOSE KINDA JOKES WITH A LADY PRESENT.
SORRY, ALICE.

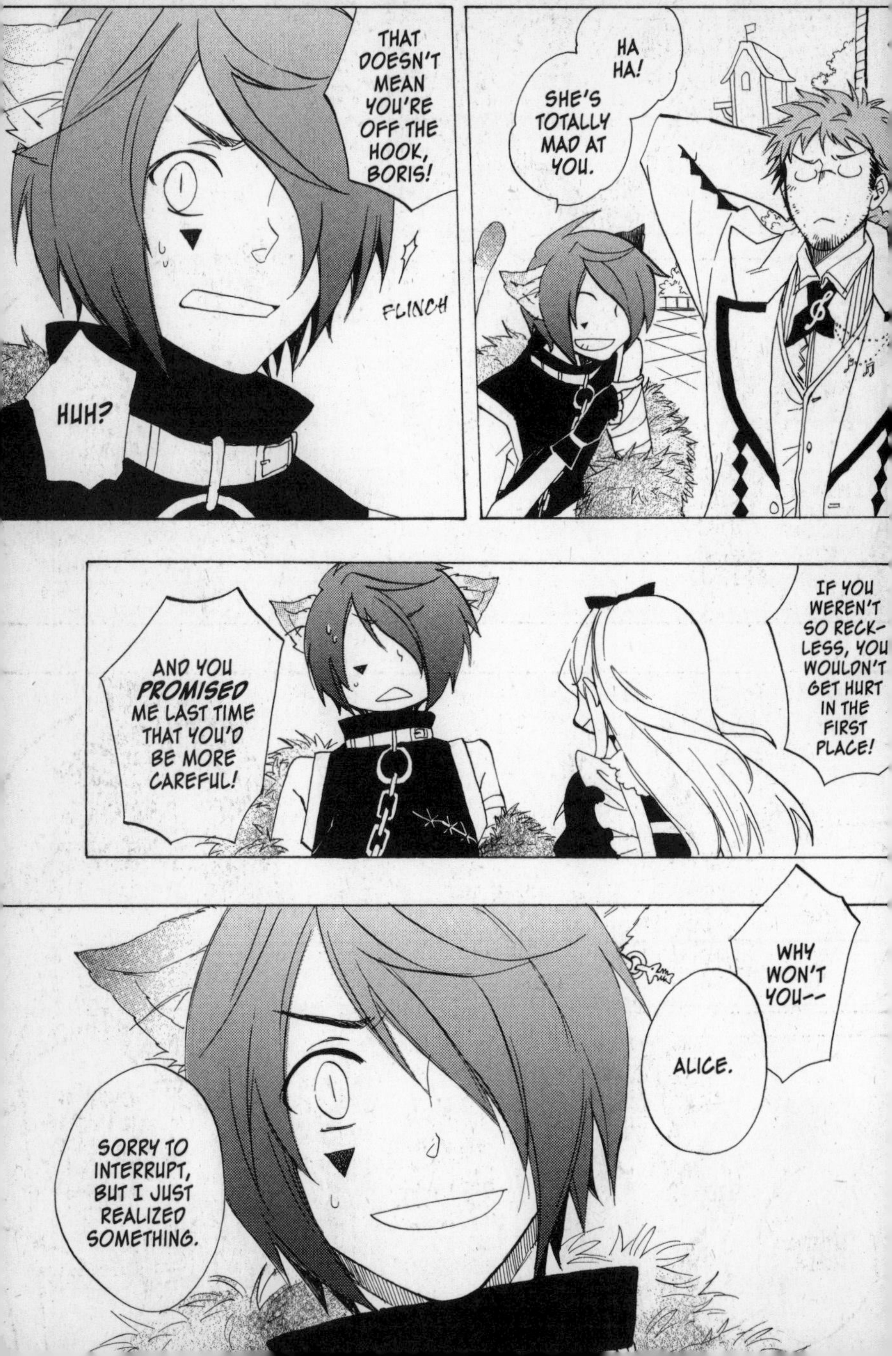
HA HA!
SHE'S TOTALLY MAD AT YOU.
THAT DOESN'T MEAN YOU'RE OFF THE HOOK, BORIS!
FLINCH
HUH?
IF YOU WEREN'T SO RECK-LESS, YOU WOULDN'T GET HURT IN THE FIRST PLACE!
AND YOU PROMISED ME LAST TIME THAT YOU'D BE MORE CAREFUL!
WHY WON'T YOU--
ALICE.
SORRY TO INTERRUPT, BUT I JUST REALIZED SOMETHING.

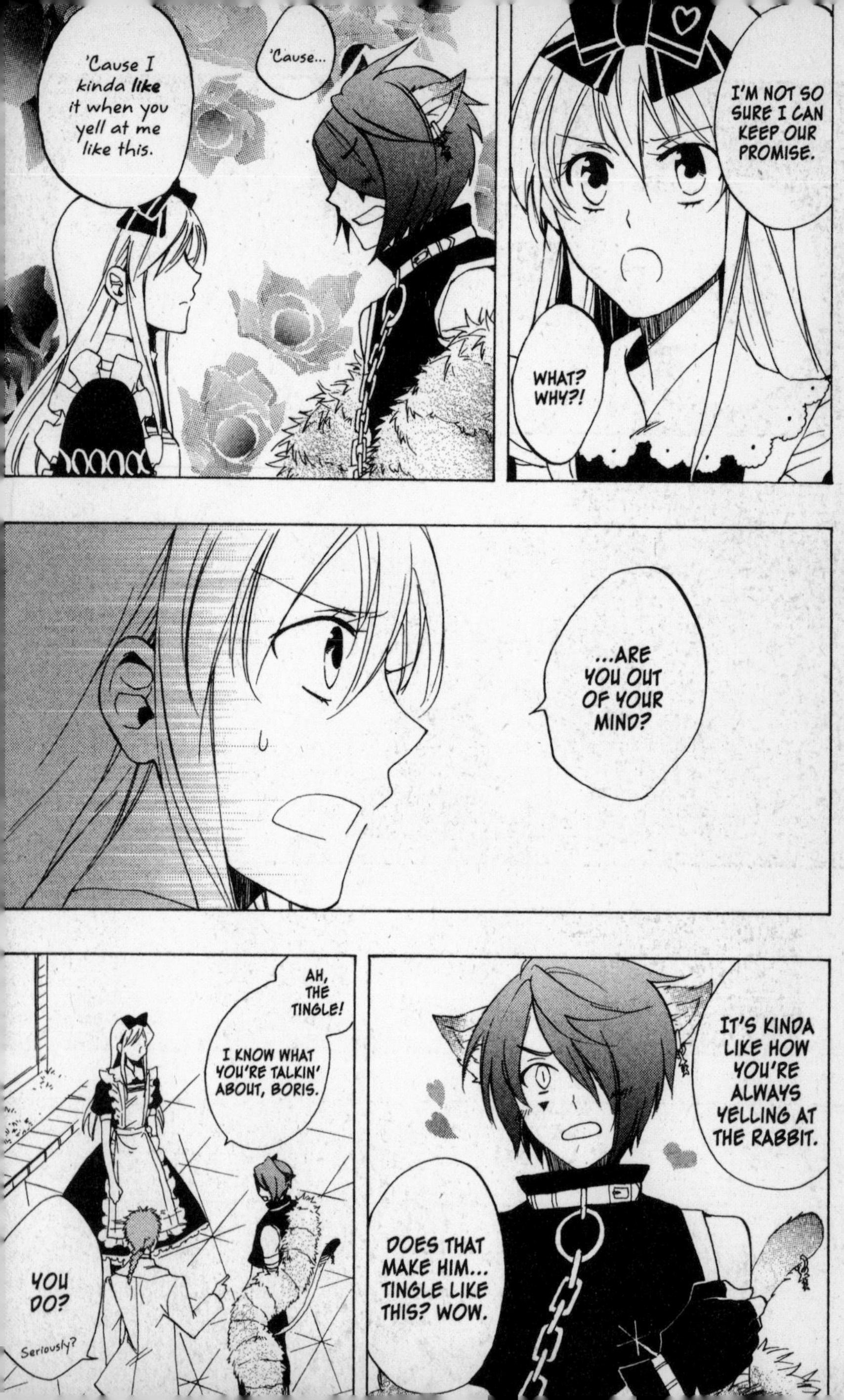
I'M NOT SO SURE I CAN KEEP OUR PROMISE.
WHAT? WHY?!
'Cause...
'Cause I kinda **like** it when you yell at me like this.
...ARE YOU OUT OF YOUR MIND?
IT'S KINDA LIKE HOW YOU'RE ALWAYS YELLING AT THE RABBIT.
DOES THAT MAKE HIM... TINGLE LIKE THIS? WOW.
AH, THE TINGLE!
I KNOW WHAT YOU'RE TALKIN' ABOUT, BORIS.
YOU DO?
Seriously?

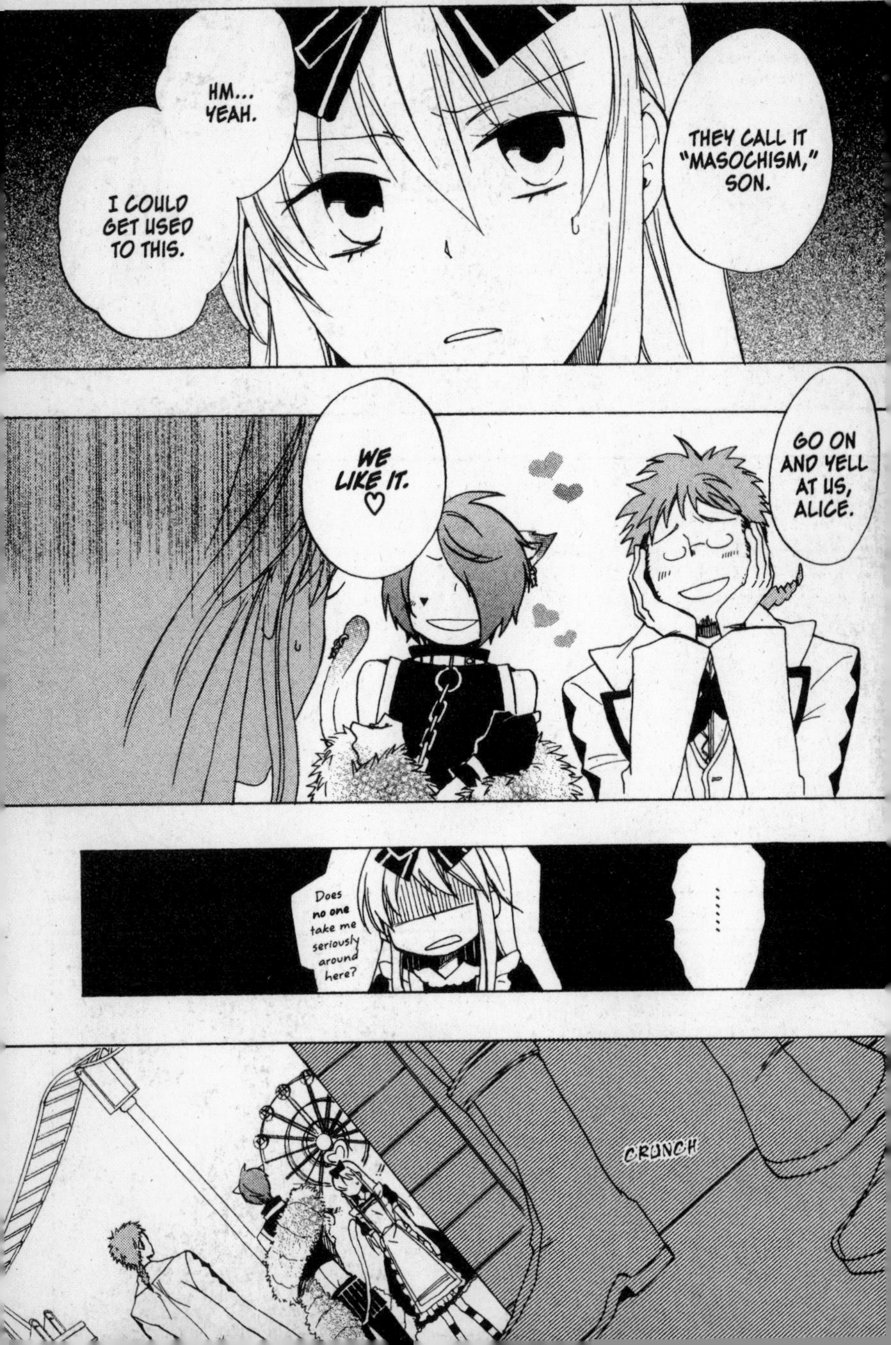
THEY CALL IT "MASOCHISM," SON.
HM... YEAH.
I COULD GET USED TO THIS.
GO ON AND YELL AT US, ALICE.
WE LIKE IT. ♡
......
Does no one take me seriously around here?
CRUNCH

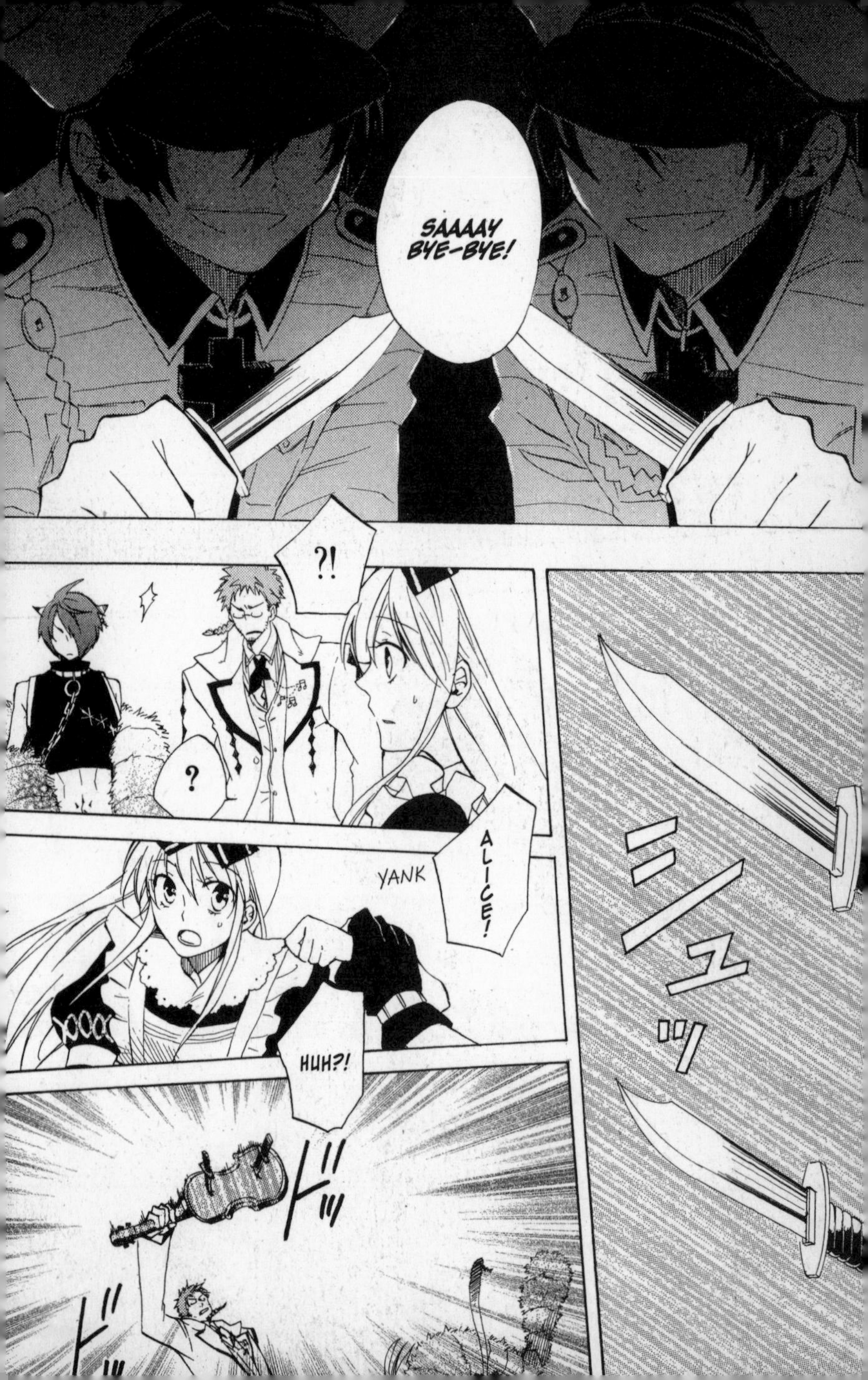
SAAAAY BYE-BYE!
シュッ
?!
?
ALICE!
YANK
HUH?!
ドッ
ドッ

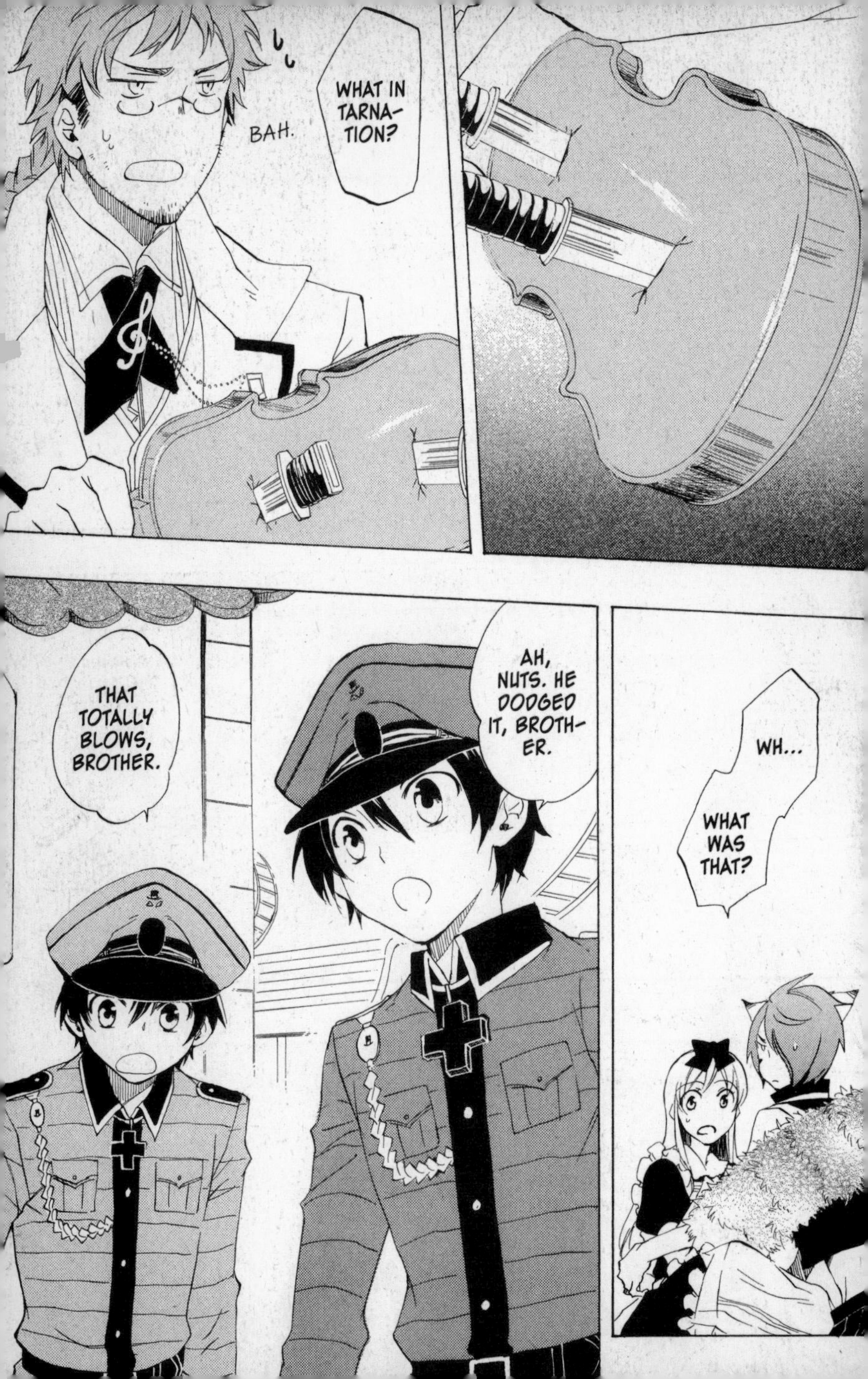
WHAT IN TARNA-TION?
BAH.
WH...
WHAT WAS THAT?
AH, NUTS. HE DODGED IT, BROTH-ER.
THAT TOTALLY BLOWS, BROTHER.

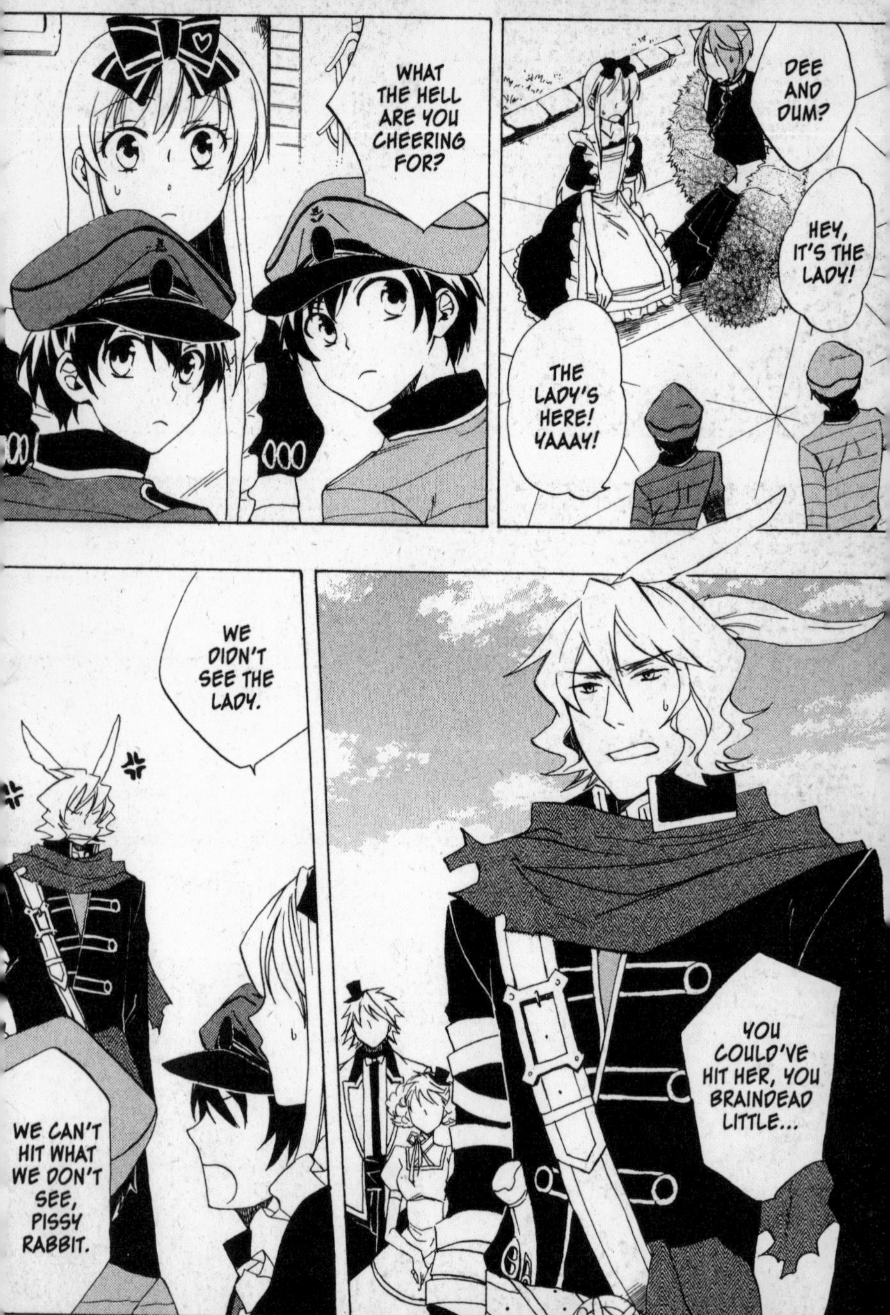
DEE AND DUM?
HEY, IT'S THE LADY!
THE LADY'S HERE! YAAAY!
WHAT THE HELL ARE YOU CHEERING FOR?
YOU COULD'VE HIT HER, YOU BRAINDEAD LITTLE...
WE DIDN'T SEE THE LADY.
WE CAN'T HIT WHAT WE DON'T SEE, PISSY RABBIT.

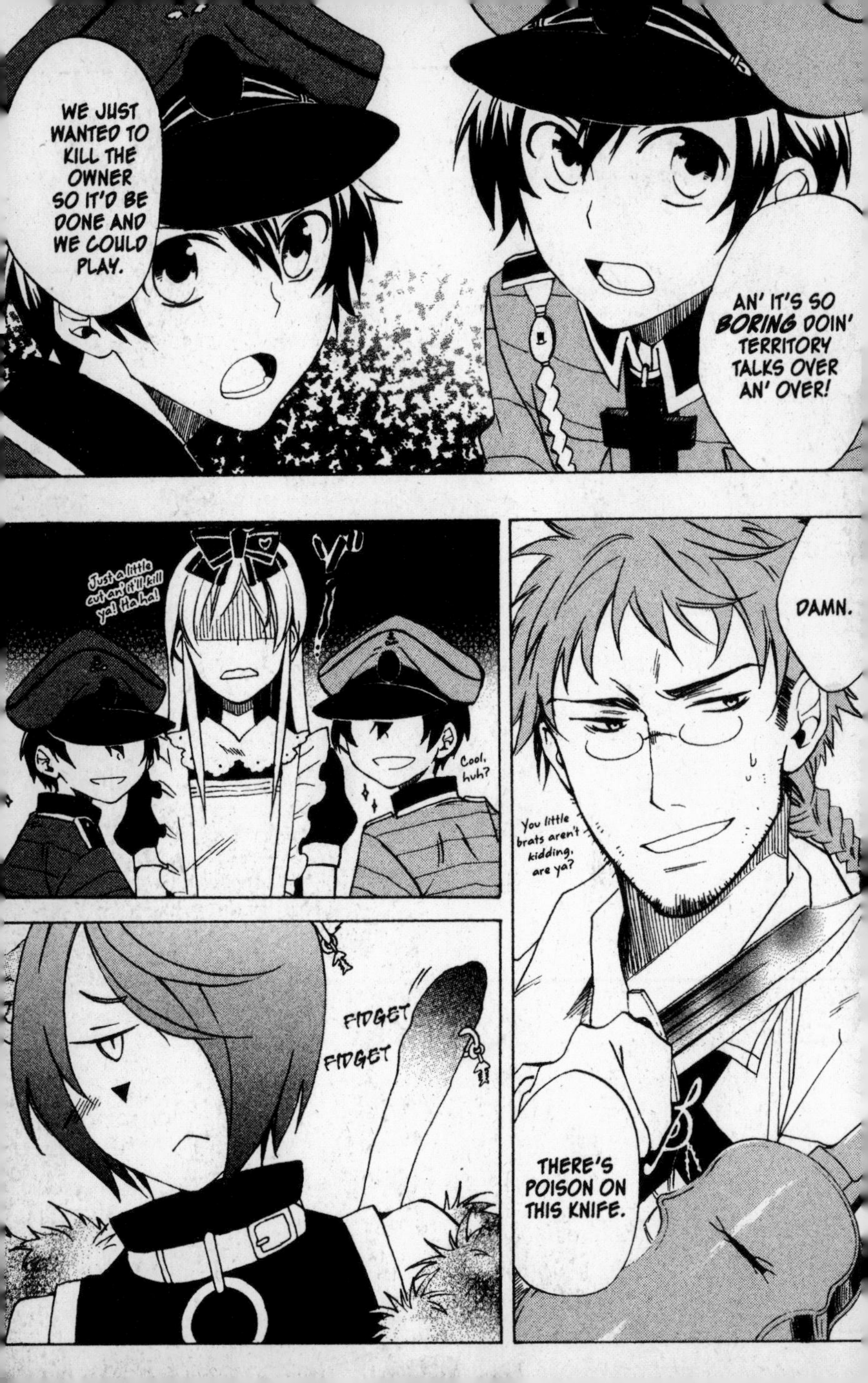
WE JUST WANTED TO KILL THE OWNER SO IT'D BE DONE AND WE COULD PLAY.
AN' IT'S SO BORING DOIN' TERRITORY TALKS OVER AN' OVER!
DAMN.
You little brats aren't kidding, are ya?
THERE'S POISON ON THIS KNIFE.
Cool, huh?
Just a little cut an' it'll kill ya! Ha ha!
FIDGET
FIDGET

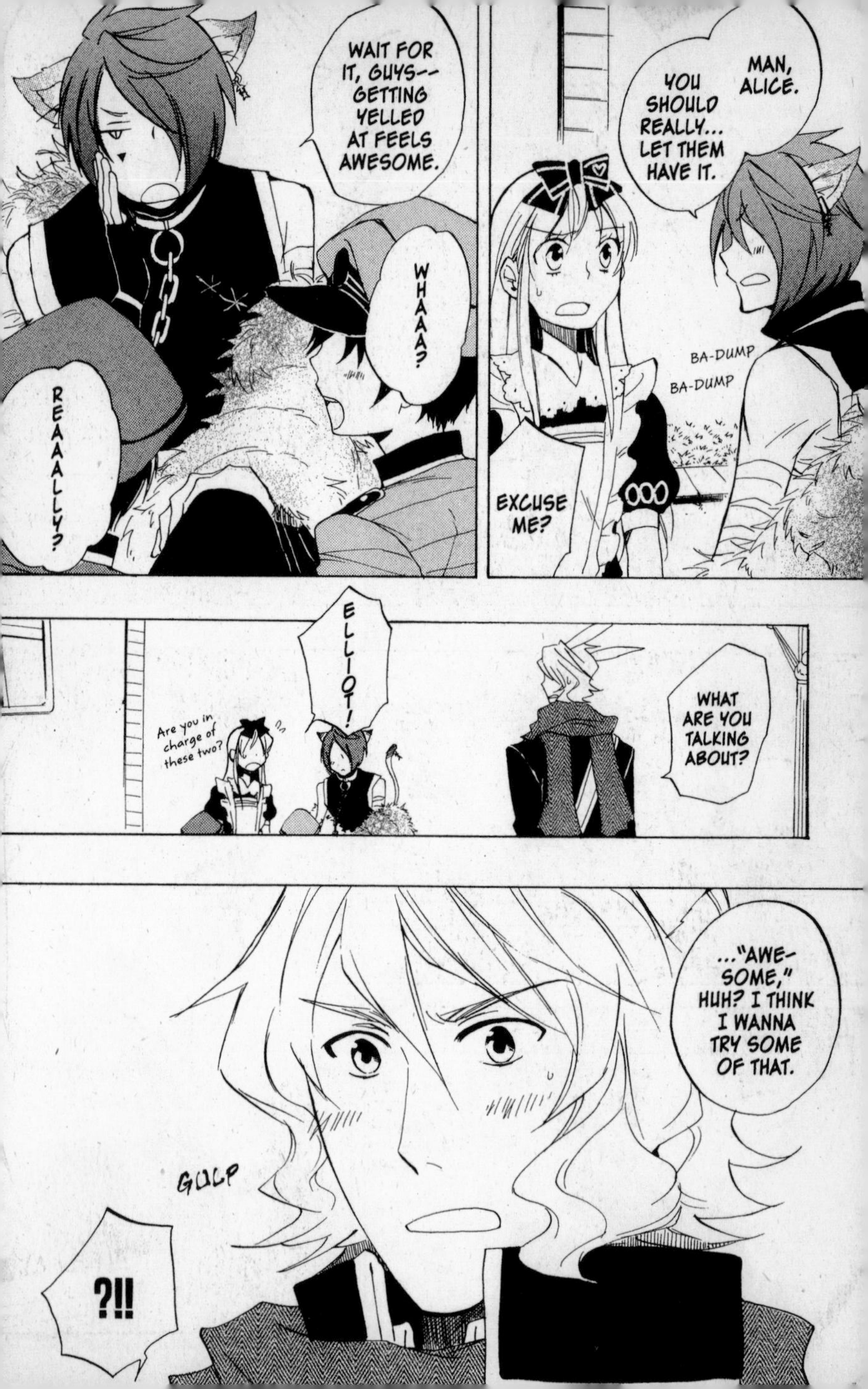
MAN, ALICE.
YOU SHOULD REALLY... LET THEM HAVE IT.
BA-DUMP
BA-DUMP
EXCUSE ME?
WAIT FOR IT, GUYS-- GETTING YELLED AT FEELS AWESOME.
WHAAAA?
REAAAALLY?
WHAT ARE YOU TALKING ABOUT?
ELLIOT!
Are you in charge of these two?
..."AWE-SOME," HUH? I THINK I WANNA TRY SOME OF THAT.
GULP
?!!

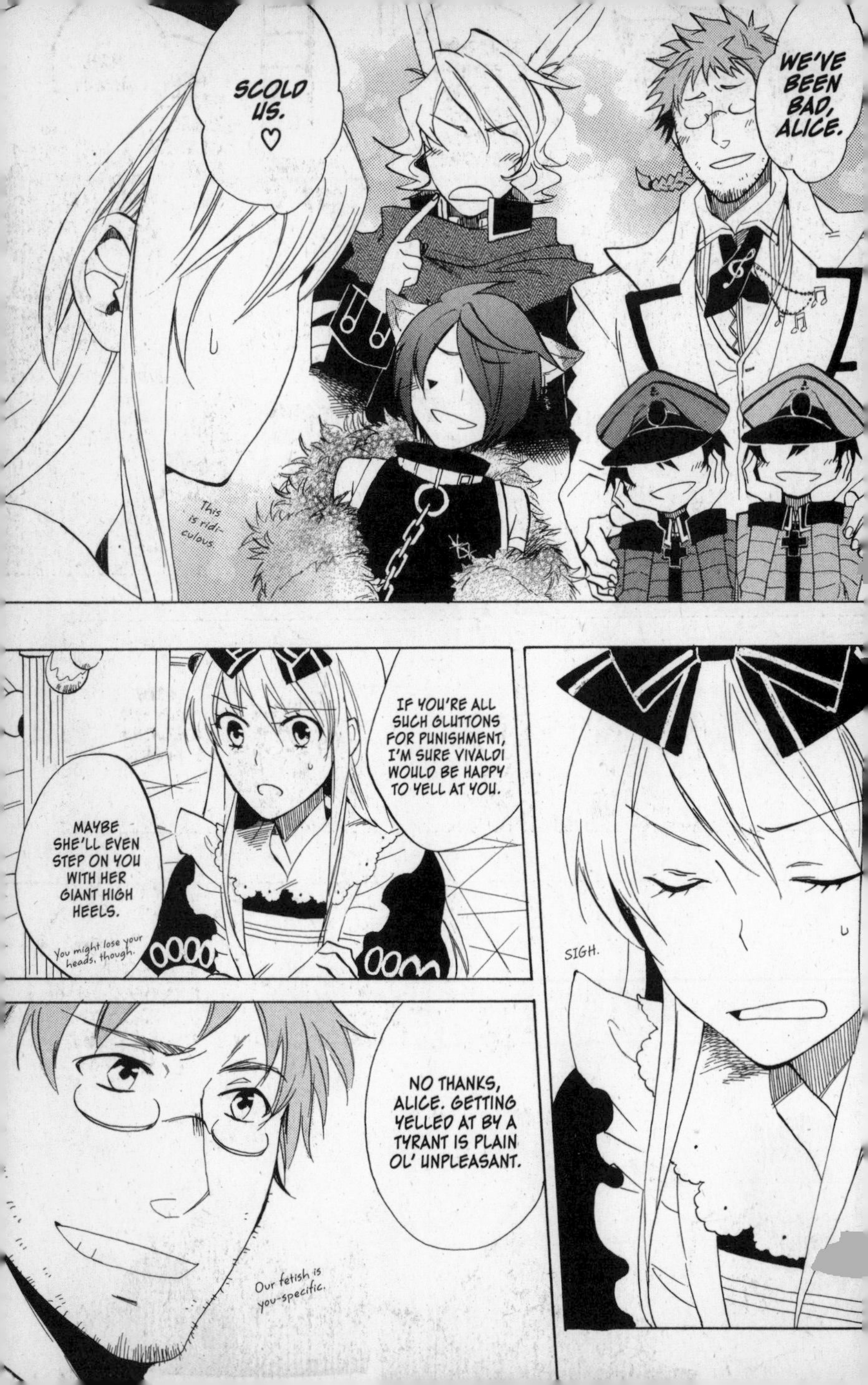
WE'VE BEEN BAD, ALICE.
SCOLD US. ♡
This is ridiculous.
SIGH.
IF YOU'RE ALL SUCH GLUTTONS FOR PUNISHMENT, I'M SURE VIVALDI WOULD BE HAPPY TO YELL AT YOU.
MAYBE SHE'LL EVEN STEP ON YOU WITH HER GIANT HIGH HEELS.
You might lose your heads, though.
NO THANKS, ALICE. GETTING YELLED AT BY A TYRANT IS PLAIN OL' UNPLEASANT.
Our fetish is you-specific.

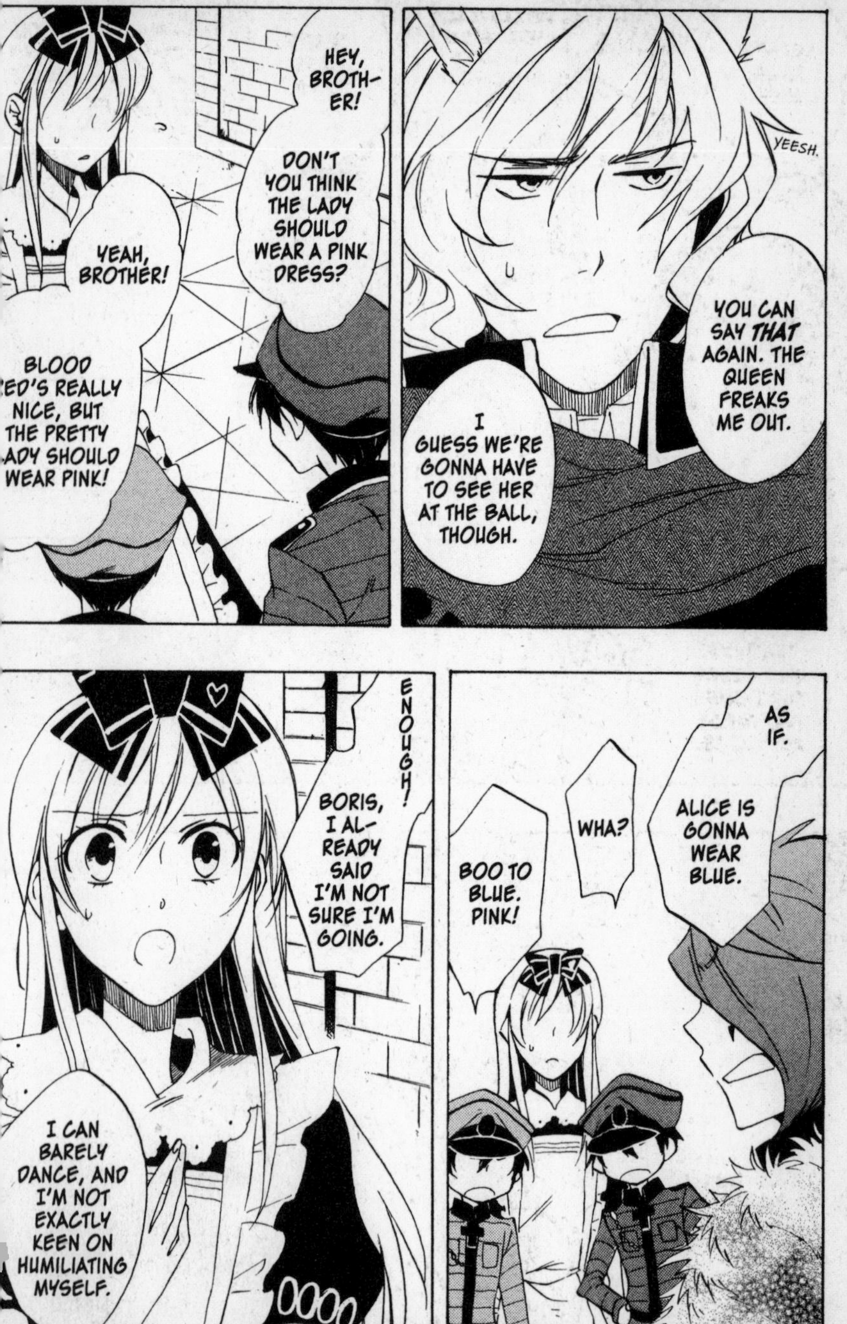
YEESH.
YOU CAN SAY THAT AGAIN. THE QUEEN FREAKS ME OUT.
I GUESS WE'RE GONNA HAVE TO SEE HER AT THE BALL, THOUGH.
HEY, BROTHER!
DON'T YOU THINK THE LADY SHOULD WEAR A PINK DRESS?
YEAH, BROTHER!
BLOOD ED'S REALLY NICE, BUT THE PRETTY ADY SHOULD WEAR PINK!
AS IF.
ALICE IS GONNA WEAR BLUE.
WHA?
BOO TO BLUE. PINK!
ENOUGH!
BORIS, I AL-READY SAID I'M NOT SURE I'M GOING.
I CAN BARELY DANCE, AND I'M NOT EXACTLY KEEN ON HUMILIATING MYSELF.

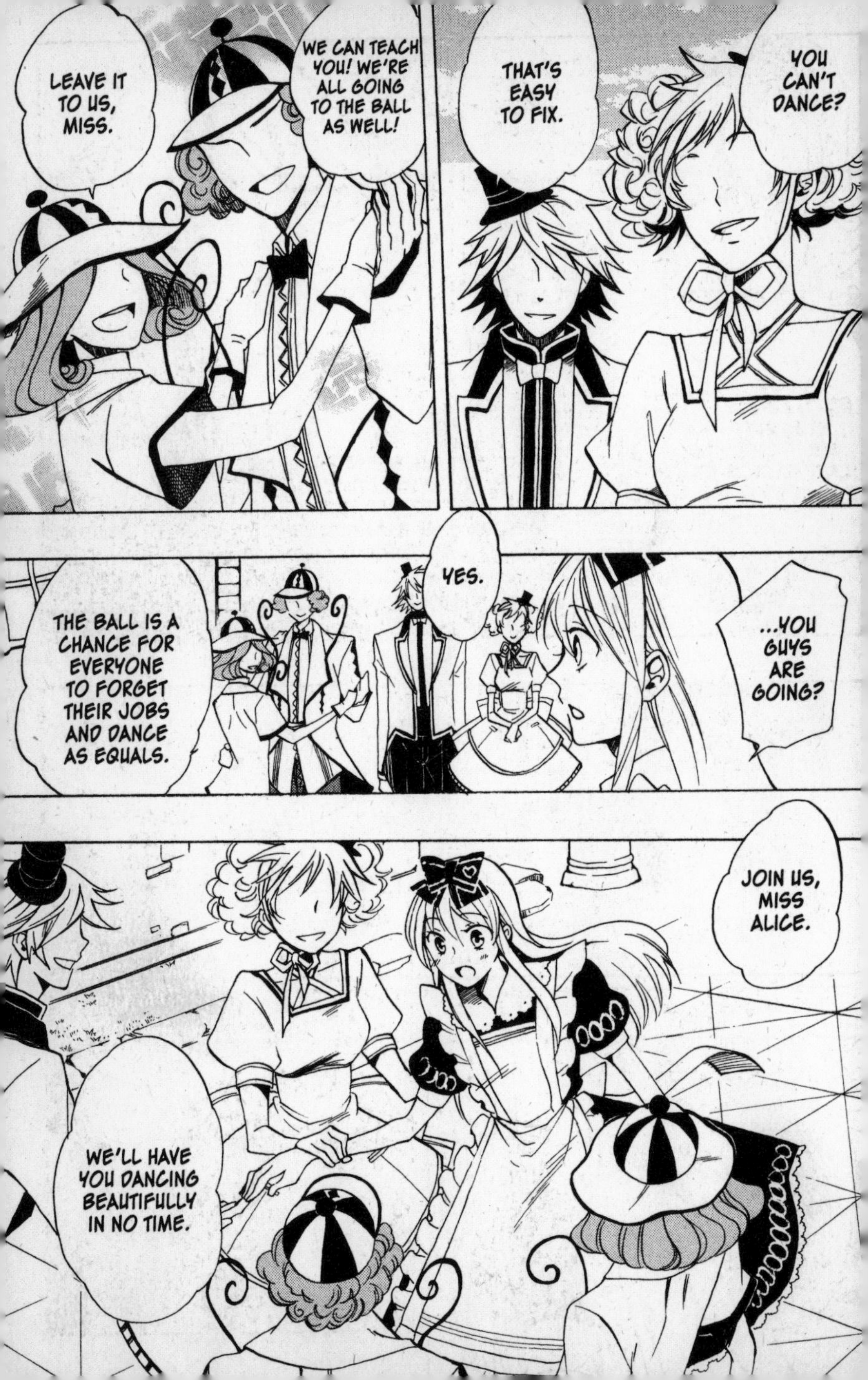
YOU CAN'T DANCE?
THAT'S EASY TO FIX.
WE CAN TEACH YOU! WE'RE ALL GOING TO THE BALL AS WELL!
LEAVE IT TO US, MISS.
...YOU GUYS ARE GOING?
YES.
THE BALL IS A CHANCE FOR EVERYONE TO FORGET THEIR JOBS AND DANCE AS EQUALS.
JOIN US, MISS ALICE.
WE'LL HAVE YOU DANCING BEAUTIFULLY IN NO TIME.

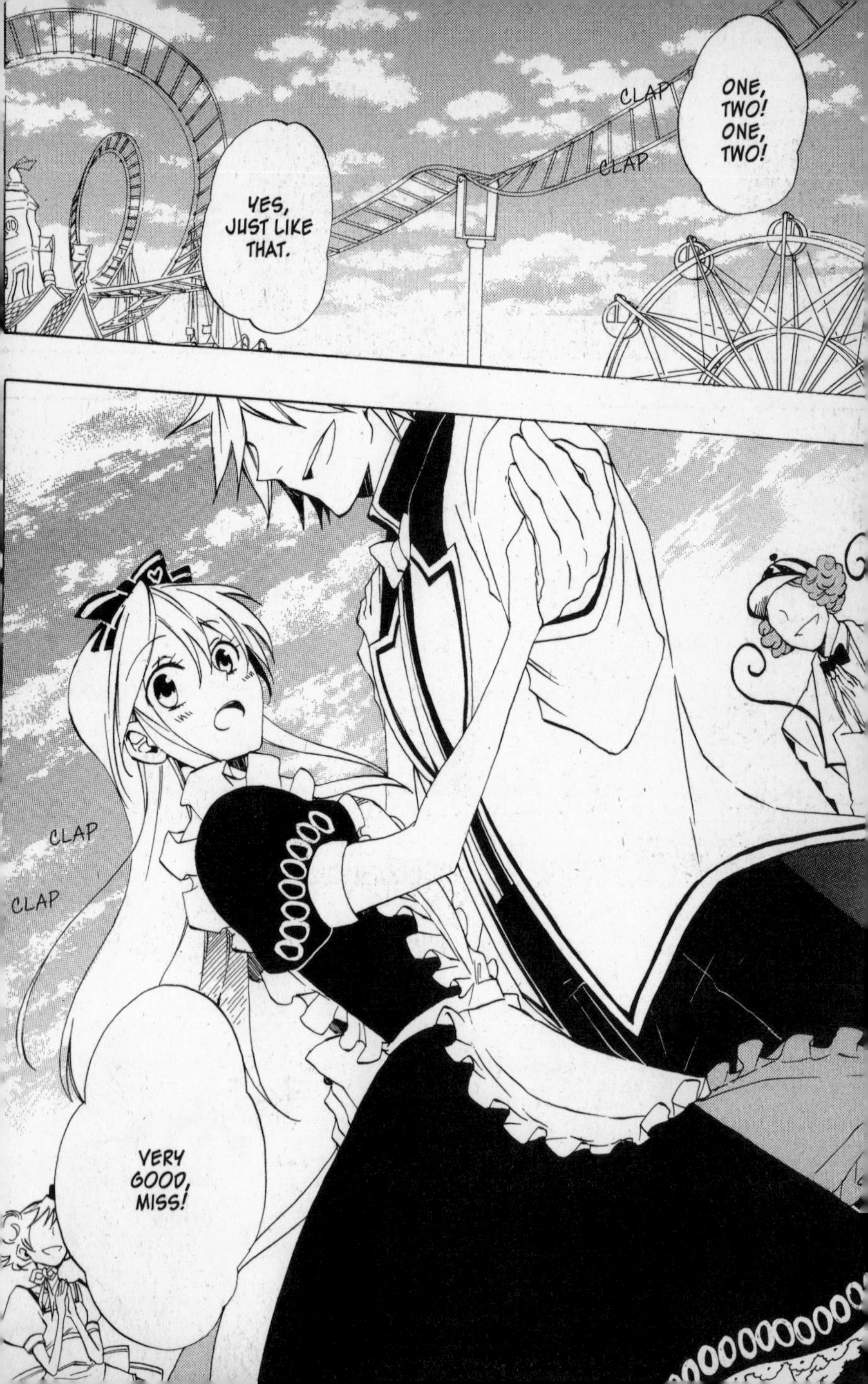
ONE, TWO! ONE, TWO!
CLAP
CLAP
YES, JUST LIKE THAT.
CLAP
CLAP
VERY GOOD, MISS!

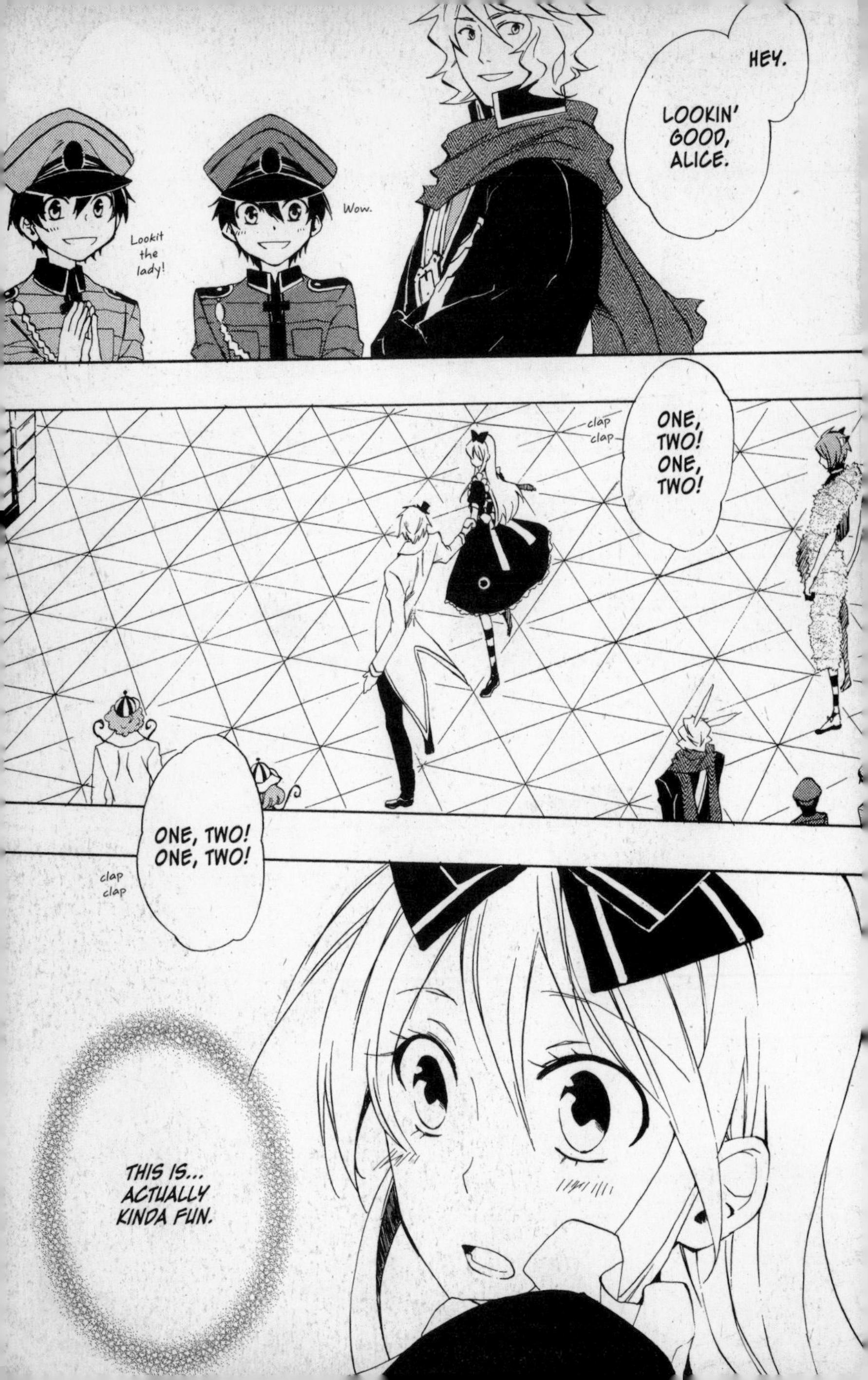
HEY.
LOOKIN' GOOD, ALICE.
Wow.
Lookit the lady!
ONE, TWO! ONE, TWO!
clap clap
ONE, TWO! ONE, TWO!
clap clap
THIS IS... ACTUALLY KINDA FUN.

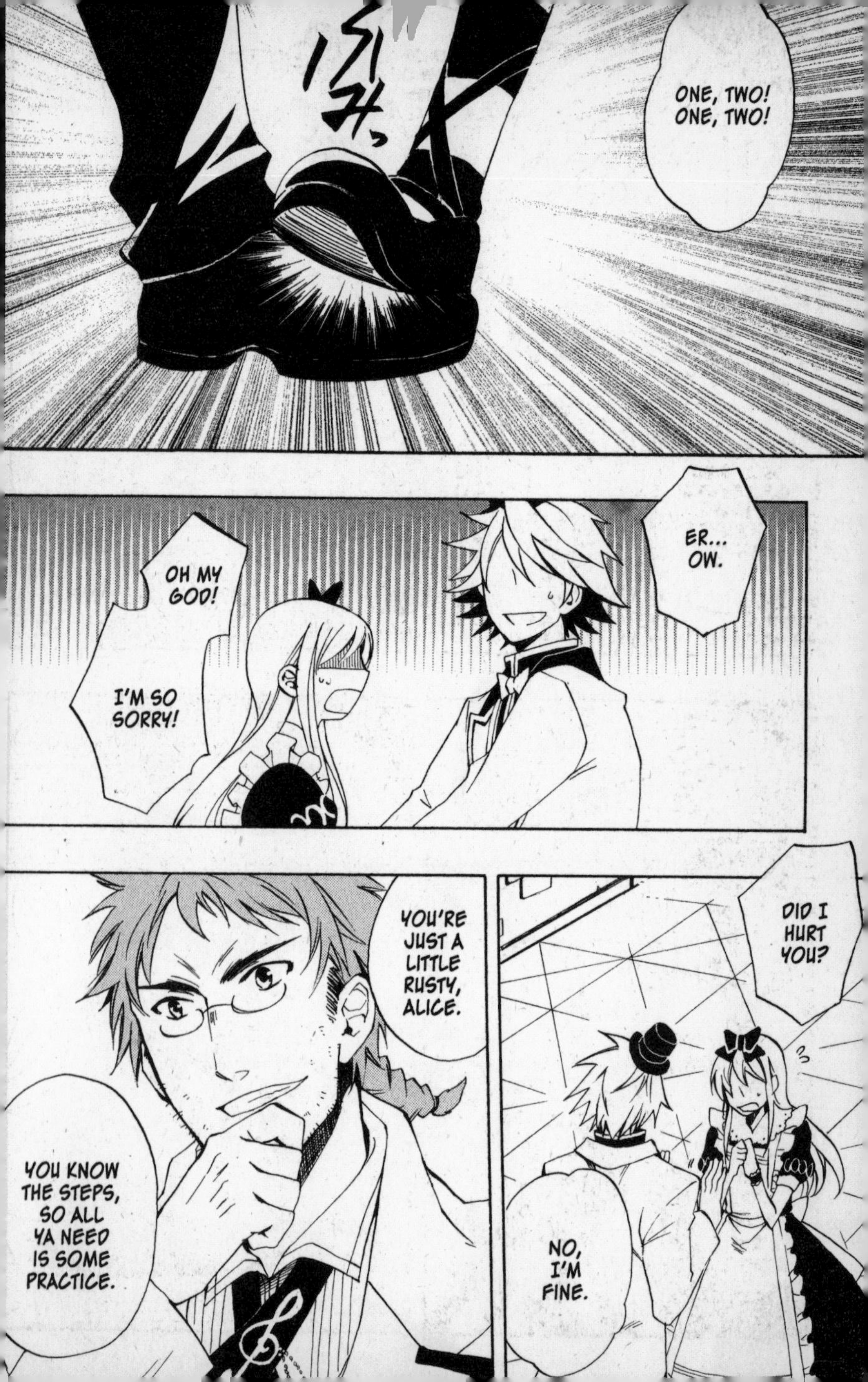
ふみっ
ONE, TWO! ONE, TWO!
ER... OW.
OH MY GOD!
I'M SO SORRY!
DID I HURT YOU?
NO, I'M FINE.
YOU'RE JUST A LITTLE RUSTY, ALICE.
YOU KNOW THE STEPS, SO ALL YA NEED IS SOME PRACTICE.

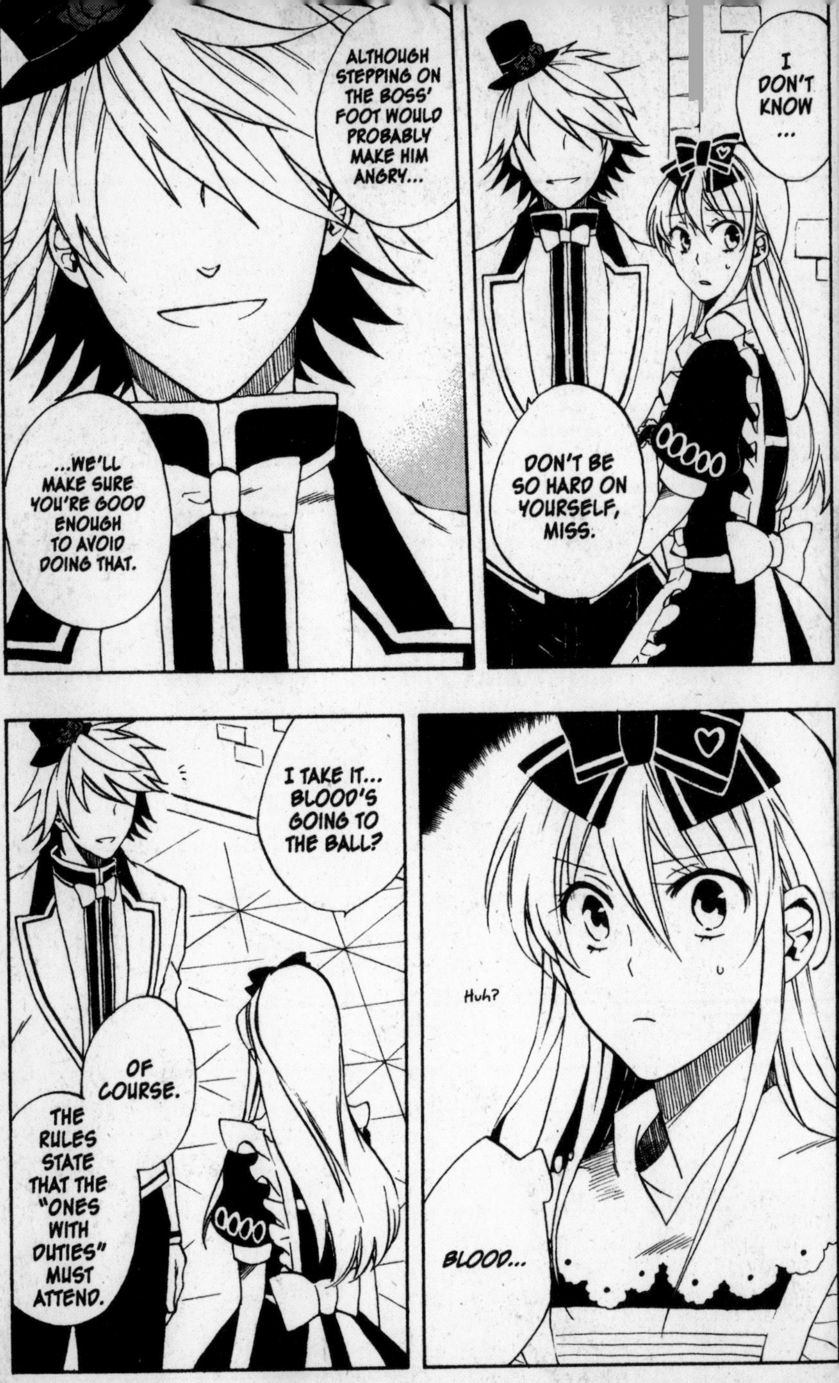
I DON'T KNOW ...
DON'T BE SO HARD ON YOURSELF, MISS.
ALTHOUGH STEPPING ON THE BOSS' FOOT WOULD PROBABLY MAKE HIM ANGRY...
...WE'LL MAKE SURE YOU'RE GOOD ENOUGH TO AVOID DOING THAT.
Huh?
BLOOD...
I TAKE IT... BLOOD'S GOING TO THE BALL?
OF COURSE.
THE RULES STATE THAT THE "ONES WITH DUTIES" MUST ATTEND.

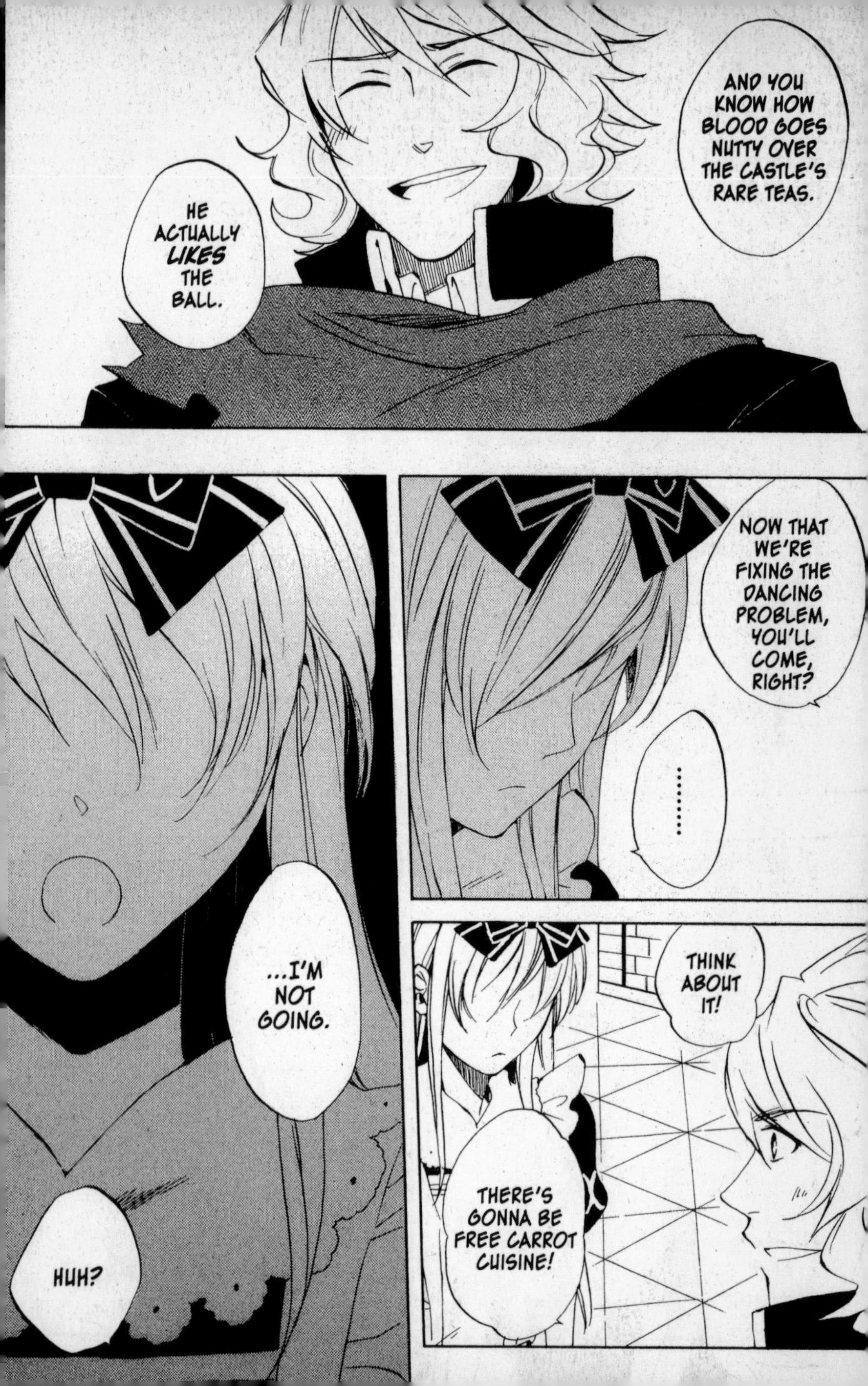

AND YOU KNOW HOW BLOOD GOES NUTTY OVER THE CASTLE'S RARE TEAS.
HE ACTUALLY *LIKES* THE BALL.
NOW THAT WE'RE FIXING THE DANCING PROBLEM, YOU'LL COME, RIGHT?
....
THINK ABOUT IT!
THERE'S GONNA BE FREE CARROT CUISINE!
...I'M NOT GOING.
HUH?

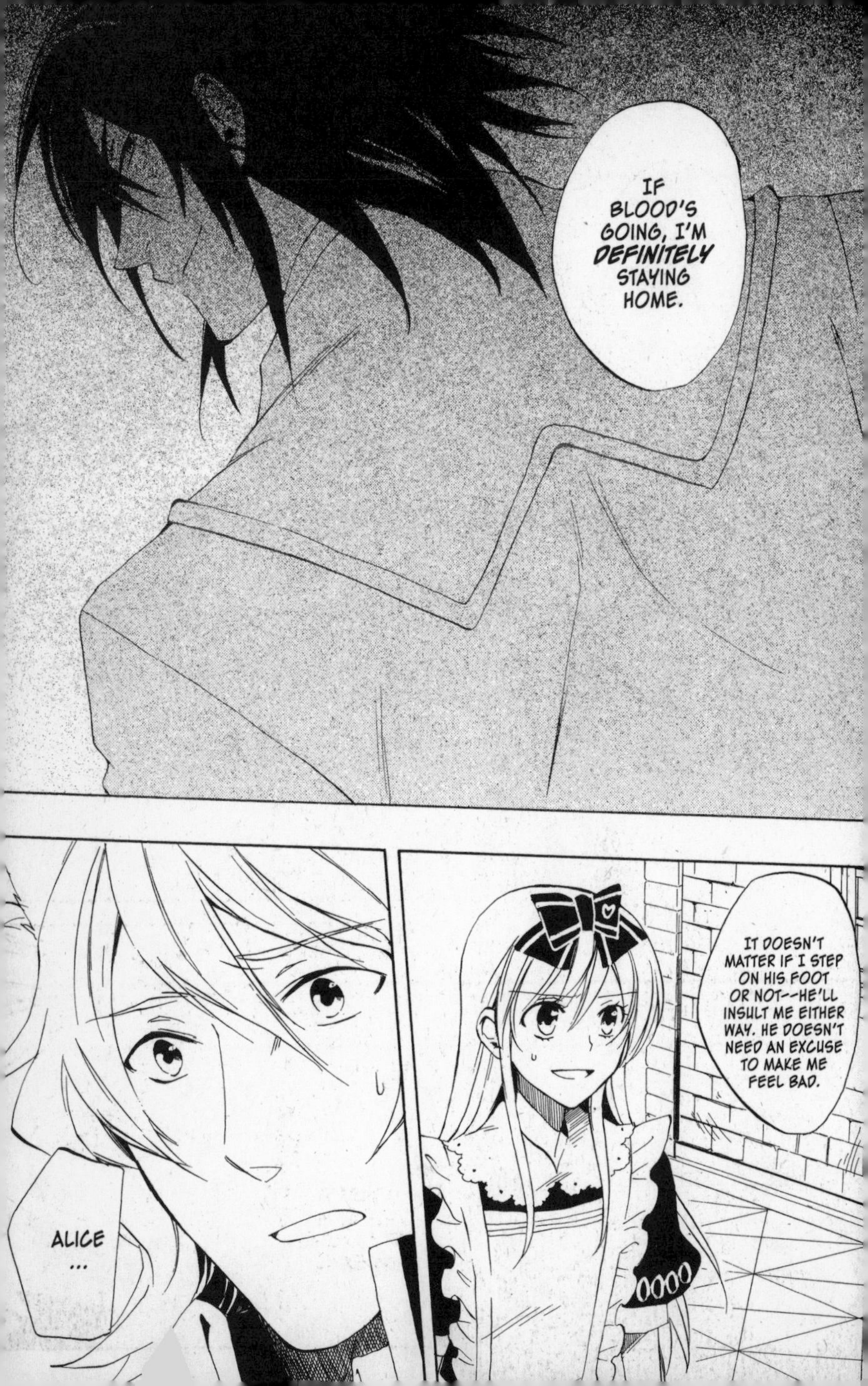
IF BLOOD'S GOING, I'M DEFINITELY STAYING HOME.
IT DOESN'T MATTER IF I STEP ON HIS FOOT OR NOT--HE'LL INSULT ME EITHER WAY. HE DOESN'T NEED AN EXCUSE TO MAKE ME FEEL BAD.
ALICE ...

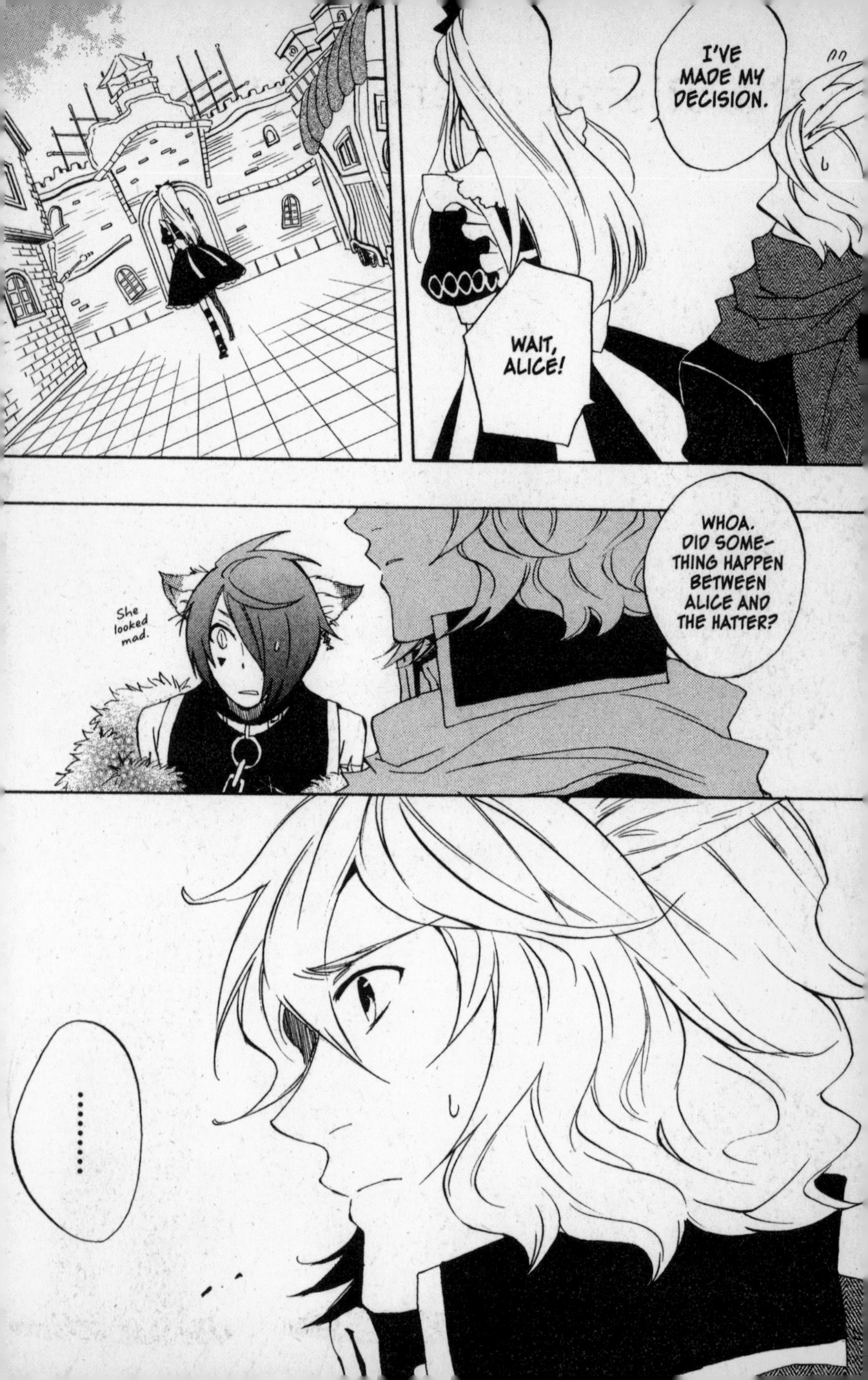
I'VE MADE MY DECISION.
WAIT, ALICE!
WHOA. DID SOMETHING HAPPEN BETWEEN ALICE AND THE HATTER?
She looked mad.
....

♥26 Rising of the Curtain

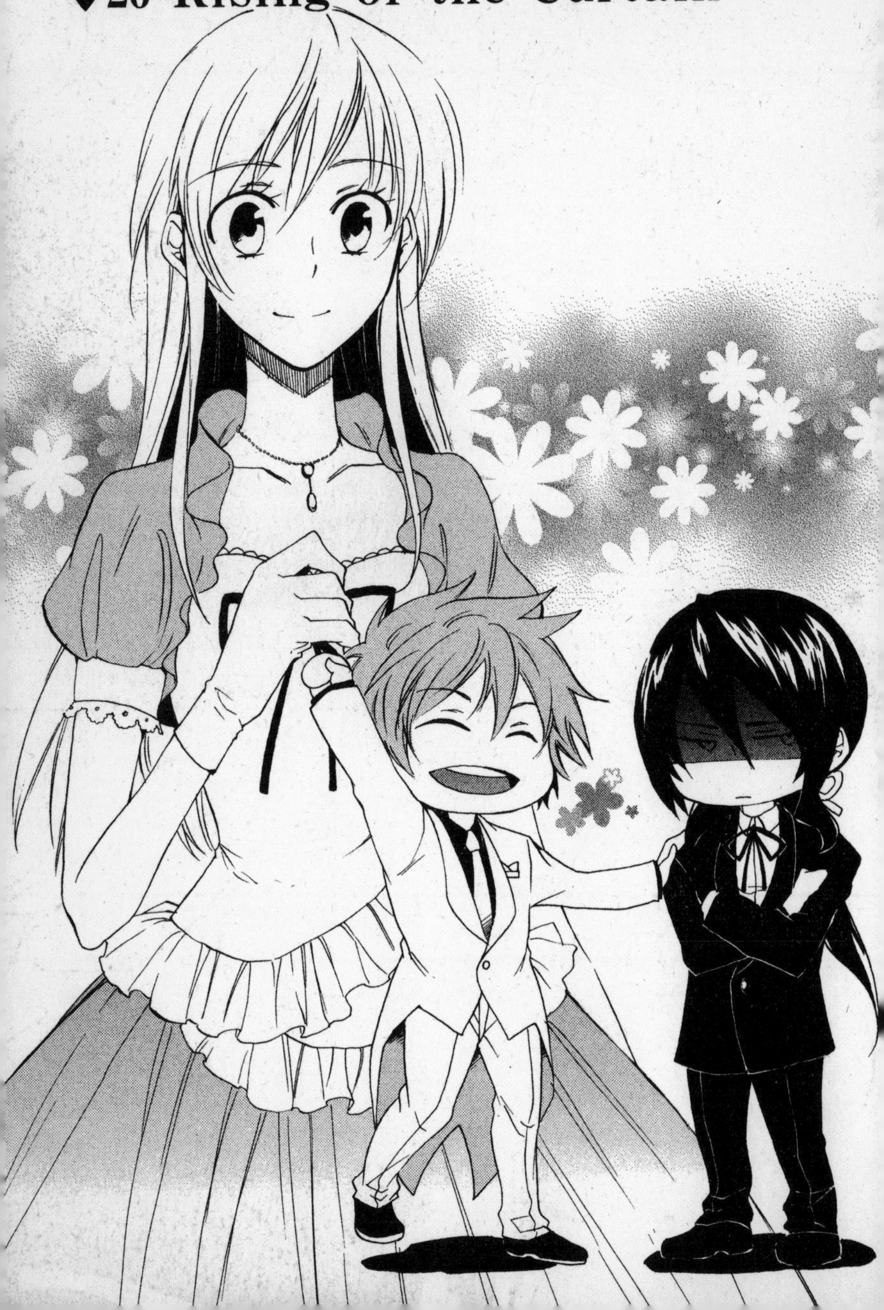

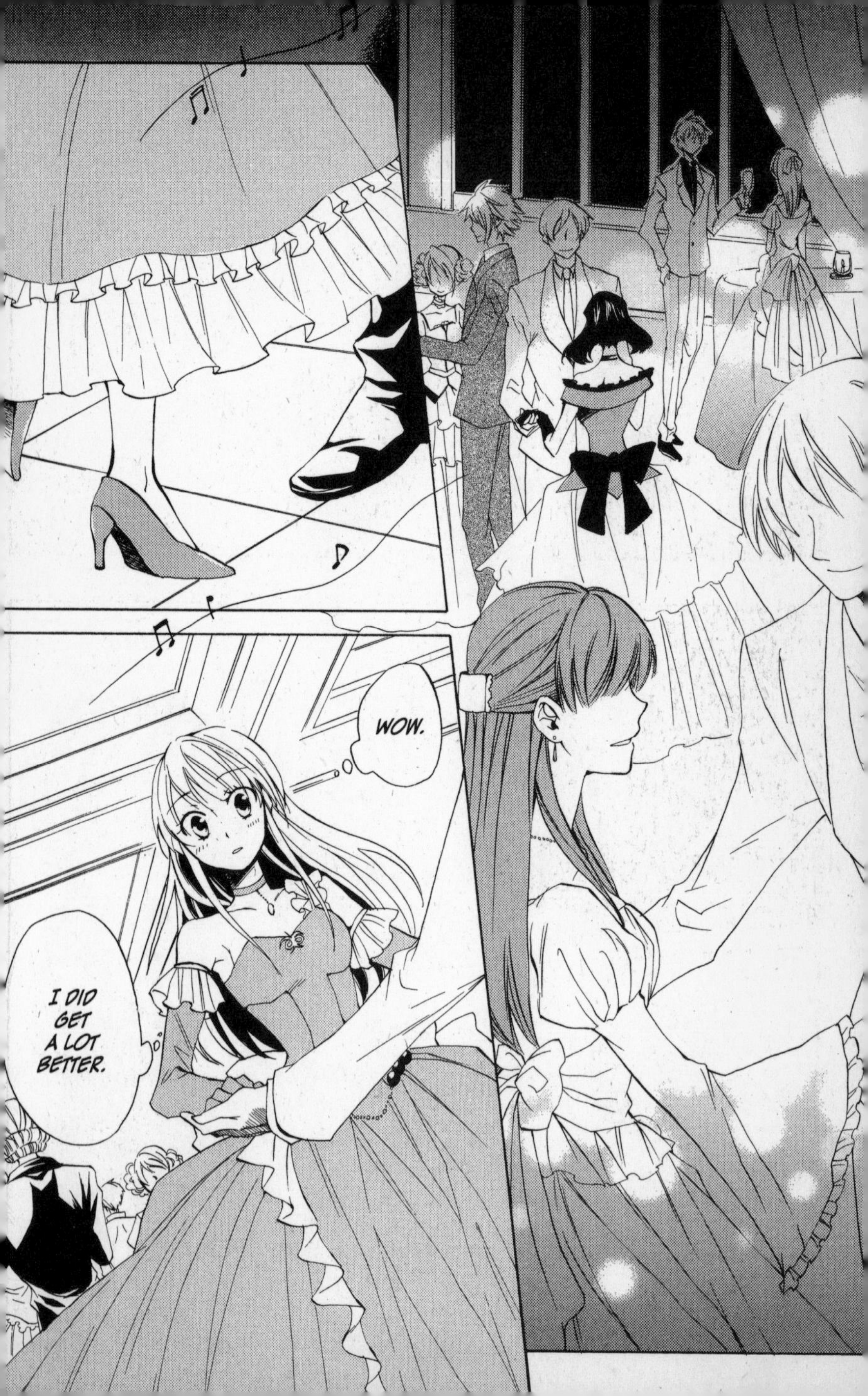
WOW.
I DID GET A LOT BETTER.

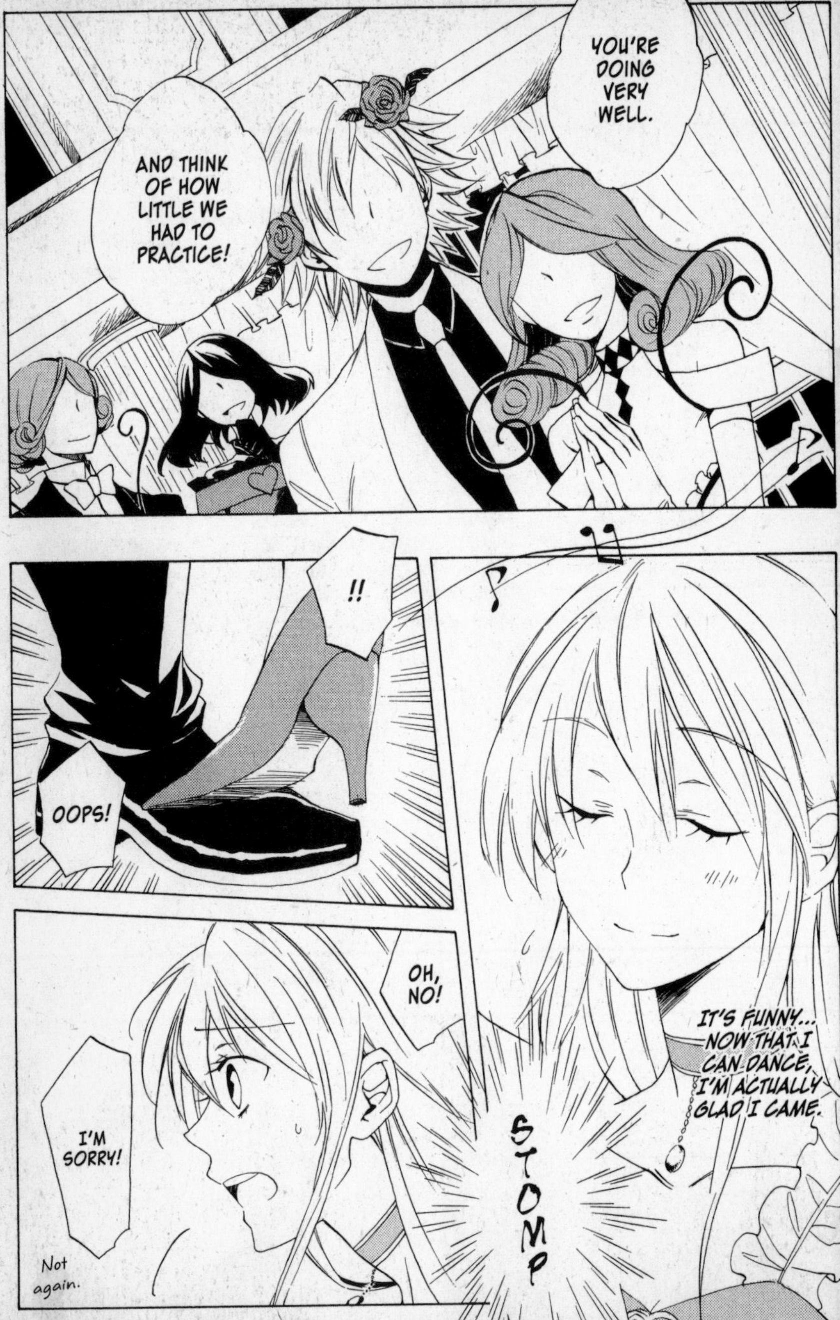
YOU'RE DOING VERY WELL.
AND THINK OF HOW LITTLE WE HAD TO PRACTICE!
IT'S FUNNY... NOW THAT I CAN DANCE, I'M ACTUALLY GLAD I CAME.
!!
OOPS!
STOMP
OH, NO!
I'M SORRY!
Not again.

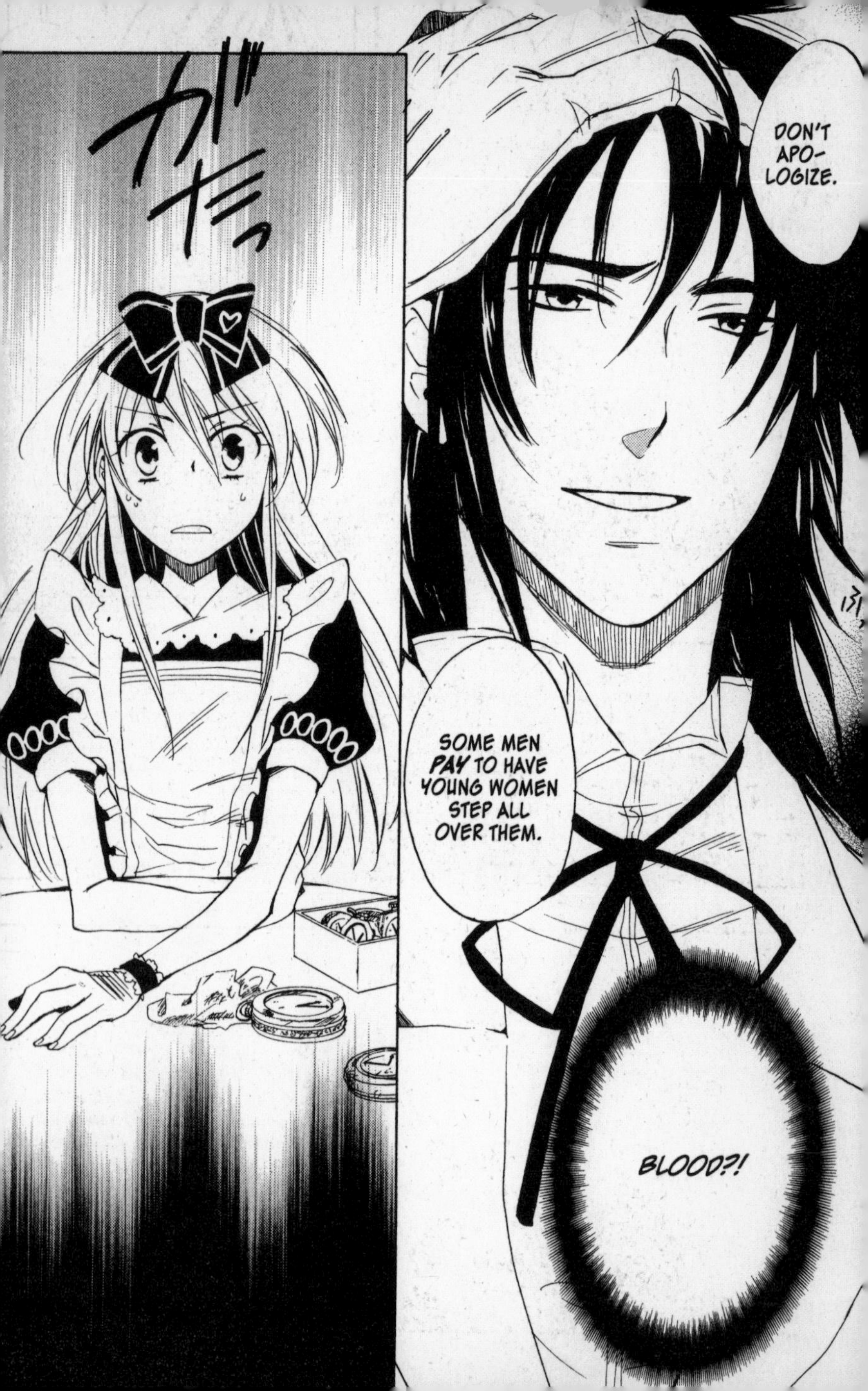
DON'T APO-LOGIZE.
SOME MEN *PAY* TO HAVE YOUNG WOMEN STEP ALL OVER THEM.
BLOOD?!
ガタッ

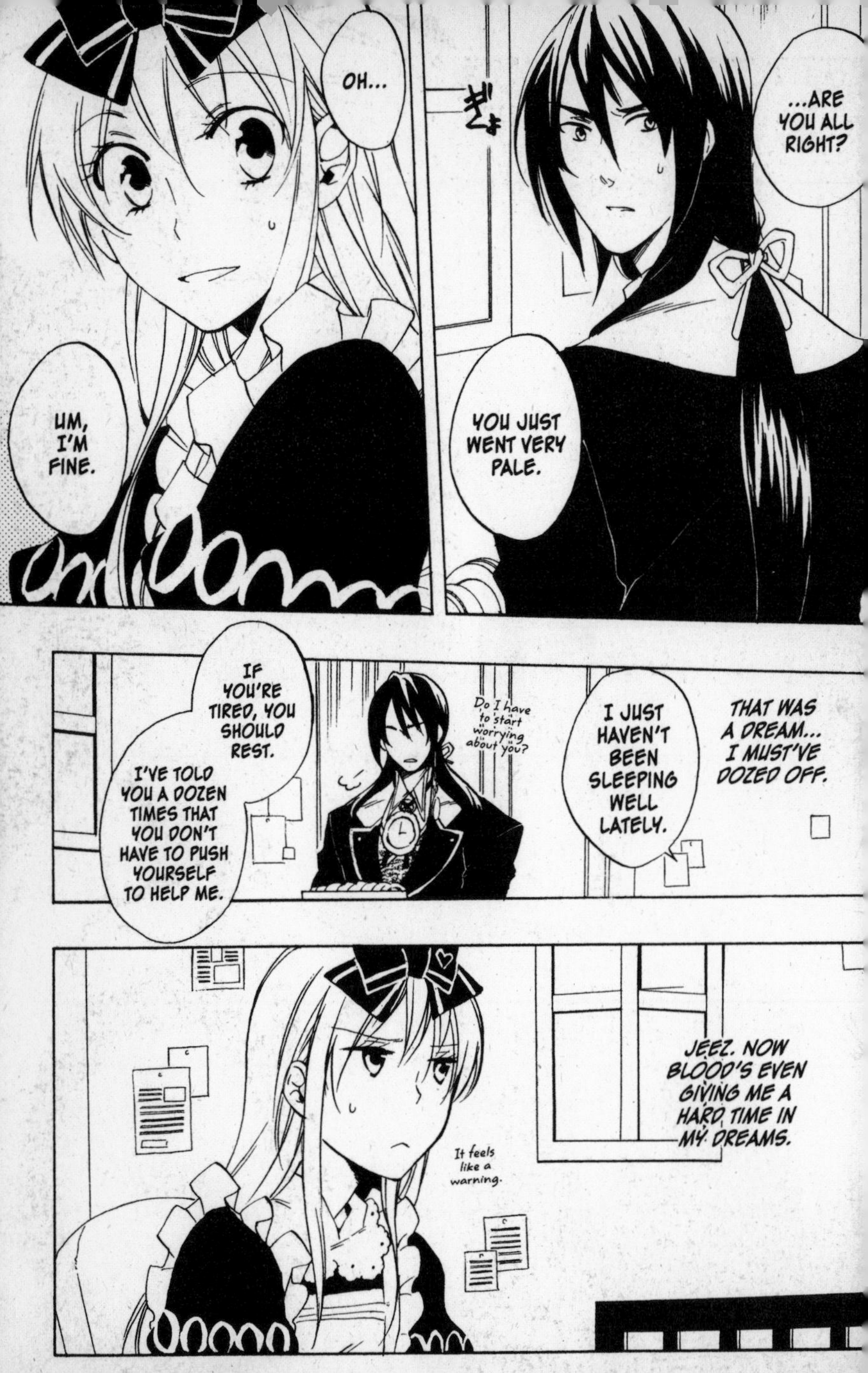
...ARE YOU ALL RIGHT?
ぎょ
YOU JUST WENT VERY PALE.
OH...
UM, I'M FINE.
THAT WAS A DREAM... I MUST'VE DOZED OFF.
I JUST HAVEN'T BEEN SLEEPING WELL LATELY.
Do I have to start worrying about you?
IF YOU'RE TIRED, YOU SHOULD REST.
I'VE TOLD YOU A DOZEN TIMES THAT YOU DON'T HAVE TO PUSH YOURSELF TO HELP ME.
JEEZ. NOW BLOOD'S EVEN GIVING ME A HARD TIME IN MY DREAMS.
It feels like a warning.

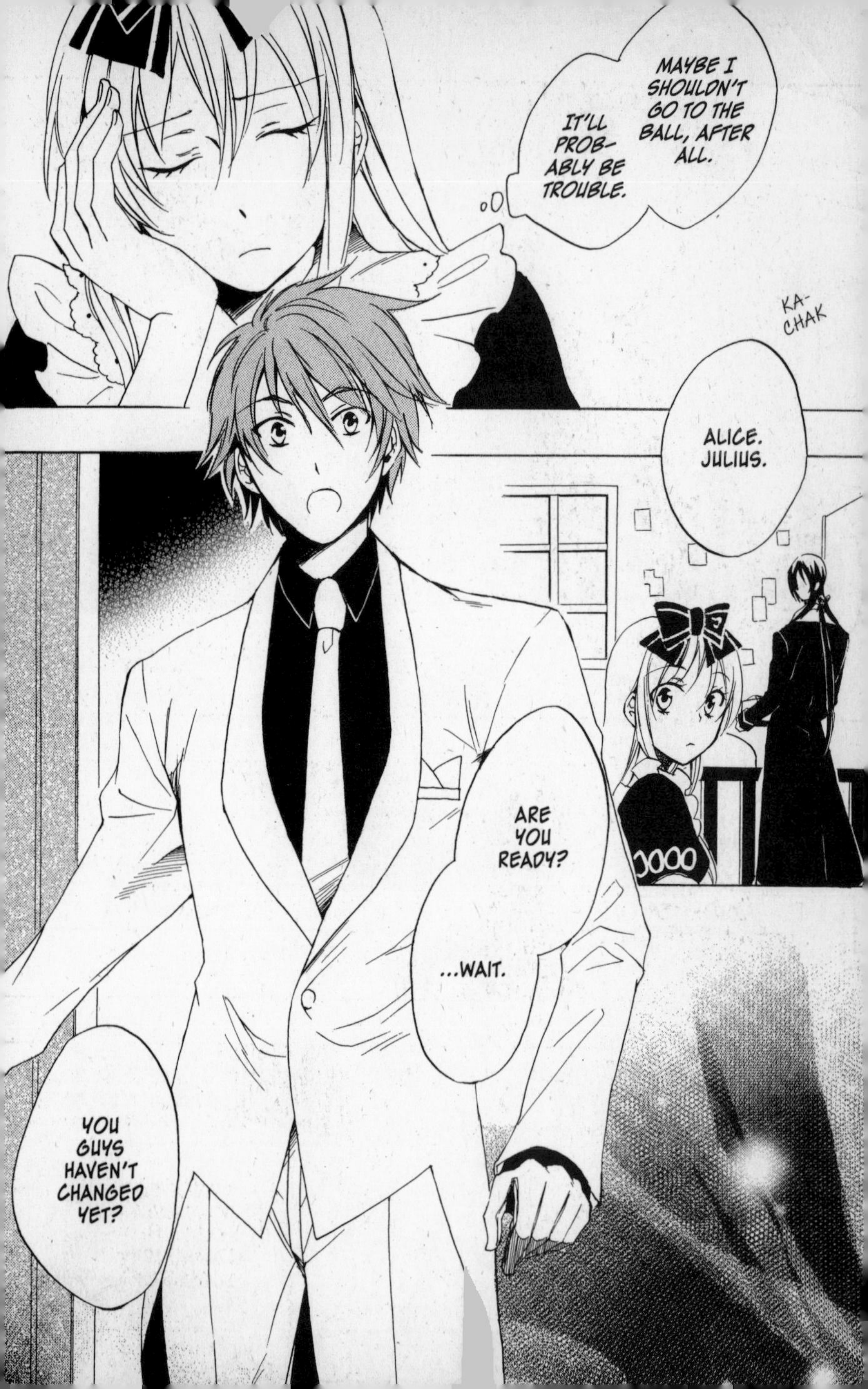
MAYBE I SHOULDN'T GO TO THE BALL, AFTER ALL.
IT'LL PROBABLY BE TROUBLE.
KA-CHAK
ALICE. JULIUS.
ARE YOU READY?
...WAIT.
YOU GUYS HAVEN'T CHANGED YET?

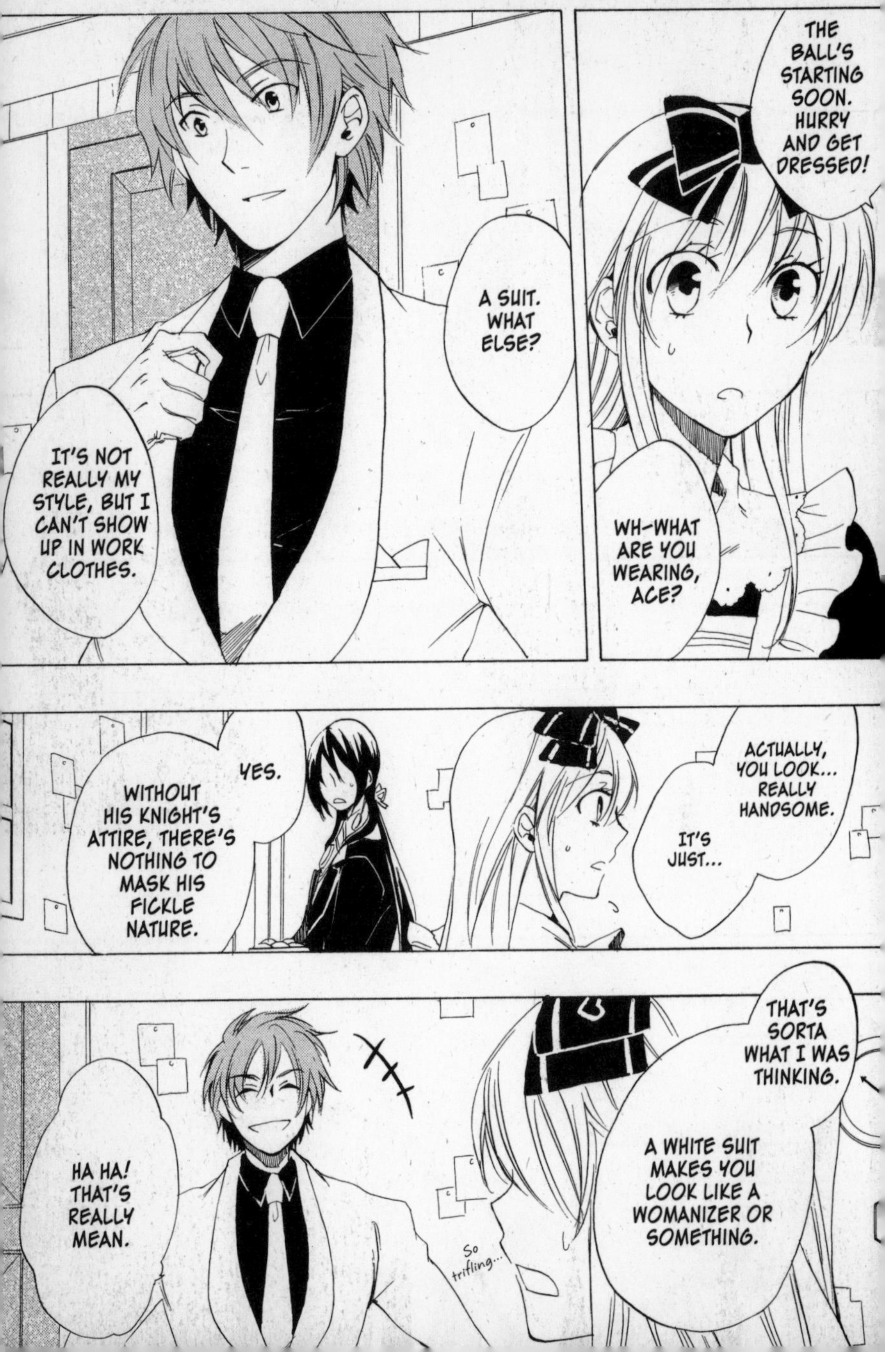
THE BALL'S STARTING SOON. HURRY AND GET DRESSED!
WH-WHAT ARE YOU WEARING, ACE?
A SUIT. WHAT ELSE?
IT'S NOT REALLY MY STYLE, BUT I CAN'T SHOW UP IN WORK CLOTHES.
ACTUALLY, YOU LOOK... REALLY HANDSOME.
IT'S JUST...
YES.
WITHOUT HIS KNIGHT'S ATTIRE, THERE'S NOTHING TO MASK HIS FICKLE NATURE.
THAT'S SORTA WHAT I WAS THINKING.
A WHITE SUIT MAKES YOU LOOK LIKE A WOMANIZER OR SOMETHING.
So trifling...
HA HA! THAT'S REALLY MEAN.

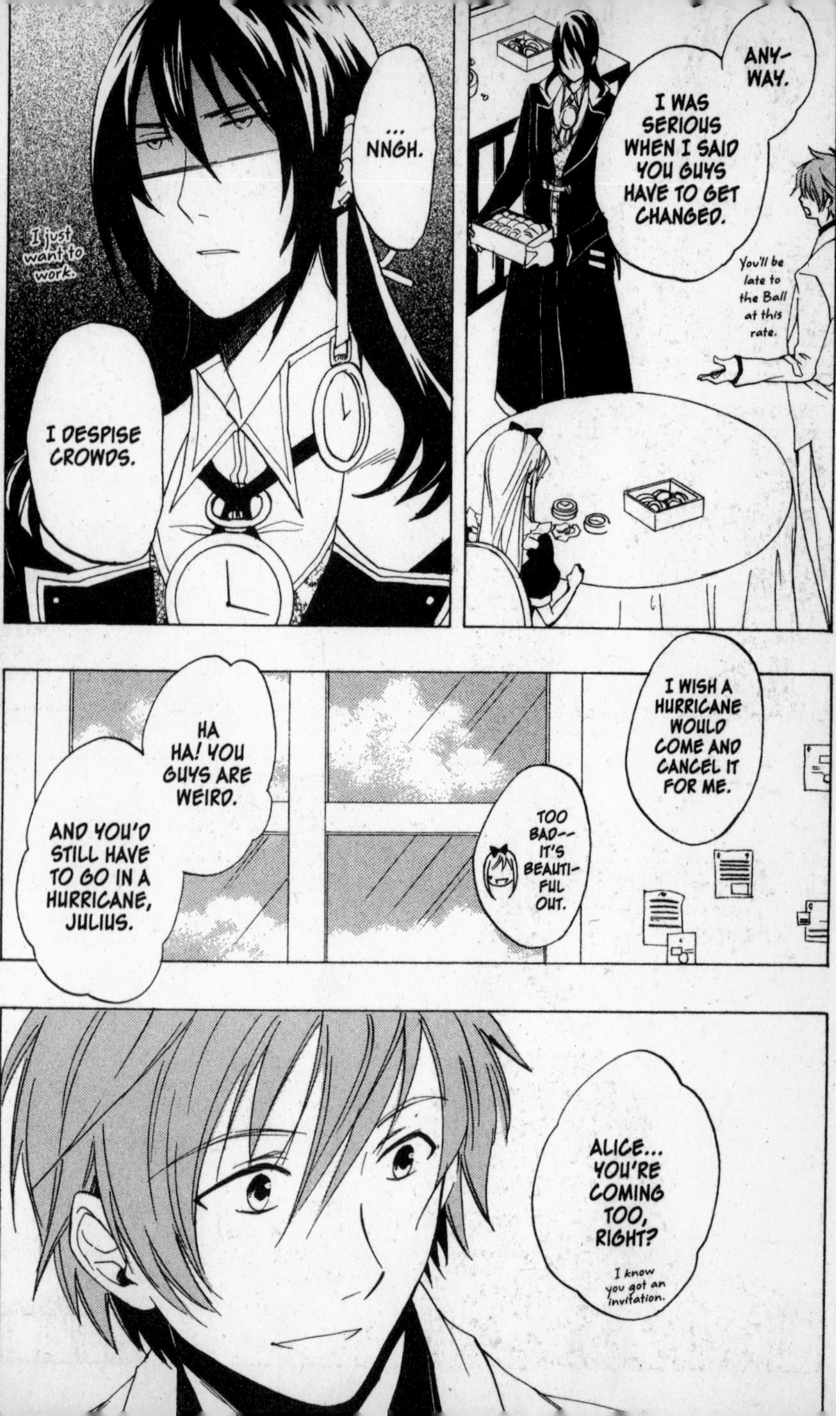
ANY-WAY.
I WAS SERIOUS WHEN I SAID YOU GUYS HAVE TO GET CHANGED.
You'll be late to the Ball at this rate.
... NNGH.
I just want to work.
I DESPISE CROWDS.
I WISH A HURRICANE WOULD COME AND CANCEL IT FOR ME.
TOO BAD-- IT'S BEAUTI-FUL OUT.
HA HA! YOU GUYS ARE WEIRD.
AND YOU'D STILL HAVE TO GO IN A HURRICANE, JULIUS.
ALICE... YOU'RE COMING TOO, RIGHT?
I know you got an invitation.

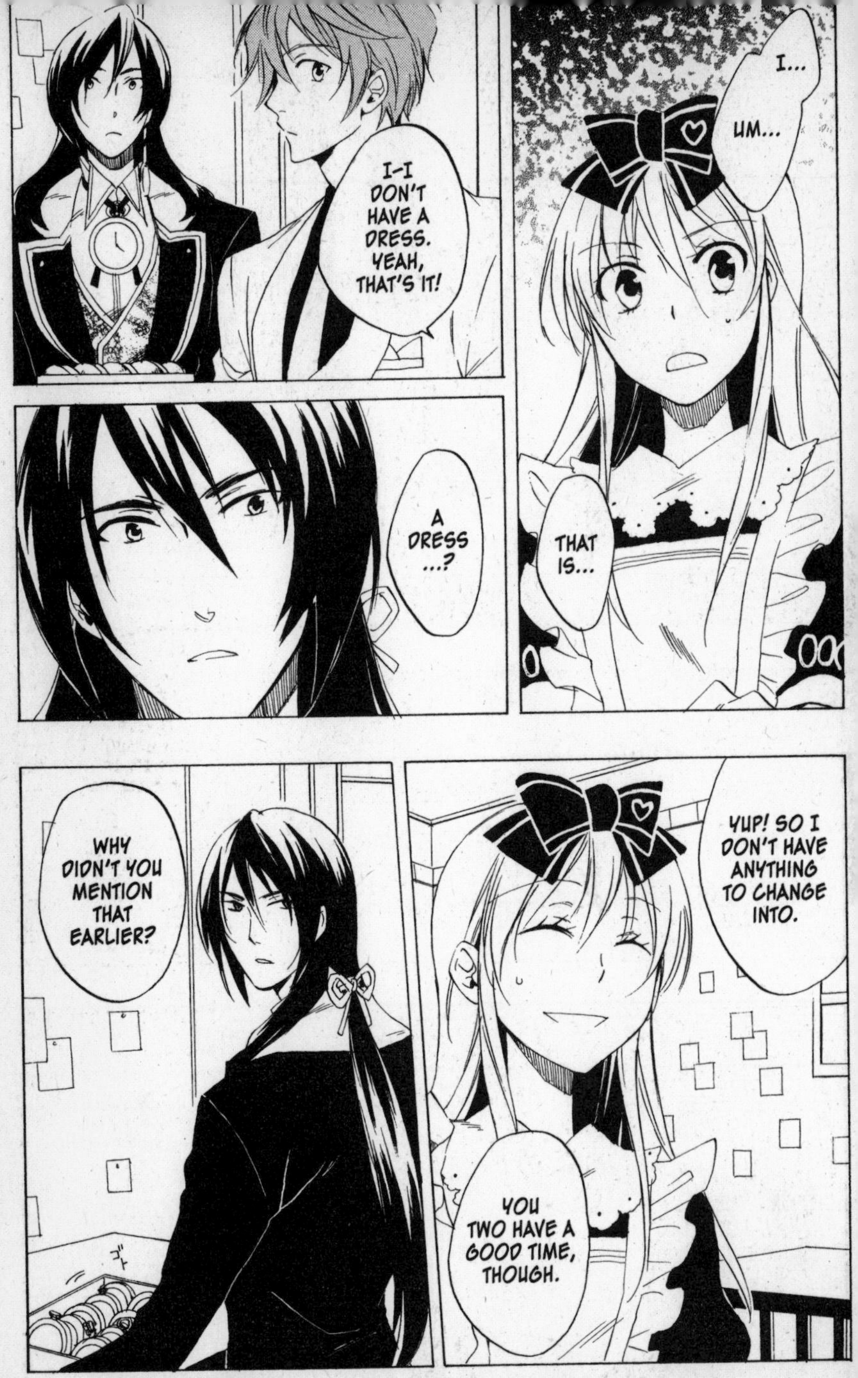
I...
UM...
THAT IS...
I-I DON'T HAVE A DRESS. YEAH, THAT'S IT!
A DRESS ...?
YUP! SO I DON'T HAVE ANYTHING TO CHANGE INTO.
YOU TWO HAVE A GOOD TIME, THOUGH.
WHY DIDN'T YOU MENTION THAT EARLIER?
ゴト

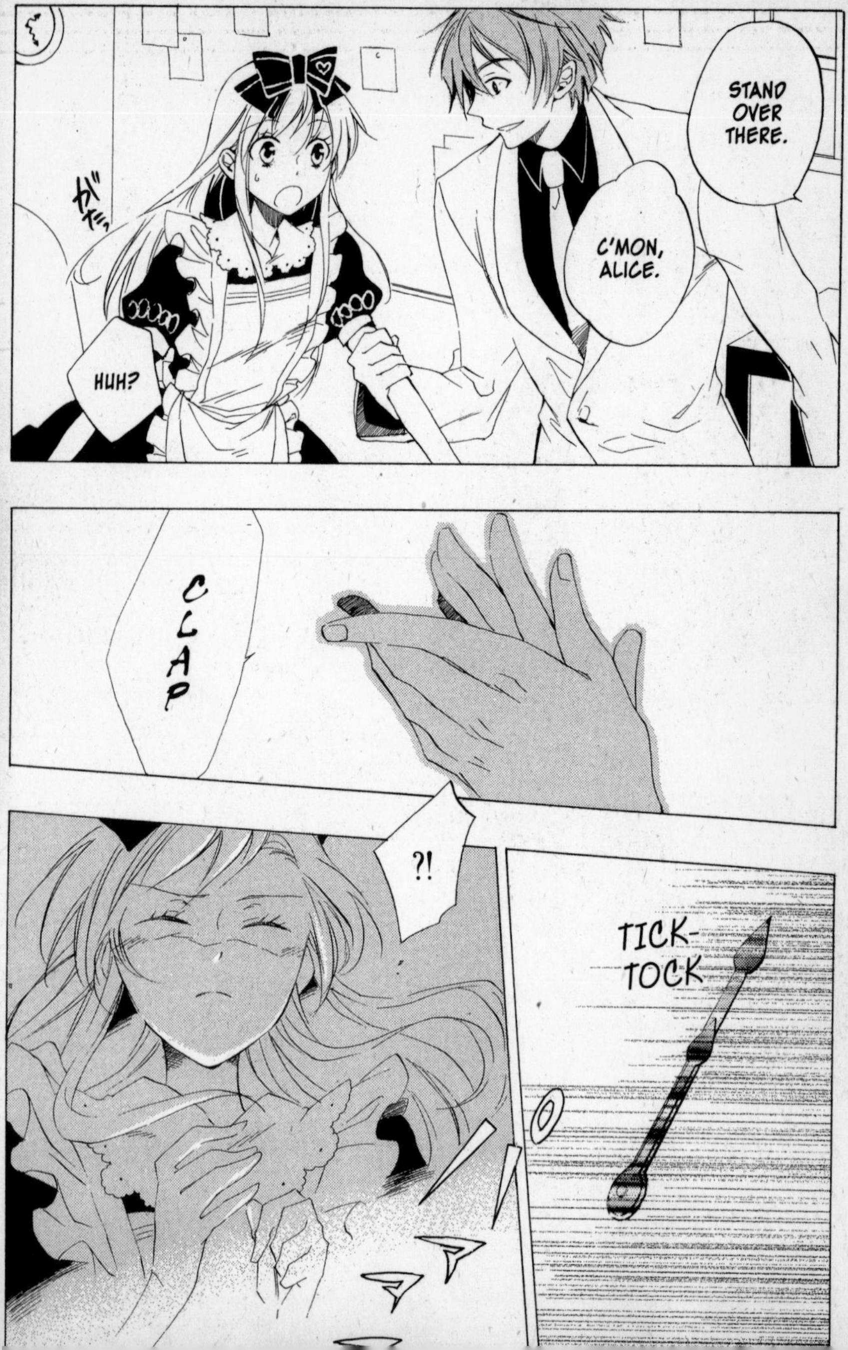
STAND OVER THERE.
C'MON, ALICE.
HUH?
CLAP
TICK-TOCK
?!

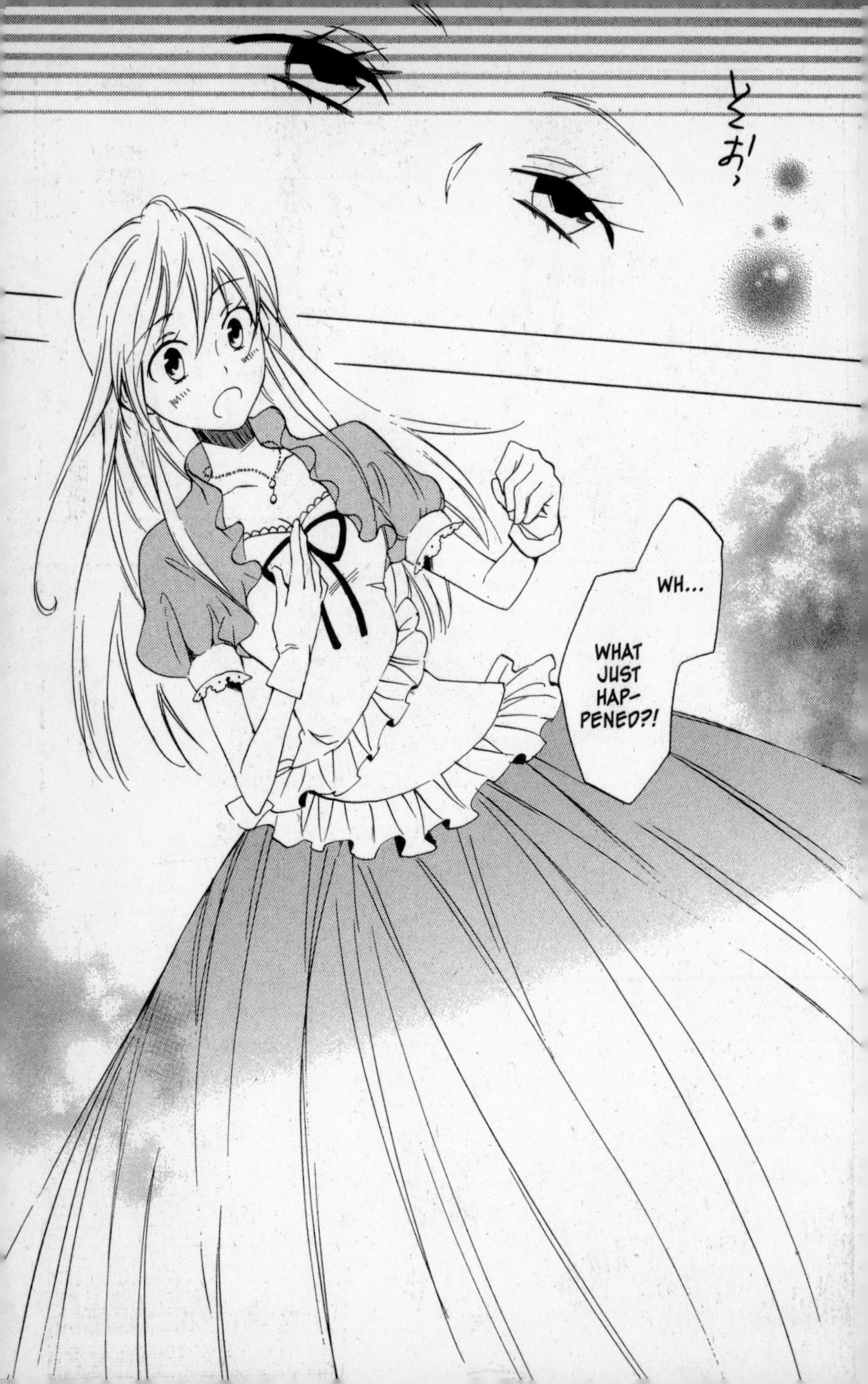

とお、
WH...
WHAT JUST HAP-PENED?!

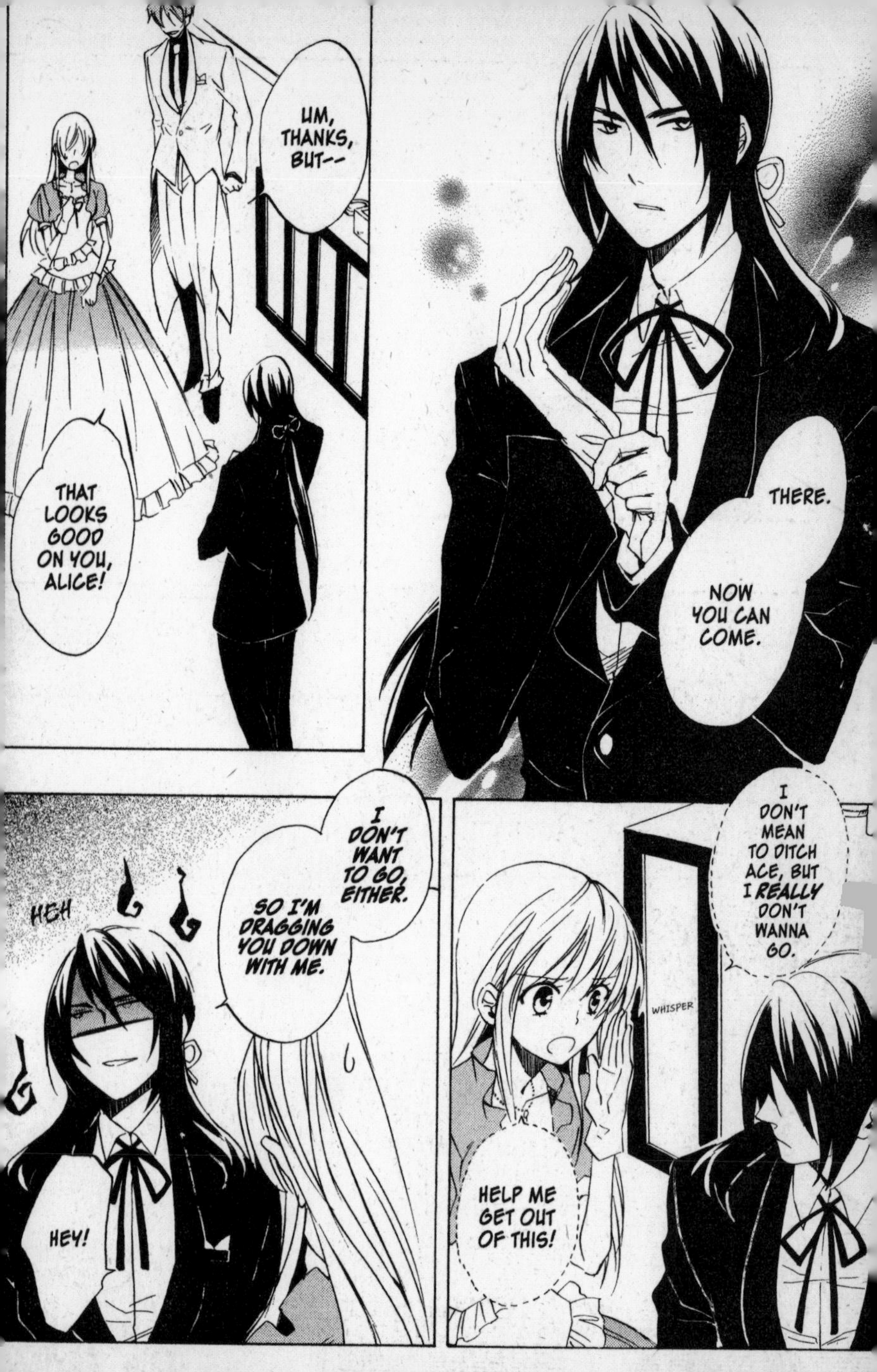
THERE.
NOW YOU CAN COME.
UM, THANKS, BUT--
THAT LOOKS GOOD ON YOU, ALICE!
I DON'T MEAN TO DITCH ACE, BUT I REALLY DON'T WANNA GO.
WHISPER
HELP ME GET OUT OF THIS!
I DON'T WANT TO GO, EITHER.
SO I'M DRAGGING YOU DOWN WITH ME.
HEH
HEY!

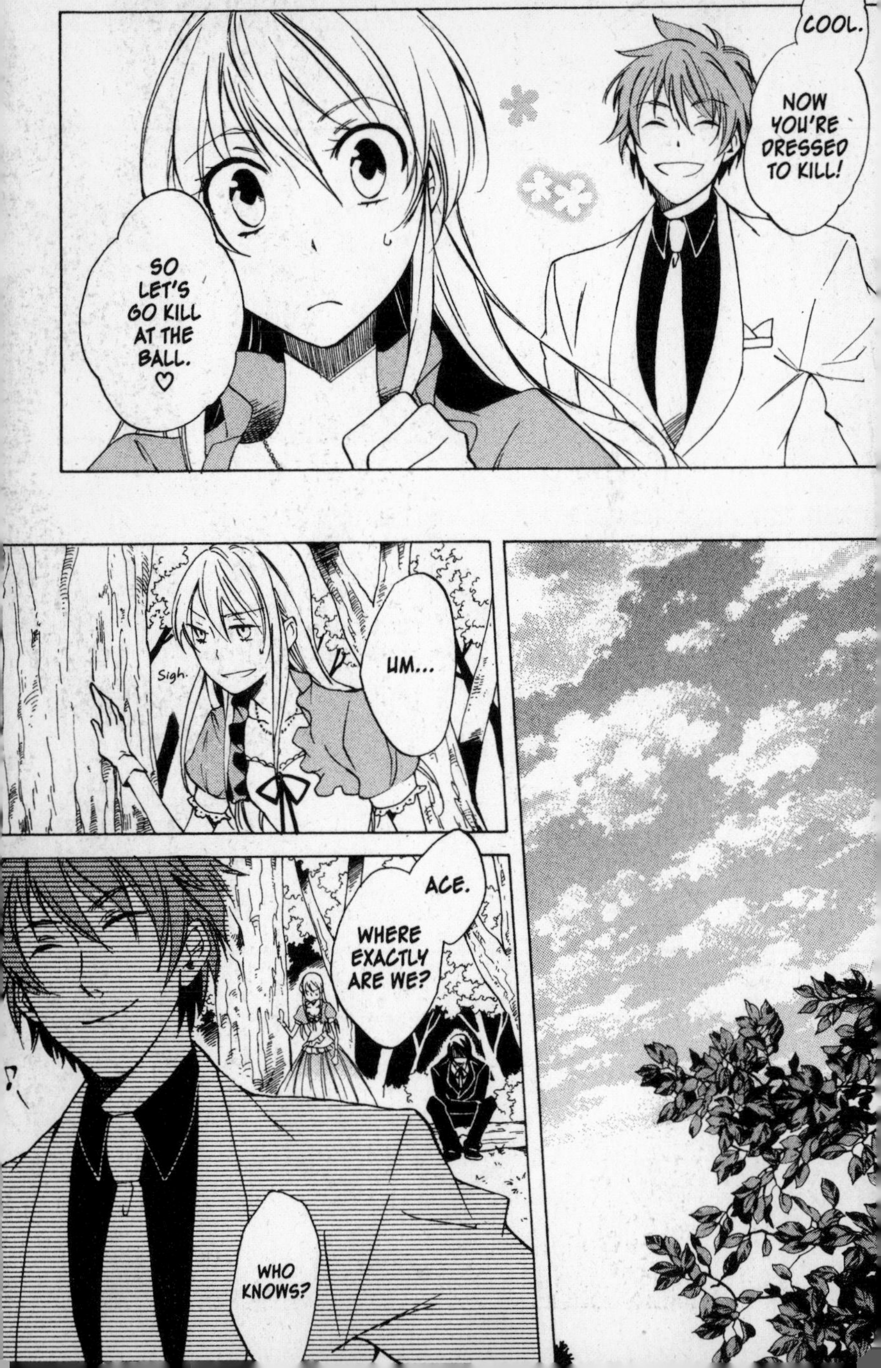
COOL.
NOW YOU'RE DRESSED TO KILL!
SO LET'S GO KILL AT THE BALL. ♡
UM...
Sigh.
ACE.
WHERE EXACTLY ARE WE?
WHO KNOWS?

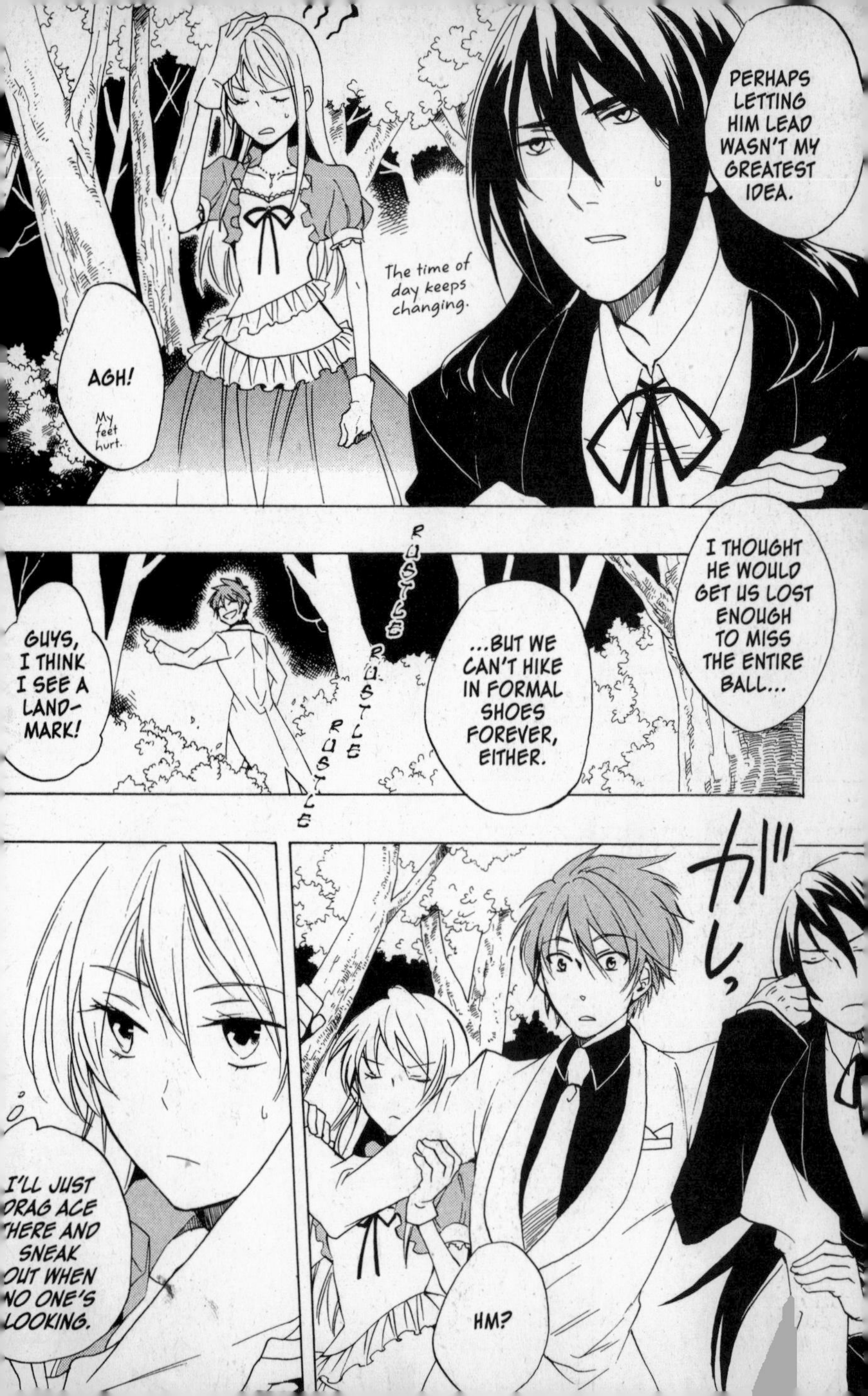

PERHAPS LETTING HIM LEAD WASN'T MY GREATEST IDEA.
The time of day keeps changing.
AGH!
My feet hurt.
I THOUGHT HE WOULD GET US LOST ENOUGH TO MISS THE ENTIRE BALL...
...BUT WE CAN'T HIKE IN FORMAL SHOES FOREVER, EITHER.
RUSTLE
RUSTLE
RUSTLE
GUYS, I THINK I SEE A LAND-MARK!
ガしっ
HM?
I'LL JUST DRAG ACE THERE AND SNEAK OUT WHEN NO ONE'S LOOKING.

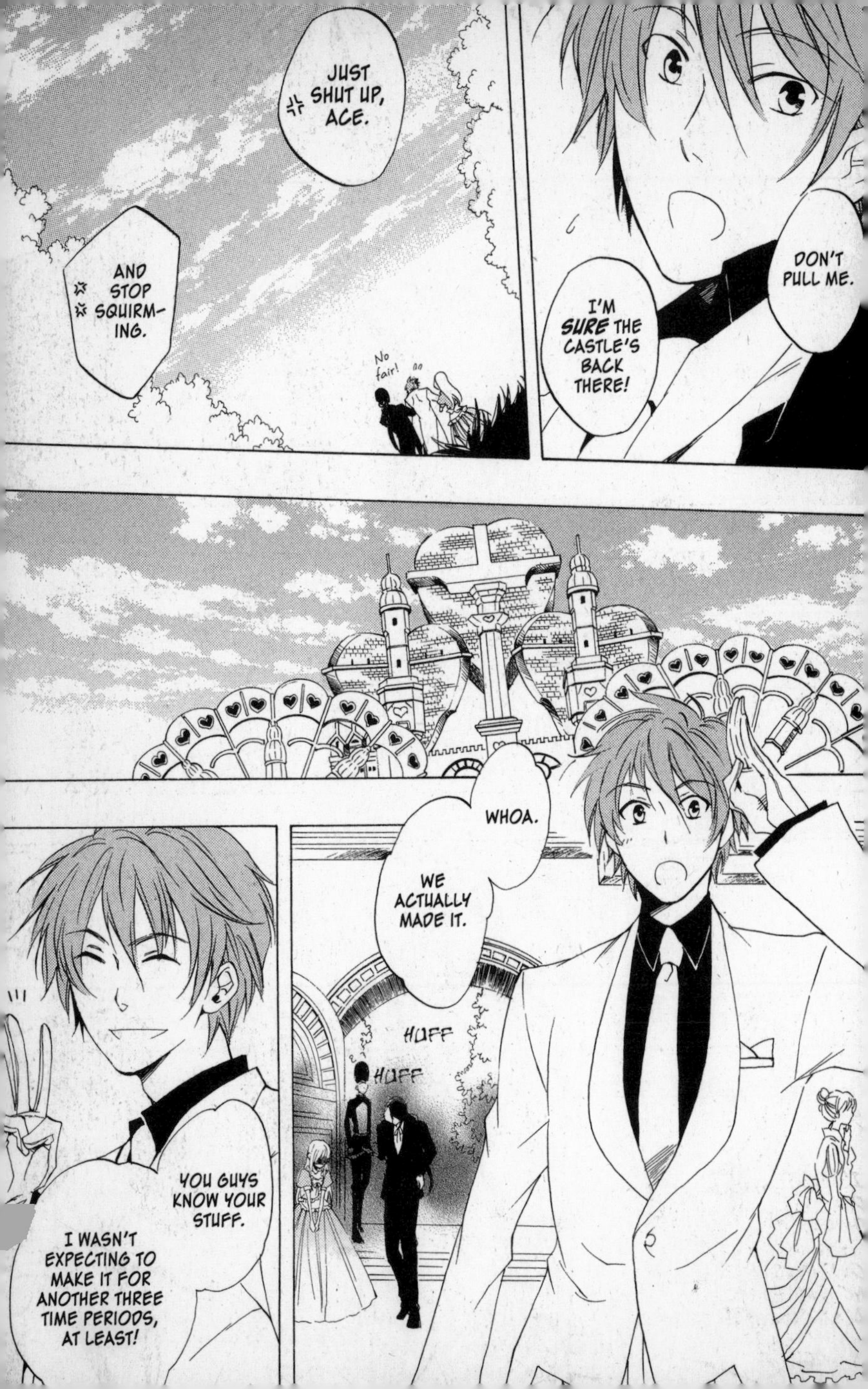
DON'T PULL ME.
I'M *SURE* THE CASTLE'S BACK THERE!
JUST SHUT UP, ACE.
AND STOP SQUIRMING.
No fair!
WHOA.
WE ACTUALLY MADE IT.
HUFF
HUFF
YOU GUYS KNOW YOUR STUFF.
I WASN'T EXPECTING TO MAKE IT FOR ANOTHER THREE TIME PERIODS, AT LEAST!

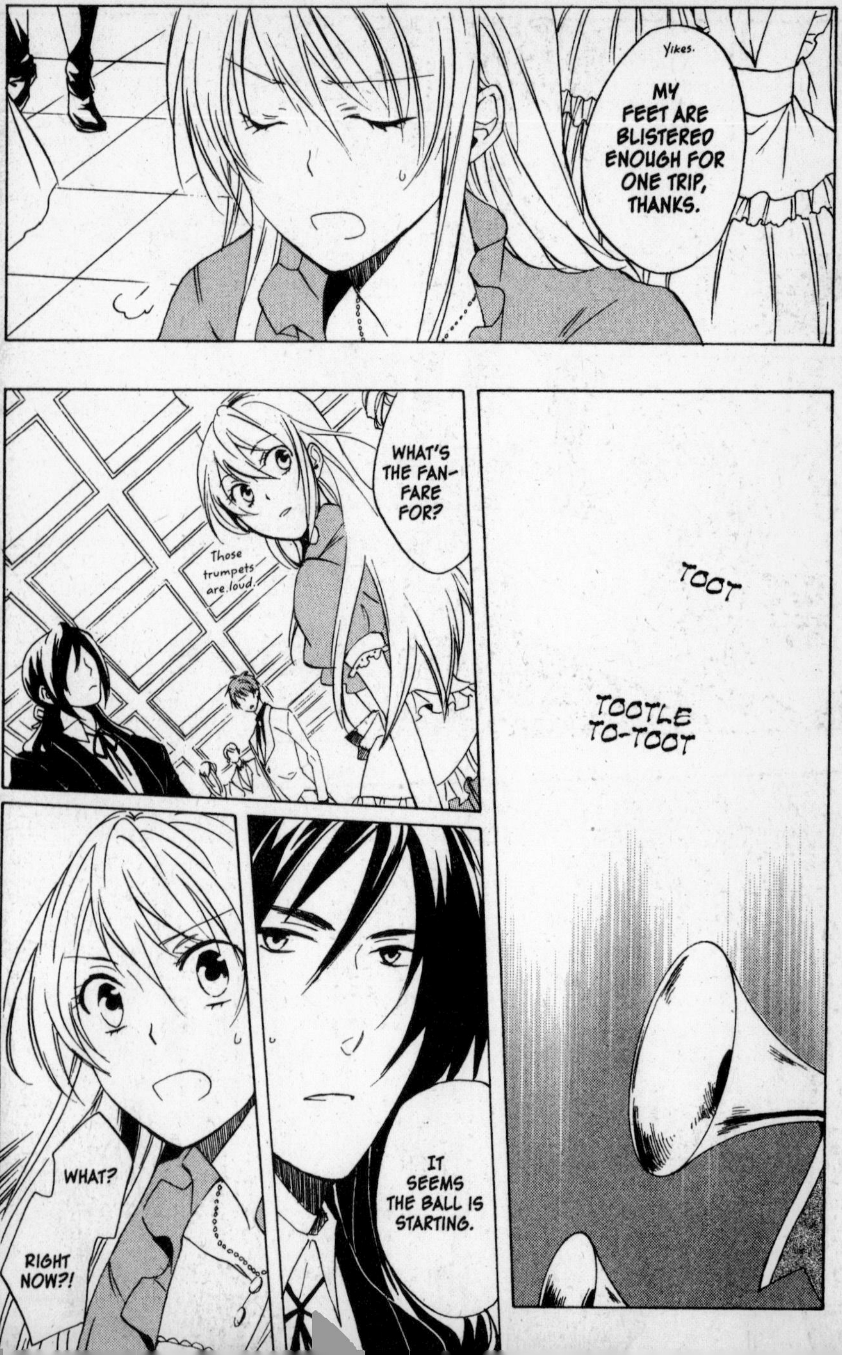
Yikes.
MY FEET ARE BLISTERED ENOUGH FOR ONE TRIP, THANKS.
TOOT
TOOTLE TO-TOOT
WHAT'S THE FAN-FARE FOR?
Those trumpets are loud.
IT SEEMS THE BALL IS STARTING.
WHAT?
RIGHT NOW?!

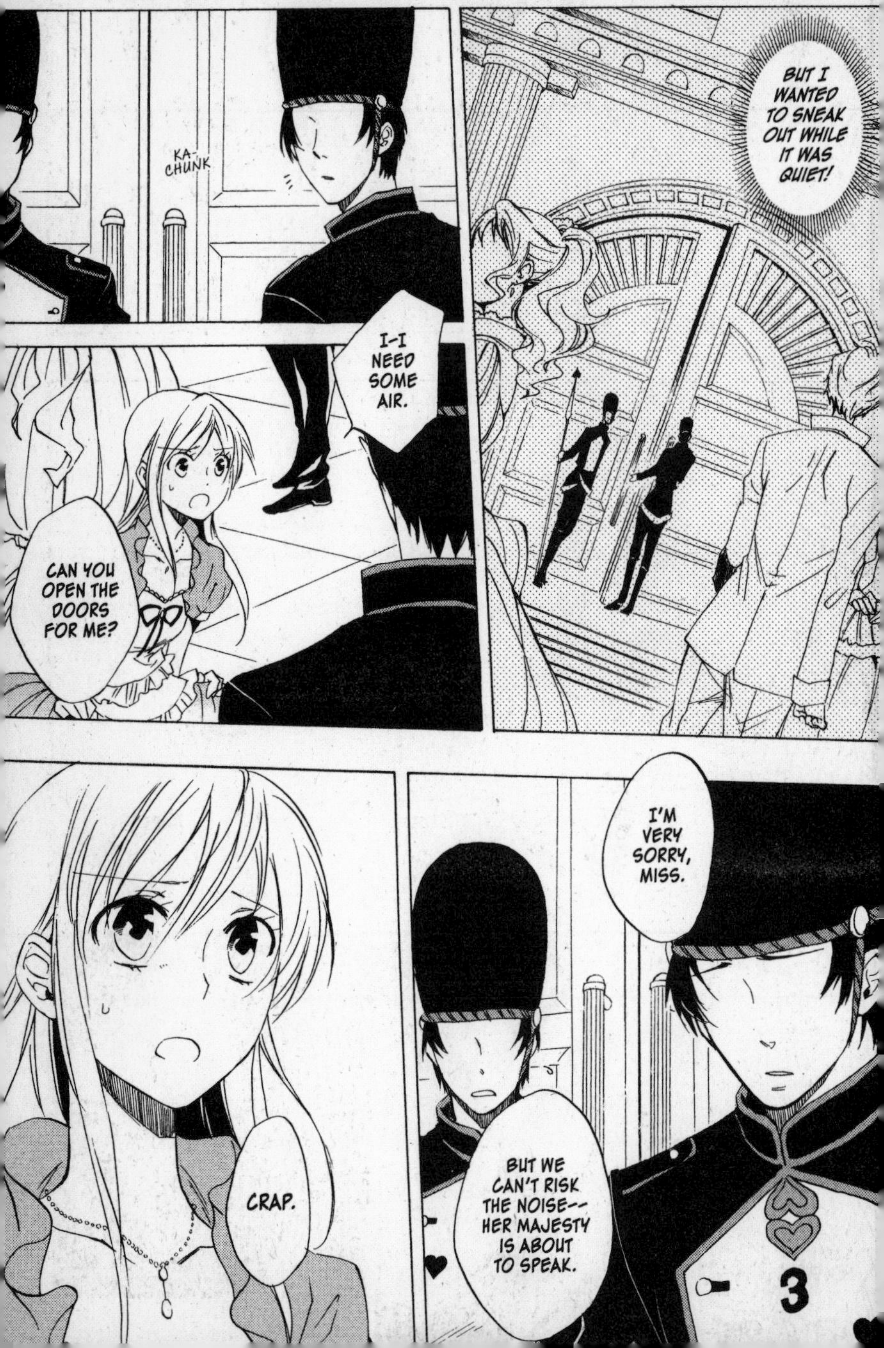
BUT I WANTED TO SNEAK OUT WHILE IT WAS QUIET!
KA-CHUNK
I-I NEED SOME AIR.
CAN YOU OPEN THE DOORS FOR ME?
I'M VERY SORRY, MISS.
BUT WE CAN'T RISK THE NOISE--HER MAJESTY IS ABOUT TO SPEAK.
3
CRAP.

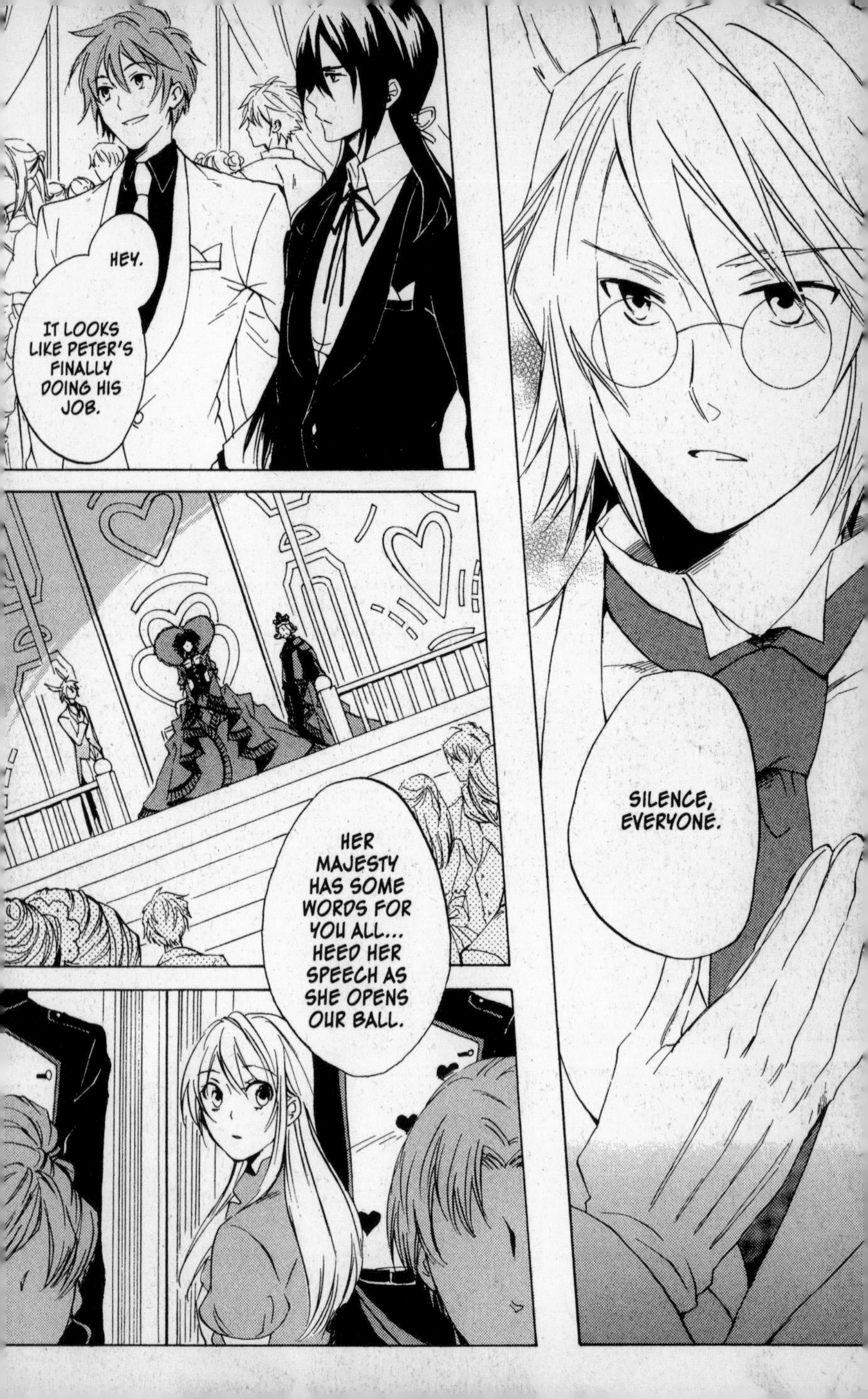
SILENCE, EVERYONE.
HEY.
IT LOOKS LIKE PETER'S FINALLY DOING HIS JOB.
HER MAJESTY HAS SOME WORDS FOR YOU ALL... HEED HER SPEECH AS SHE OPENS OUR BALL.

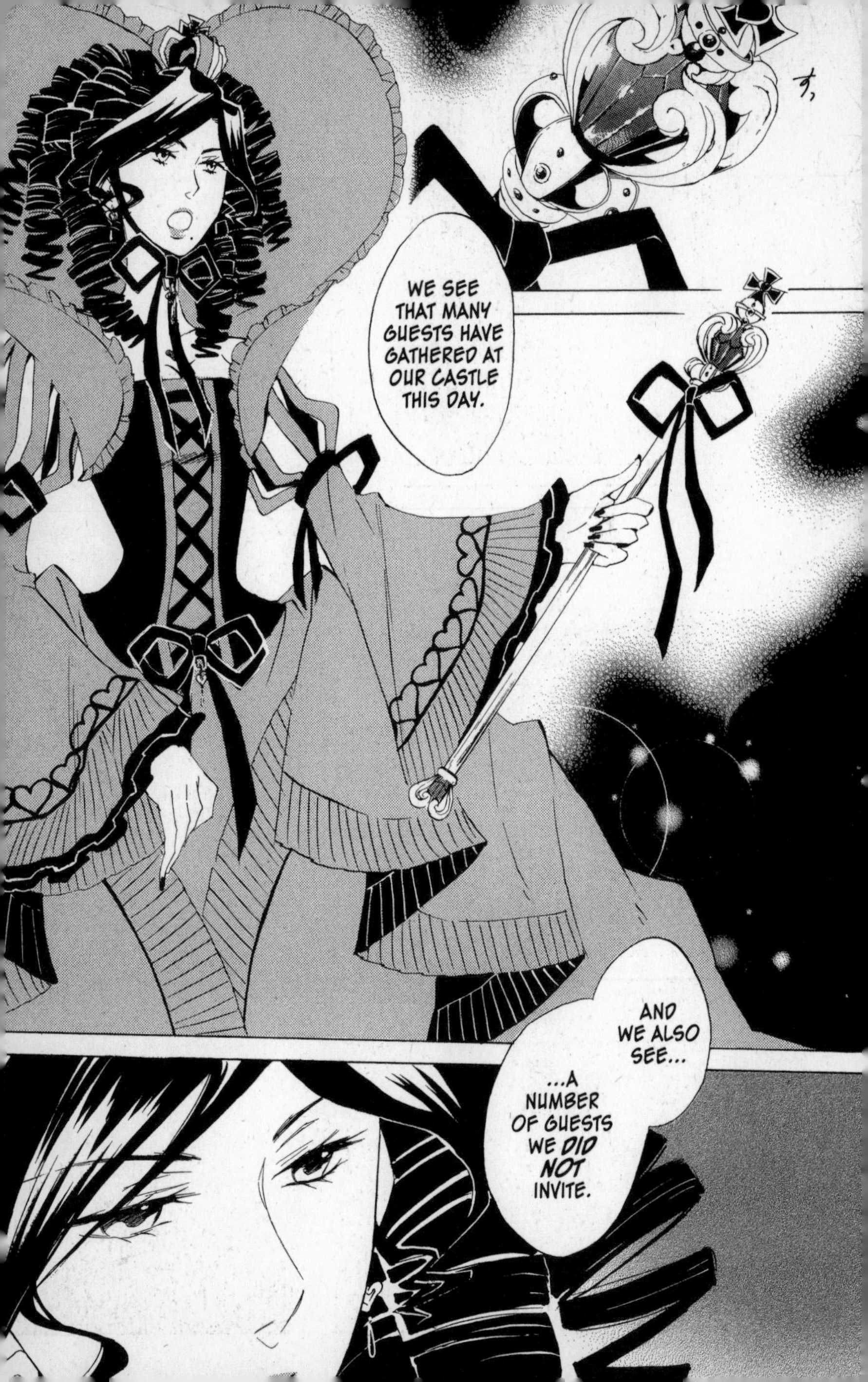
すっ
WE SEE THAT MANY GUESTS HAVE GATHERED AT OUR CASTLE THIS DAY.
AND WE ALSO SEE...
...A NUMBER OF GUESTS WE *DID NOT* INVITE.

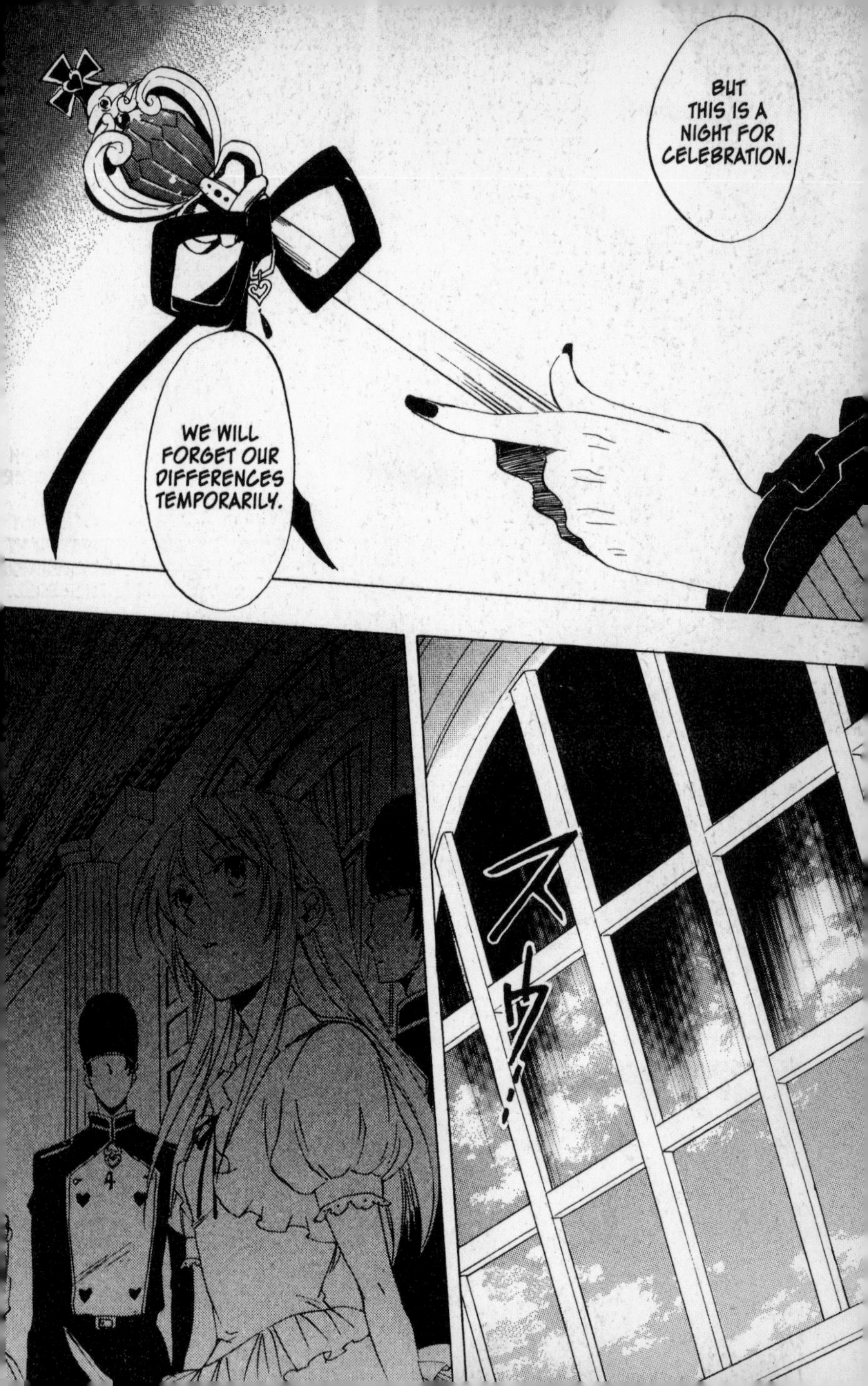
BUT THIS IS A NIGHT FOR CELEBRATION.
WE WILL FORGET OUR DIFFERENCES TEMPORARILY.

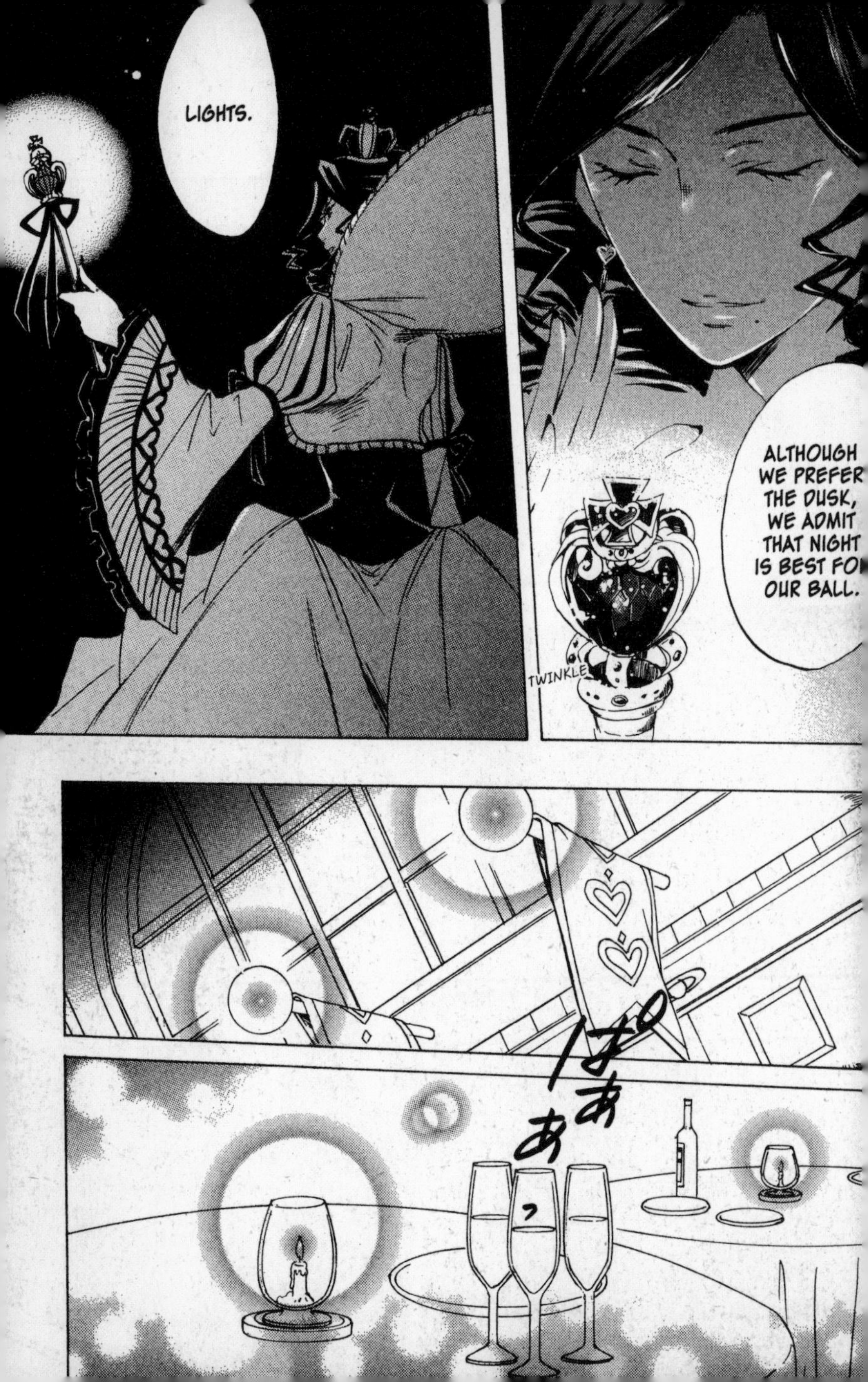
ALTHOUGH WE PREFER THE DUSK, WE ADMIT THAT NIGHT IS BEST FO OUR BALL.
TWINKLE
LIGHTS.
ぱぁぁっ

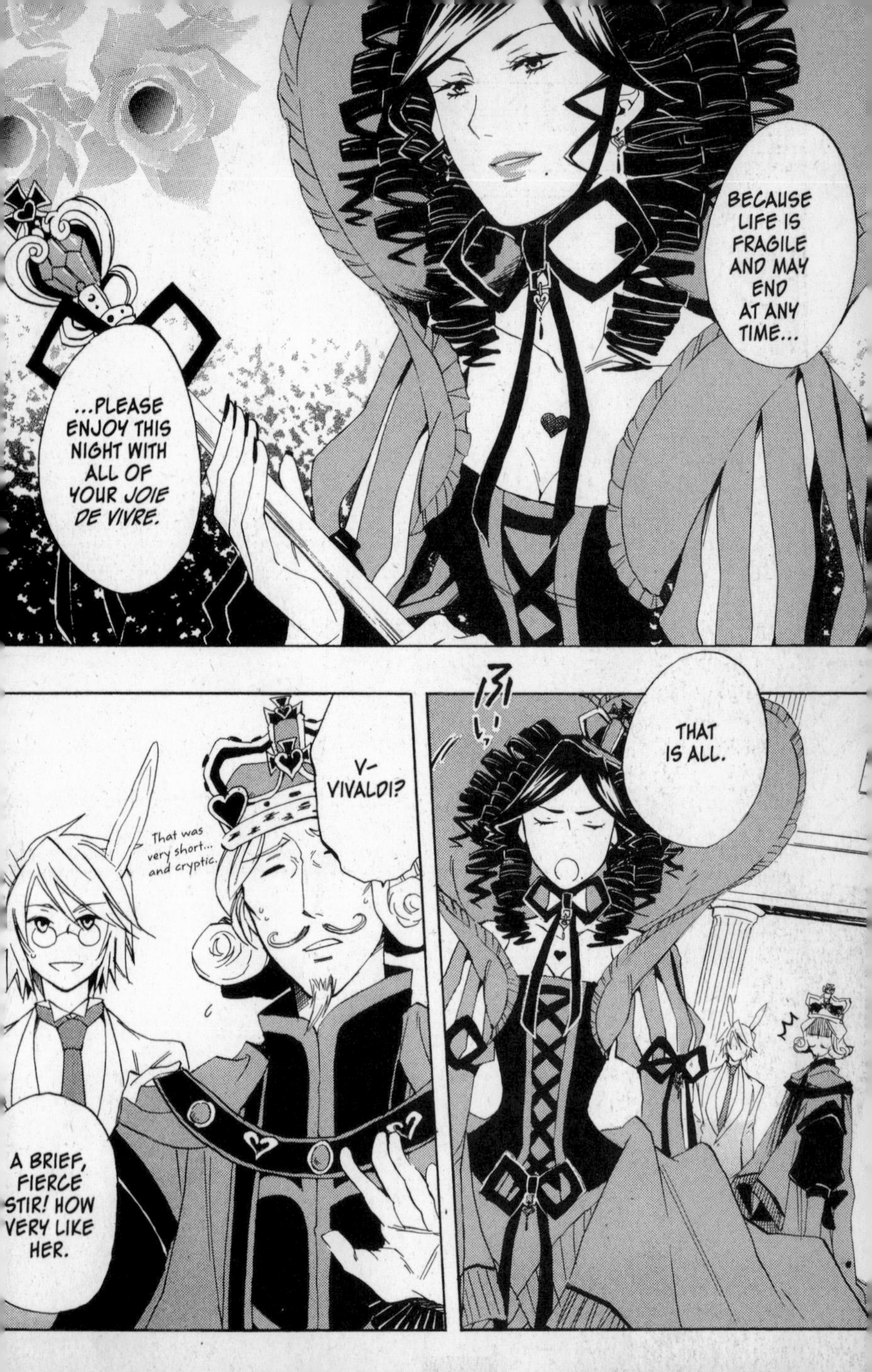
BECAUSE LIFE IS FRAGILE AND MAY END AT ANY TIME...
...PLEASE ENJOY THIS NIGHT WITH ALL OF YOUR JOIE DE VIVRE.
THAT IS ALL.
V-VIVALDI?
That was very short... and cryptic.
A BRIEF, FIERCE STIR! HOW VERY LIKE HER.

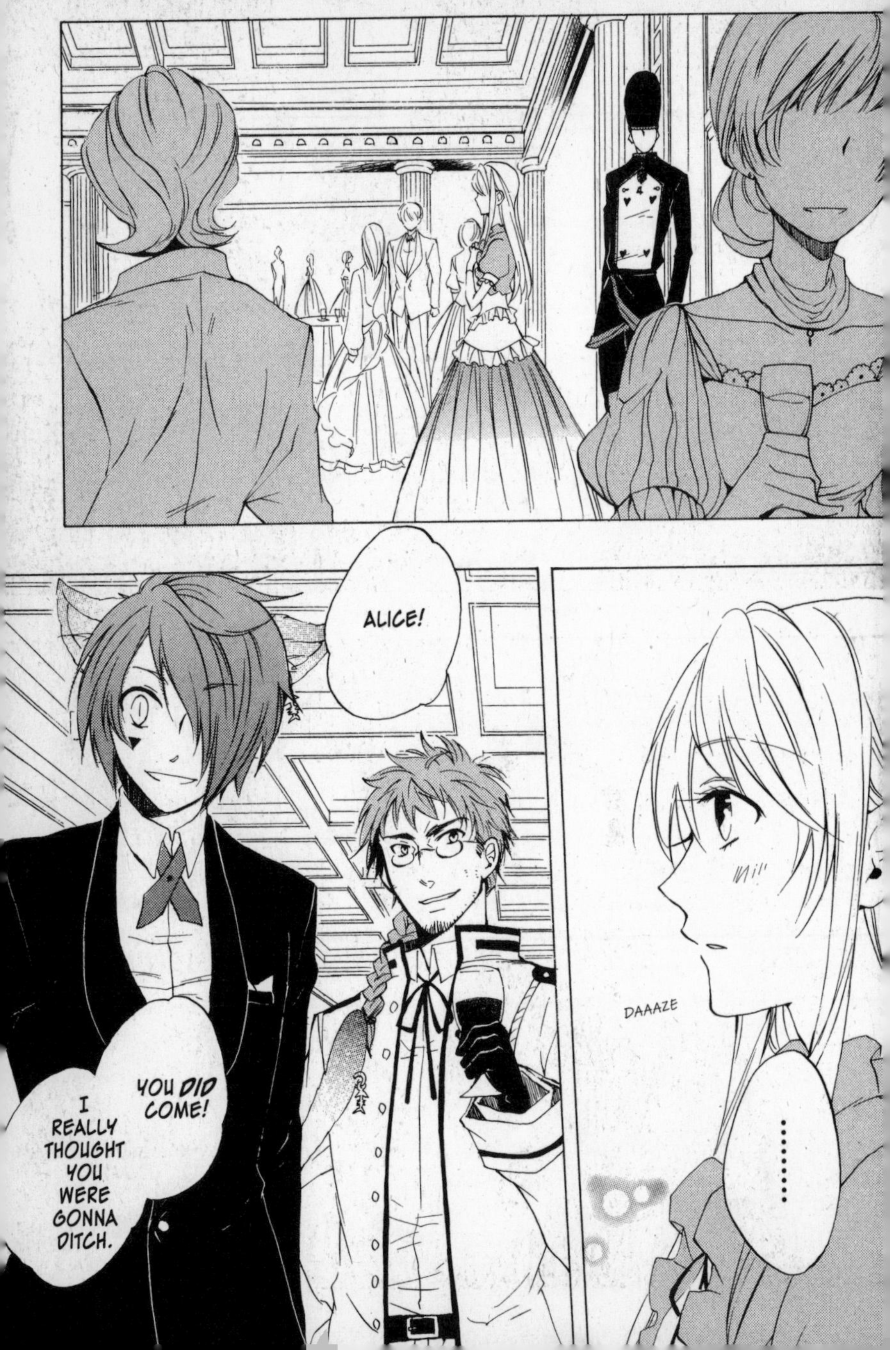
DAAAZE
......
ALICE!
YOU DID COME!
I REALLY THOUGHT YOU WERE GONNA DITCH.

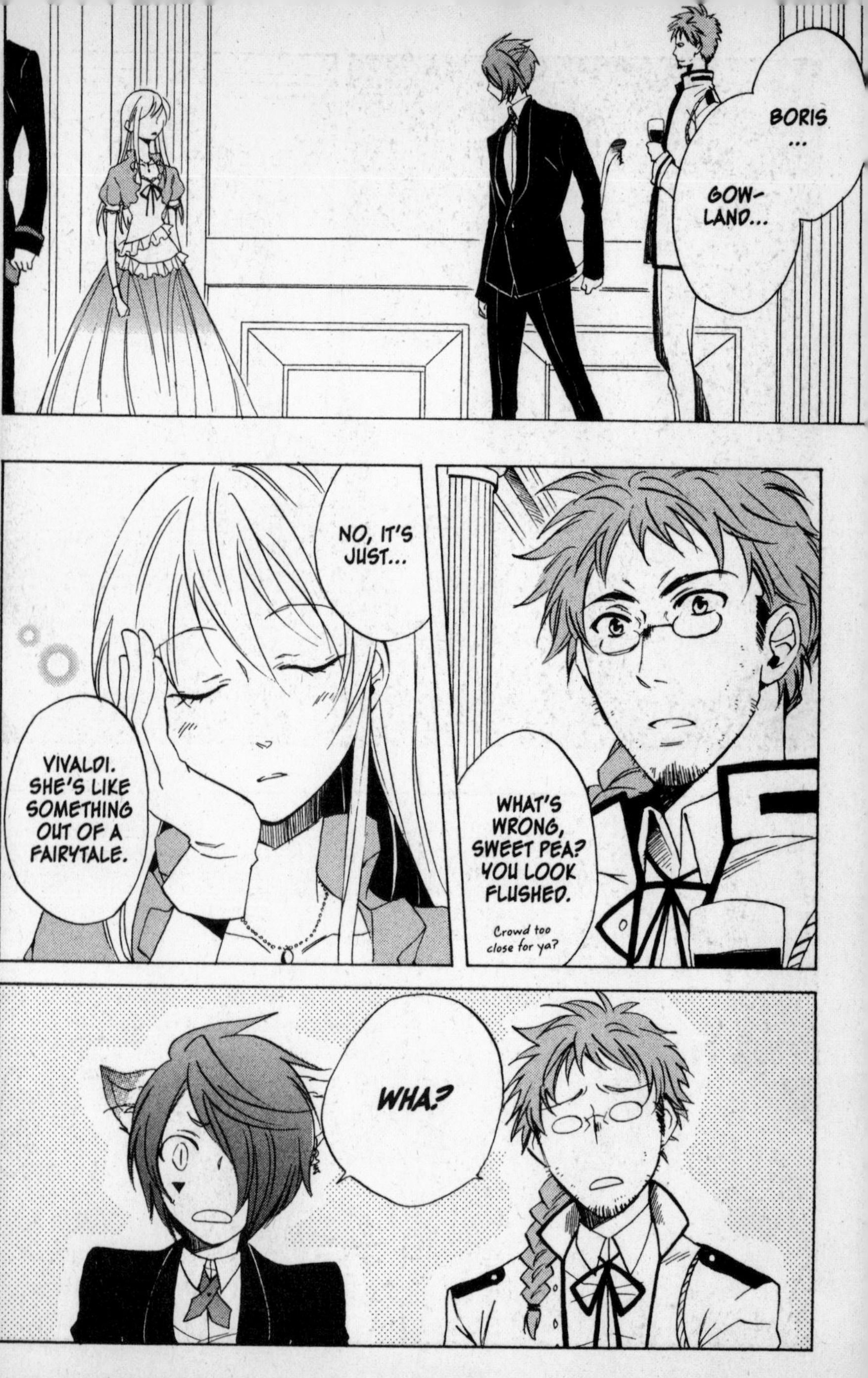
BORIS ... GOW-LAND...
WHAT'S WRONG, SWEET PEA? YOU LOOK FLUSHED.
Crowd too close for ya?
NO, IT'S JUST...
VIVALDI. SHE'S LIKE SOMETHING OUT OF A FAIRYTALE.
WHA?

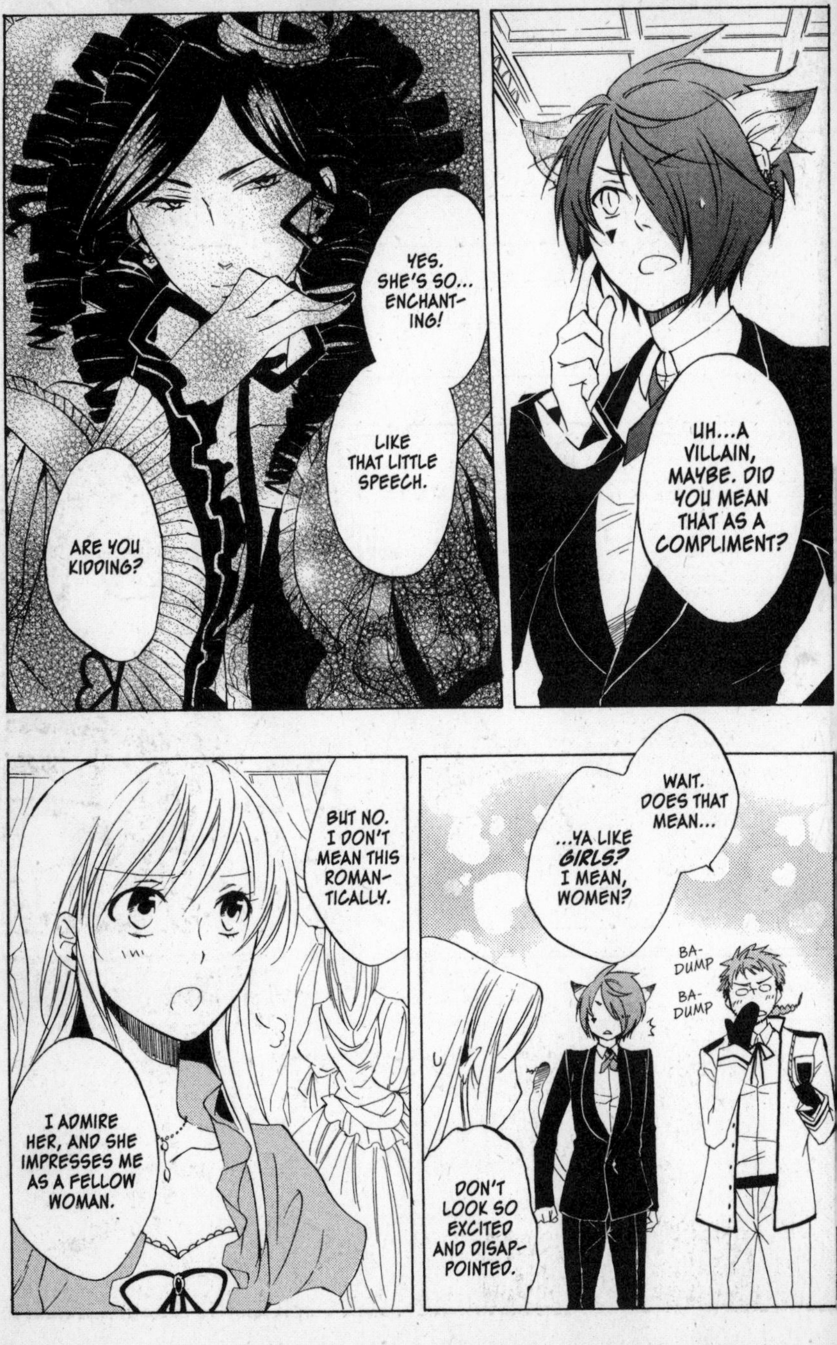
UH...A VILLAIN, MAYBE. DID YOU MEAN THAT AS A COMPLIMENT?
YES. SHE'S SO... ENCHANT-ING!
LIKE THAT LITTLE SPEECH.
ARE YOU KIDDING?
WAIT. DOES THAT MEAN...
...YA LIKE GIRLS? I MEAN, WOMEN?
BA-DUMP
BA-DUMP
DON'T LOOK SO EXCITED AND DISAP-POINTED.
BUT NO. I DON'T MEAN THIS ROMAN-TICALLY.
I ADMIRE HER, AND SHE IMPRESSES ME AS A FELLOW WOMAN.

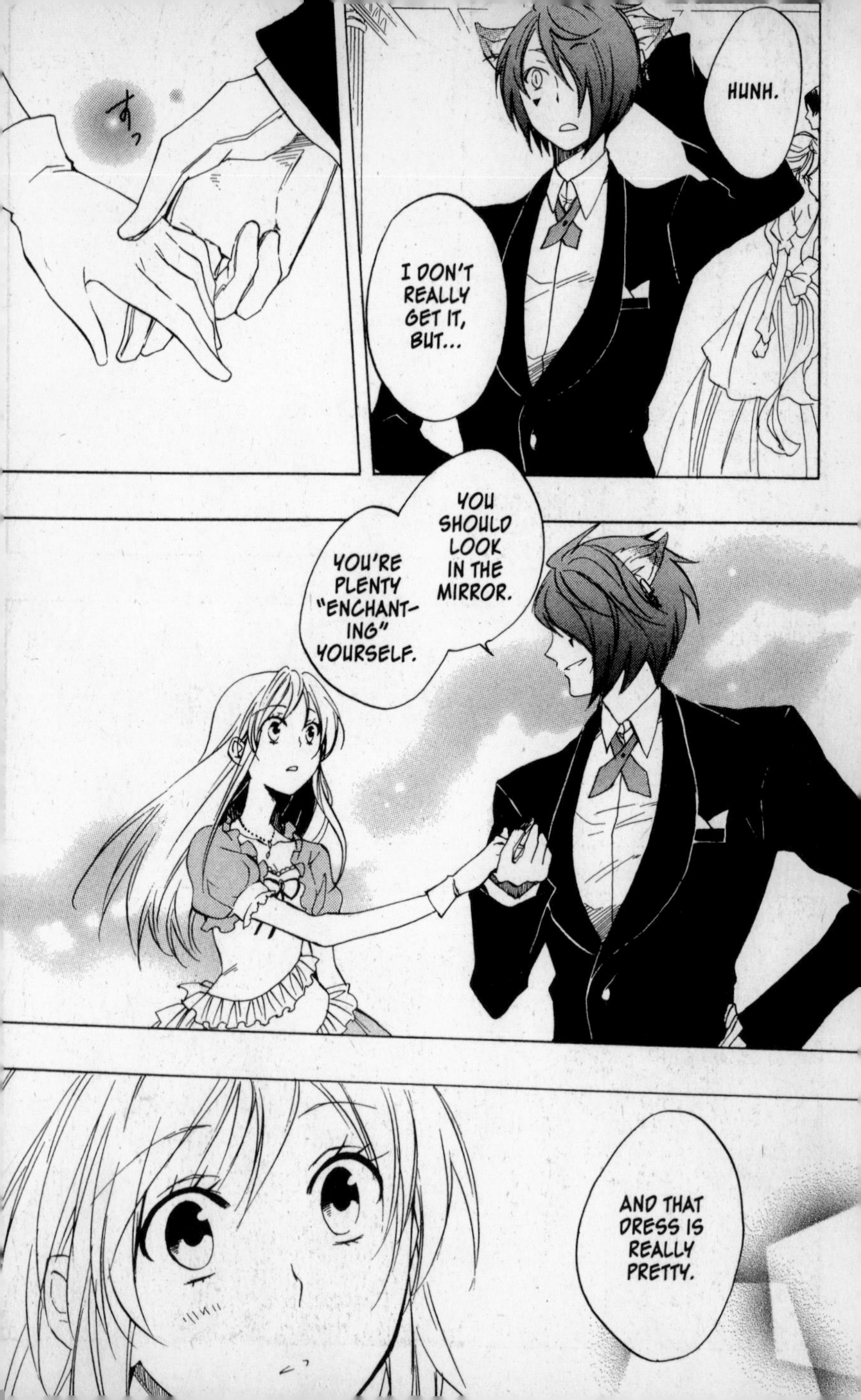
HUNH.
I DON'T REALLY GET IT, BUT...
すっ
YOU SHOULD LOOK IN THE MIRROR.
YOU'RE PLENTY "ENCHANTING" YOURSELF.
AND THAT DRESS IS REALLY PRETTY.

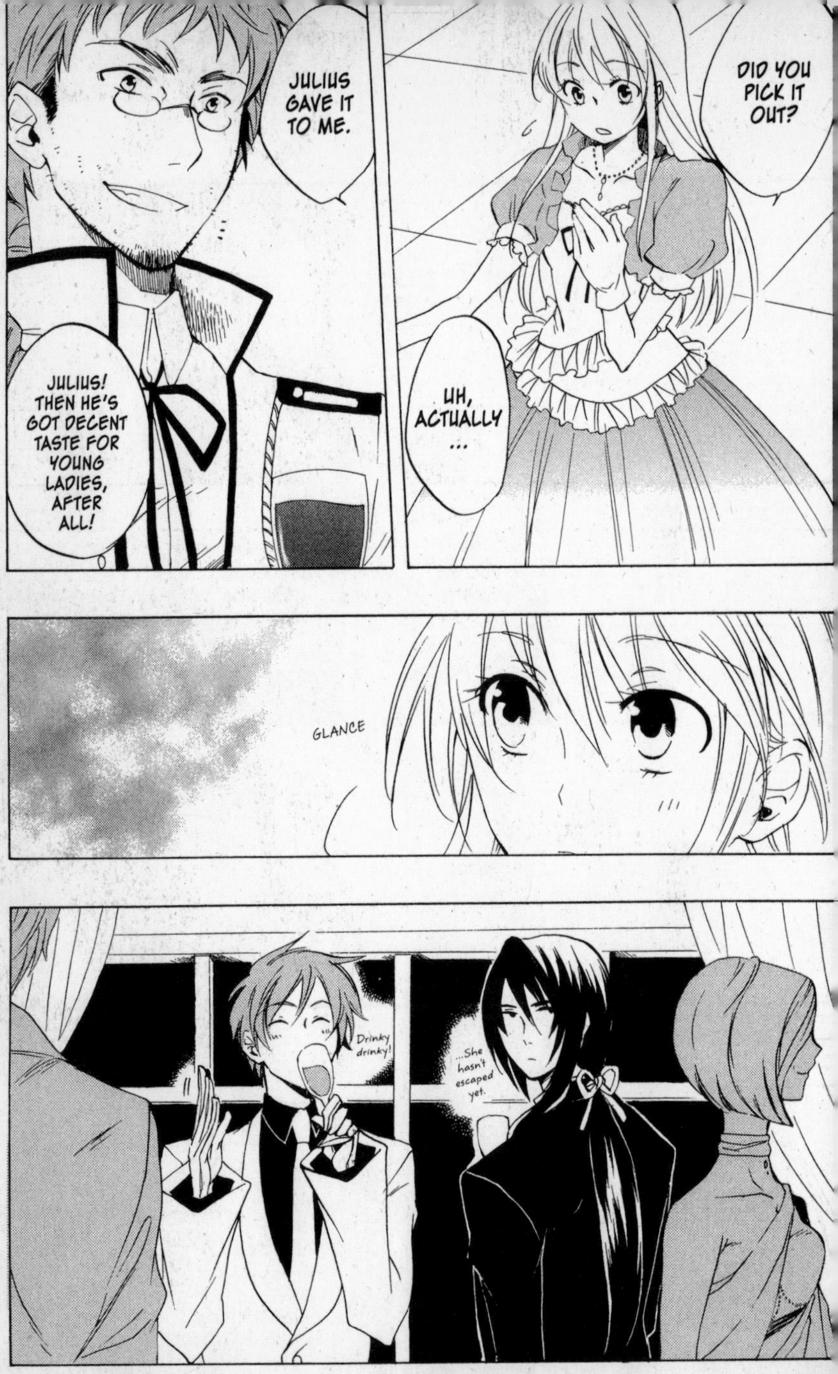
DID YOU PICK IT OUT?
UH, ACTUALLY ...
JULIUS GAVE IT TO ME.
JULIUS! THEN HE'S GOT DECENT TASTE FOR YOUNG LADIES, AFTER ALL!
GLANCE
...She hasn't escaped yet.
Drinky drinky!

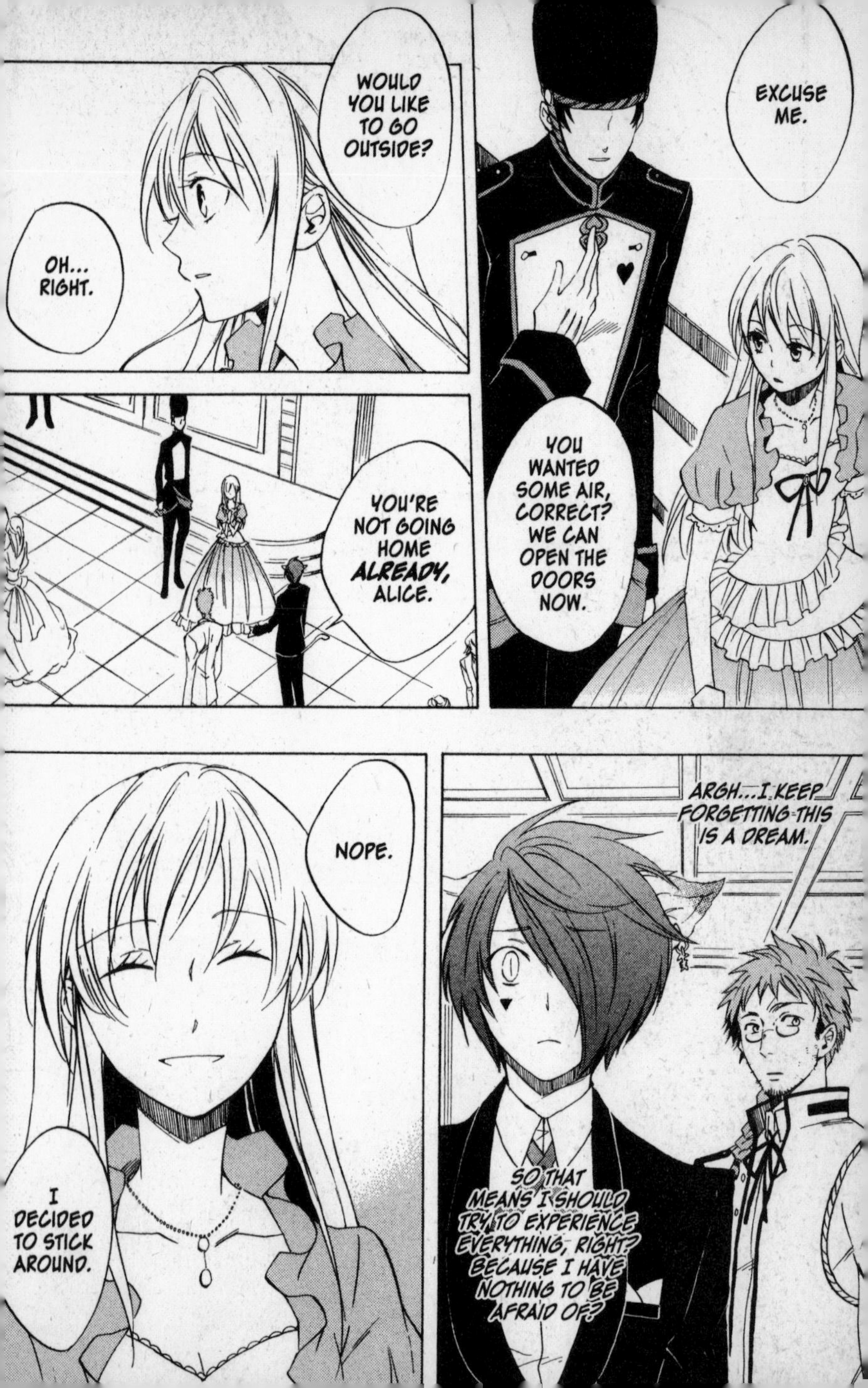
EXCUSE ME.
YOU WANTED SOME AIR, CORRECT? WE CAN OPEN THE DOORS NOW.
WOULD YOU LIKE TO GO OUTSIDE?
OH... RIGHT.
YOU'RE NOT GOING HOME **ALREADY**, ALICE.
ARGH...I KEEP FORGETTING THIS IS A DREAM.
SO THAT MEANS I SHOULD TRY TO EXPERIENCE EVERYTHING, RIGHT? BECAUSE I HAVE NOTHING TO BE AFRAID OF?
NOPE.
I DECIDED TO STICK AROUND.

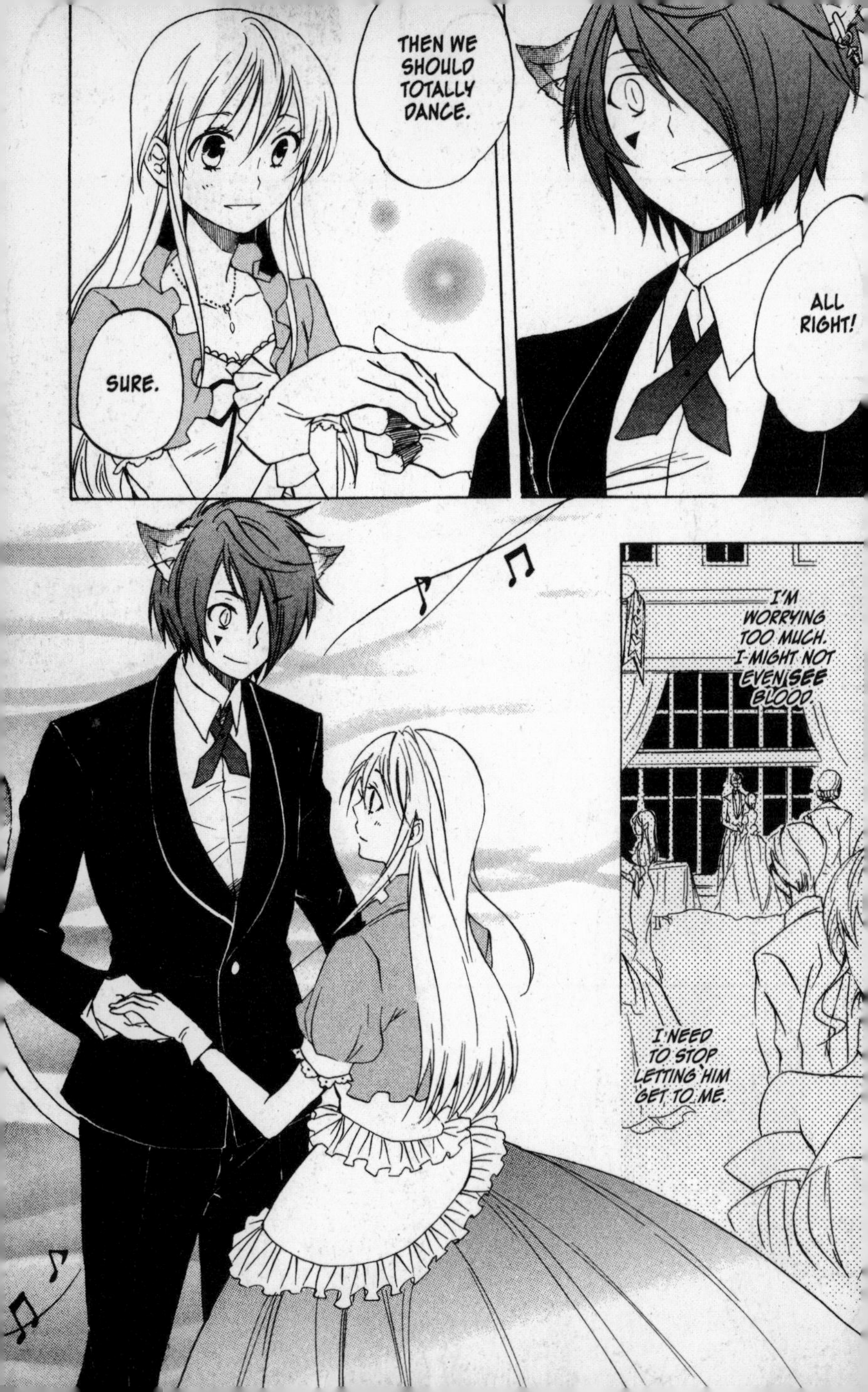
ALL RIGHT!
THEN WE SHOULD TOTALLY DANCE.
SURE.
I'M WORRYING TOO MUCH. I MIGHT NOT EVEN SEE BLOOD.
I NEED TO STOP LETTING HIM GET TO ME.

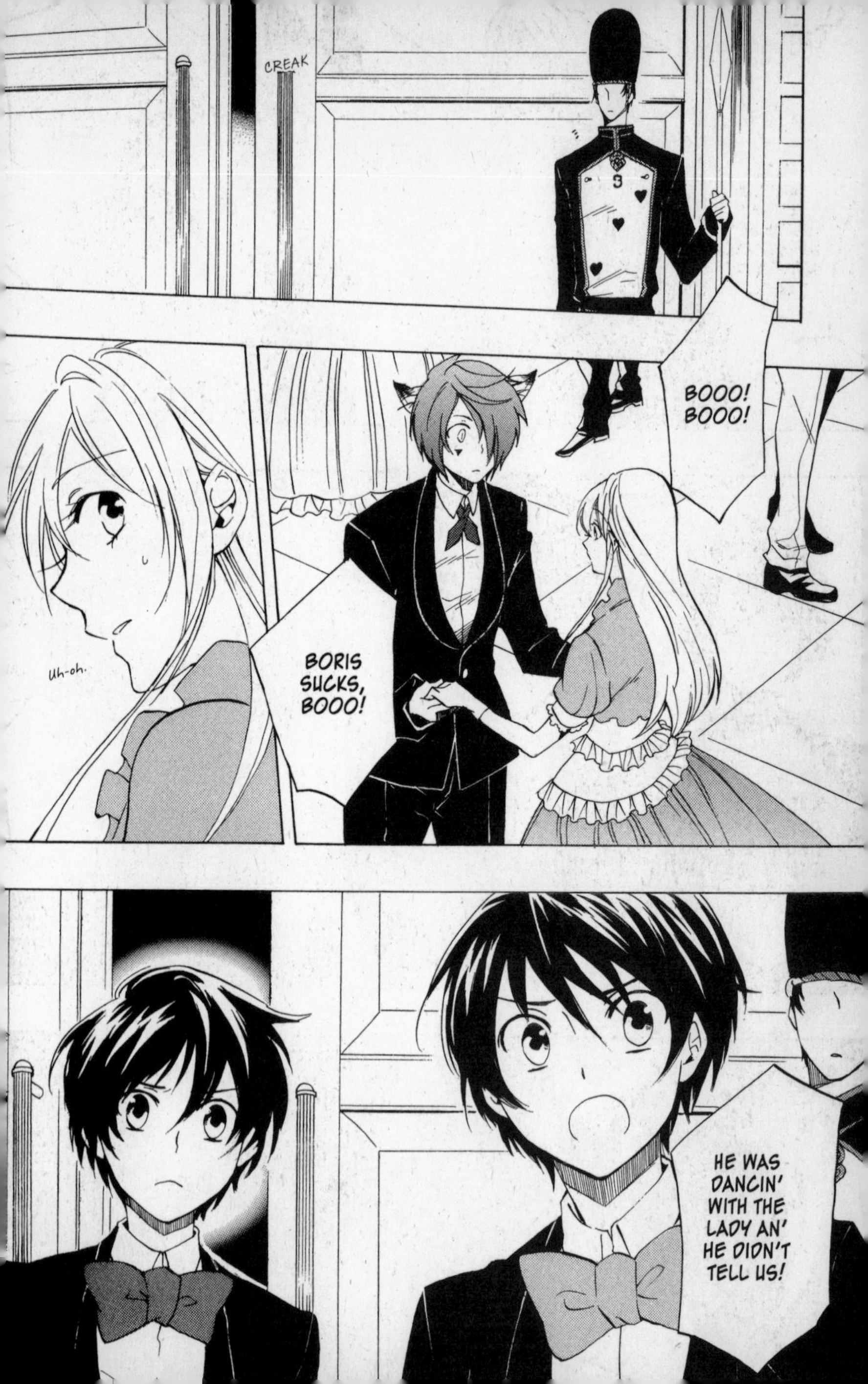
CREAK
BOOO! BOOO!
BORIS SUCKS, BOOO!
Uh-oh.
HE WAS DANCIN' WITH THE LADY AN' HE DIDN'T TELL US!

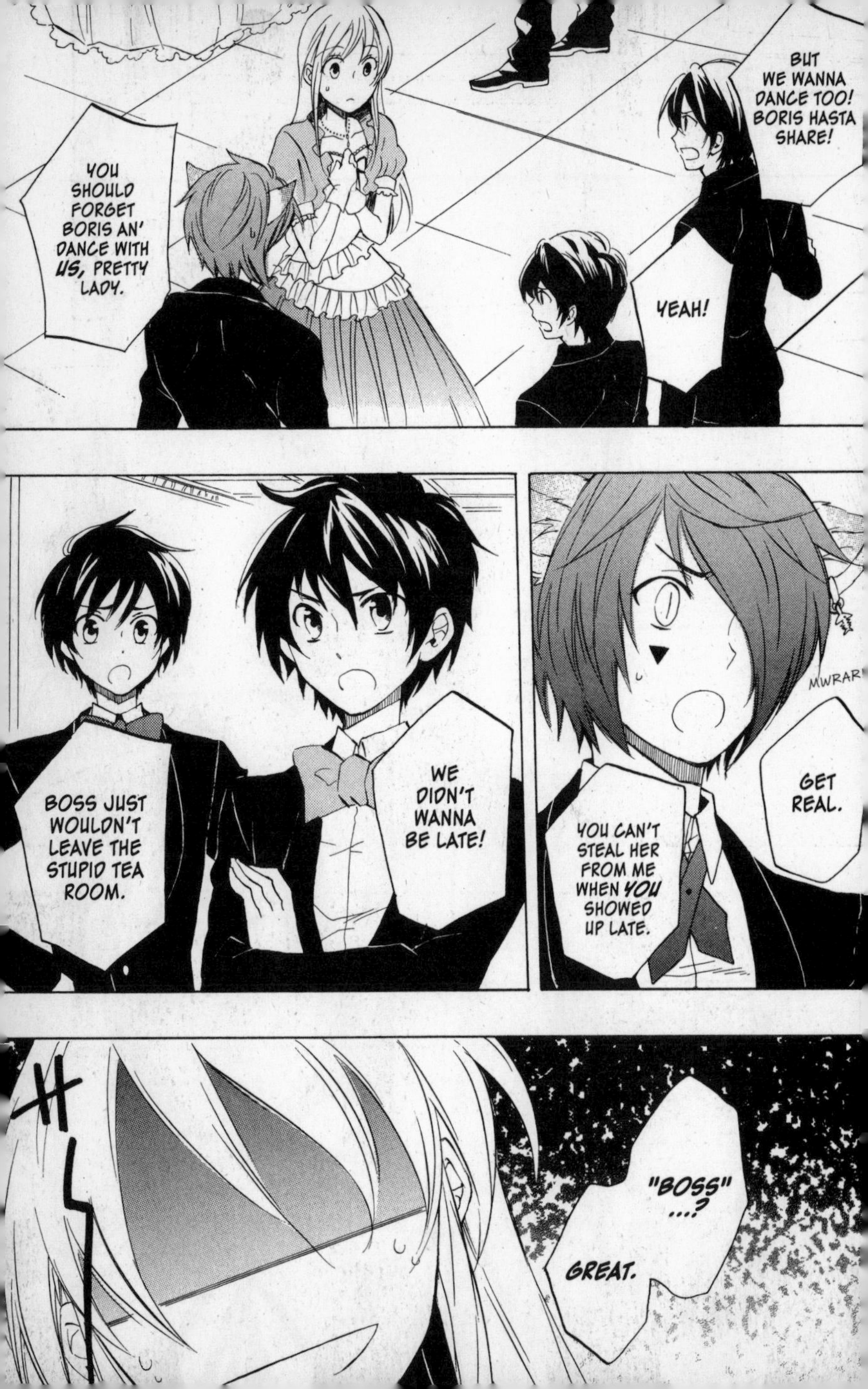
BUT WE WANNA DANCE TOO! BORIS HASTA SHARE!
YEAH!
YOU SHOULD FORGET BORIS AN' DANCE WITH US, PRETTY LADY.
MWRAR
GET REAL.
YOU CAN'T STEAL HER FROM ME WHEN YOU SHOWED UP LATE.
WE DIDN'T WANNA BE LATE!
BOSS JUST WOULDN'T LEAVE THE STUPID TEA ROOM.
"BOSS" ....?
GREAT.

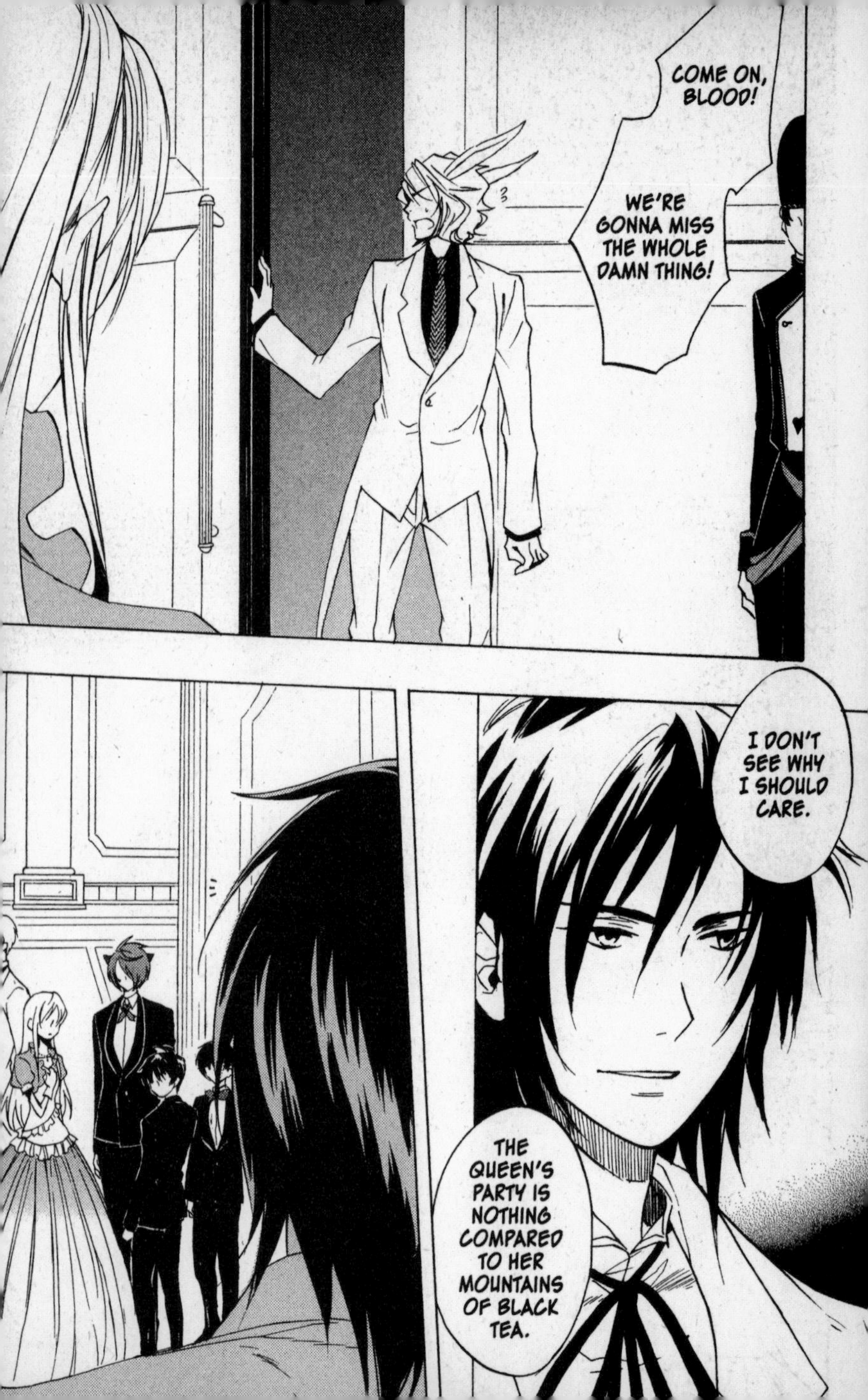
COME ON, BLOOD!
WE'RE GONNA MISS THE WHOLE DAMN THING!
I DON'T SEE WHY I SHOULD CARE.
THE QUEEN'S PARTY IS NOTHING COMPARED TO HER MOUNTAINS OF BLACK TEA.

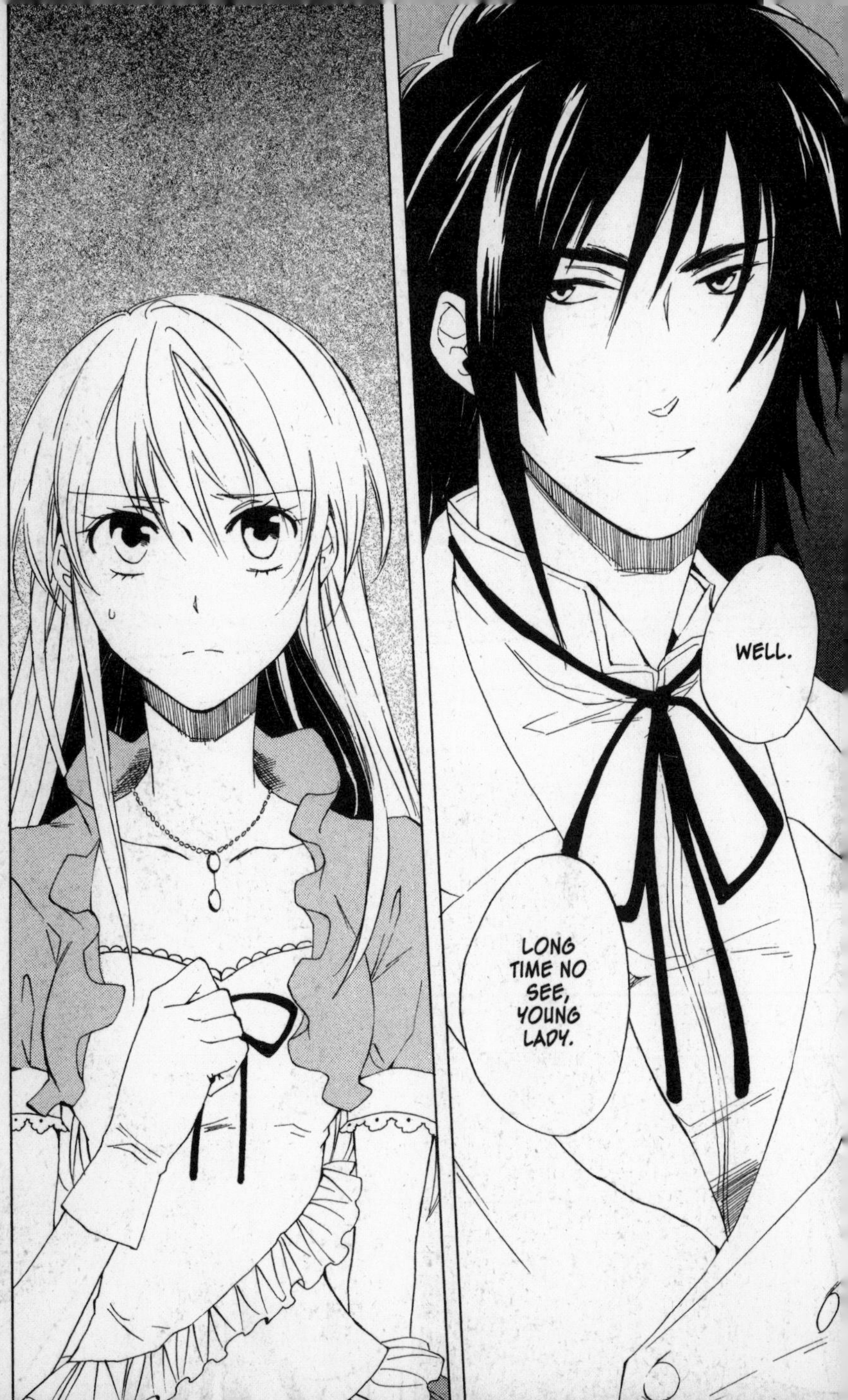
WELL.
LONG TIME NO SEE, YOUNG LADY.

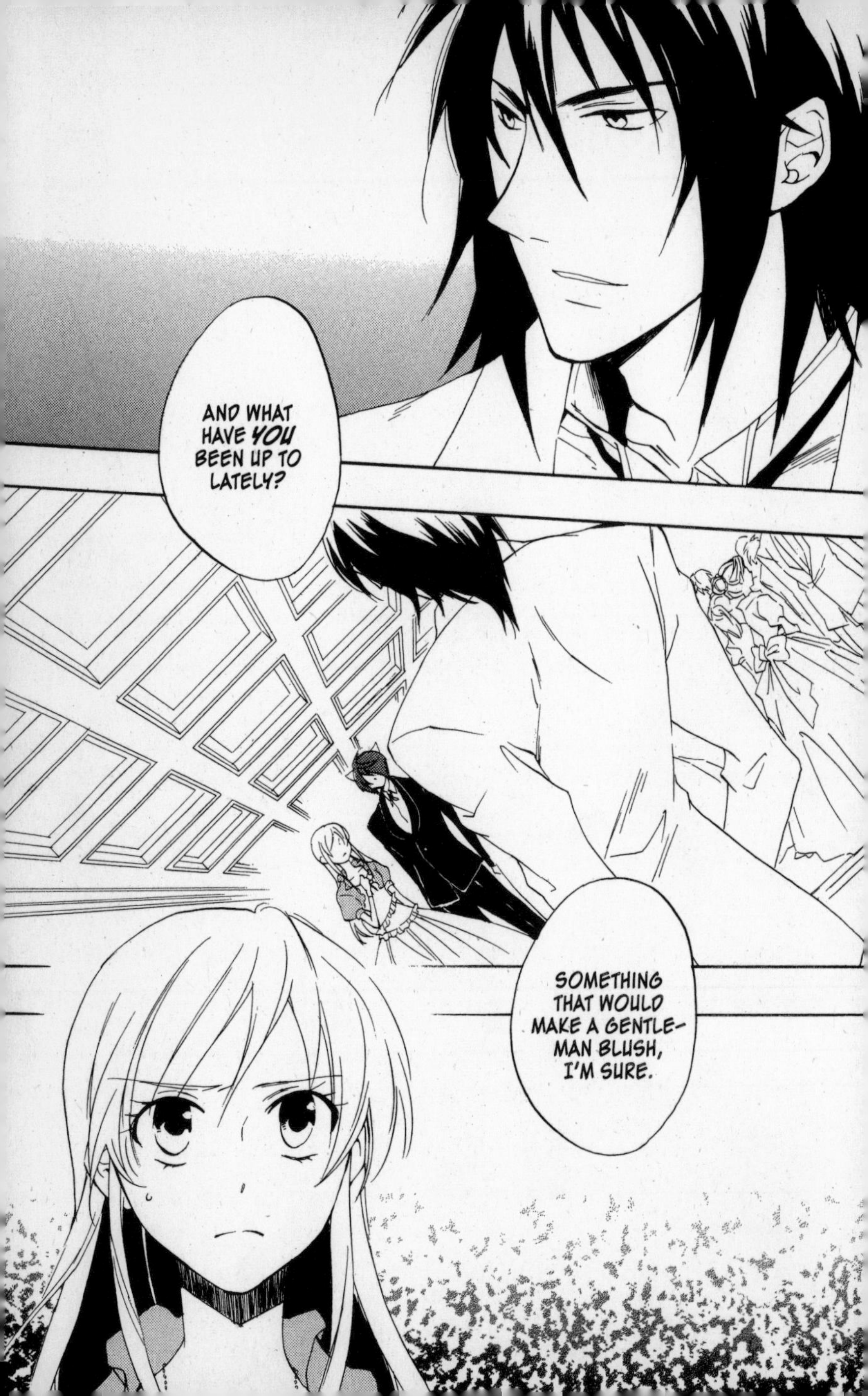
AND WHAT HAVE *YOU* BEEN UP TO LATELY?
SOMETHING THAT WOULD MAKE A GENTLE-MAN BLUSH, I'M SURE.

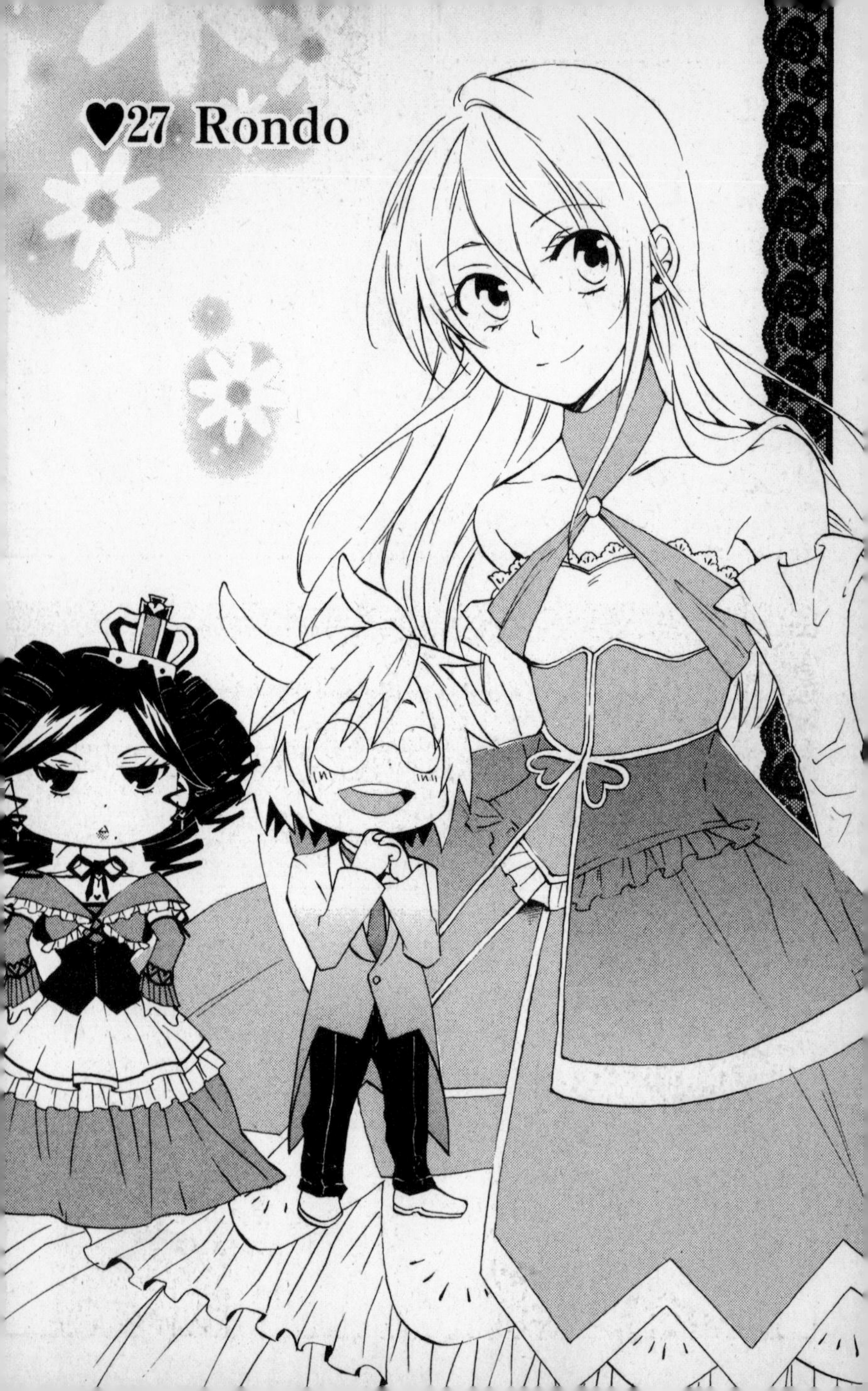
♥27 Rondo

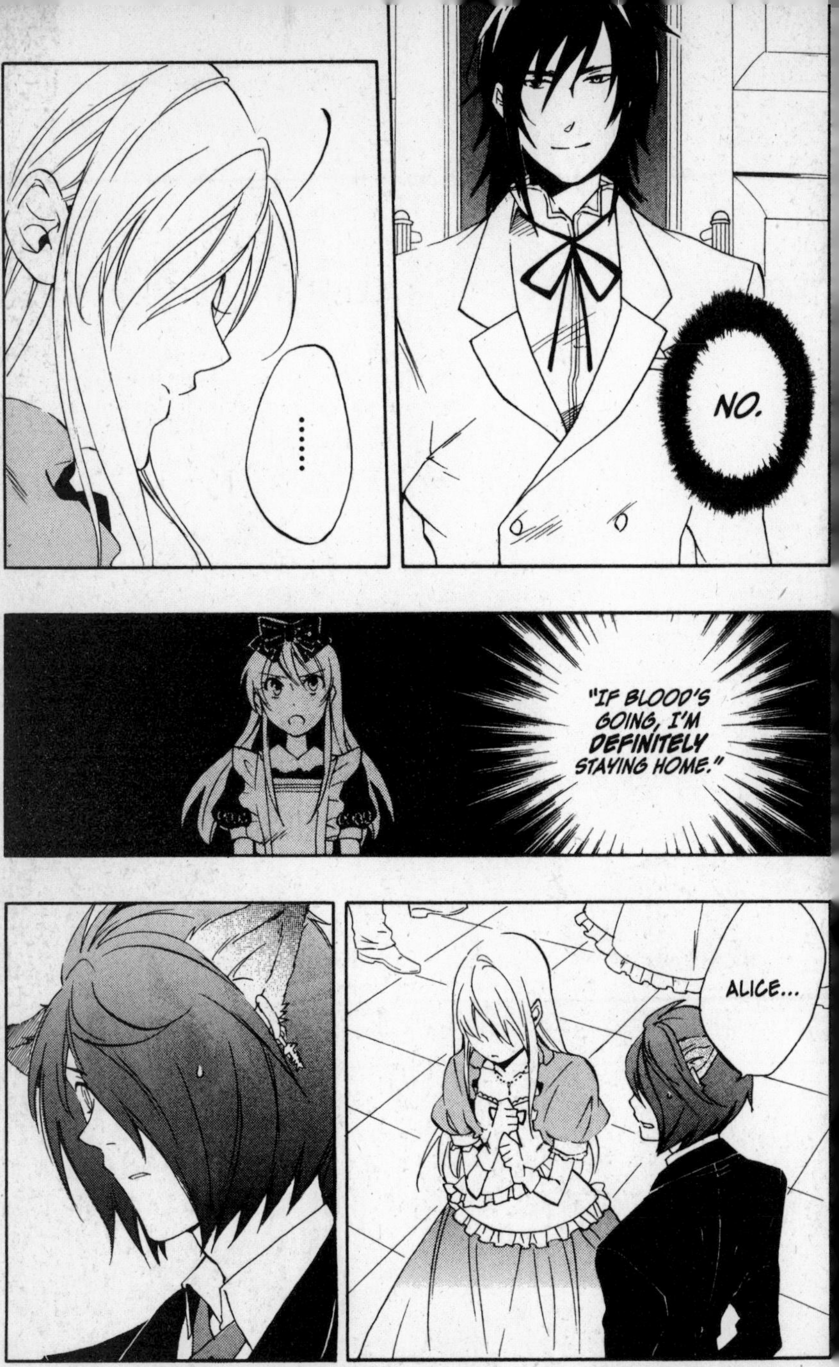
NO.
......
"IF BLOOD'S GOING, I'M DEFINITELY STAYING HOME."
ALICE...

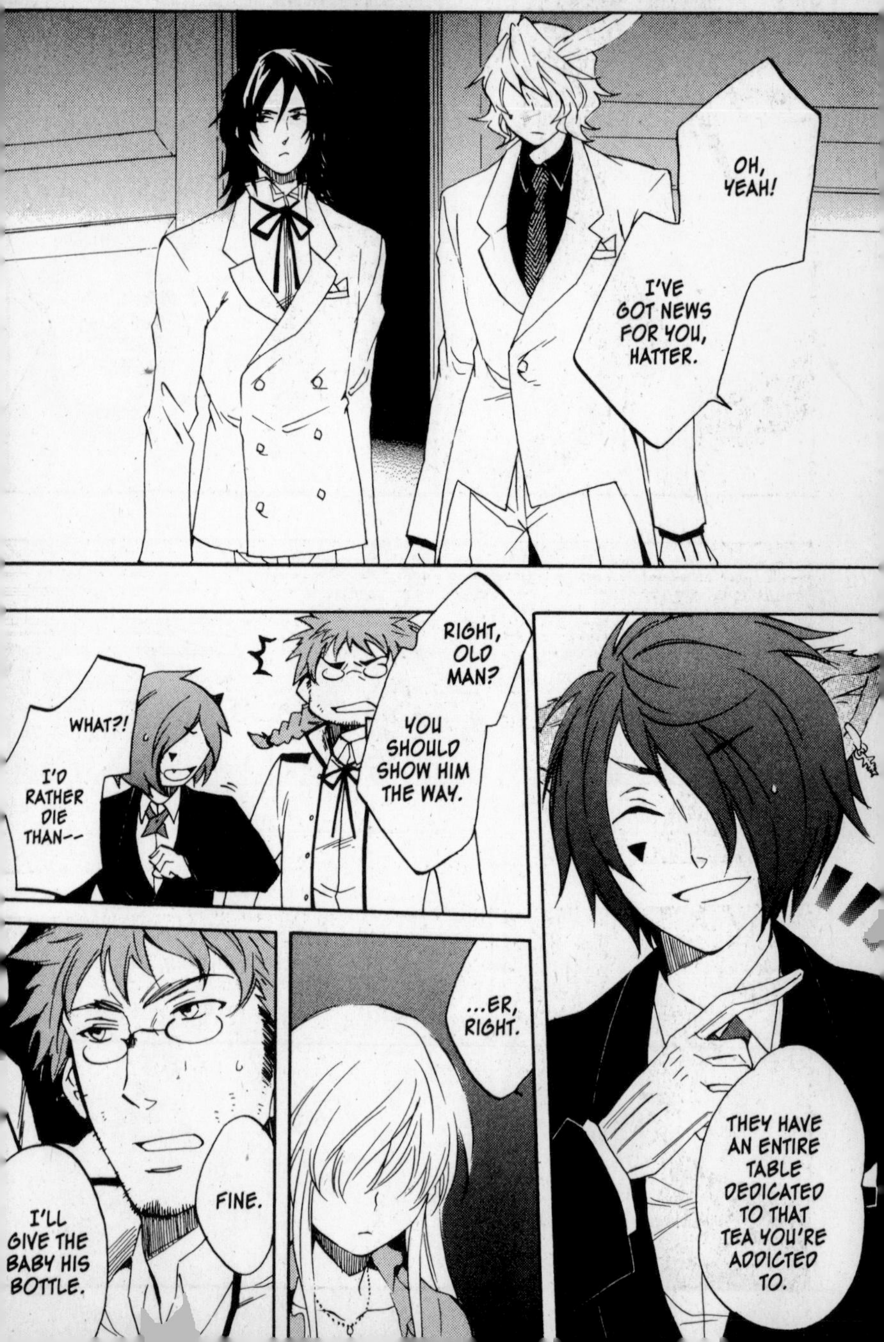
OH, YEAH!
I'VE GOT NEWS FOR YOU, HATTER.
THEY HAVE AN ENTIRE TABLE DEDICATED TO THAT TEA YOU'RE ADDICTED TO.
RIGHT, OLD MAN?
YOU SHOULD SHOW HIM THE WAY.
WHAT?!
I'D RATHER DIE THAN--
...ER, RIGHT.
FINE.
I'LL GIVE THE BABY HIS BOTTLE.

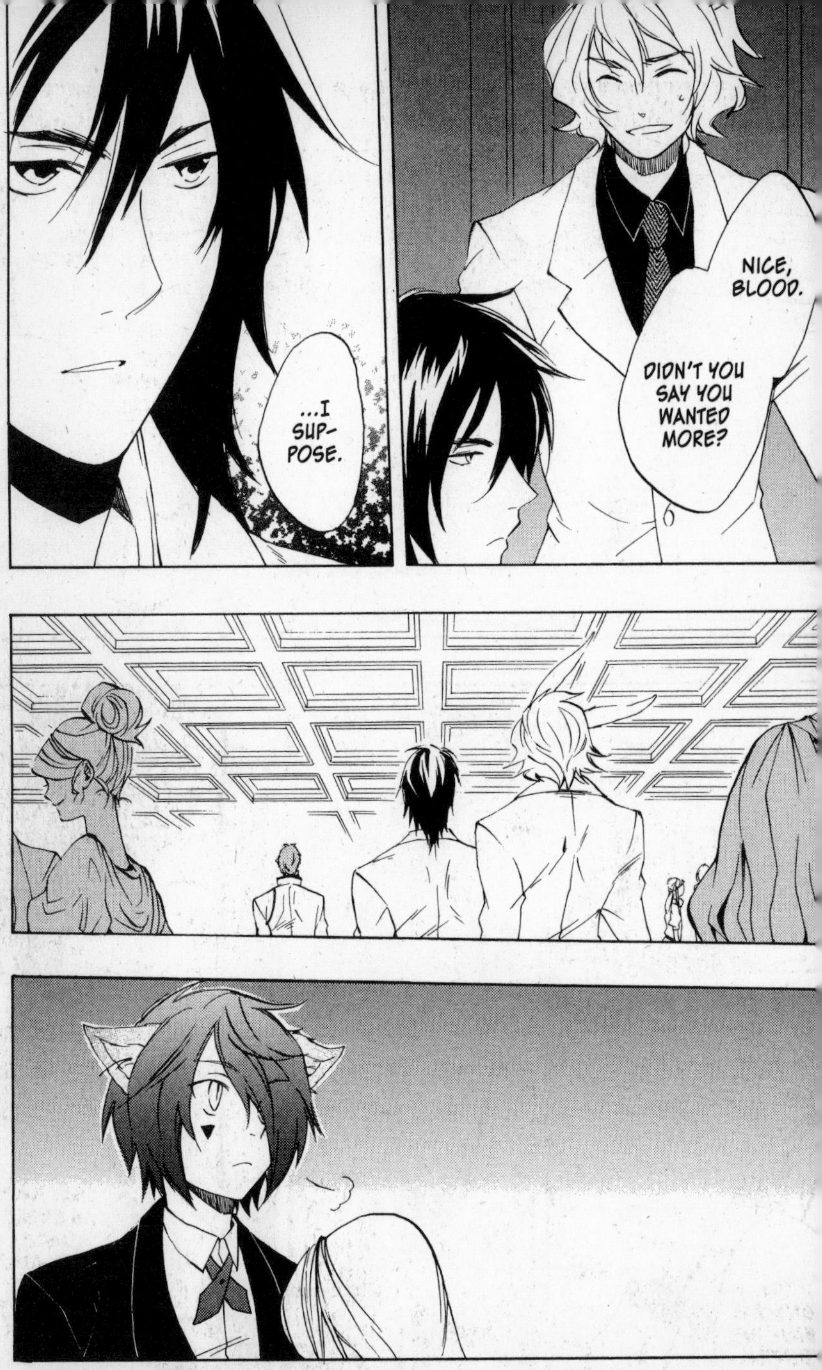
NICE, BLOOD.
DIDN'T YOU SAY YOU WANTED MORE?
...I SUP-POSE.

I DON'T MEAN TO BE SO DIFFICULT.

I'M SORRY.

BORIS...

I JUST WANNA KEEP DANCING, AND THAT GUY CRAMPS OUR STYLE.

NO WORRIES, ALICE.

C'MON-- THE SONG'S STILL GOING!

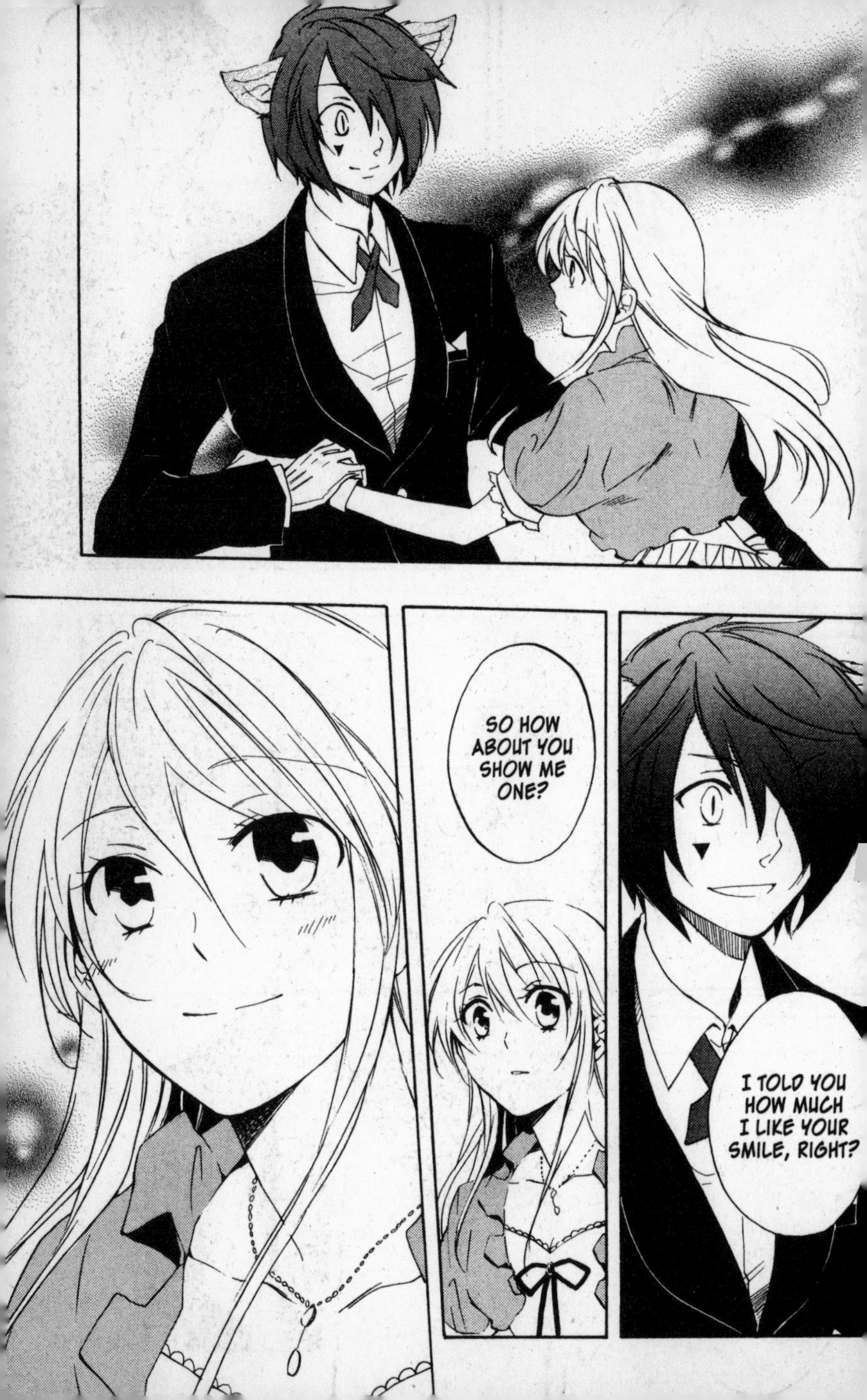
I TOLD YOU HOW MUCH I LIKE YOUR SMILE, RIGHT?
SO HOW ABOUT YOU SHOW ME ONE?

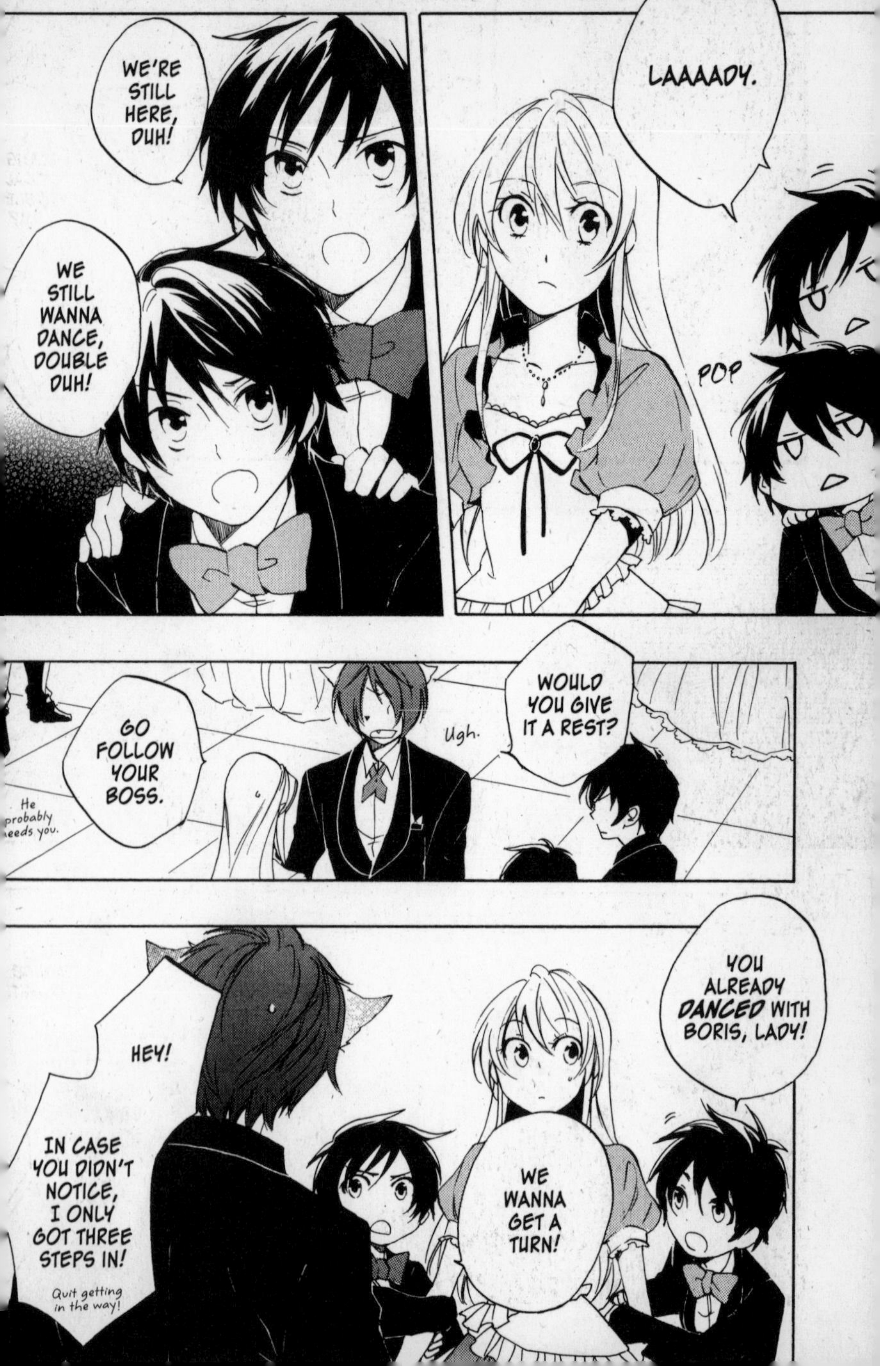
LAAAADY.
POP
WE'RE STILL HERE, DUH!
WE STILL WANNA DANCE, DOUBLE DUH!
WOULD YOU GIVE IT A REST?
Ugh.
GO FOLLOW YOUR BOSS.
He probably needs you.
YOU ALREADY DANCED WITH BORIS, LADY!
WE WANNA GET A TURN!
HEY!
IN CASE YOU DIDN'T NOTICE, I ONLY GOT THREE STEPS IN!
Quit getting in the way!

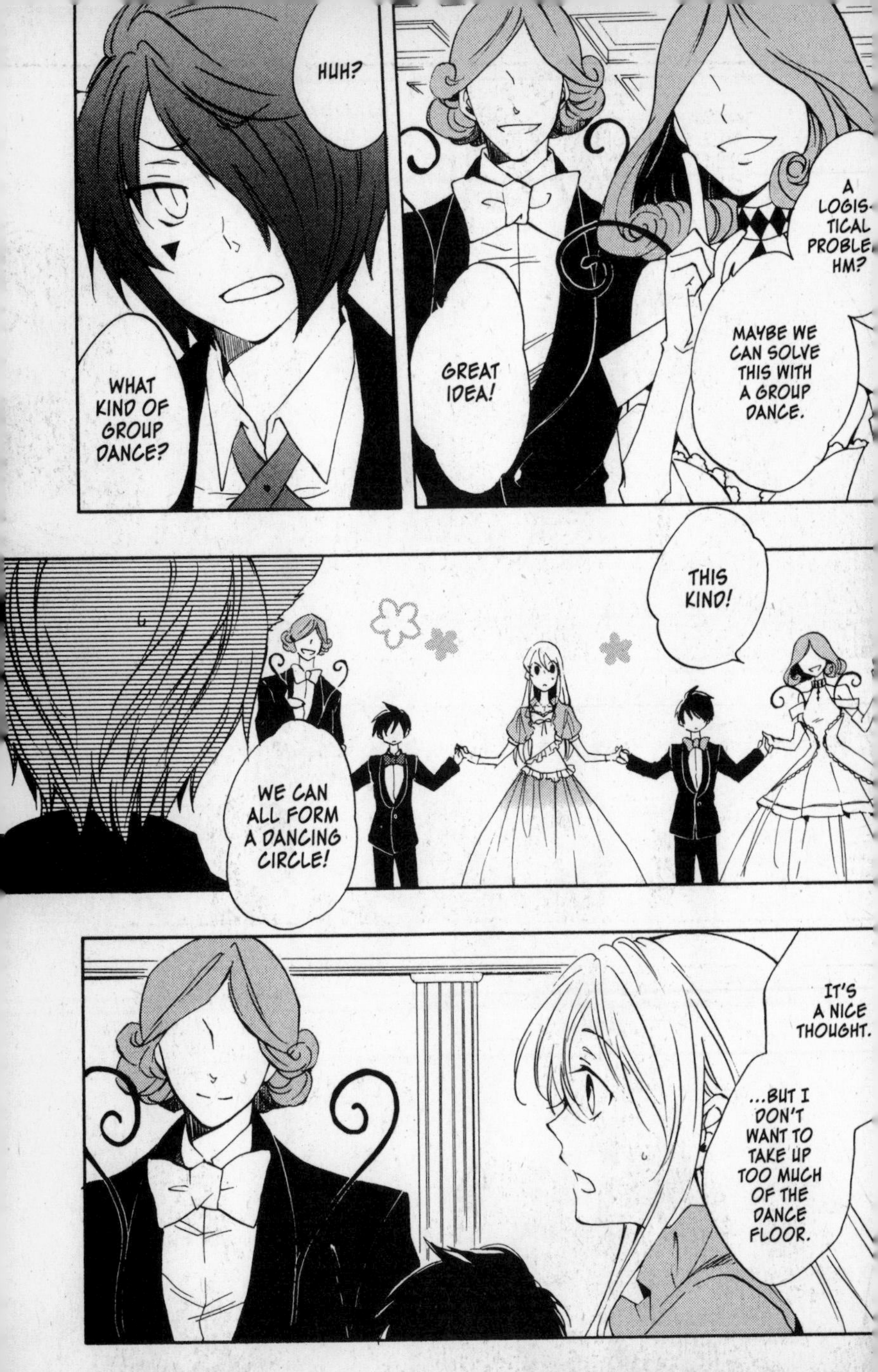
A LOGISTICAL PROBLEHM?
MAYBE WE CAN SOLVE THIS WITH A GROUP DANCE.
GREAT IDEA!
HUH?
WHAT KIND OF GROUP DANCE?
THIS KIND!
WE CAN ALL FORM A DANCING CIRCLE!
IT'S A NICE THOUGHT.
...BUT I DON'T WANT TO TAKE UP TOO MUCH OF THE DANCE FLOOR.

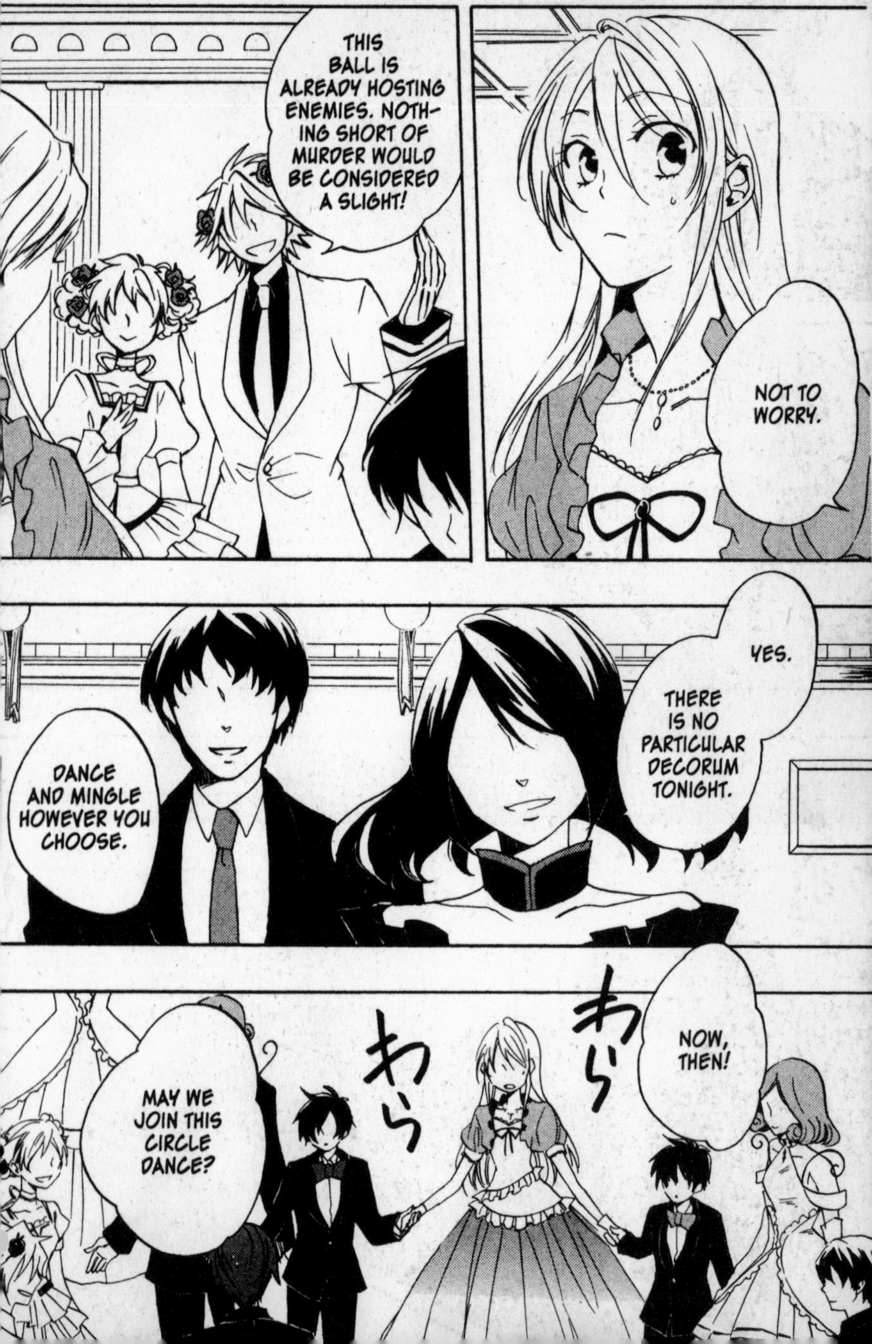
NOT TO WORRY.
THIS BALL IS ALREADY HOSTING ENEMIES. NOTHING SHORT OF MURDER WOULD BE CONSIDERED A SLIGHT!
YES.
THERE IS NO PARTICULAR DECORUM TONIGHT.
DANCE AND MINGLE HOWEVER YOU CHOOSE.
NOW, THEN!
わら
わら
MAY WE JOIN THIS CIRCLE DANCE?

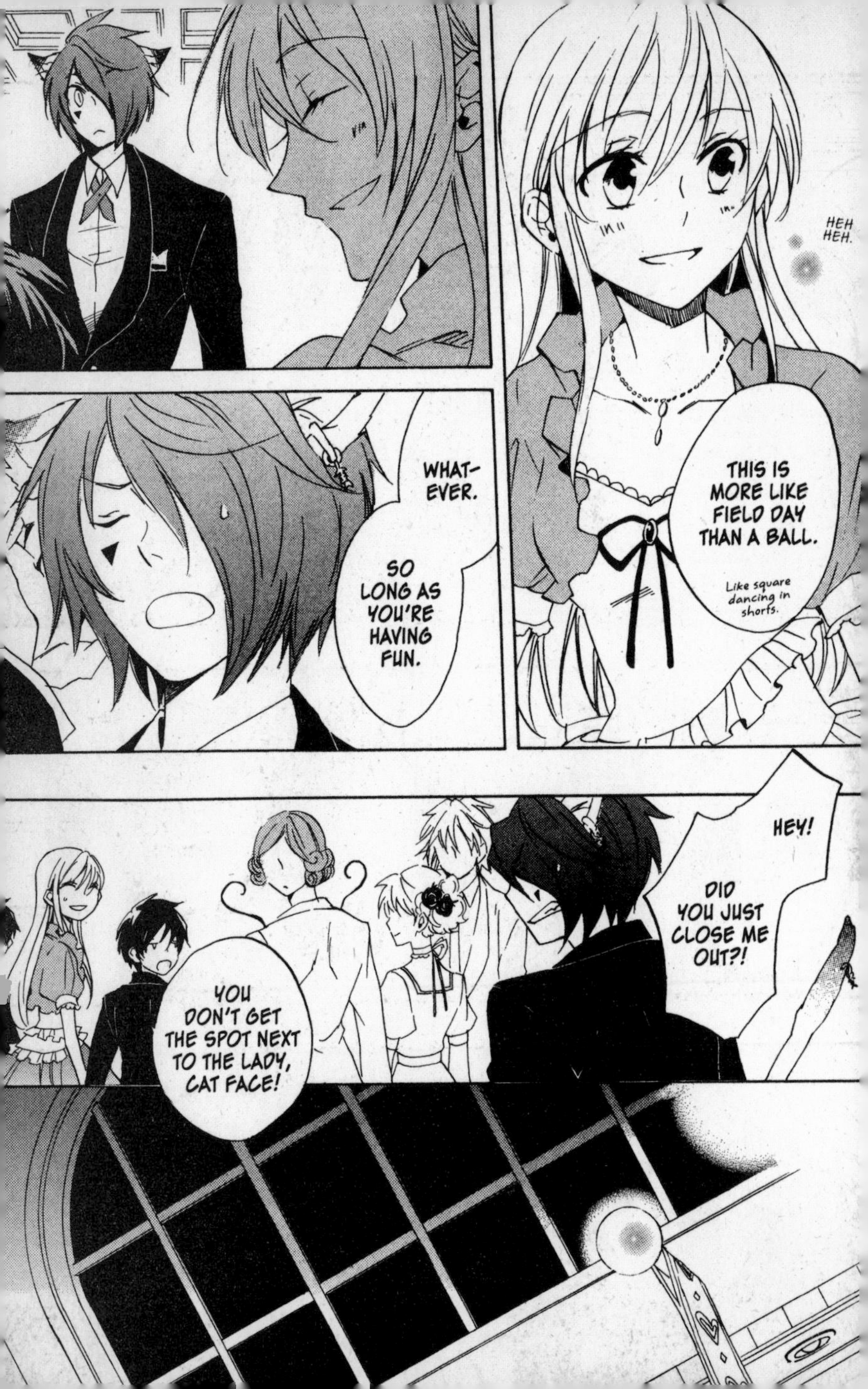
HEH HEH.
THIS IS MORE LIKE FIELD DAY THAN A BALL.
Like square dancing in shorts.
WHAT-EVER.
SO LONG AS YOU'RE HAVING FUN.
HEY!
DID YOU JUST CLOSE ME OUT?!
YOU DON'T GET THE SPOT NEXT TO THE LADY, CAT FACE!

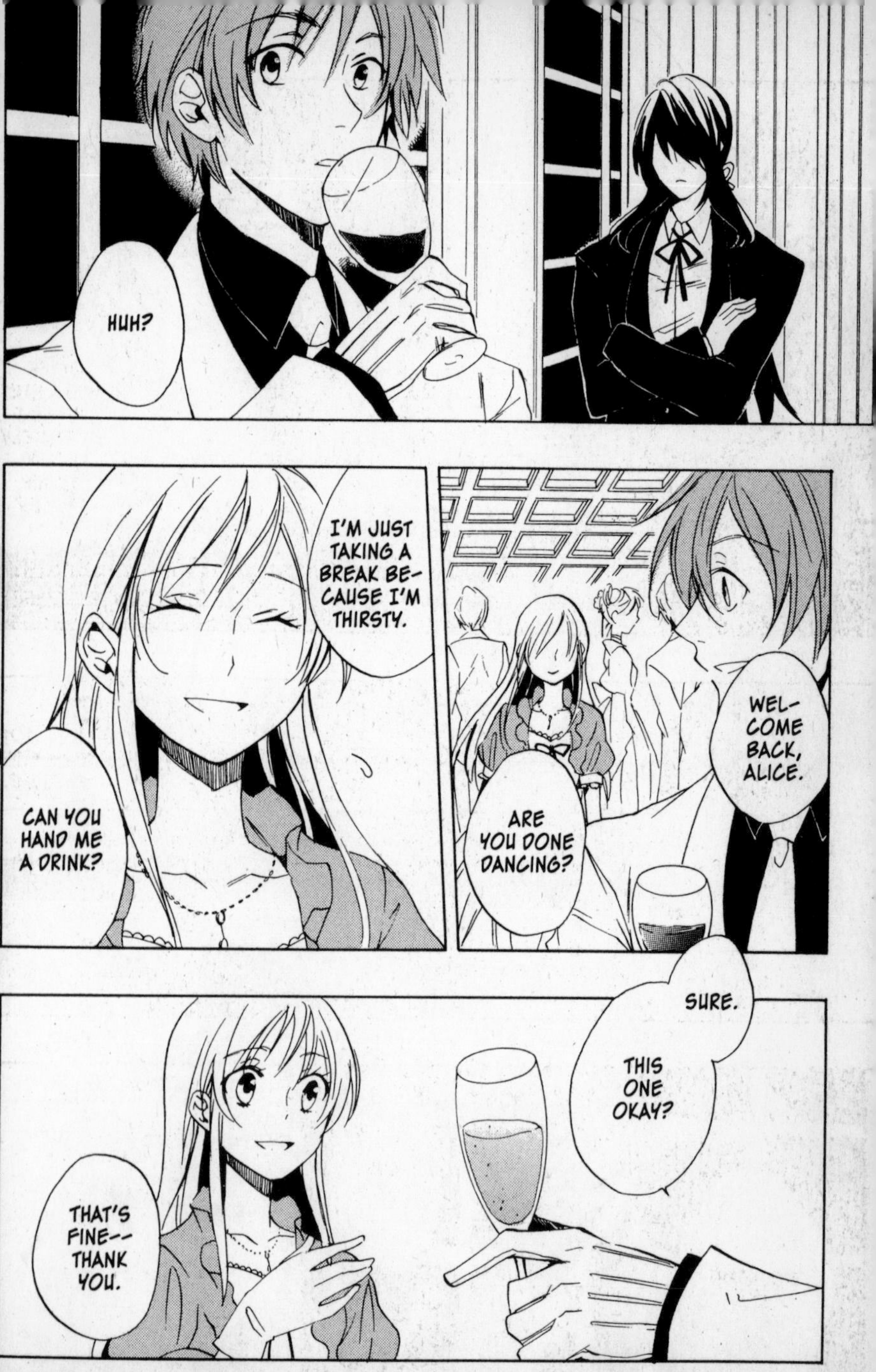
HUH?
WEL-COME BACK, ALICE.
ARE YOU DONE DANCING?
I'M JUST TAKING A BREAK BE-CAUSE I'M THIRSTY.
CAN YOU HAND ME A DRINK?
SURE.
THIS ONE OKAY?
THAT'S FINE--THANK YOU.

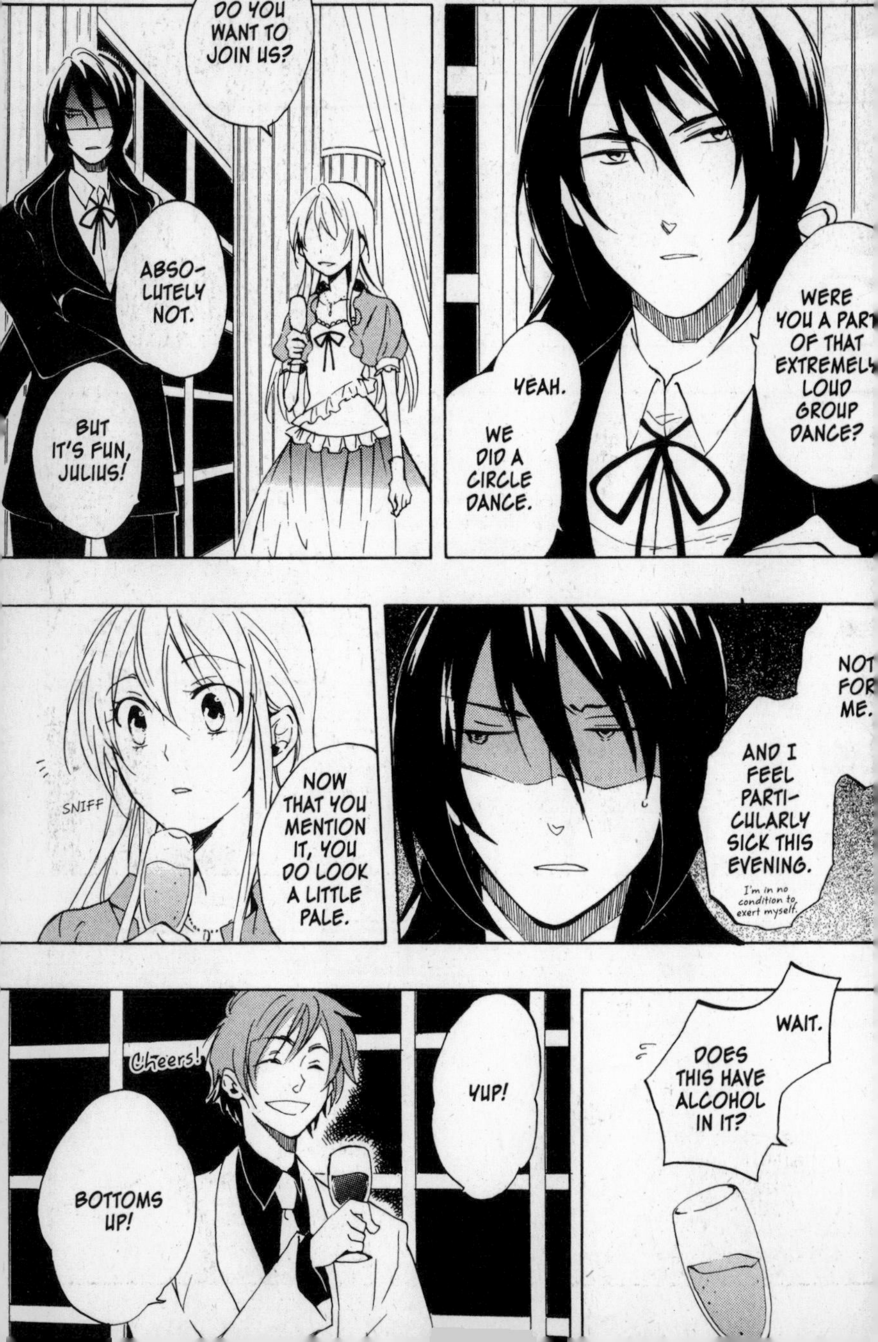
WERE YOU A PART OF THAT EXTREMELY LOUD GROUP DANCE?
YEAH.
WE DID A CIRCLE DANCE.
DO YOU WANT TO JOIN US?
ABSO-LUTELY NOT.
BUT IT'S FUN, JULIUS!
NOT FOR ME.
AND I FEEL PARTI-CULARLY SICK THIS EVENING.
I'm in no condition to exert myself.
SNIFF
NOW THAT YOU MENTION IT, YOU DO LOOK A LITTLE PALE.
WAIT.
DOES THIS HAVE ALCOHOL IN IT?
YUP!
Cheers!
BOTTOMS UP!

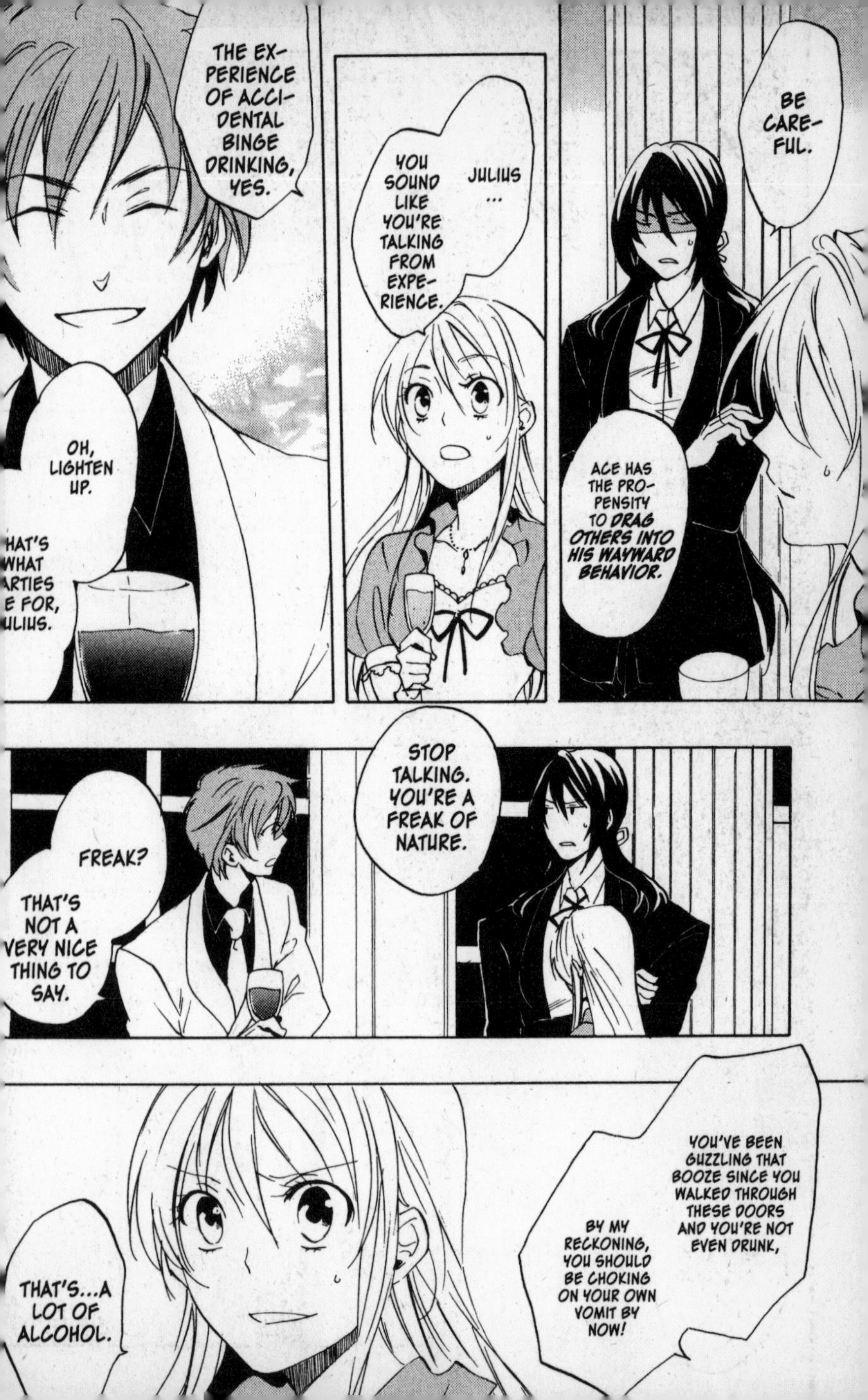
BE CAREFUL.
ACE HAS THE PROPENSITY TO DRAG OTHERS INTO HIS WAYWARD BEHAVIOR.
JULIUS...
YOU SOUND LIKE YOU'RE TALKING FROM EXPERIENCE.
THE EXPERIENCE OF ACCIDENTAL BINGE DRINKING, YES.
OH, LIGHTEN UP.
HAT'S WHAT ARTIES E FOR, ULIUS.
STOP TALKING. YOU'RE A FREAK OF NATURE.
FREAK?
THAT'S NOT A VERY NICE THING TO SAY.
YOU'VE BEEN GUZZLING THAT BOOZE SINCE YOU WALKED THROUGH THESE DOORS AND YOU'RE NOT EVEN DRUNK,
BY MY RECKONING, YOU SHOULD BE CHOKING ON YOUR OWN VOMIT BY NOW!
THAT'S...A LOT OF ALCOHOL.

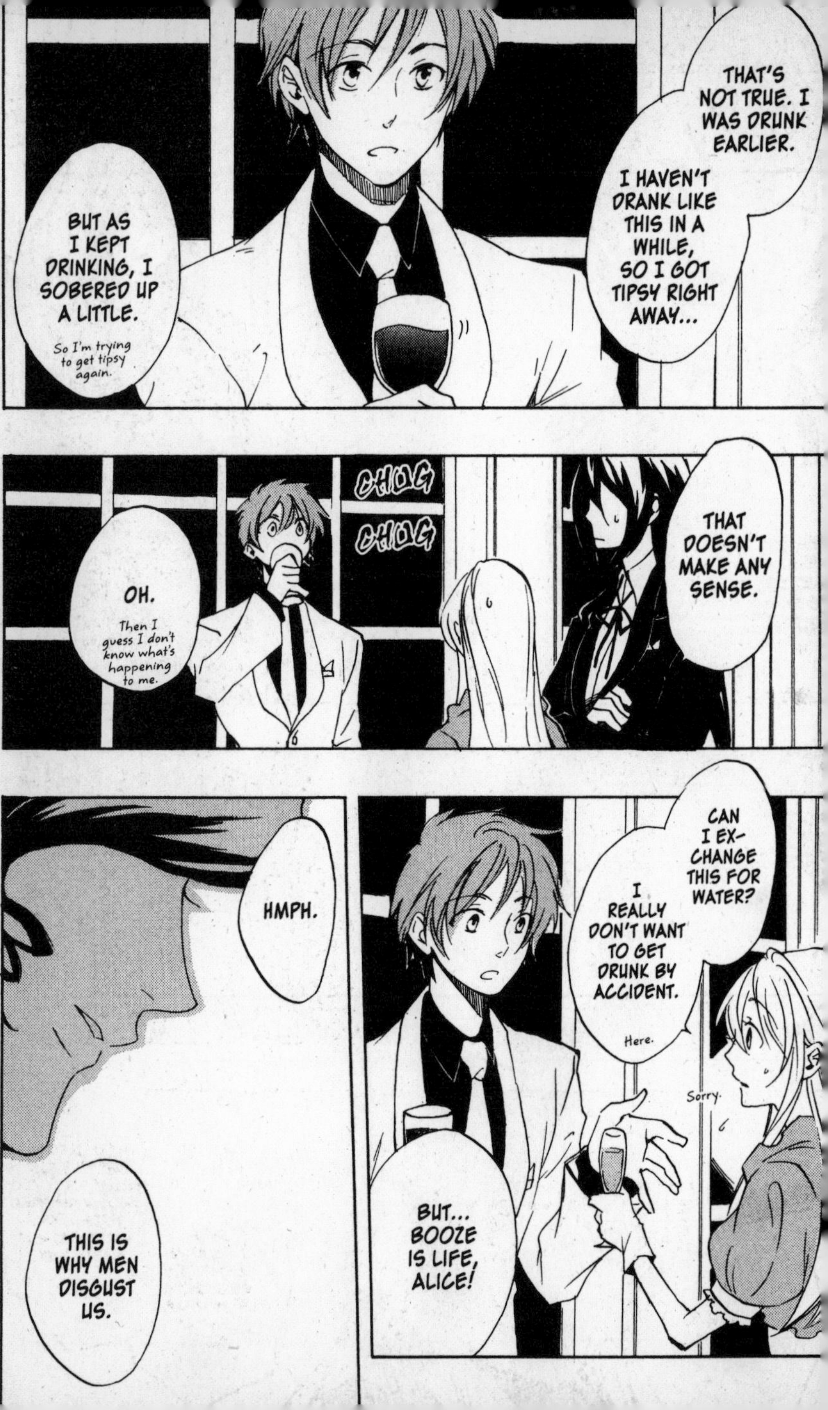
THAT'S NOT TRUE. I WAS DRUNK EARLIER.
I HAVEN'T DRANK LIKE THIS IN A WHILE, SO I GOT TIPSY RIGHT AWAY...
BUT AS I KEPT DRINKING, I SOBERED UP A LITTLE.
So I'm trying to get tipsy again.
THAT DOESN'T MAKE ANY SENSE.
CHUG
CHUG
OH.
Then I guess I don't know what's happening to me.
CAN I EXCHANGE THIS FOR WATER?
I REALLY DON'T WANT TO GET DRUNK BY ACCIDENT.
Here.
Sorry.
BUT... BOOZE IS LIFE, ALICE!
HMPH.
THIS IS WHY MEN DISGUST US.

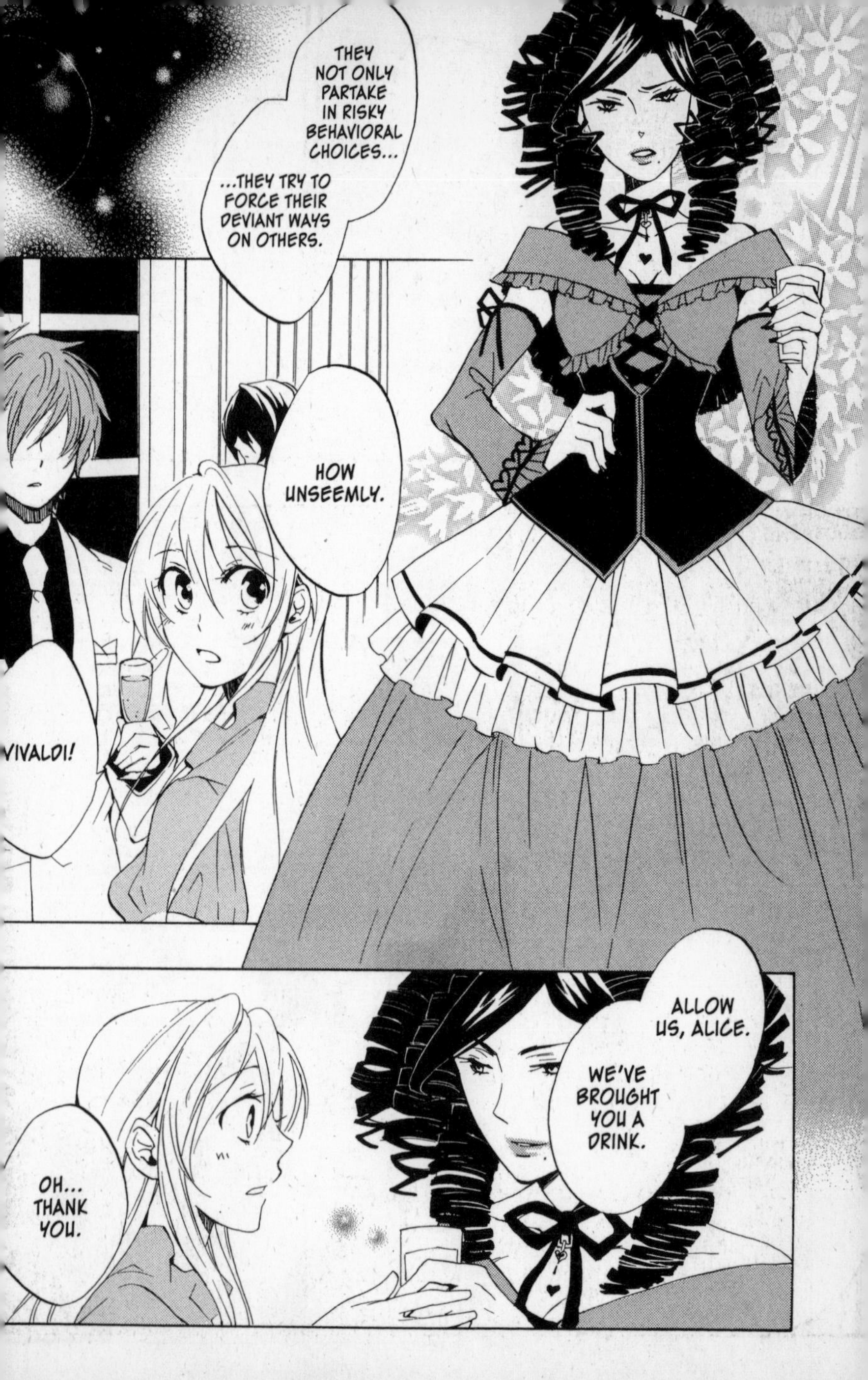
THEY NOT ONLY PARTAKE IN RISKY BEHAVIORAL CHOICES...
...THEY TRY TO FORCE THEIR DEVIANT WAYS ON OTHERS.
HOW UNSEEMLY.
VIVALDI!
ALLOW US, ALICE.
WE'VE BROUGHT YOU A DRINK.
OH... THANK YOU.

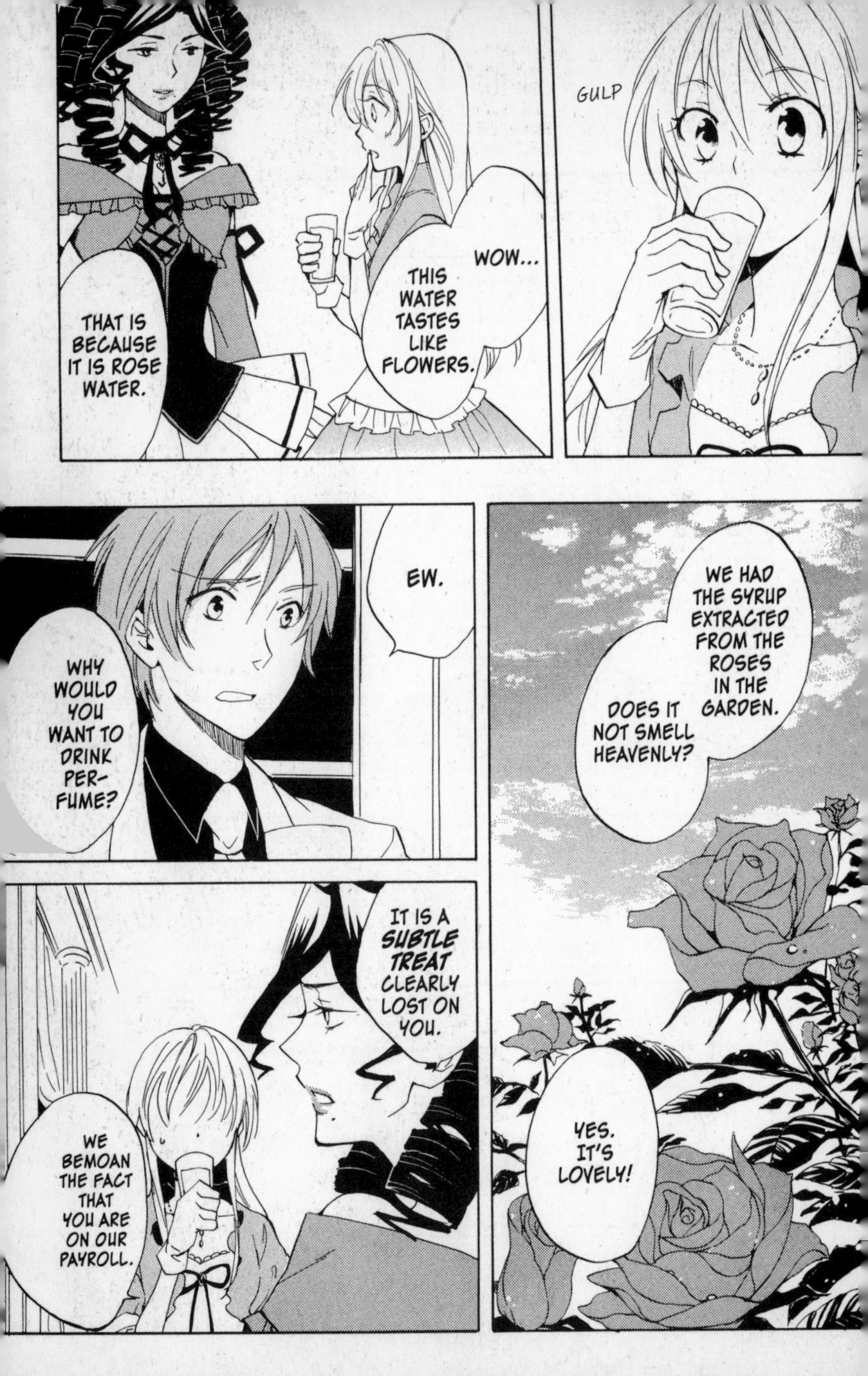
GULP
WOW...
THIS WATER TASTES LIKE FLOWERS.
THAT IS BECAUSE IT IS ROSE WATER.
WE HAD THE SYRUP EXTRACTED FROM THE ROSES IN THE GARDEN.
DOES IT NOT SMELL HEAVENLY?
YES. IT'S LOVELY!
EW.
WHY WOULD YOU WANT TO DRINK PER-FUME?
IT IS A SUBTLE TREAT CLEARLY LOST ON YOU.
WE BEMOAN THE FACT THAT YOU ARE ON OUR PAYROLL.

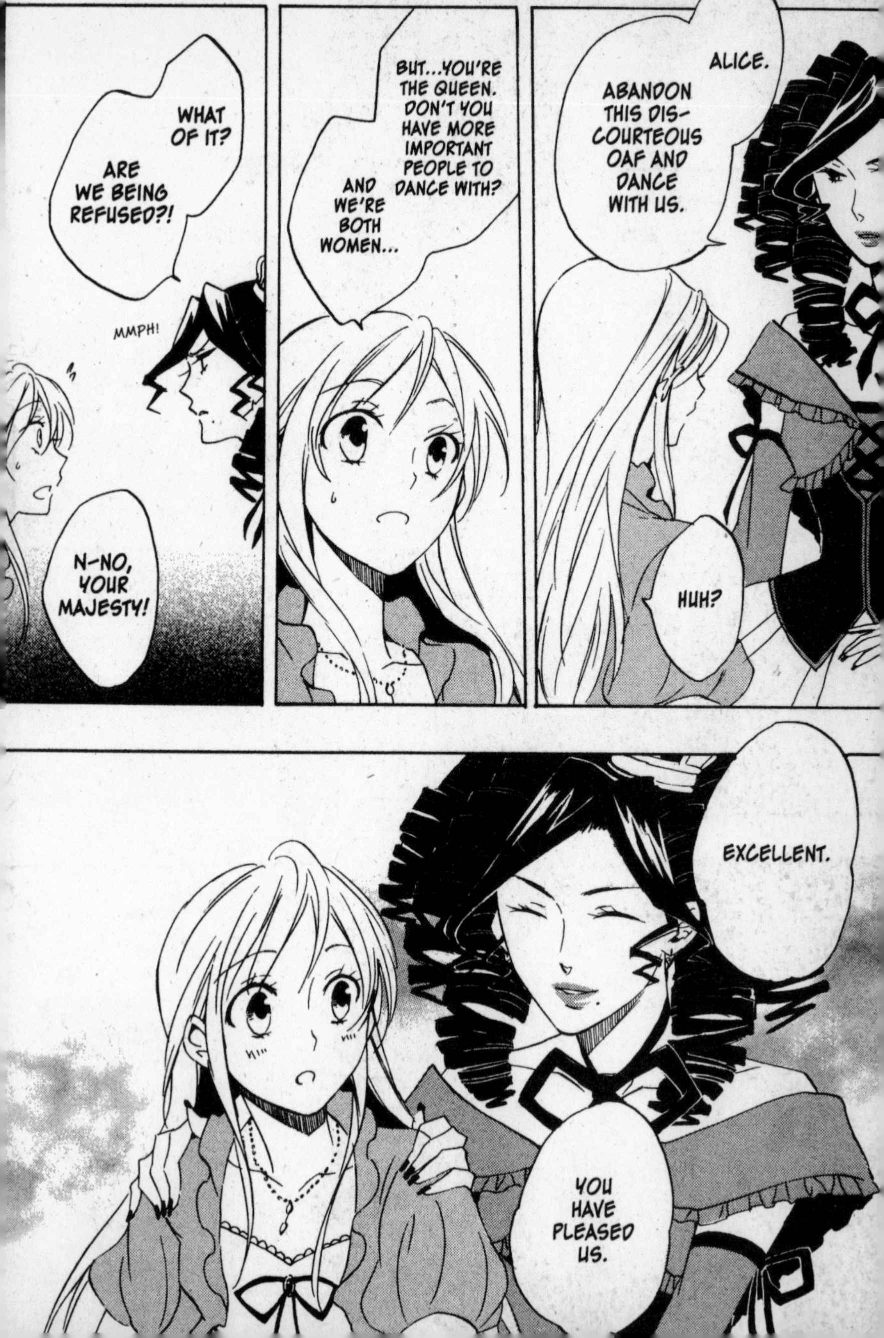
ALICE.
ABANDON THIS DIS-COURTEOUS OAF AND DANCE WITH US.
HUH?
BUT...YOU'RE THE QUEEN. DON'T YOU HAVE MORE IMPORTANT PEOPLE TO DANCE WITH?
AND WE'RE BOTH WOMEN...
WHAT OF IT?
ARE WE BEING REFUSED?!
MMPH!
N-NO, YOUR MAJESTY!
EXCELLENT.
YOU HAVE PLEASED US.

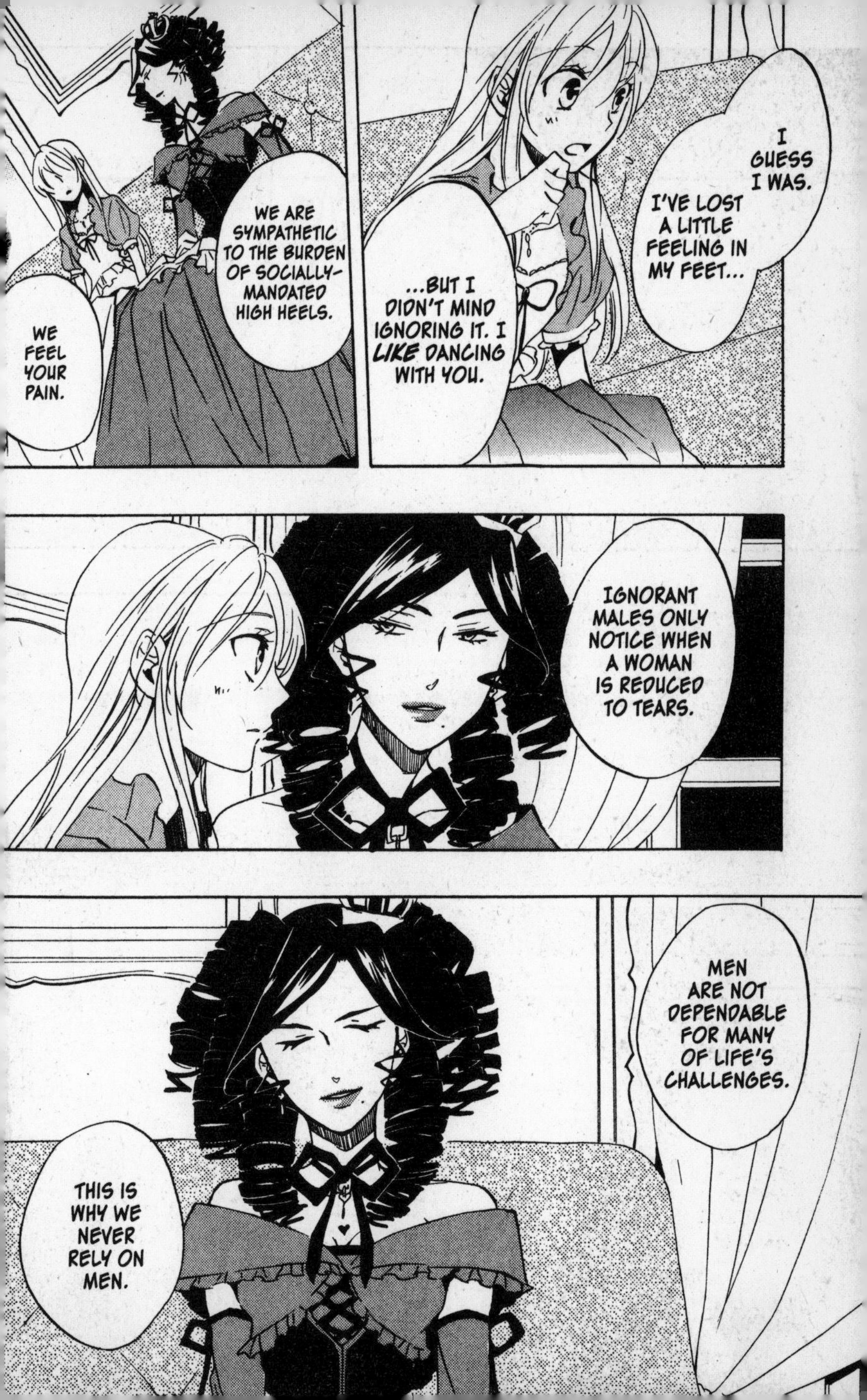
I GUESS I WAS.
I'VE LOST A LITTLE FEELING IN MY FEET...
...BUT I DIDN'T MIND IGNORING IT. I *LIKE* DANCING WITH YOU.
WE ARE SYMPATHETIC TO THE BURDEN OF SOCIALLY-MANDATED HIGH HEELS.
WE FEEL YOUR PAIN.
IGNORANT MALES ONLY NOTICE WHEN A WOMAN IS REDUCED TO TEARS.
MEN ARE NOT DEPENDABLE FOR MANY OF LIFE'S CHALLENGES.
THIS IS WHY WE NEVER RELY ON MEN.

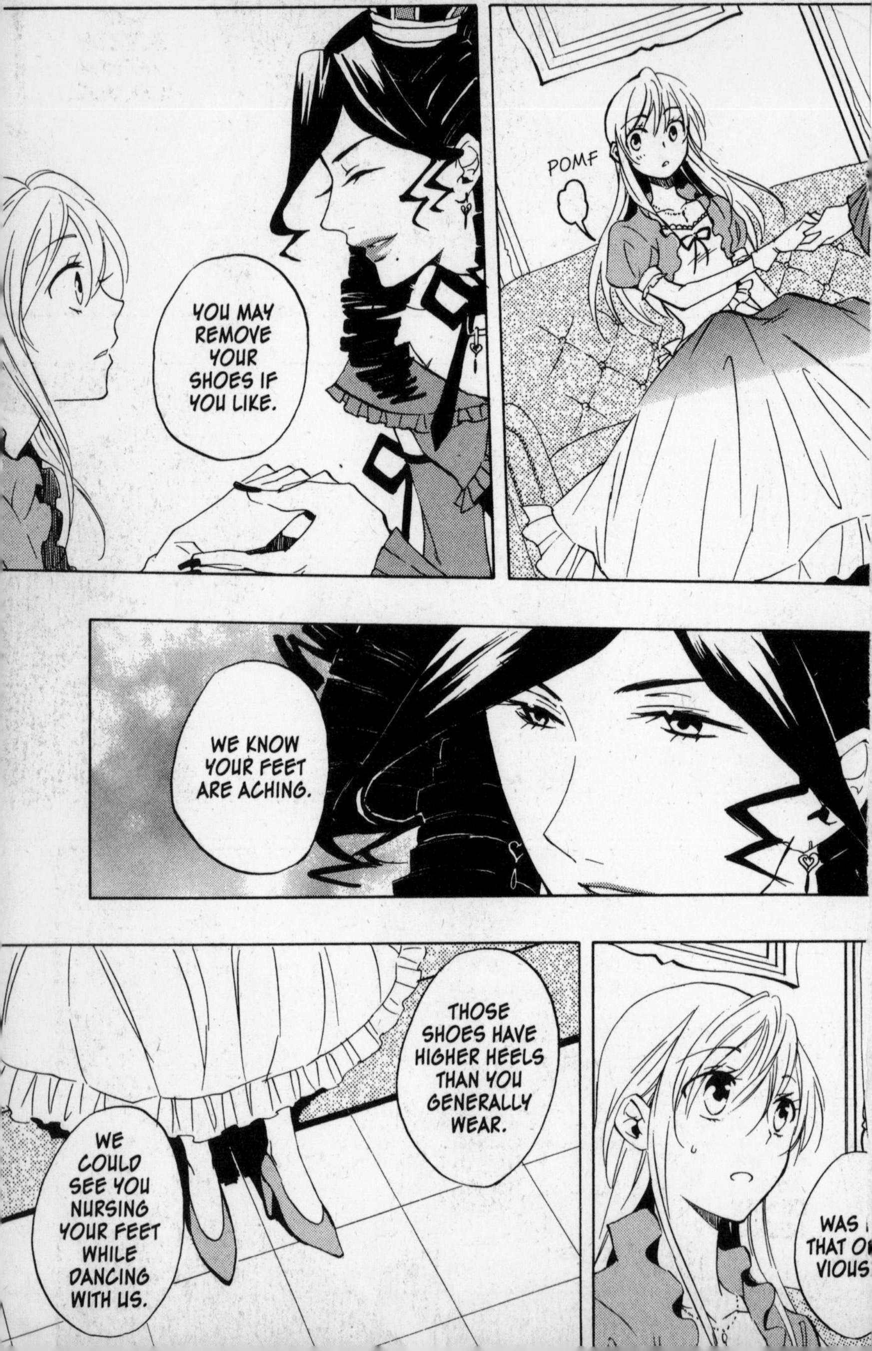
POMF
YOU MAY REMOVE YOUR SHOES IF YOU LIKE.
WE KNOW YOUR FEET ARE ACHING.
WAS THAT O VIOUS
THOSE SHOES HAVE HIGHER HEELS THAN YOU GENERALLY WEAR.
WE COULD SEE YOU NURSING YOUR FEET WHILE DANCING WITH US.

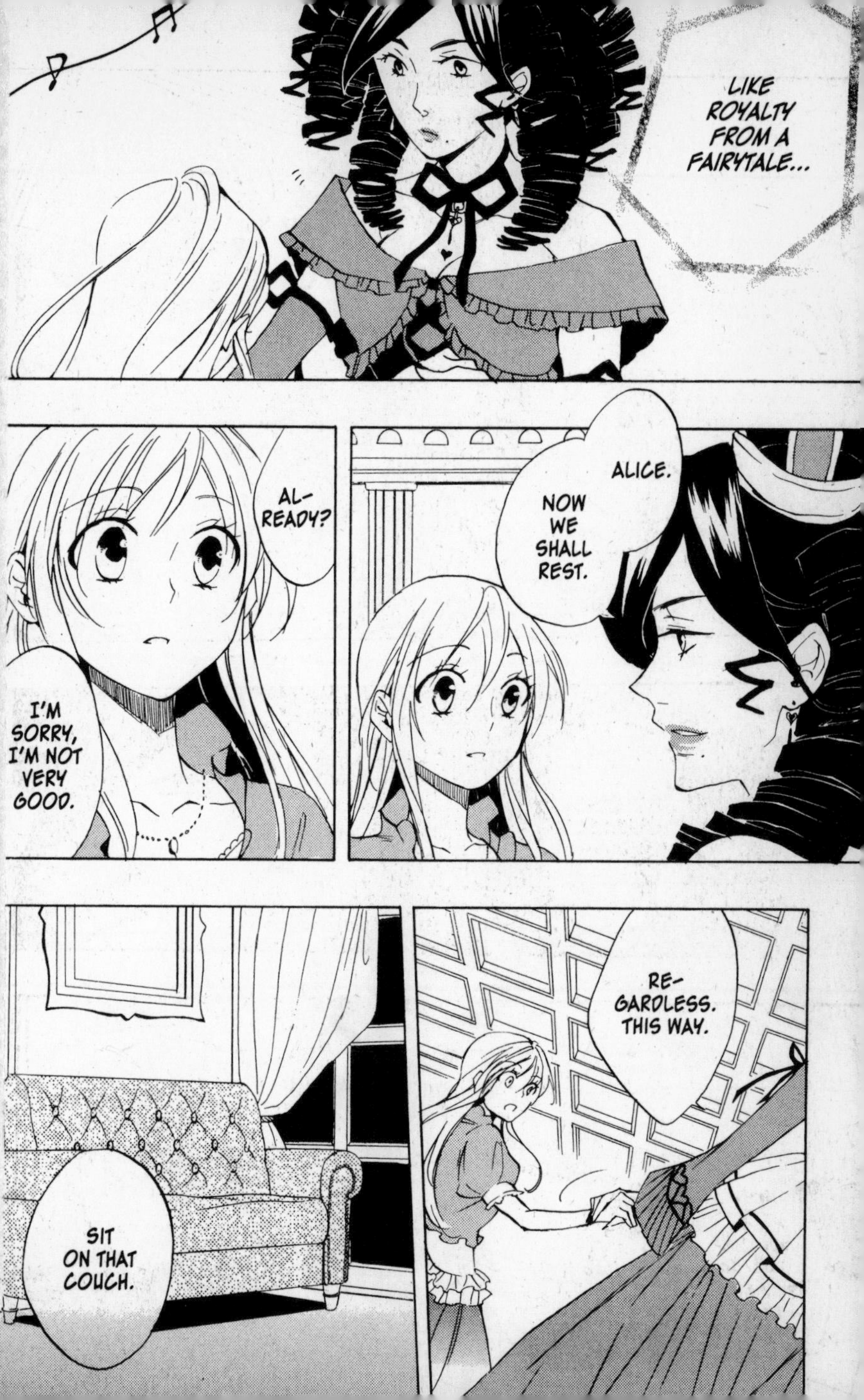
LIKE ROYALTY FROM A FAIRYTALE...
ALICE.
NOW WE SHALL REST.
AL-READY?
I'M SORRY, I'M NOT VERY GOOD.
RE-GARDLESS. THIS WAY.
SIT ON THAT COUCH.

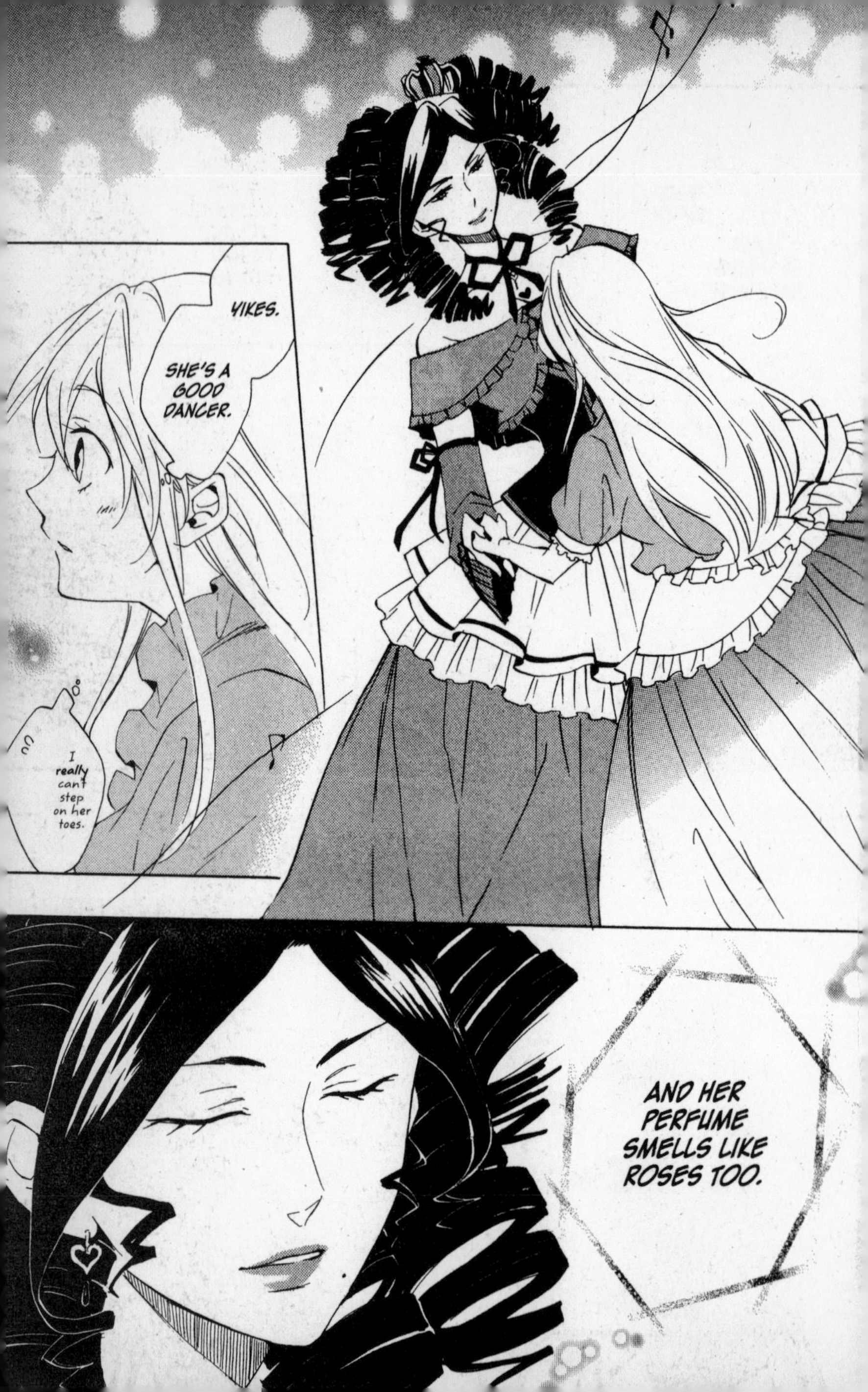
YIKES.
SHE'S A GOOD DANCER.
I really can't step on her toes.
AND HER PERFUME SMELLS LIKE ROSES TOO.

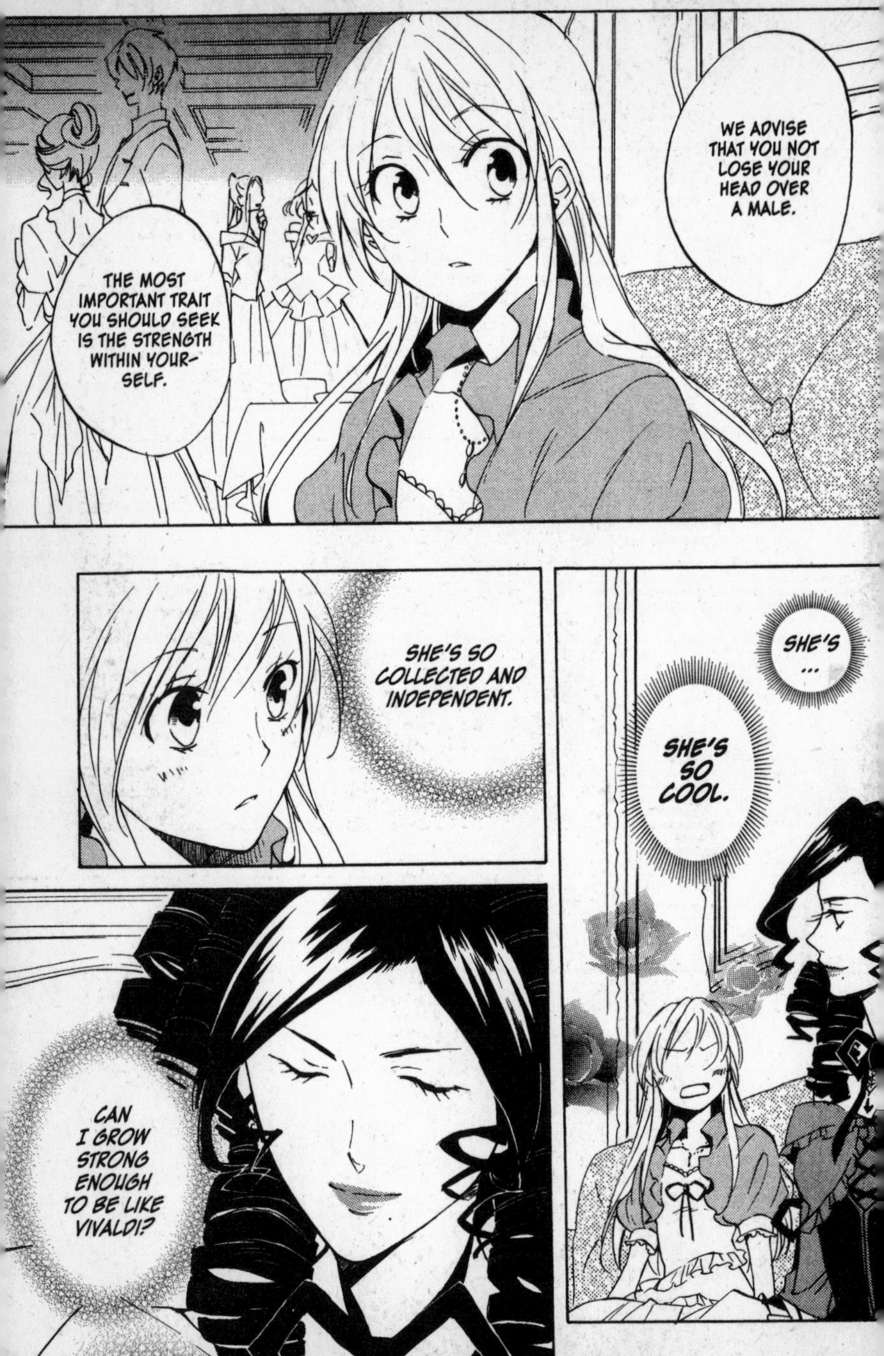
WE ADVISE THAT YOU NOT LOSE YOUR HEAD OVER A MALE.
THE MOST IMPORTANT TRAIT YOU SHOULD SEEK IS THE STRENGTH WITHIN YOUR-SELF.
SHE'S ...
SHE'S SO COOL.
SHE'S SO COLLECTED AND INDEPENDENT.
CAN I GROW STRONG ENOUGH TO BE LIKE VIVALDI?

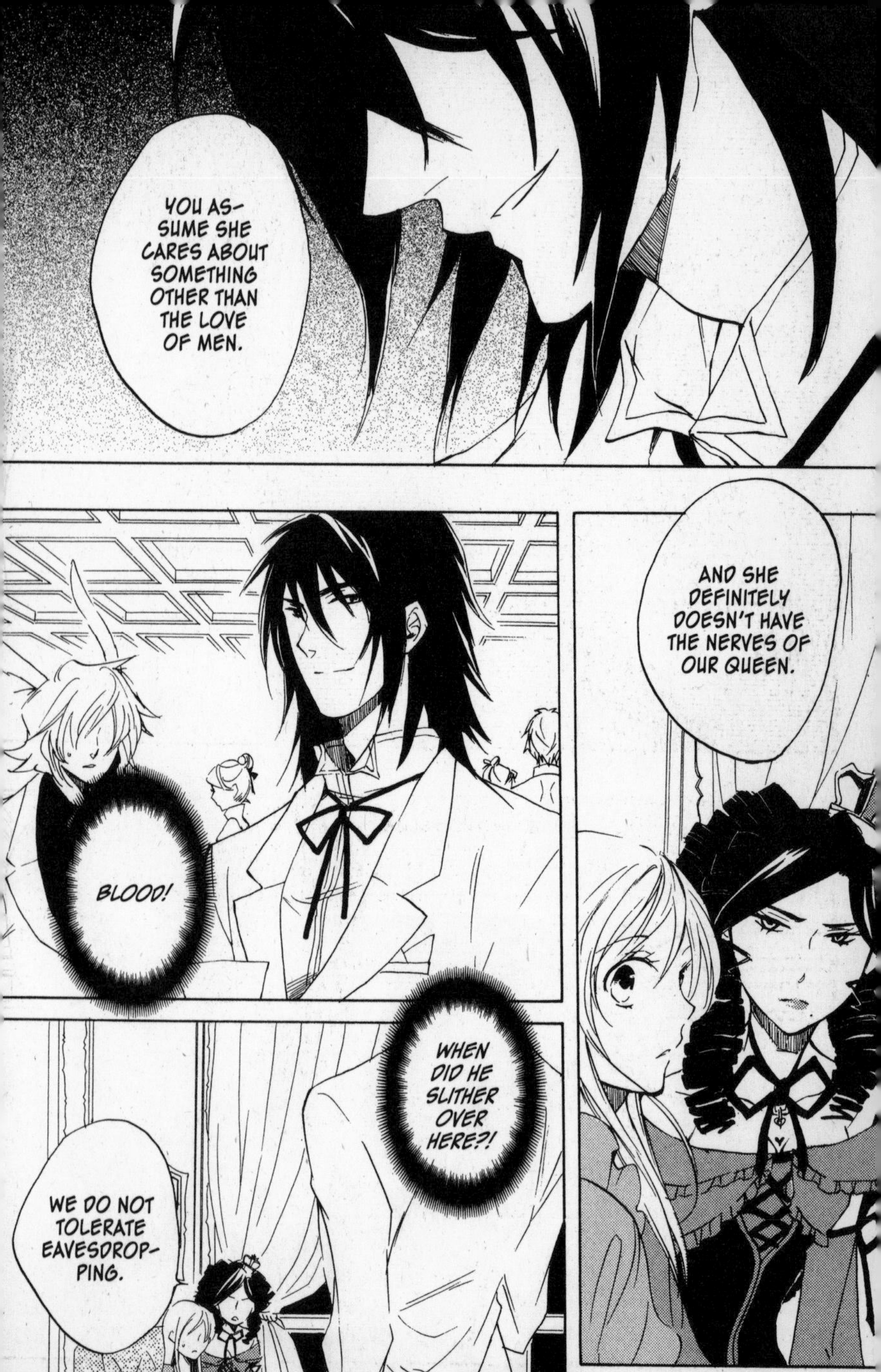
YOU AS-SUME SHE CARES ABOUT SOMETHING OTHER THAN THE LOVE OF MEN.
AND SHE DEFINITELY DOESN'T HAVE THE NERVES OF OUR QUEEN.
BLOOD!
WHEN DID HE SLITHER OVER HERE?!
WE DO NOT TOLERATE EAVESDROP-PING.

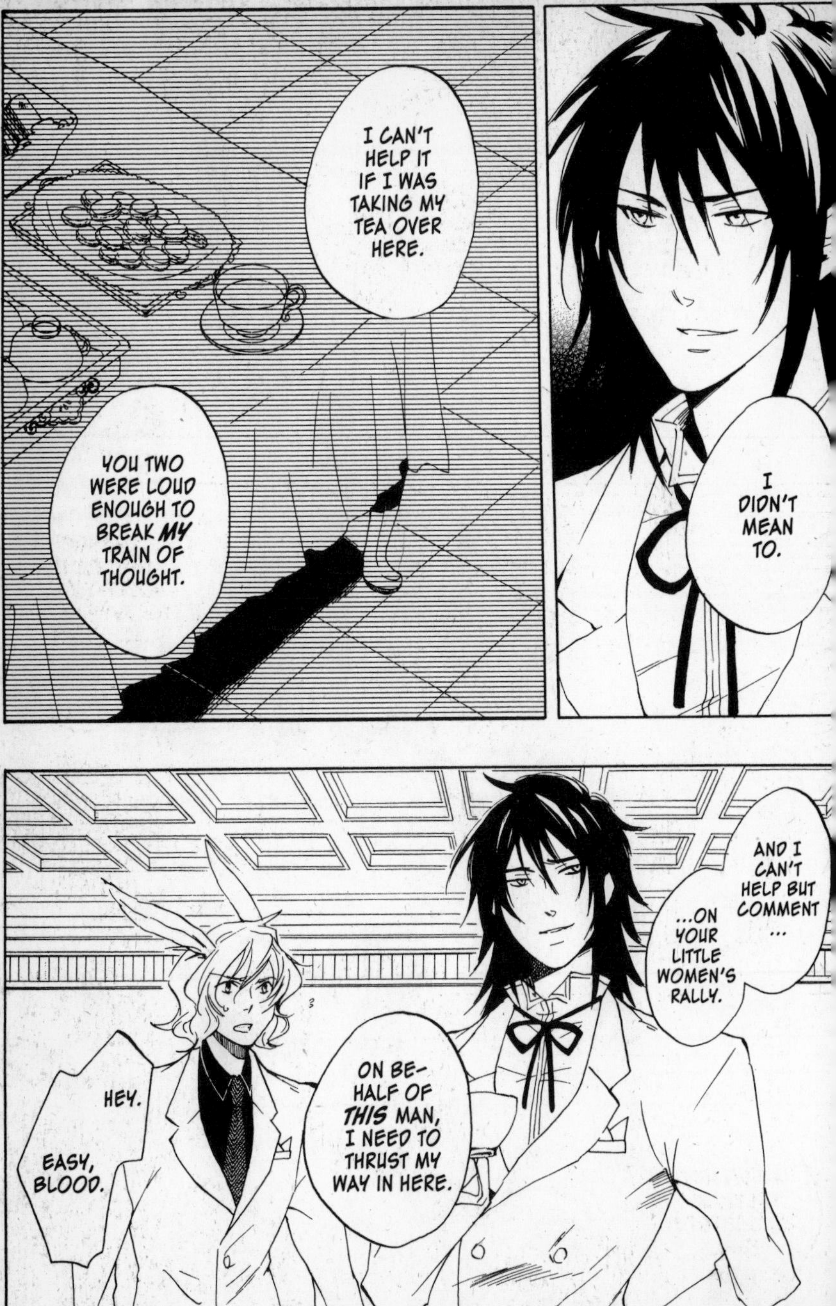
I DIDN'T MEAN TO.
I CAN'T HELP IT IF I WAS TAKING MY TEA OVER HERE.
YOU TWO WERE LOUD ENOUGH TO BREAK MY TRAIN OF THOUGHT.
AND I CAN'T HELP BUT COMMENT ...
...ON YOUR LITTLE WOMEN'S RALLY.
ON BE-HALF OF THIS MAN, I NEED TO THRUST MY WAY IN HERE.
HEY.
EASY, BLOOD.

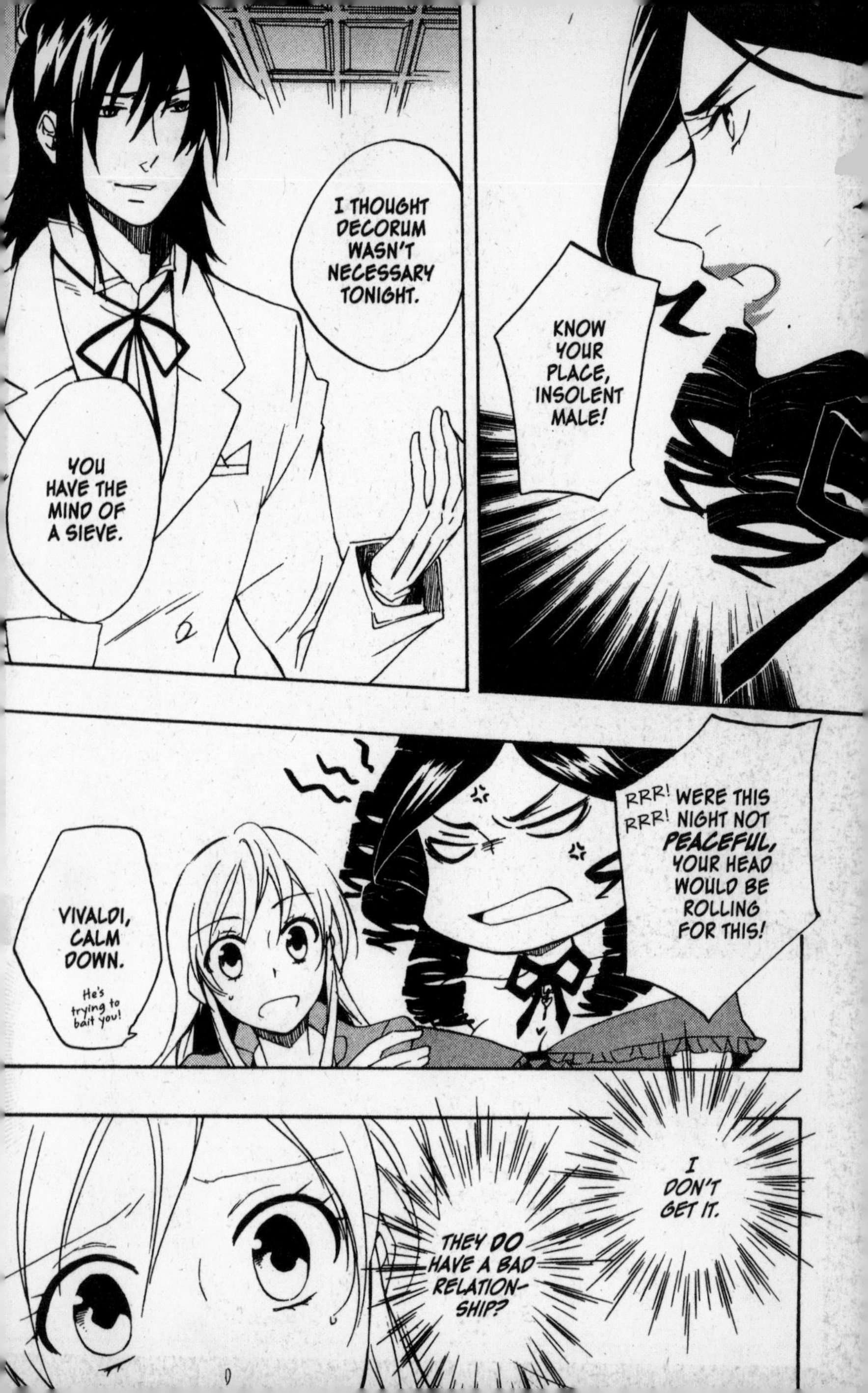
KNOW YOUR PLACE, INSOLENT MALE!
I THOUGHT DECORUM WASN'T NECESSARY TONIGHT.
YOU HAVE THE MIND OF A SIEVE.
RRR! RRR!
WERE THIS NIGHT NOT *PEACEFUL*, YOUR HEAD WOULD BE ROLLING FOR THIS!
VIVALDI, CALM DOWN.
He's trying to bait you!
I DON'T GET IT.
THEY *DO* HAVE A BAD RELATION-SHIP?

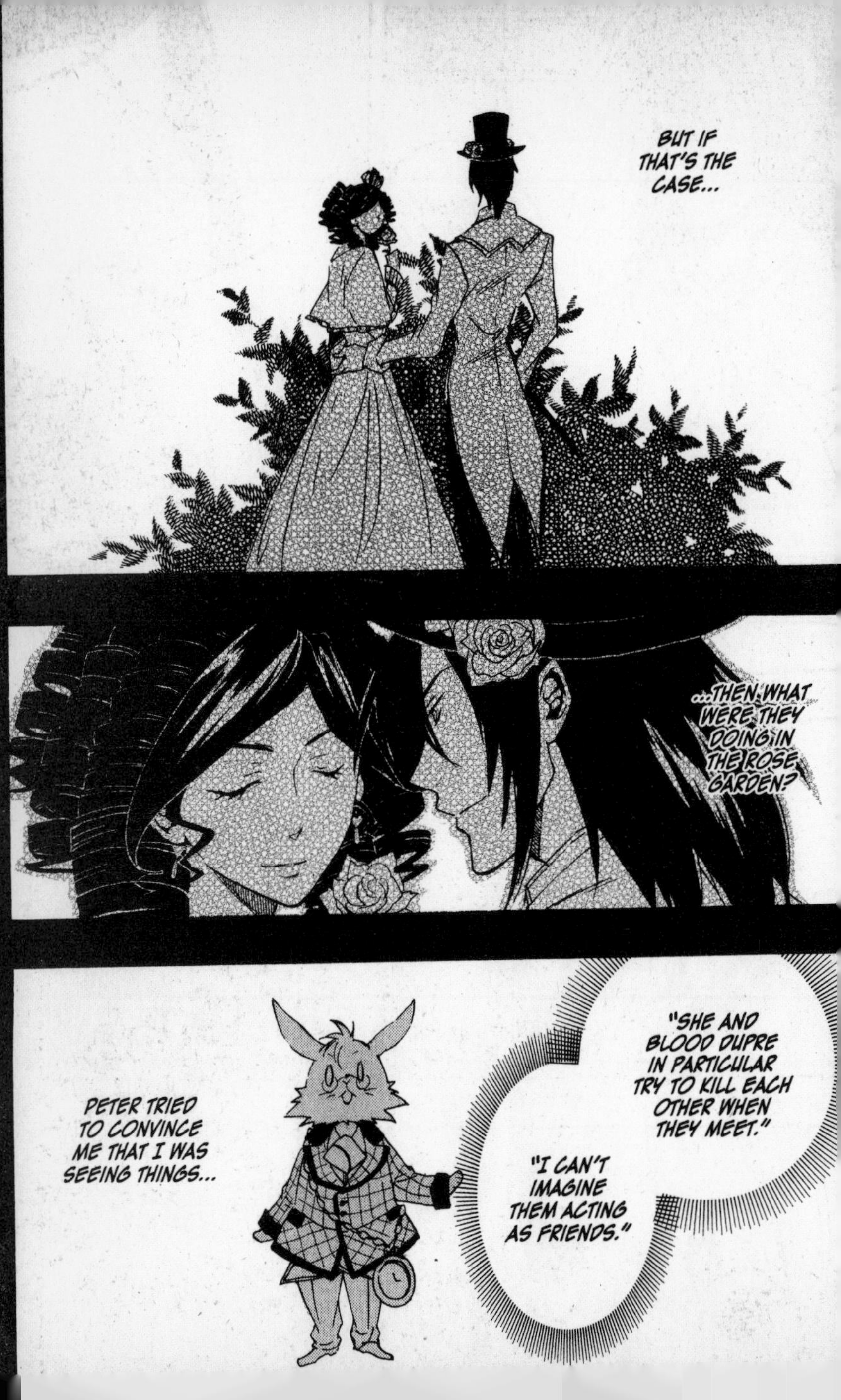
BUT IF THAT'S THE CASE...
...THEN WHAT WERE THEY DOING IN THE ROSE GARDEN?
"SHE AND BLOOD DUPRE IN PARTICULAR TRY TO KILL EACH OTHER WHEN THEY MEET."
"I CAN'T IMAGINE THEM ACTING AS FRIENDS."
PETER TRIED TO CONVINCE ME THAT I WAS SEEING THINGS...

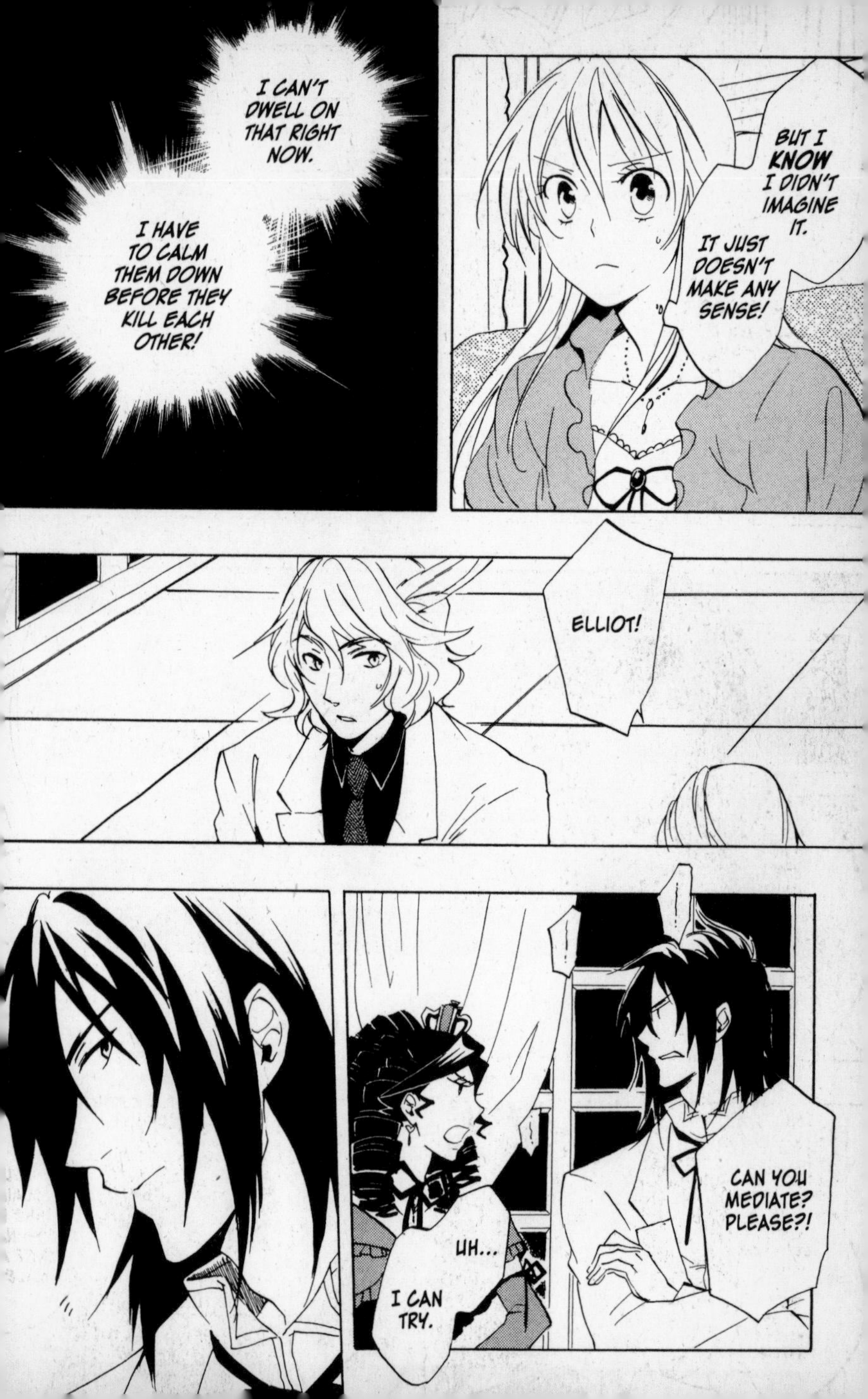
BUT I KNOW I DIDN'T IMAGINE IT.
IT JUST DOESN'T MAKE ANY SENSE!
I CAN'T DWELL ON THAT RIGHT NOW.
I HAVE TO CALM THEM DOWN BEFORE THEY KILL EACH OTHER!
ELLIOT!
CAN YOU MEDIATE? PLEASE?!
UH...
I CAN TRY.

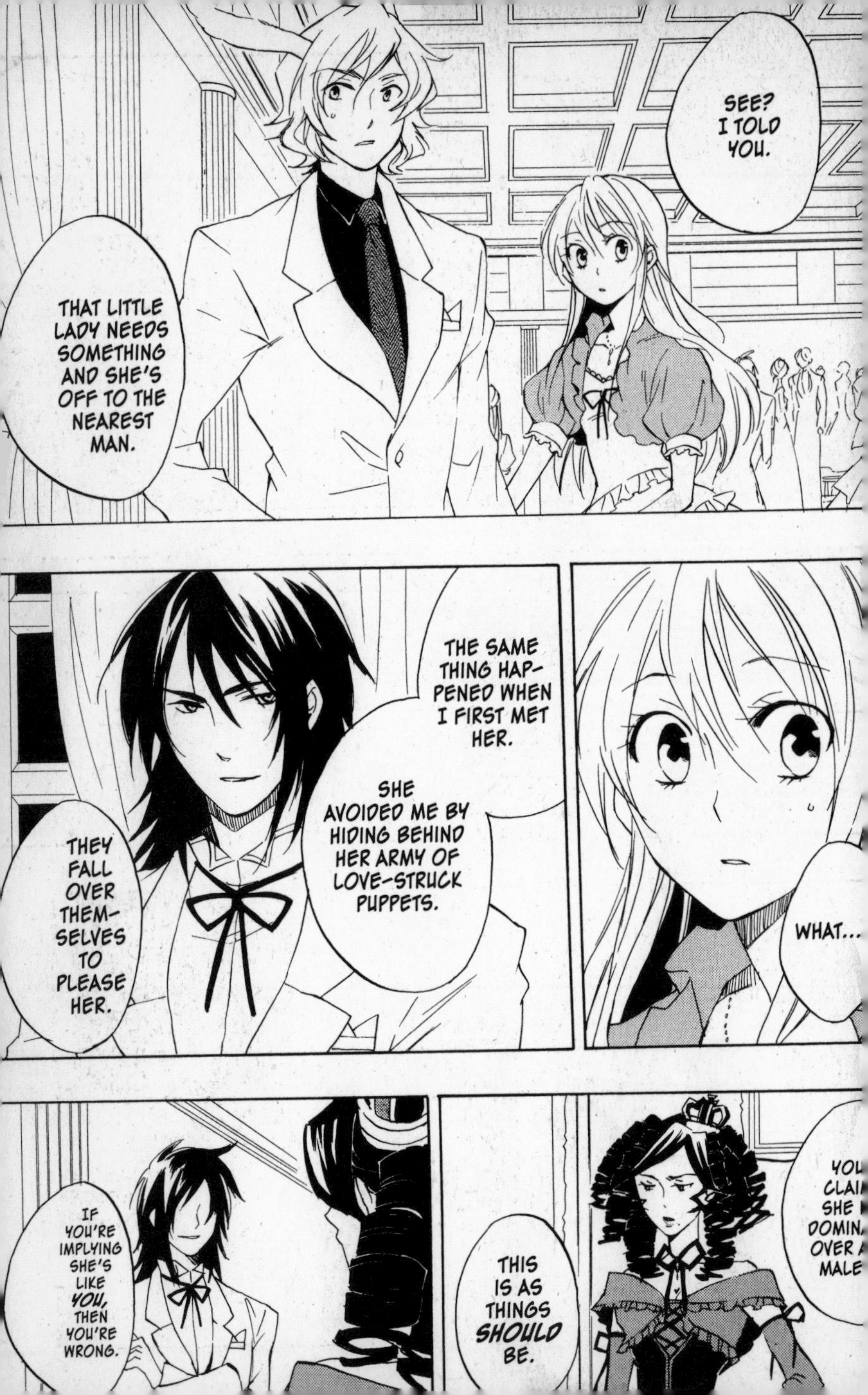
SEE? I TOLD YOU.
THAT LITTLE LADY NEEDS SOMETHING AND SHE'S OFF TO THE NEAREST MAN.
WHAT...
THE SAME THING HAP-PENED WHEN I FIRST MET HER.
SHE AVOIDED ME BY HIDING BEHIND HER ARMY OF LOVE-STRUCK PUPPETS.
THEY FALL OVER THEM-SELVES TO PLEASE HER.
YOU CLAI SHE DOMIN OVER MALE
THIS IS AS THINGS *SHOULD* BE.
IF YOU'RE IMPLYING SHE'S LIKE *YOU*, THEN YOU'RE WRONG.

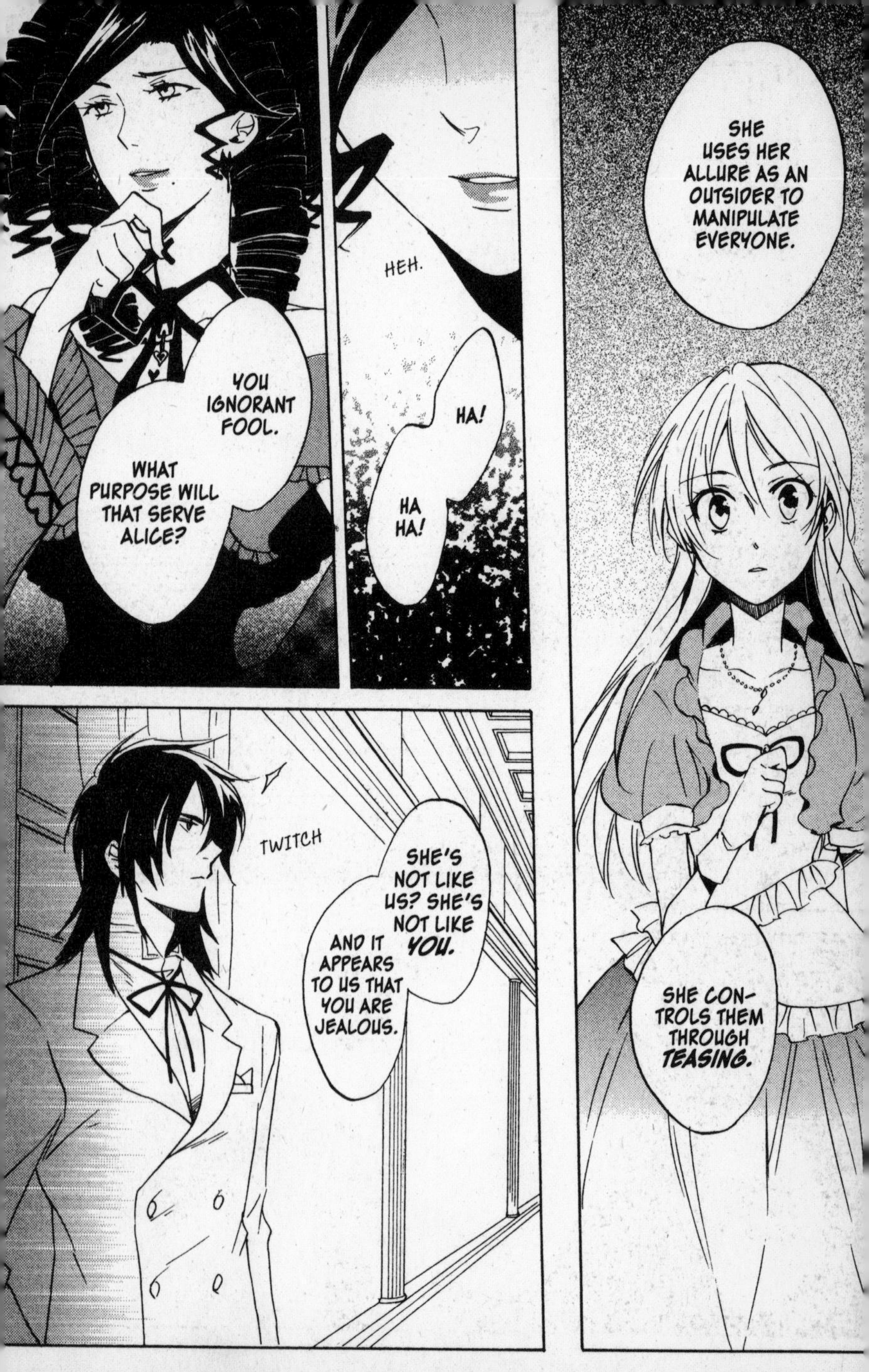
SHE USES HER ALLURE AS AN OUTSIDER TO MANIPULATE EVERYONE.
SHE CON-TROLS THEM THROUGH *TEASING.*
HEH.
HA!
HA HA!
YOU IGNORANT FOOL.
WHAT PURPOSE WILL THAT SERVE ALICE?
SHE'S NOT LIKE US? SHE'S NOT LIKE *YOU.*
AND IT APPEARS TO US THAT YOU ARE JEALOUS.
TWITCH

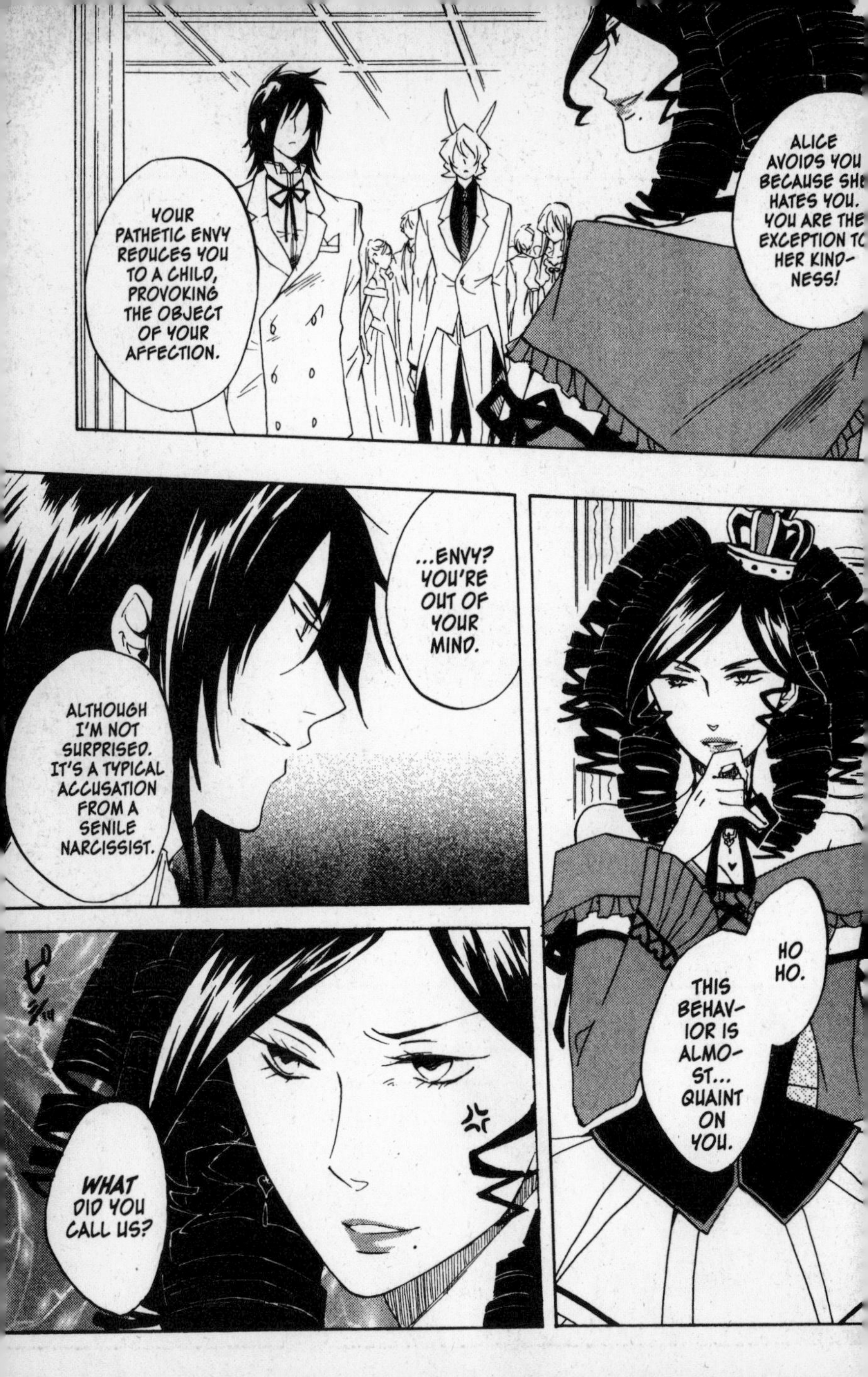
ALICE AVOIDS YOU BECAUSE SHE HATES YOU. YOU ARE THE EXCEPTION TO HER KINDNESS!
YOUR PATHETIC ENVY REDUCES YOU TO A CHILD, PROVOKING THE OBJECT OF YOUR AFFECTION.
HO HO.
THIS BEHAVIOR IS ALMOST... QUAINT ON YOU.
...ENVY? YOU'RE OUT OF YOUR MIND.
ALTHOUGH I'M NOT SURPRISED. IT'S A TYPICAL ACCUSATION FROM A SENILE NARCISSIST.
WHAT DID YOU CALL US?

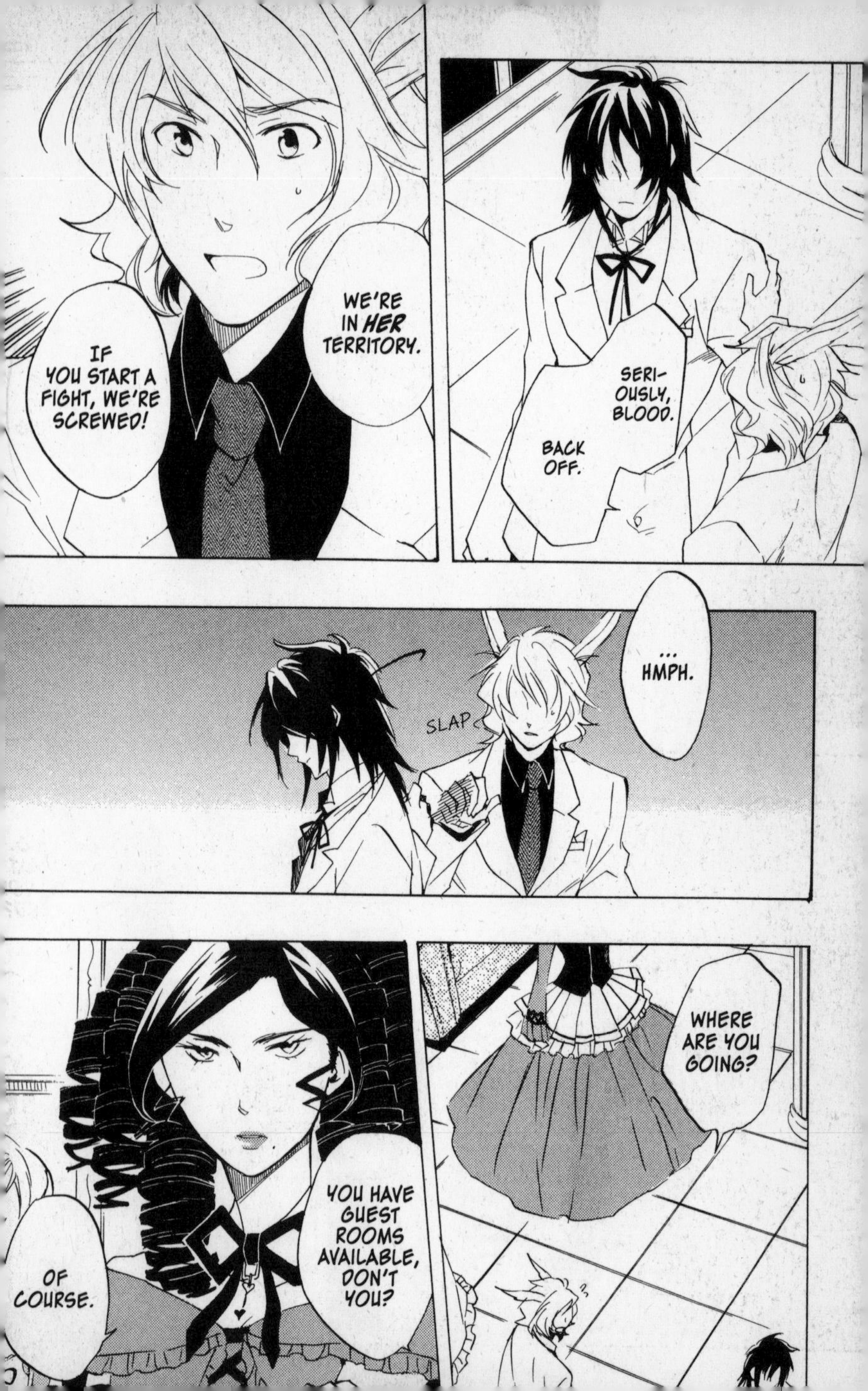
SERI-OUSLY, BLOOD.
BACK OFF.
WE'RE IN HER TERRITORY.
IF YOU START A FIGHT, WE'RE SCREWED!
... HMPH.
SLAP
WHERE ARE YOU GOING?
YOU HAVE GUEST ROOMS AVAILABLE, DON'T YOU?
OF COURSE.

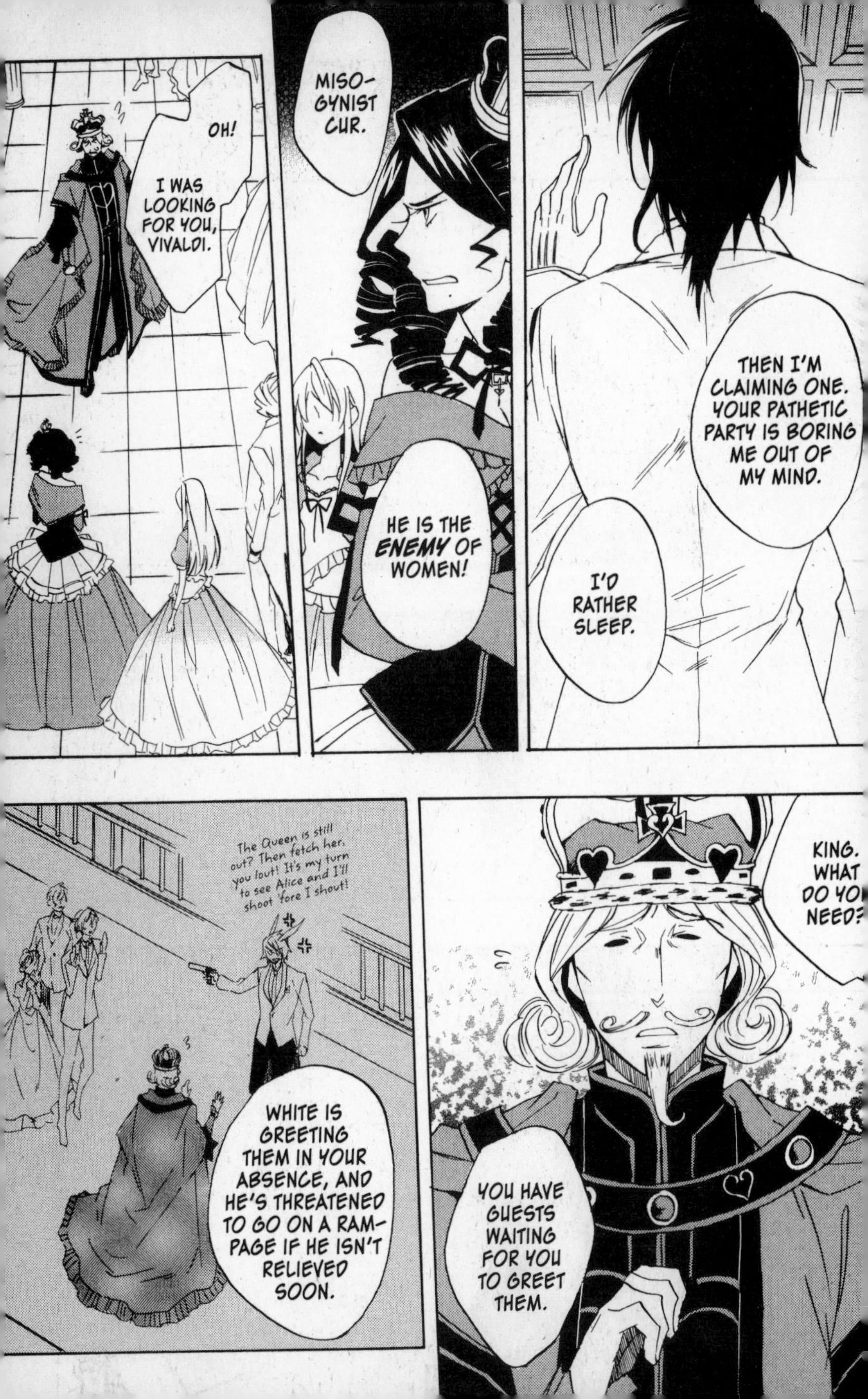
THEN I'M CLAIMING ONE. YOUR PATHETIC PARTY IS BORING ME OUT OF MY MIND.
I'D RATHER SLEEP.
MISO-GYNIST CUR.
HE IS THE ENEMY OF WOMEN!
OH!
I WAS LOOKING FOR YOU, VIVALDI.
KING. WHAT DO YO NEED?
YOU HAVE GUESTS WAITING FOR YOU TO GREET THEM.
The Queen is still out? Then fetch her, you lout! It's my turn to see Alice and I'll shoot 'fore I shout!
WHITE IS GREETING THEM IN YOUR ABSENCE, AND HE'S THREATENED TO GO ON A RAM-PAGE IF HE ISN'T RELIEVED SOON.

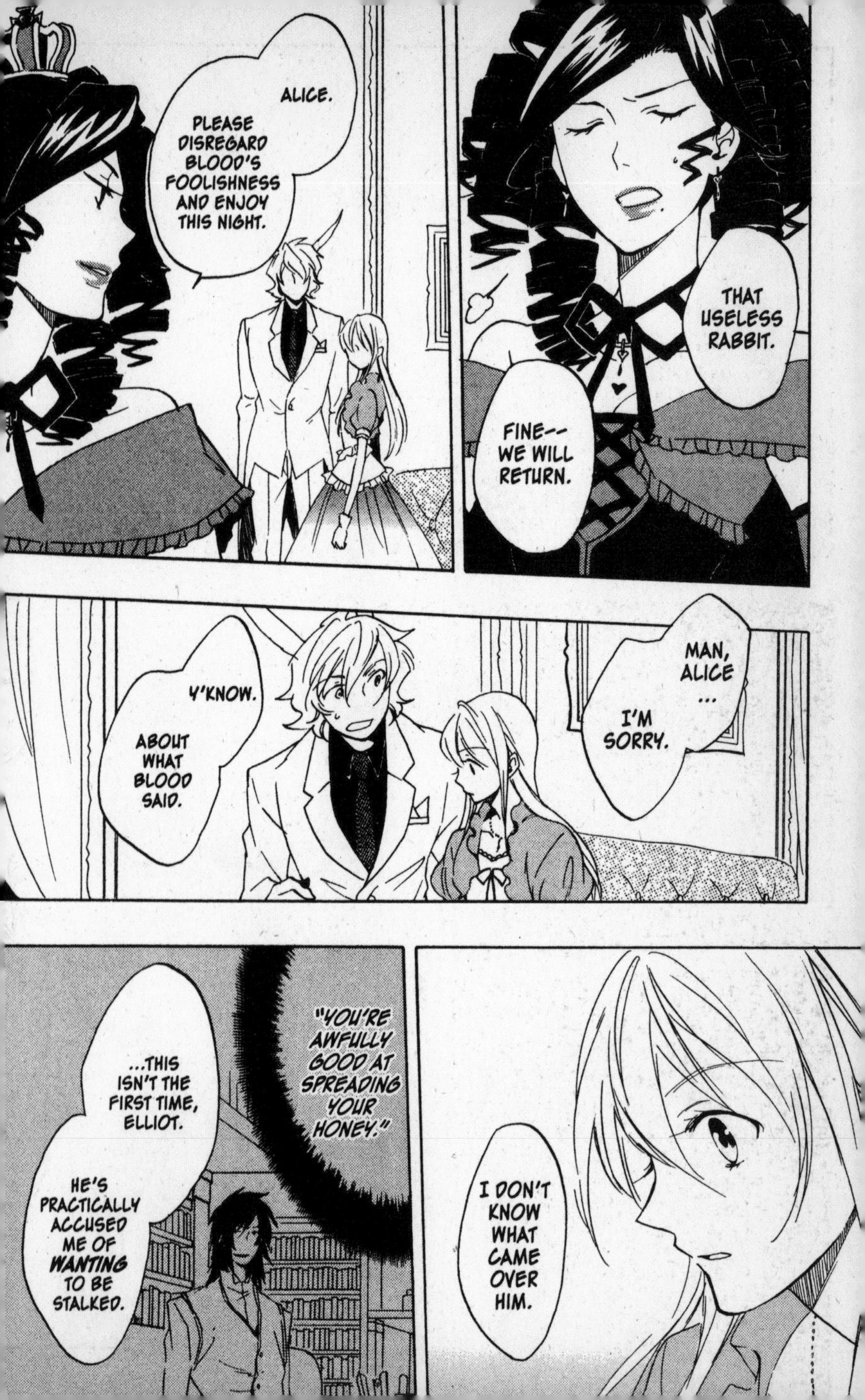
THAT USELESS RABBIT.
FINE-- WE WILL RETURN.
ALICE.
PLEASE DISREGARD BLOOD'S FOOLISHNESS AND ENJOY THIS NIGHT.
MAN, ALICE ...
I'M SORRY.
Y'KNOW.
ABOUT WHAT BLOOD SAID.
I DON'T KNOW WHAT CAME OVER HIM.
"YOU'RE AWFULLY GOOD AT SPREADING YOUR HONEY."
...THIS ISN'T THE FIRST TIME, ELLIOT.
HE'S PRACTICALLY ACCUSED ME OF *WANTING* TO BE STALKED.

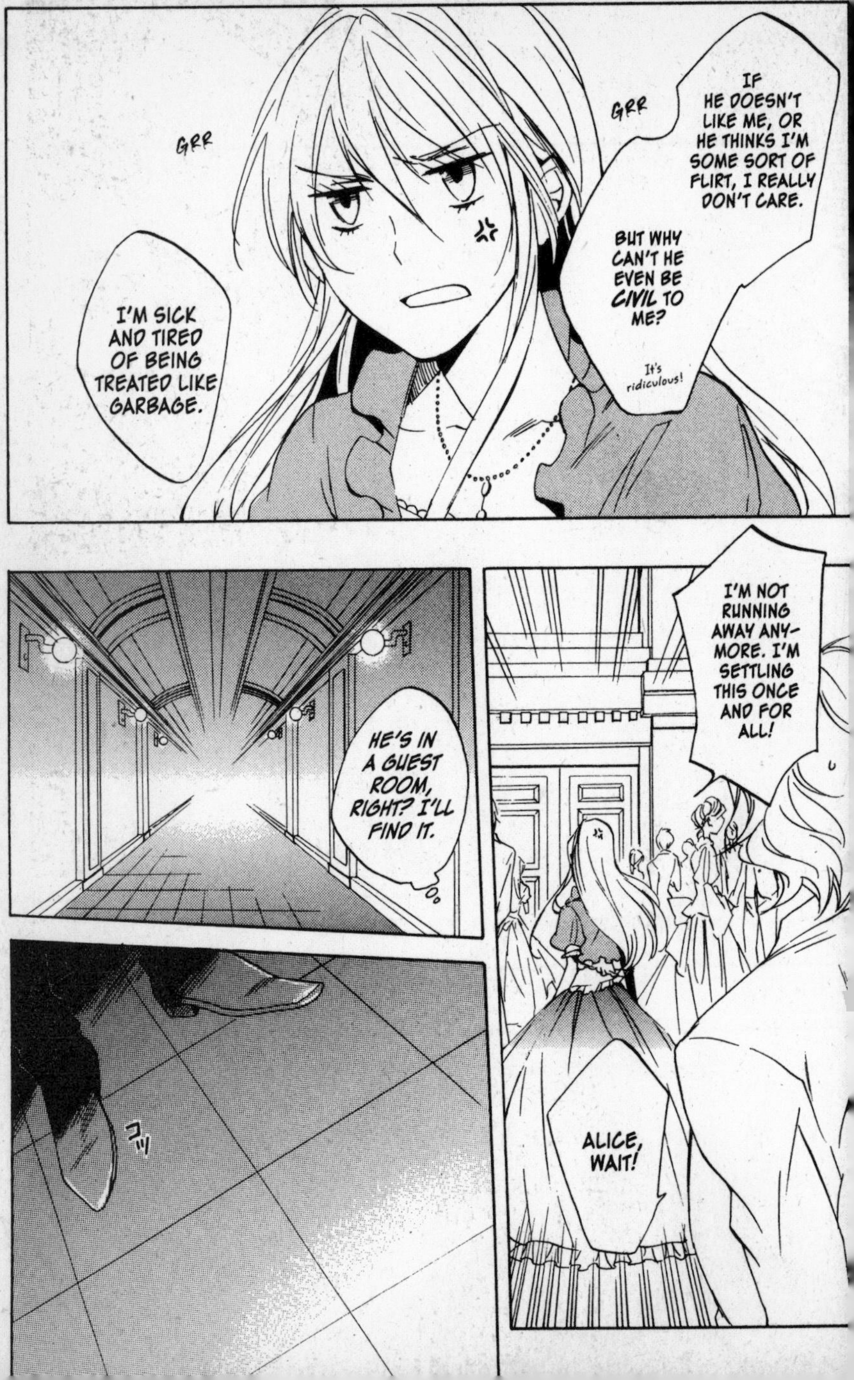
IF HE DOESN'T LIKE ME, OR HE THINKS I'M SOME SORT OF FLIRT, I REALLY DON'T CARE.
GRR
BUT WHY CAN'T HE EVEN BE CIVIL TO ME?
It's ridiculous!
GRR
I'M SICK AND TIRED OF BEING TREATED LIKE GARBAGE.
I'M NOT RUNNING AWAY ANY-MORE. I'M SETTLING THIS ONCE AND FOR ALL!
ALICE, WAIT!
HE'S IN A GUEST ROOM, RIGHT? I'LL FIND IT.
コッ

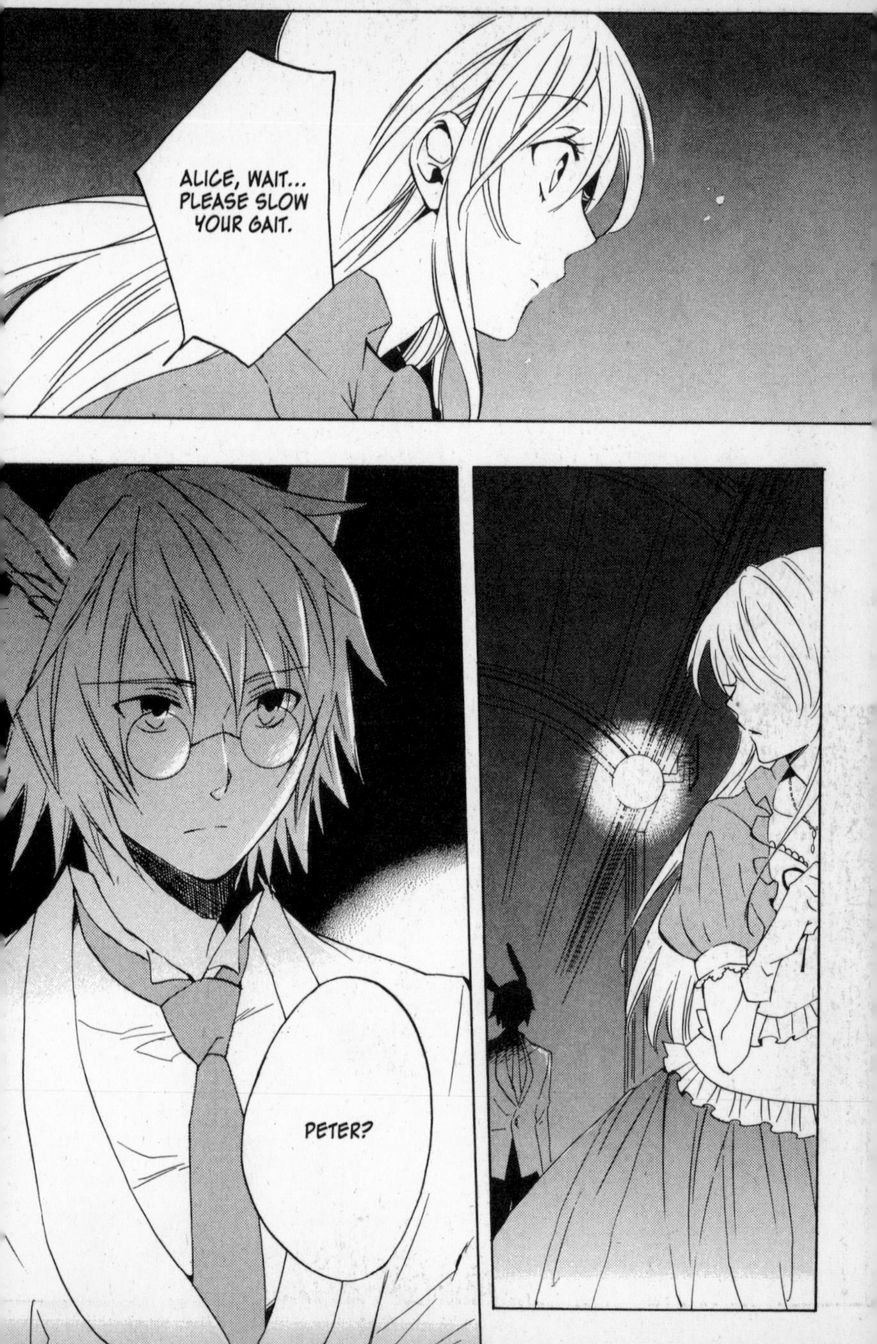
ALICE, WAIT... PLEASE SLOW YOUR GAIT.
PETER?

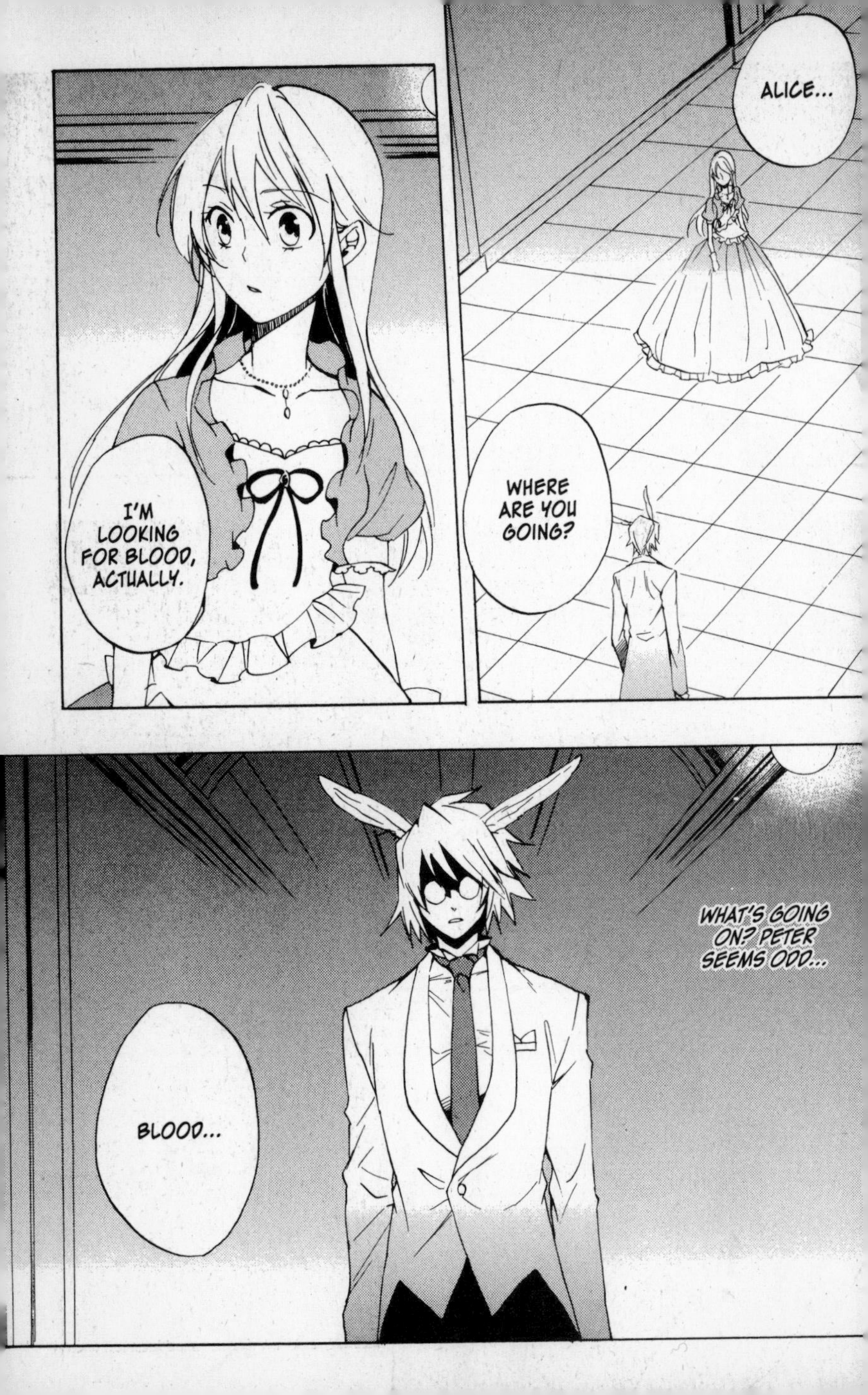
ALICE...
WHERE ARE YOU GOING?
I'M LOOKING FOR BLOOD, ACTUALLY.
WHAT'S GOING ON? PETER SEEMS ODD...
BLOOD...

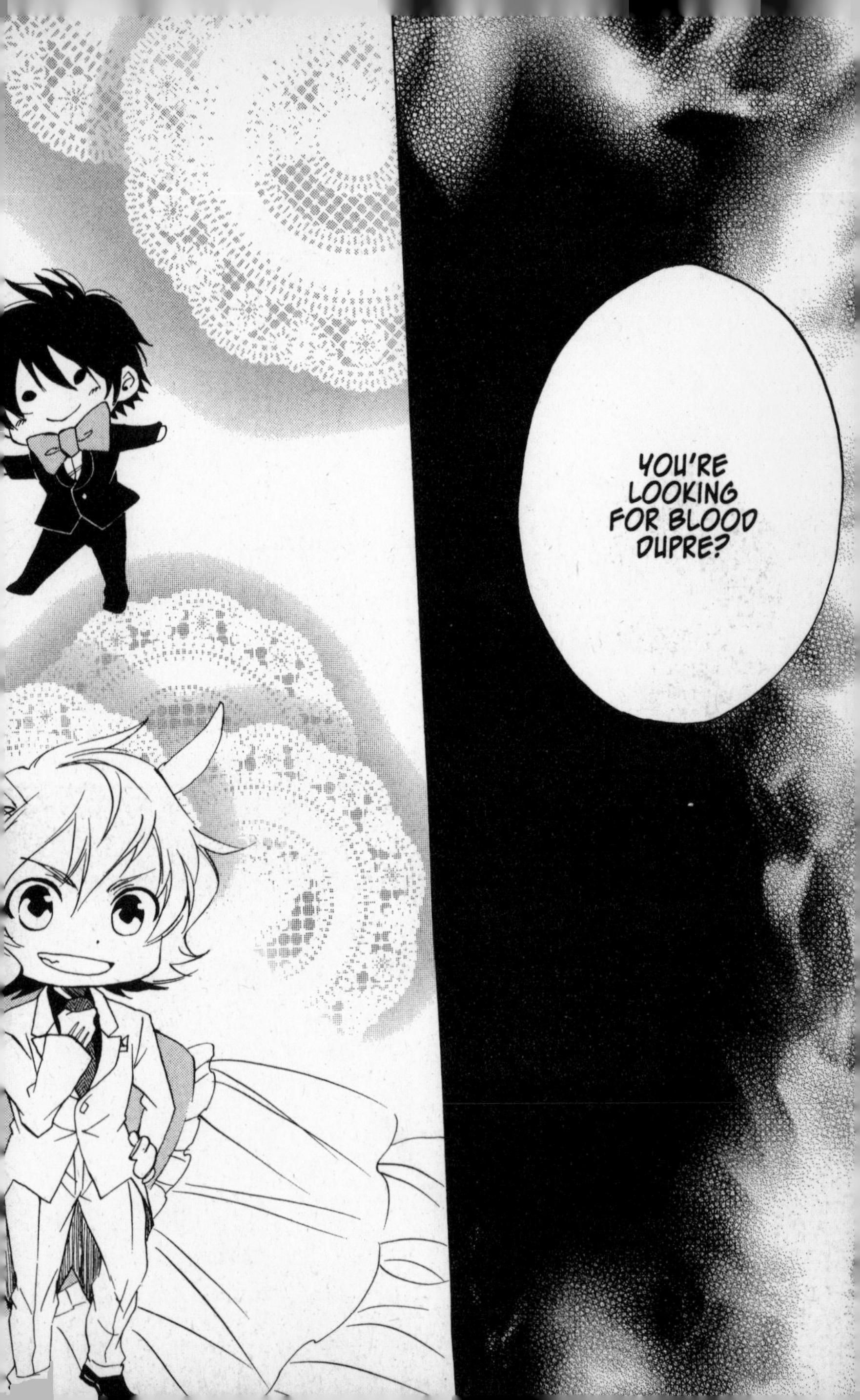
YOU'RE LOOKING FOR BLOOD DUPRE?

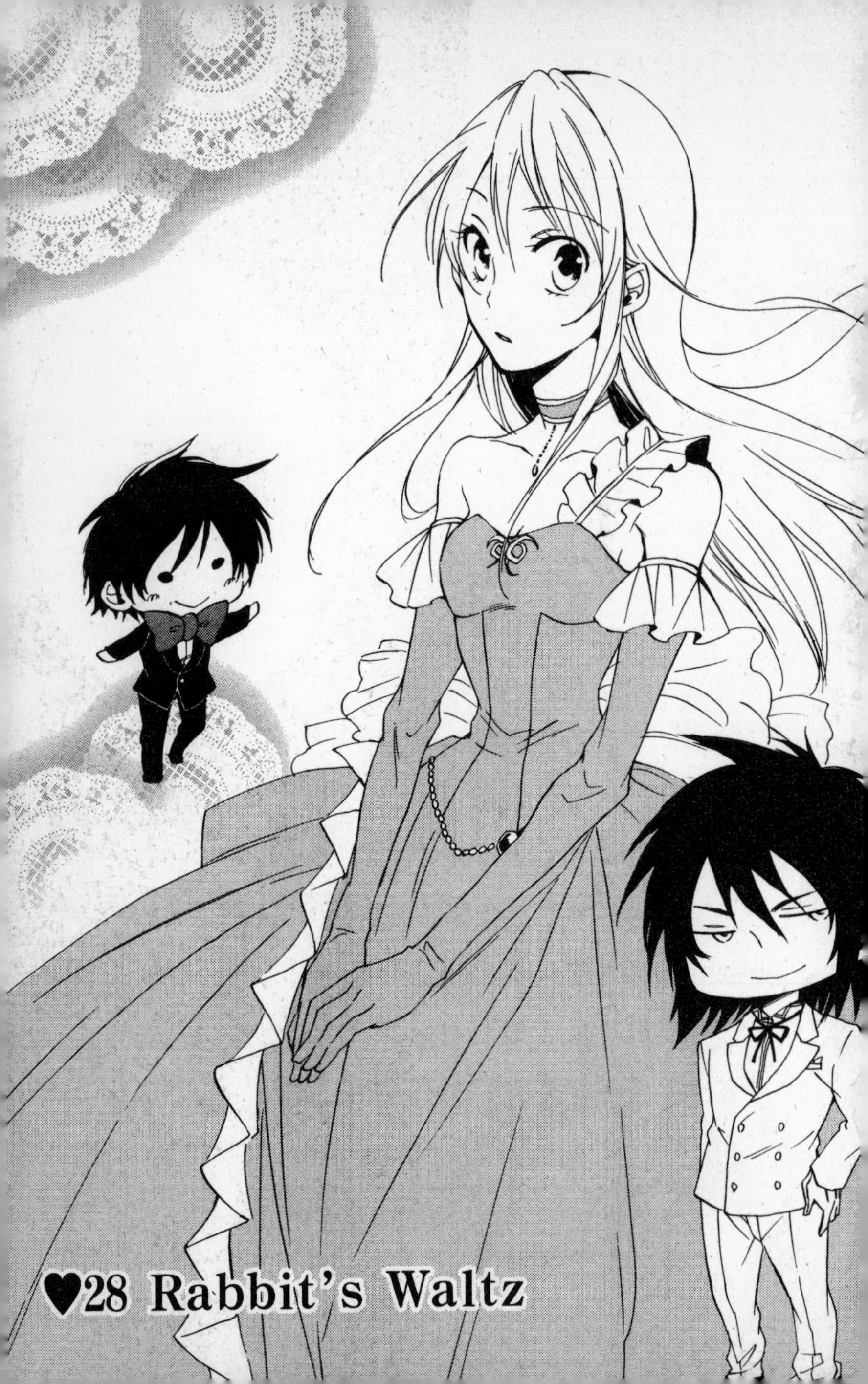

♥28 Rabbit's Waltz

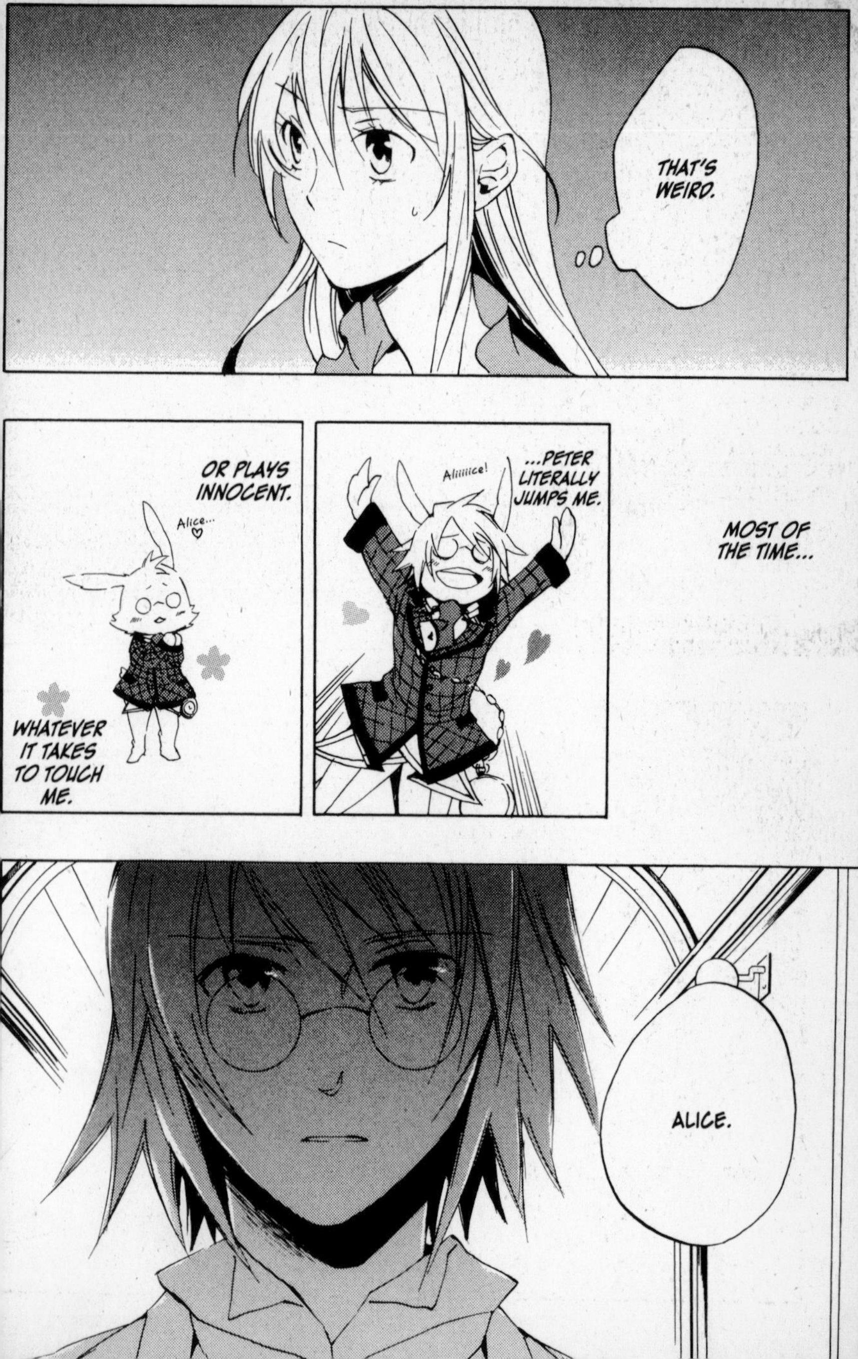
THAT'S WEIRD.
MOST OF THE TIME...
...PETER LITERALLY JUMPS ME.
Aliiiiice!
OR PLAYS INNOCENT.
Alice...
WHATEVER IT TAKES TO TOUCH ME.
ALICE.

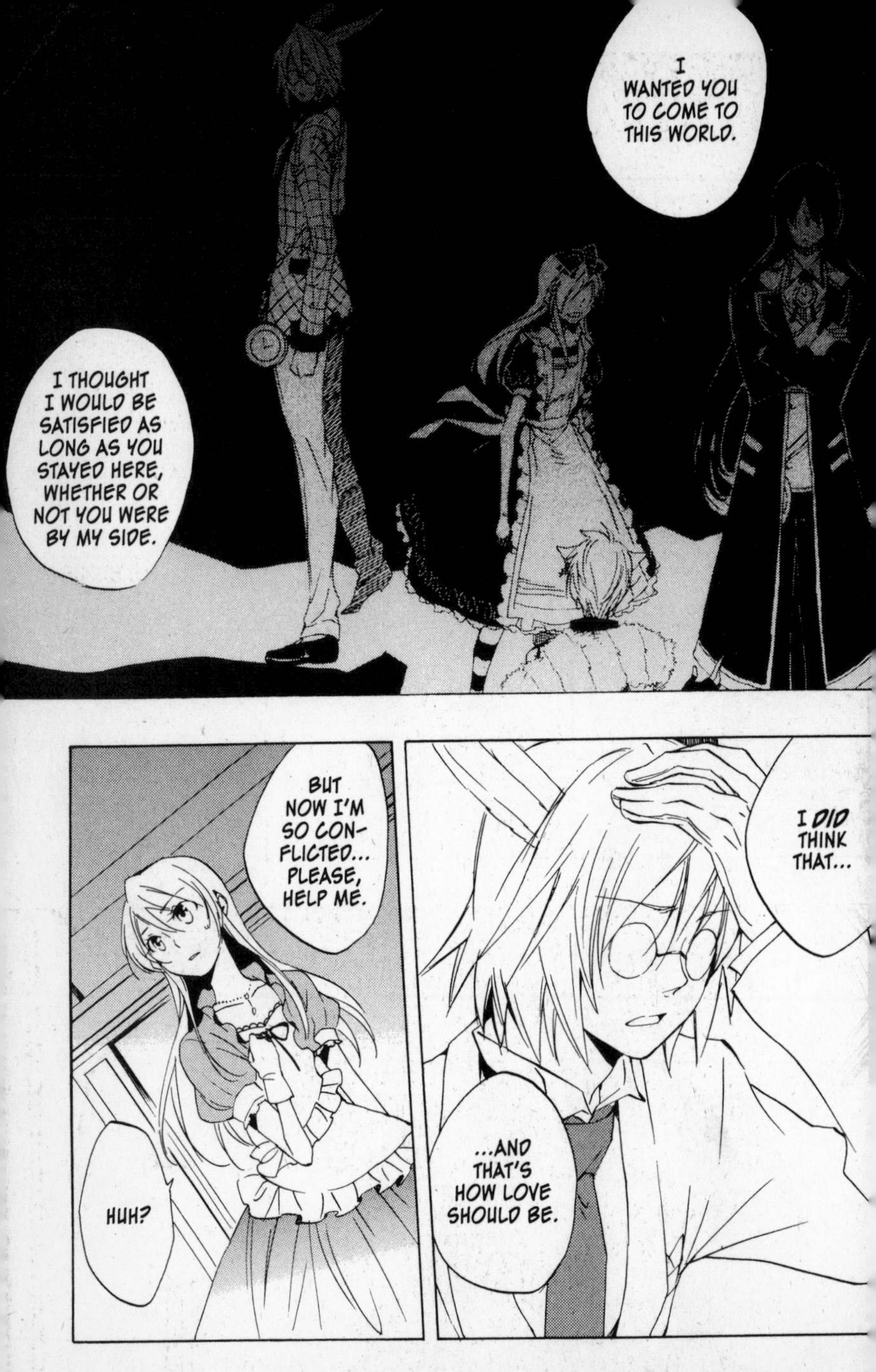
I WANTED YOU TO COME TO THIS WORLD.
I THOUGHT I WOULD BE SATISFIED AS LONG AS YOU STAYED HERE, WHETHER OR NOT YOU WERE BY MY SIDE.
I *DID* THINK THAT...
...AND THAT'S HOW LOVE SHOULD BE.
BUT NOW I'M SO CON-FLICTED... PLEASE, HELP ME.
HUH?

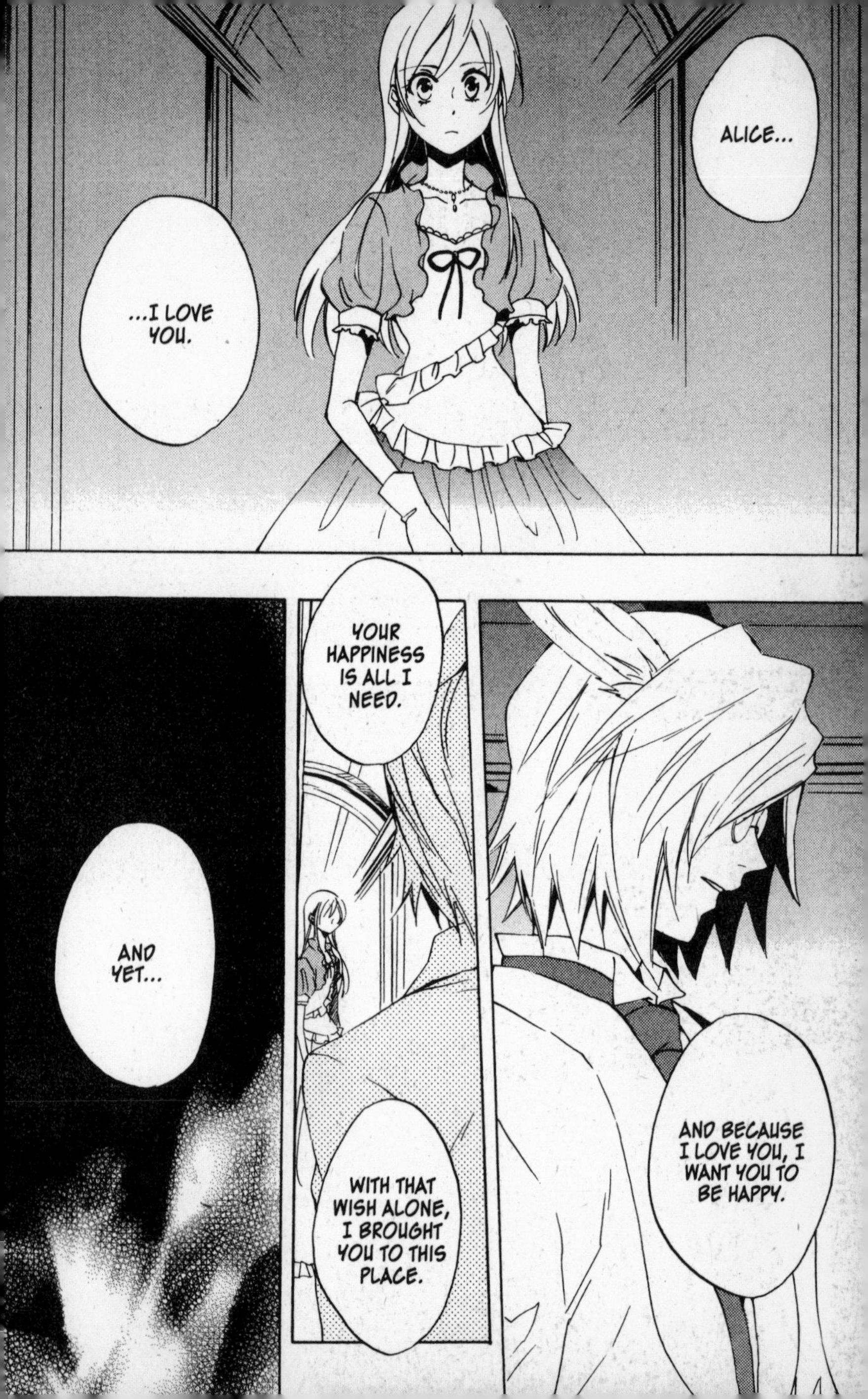
ALICE...
...I LOVE YOU.
AND BECAUSE I LOVE YOU, I WANT YOU TO BE HAPPY.
YOUR HAPPINESS IS ALL I NEED.
WITH THAT WISH ALONE, I BROUGHT YOU TO THIS PLACE.
AND YET...

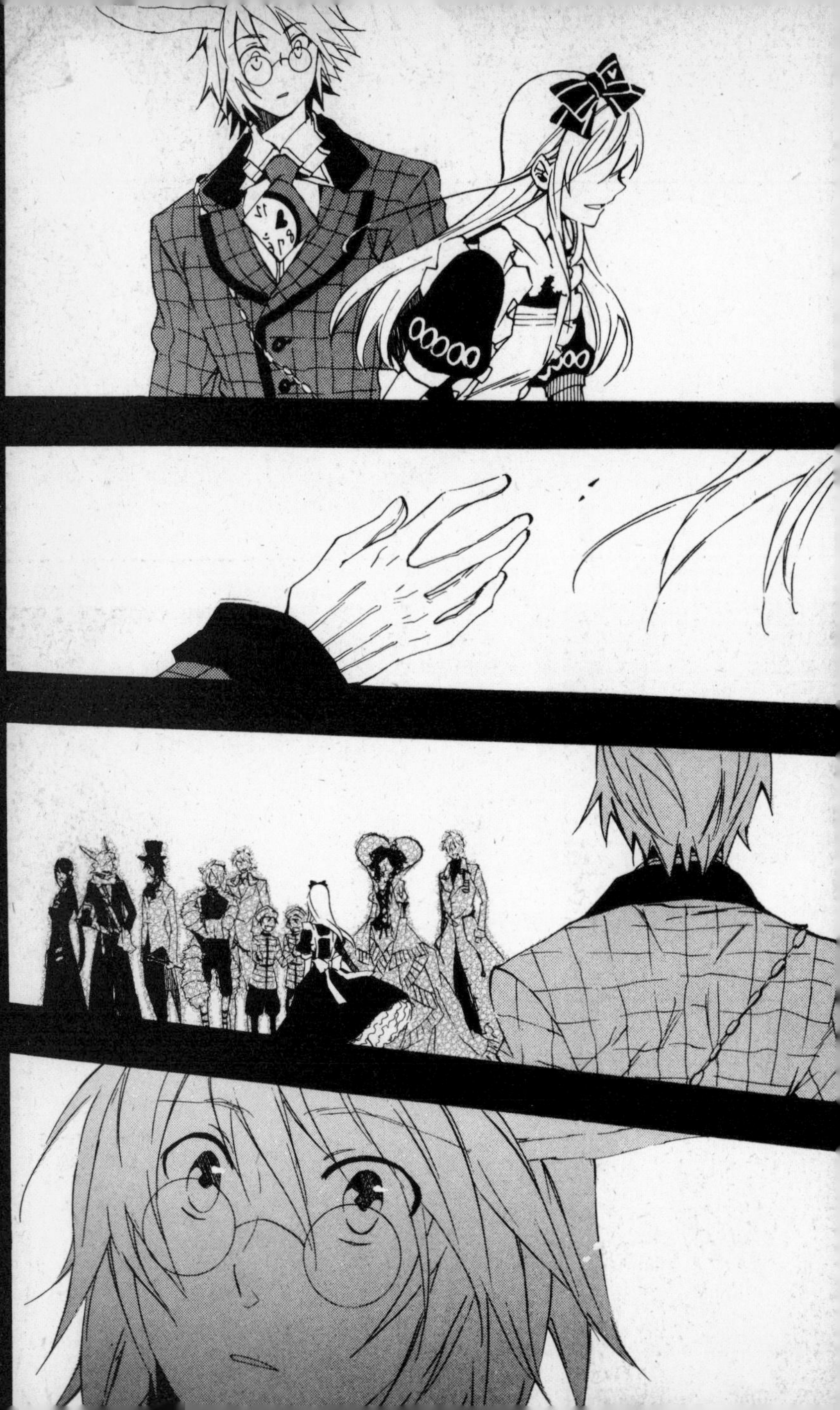

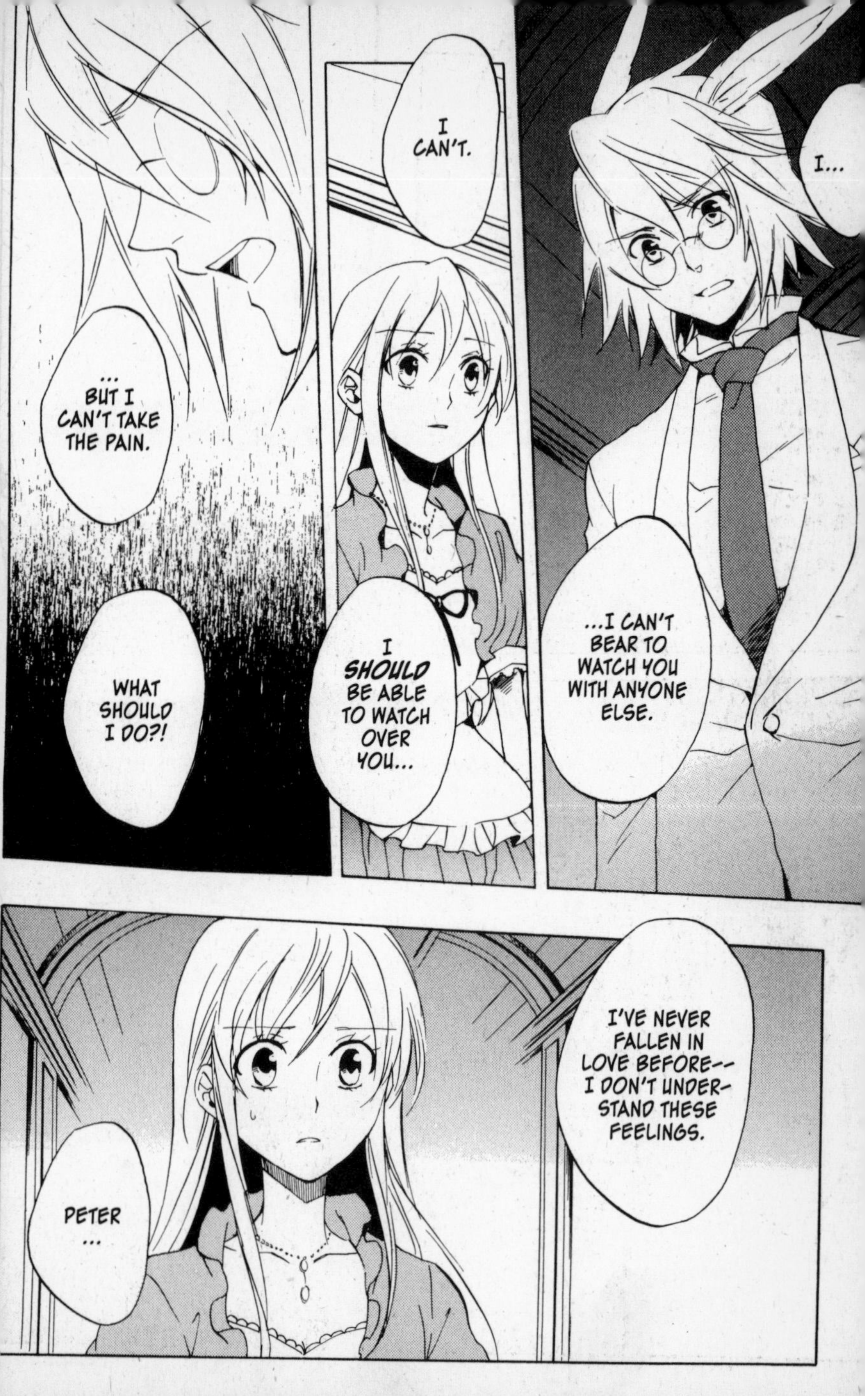
I...
...I CAN'T BEAR TO WATCH YOU WITH ANYONE ELSE.
I CAN'T.
I *SHOULD* BE ABLE TO WATCH OVER YOU...
...BUT I CAN'T TAKE THE PAIN.
WHAT SHOULD I DO?!
I'VE NEVER FALLEN IN LOVE BEFORE--I DON'T UNDER-STAND THESE FEELINGS.
PETER ...

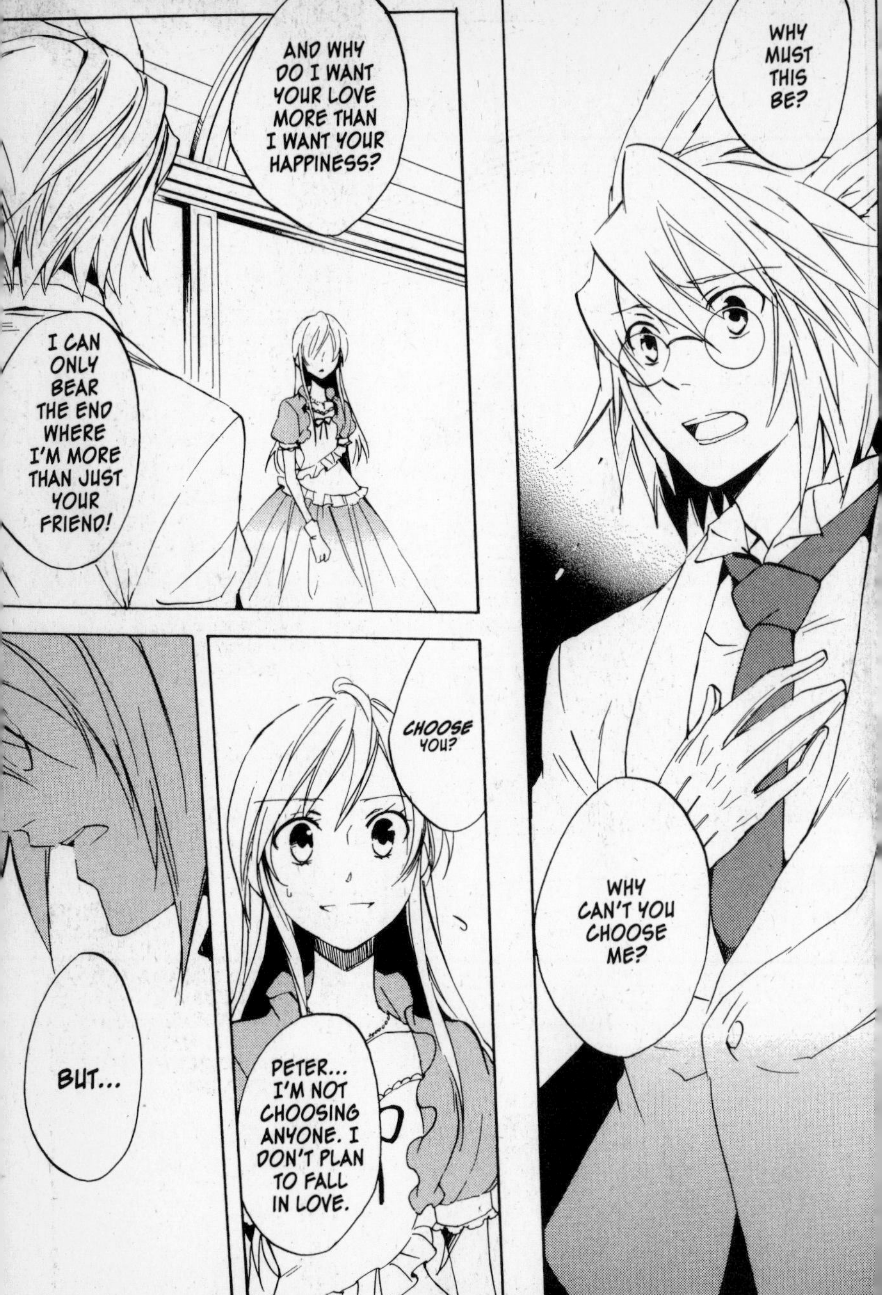
WHY MUST THIS BE?
WHY CAN'T YOU CHOOSE ME?
AND WHY DO I WANT YOUR LOVE MORE THAN I WANT YOUR HAPPINESS?
I CAN ONLY BEAR THE END WHERE I'M MORE THAN JUST YOUR FRIEND!
CHOOSE YOU?
PETER... I'M NOT CHOOSING ANYONE. I DON'T PLAN TO FALL IN LOVE.
BUT...

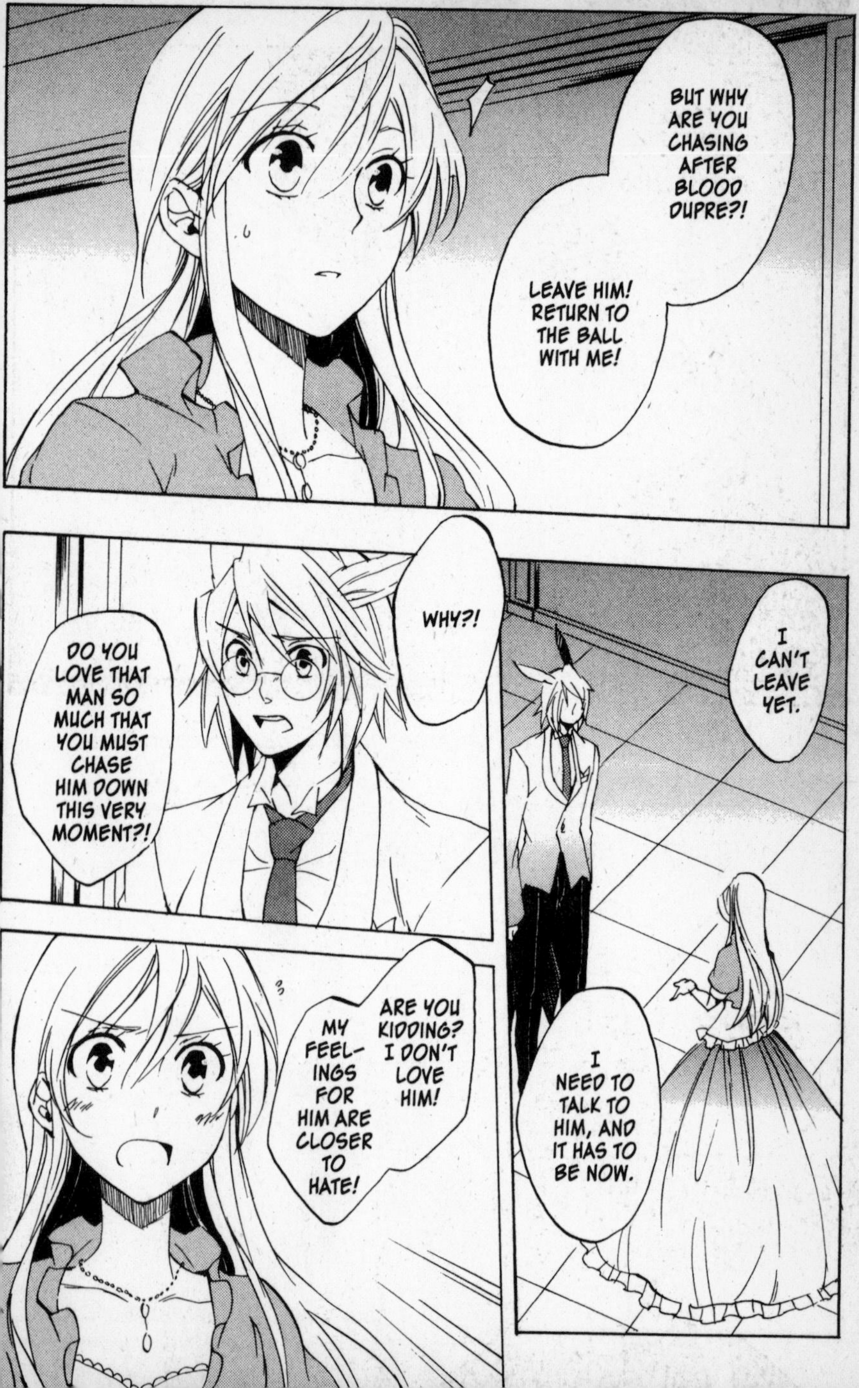
BUT WHY ARE YOU CHASING AFTER BLOOD DUPRE?!
LEAVE HIM! RETURN TO THE BALL WITH ME!
I CAN'T LEAVE YET.
I NEED TO TALK TO HIM, AND IT HAS TO BE NOW.
WHY?!
DO YOU LOVE THAT MAN SO MUCH THAT YOU MUST CHASE HIM DOWN THIS VERY MOMENT?!
ARE YOU KIDDING? I DON'T LOVE HIM!
MY FEEL-INGS FOR HIM ARE CLOSER TO HATE!

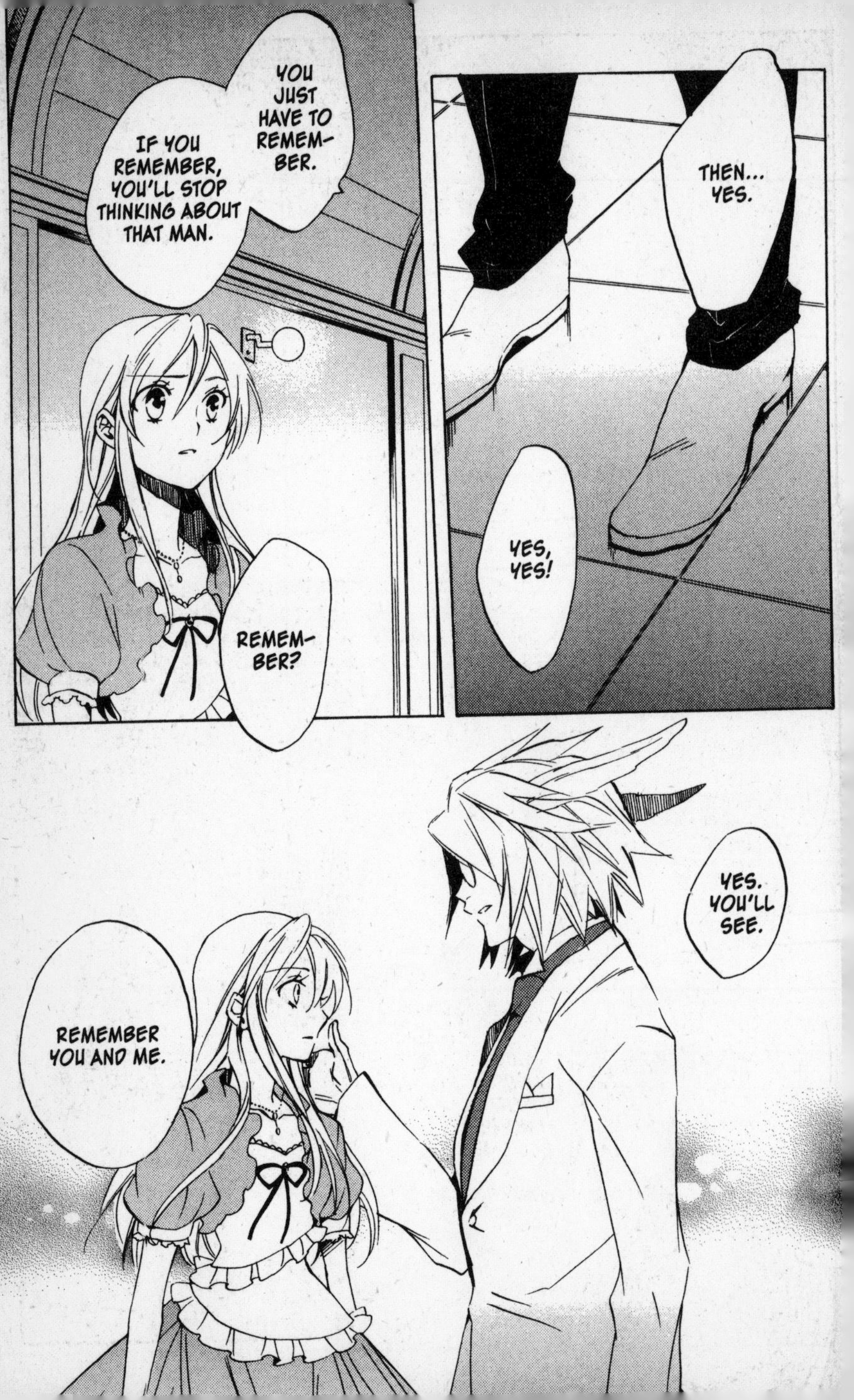
THEN... YES.
YES, YES!
YOU JUST HAVE TO REMEMBER.
IF YOU REMEMBER, YOU'LL STOP THINKING ABOUT THAT MAN.
REMEMBER?
YES. YOU'LL SEE.
REMEMBER YOU AND ME.

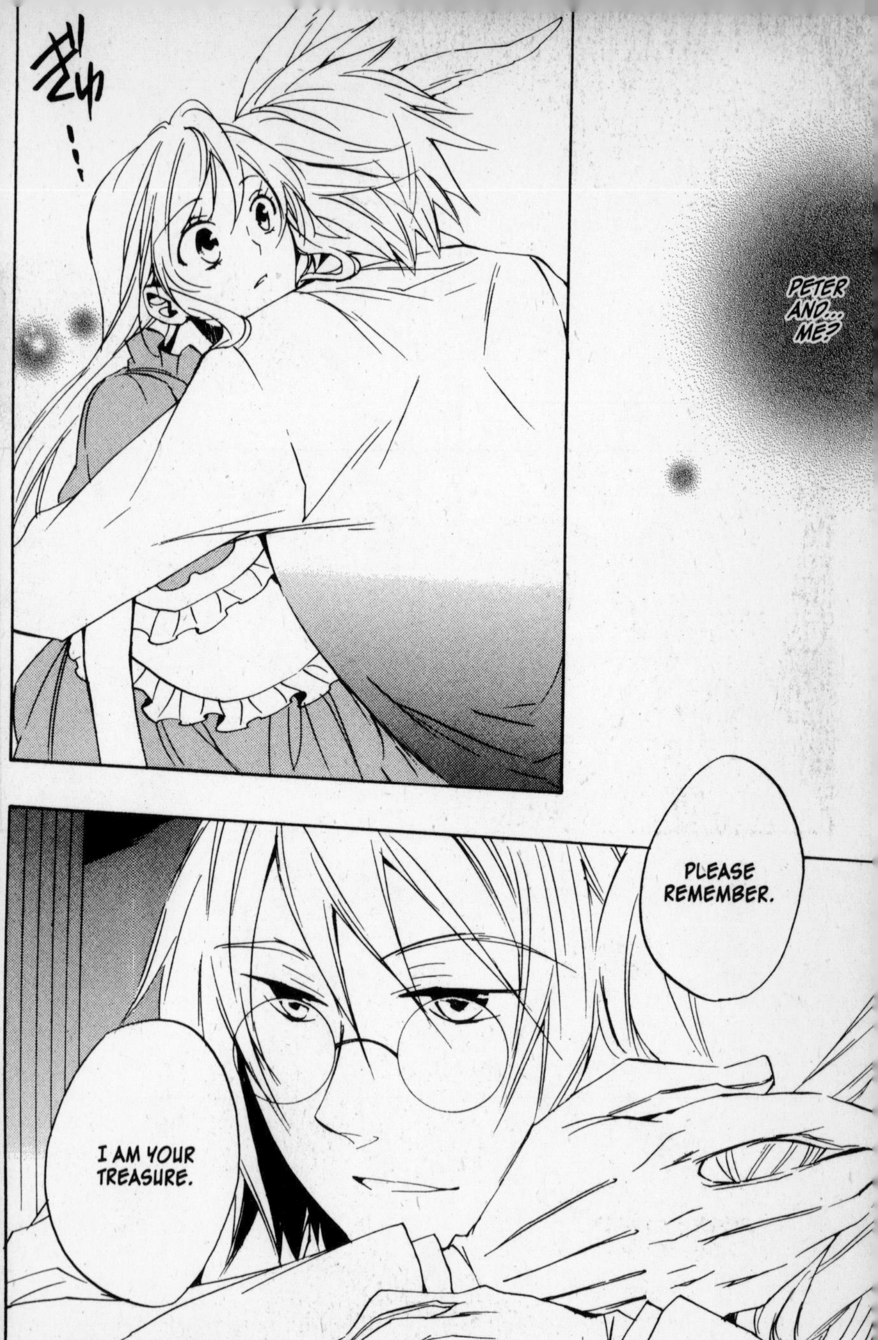
PETER AND... ME?
ぎゅ…
PLEASE REMEMBER.
I AM YOUR TREASURE.

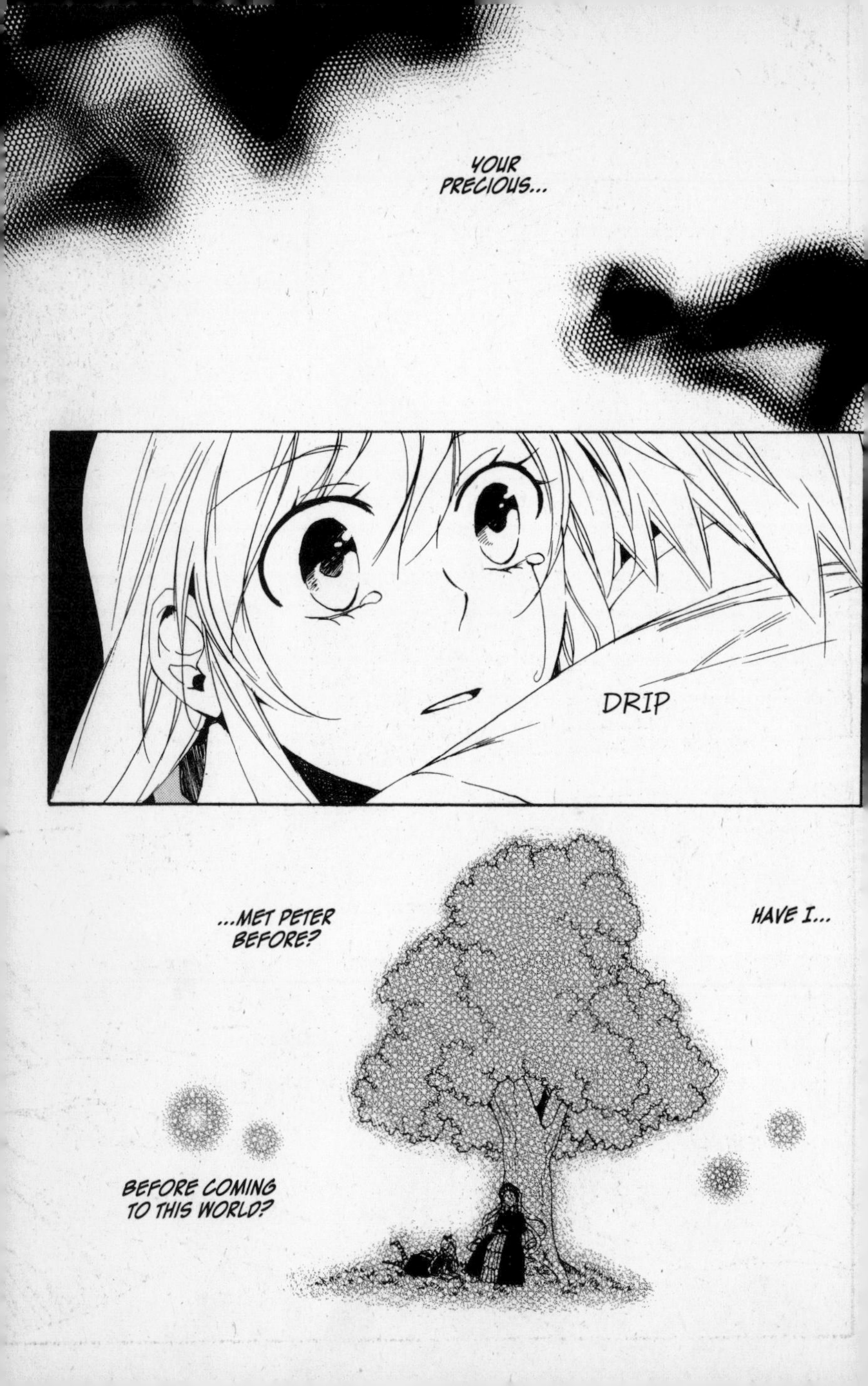
YOUR PRECIOUS...
DRIP
HAVE I...
...MET PETER BEFORE?
BEFORE COMING TO THIS WORLD?

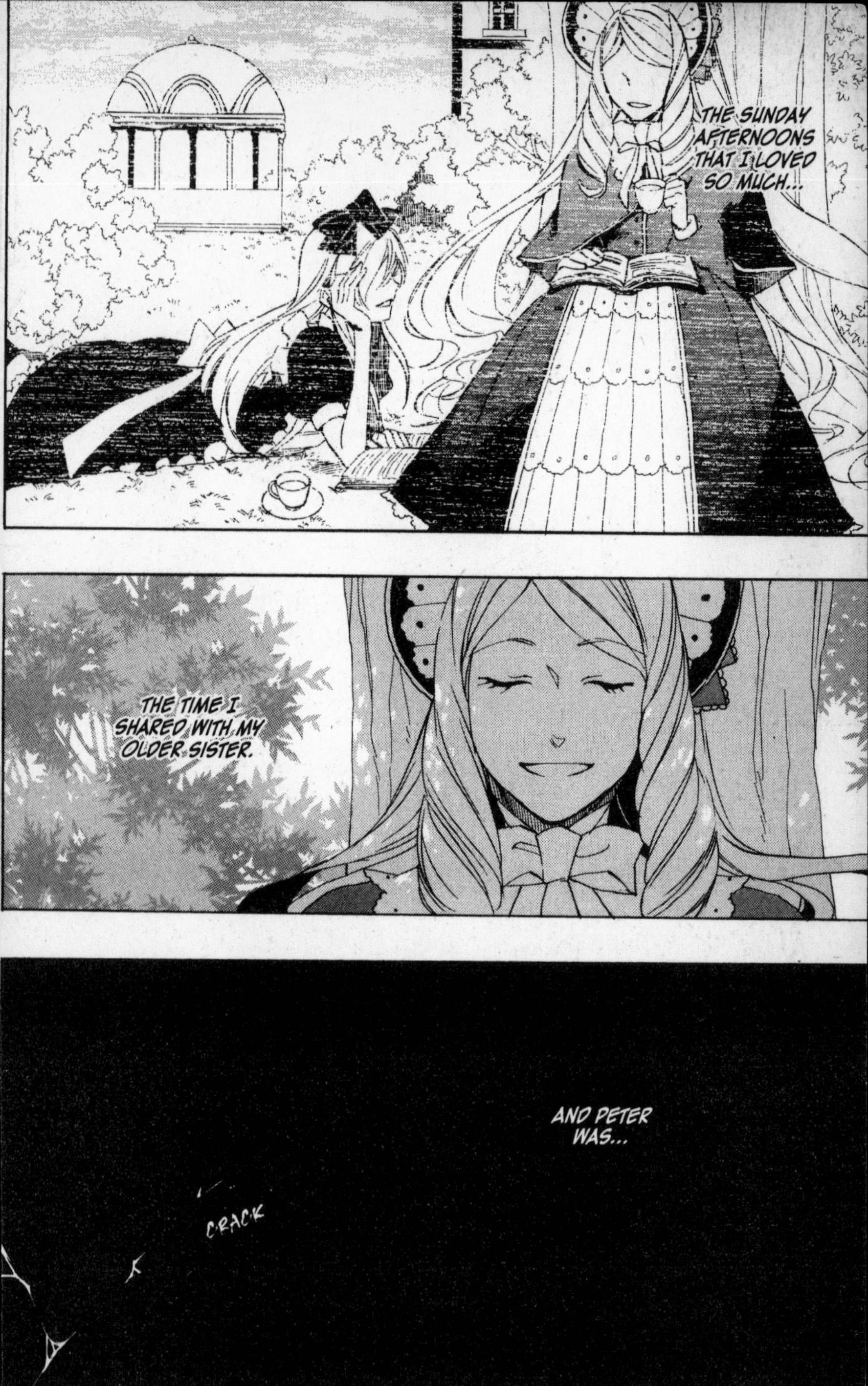
THE SUNDAY AFTERNOONS THAT I LOVED SO MUCH...
THE TIME I SHARED WITH MY OLDER SISTER.
AND PETER WAS...
CRACK

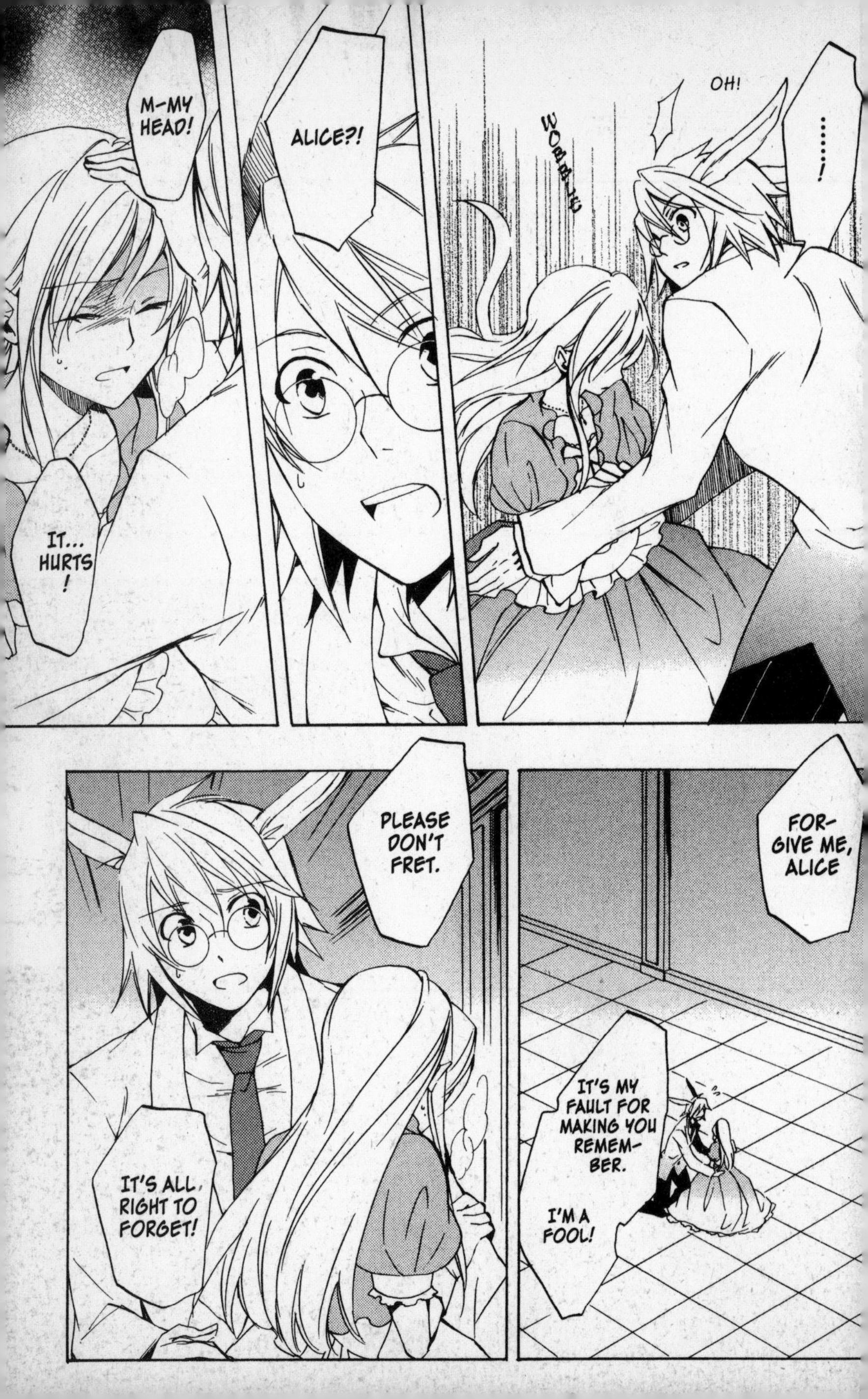
......!
OH!
WOBBLE
ALICE?!
M-MY HEAD!
IT... HURTS!
FOR-GIVE ME, ALICE
IT'S MY FAULT FOR MAKING YOU REMEM-BER.
I'M A FOOL!
PLEASE DON'T FRET.
IT'S ALL RIGHT TO FORGET!

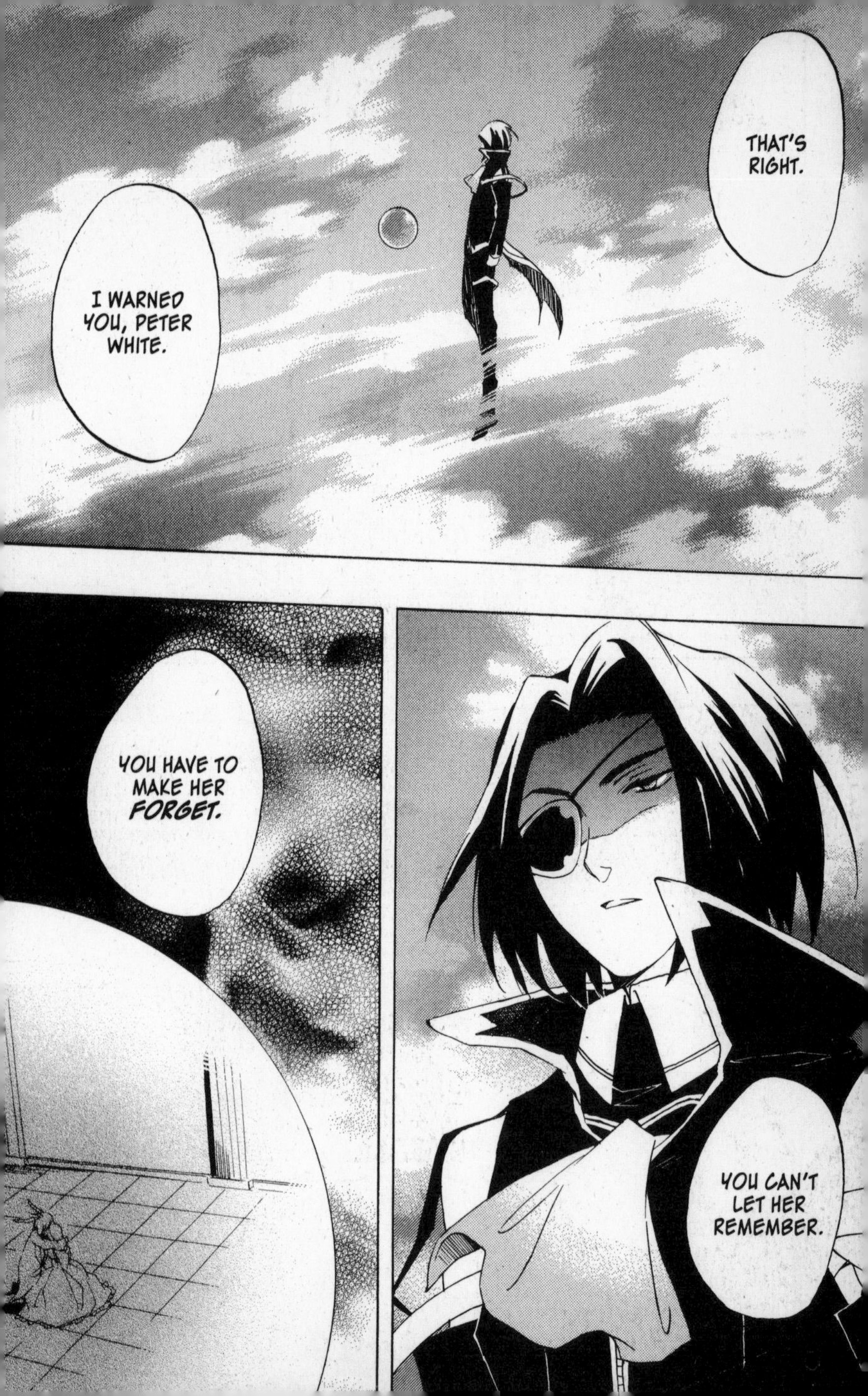
THAT'S RIGHT.
I WARNED YOU, PETER WHITE.
YOU CAN'T LET HER REMEMBER.
YOU HAVE TO MAKE HER *FORGET.*

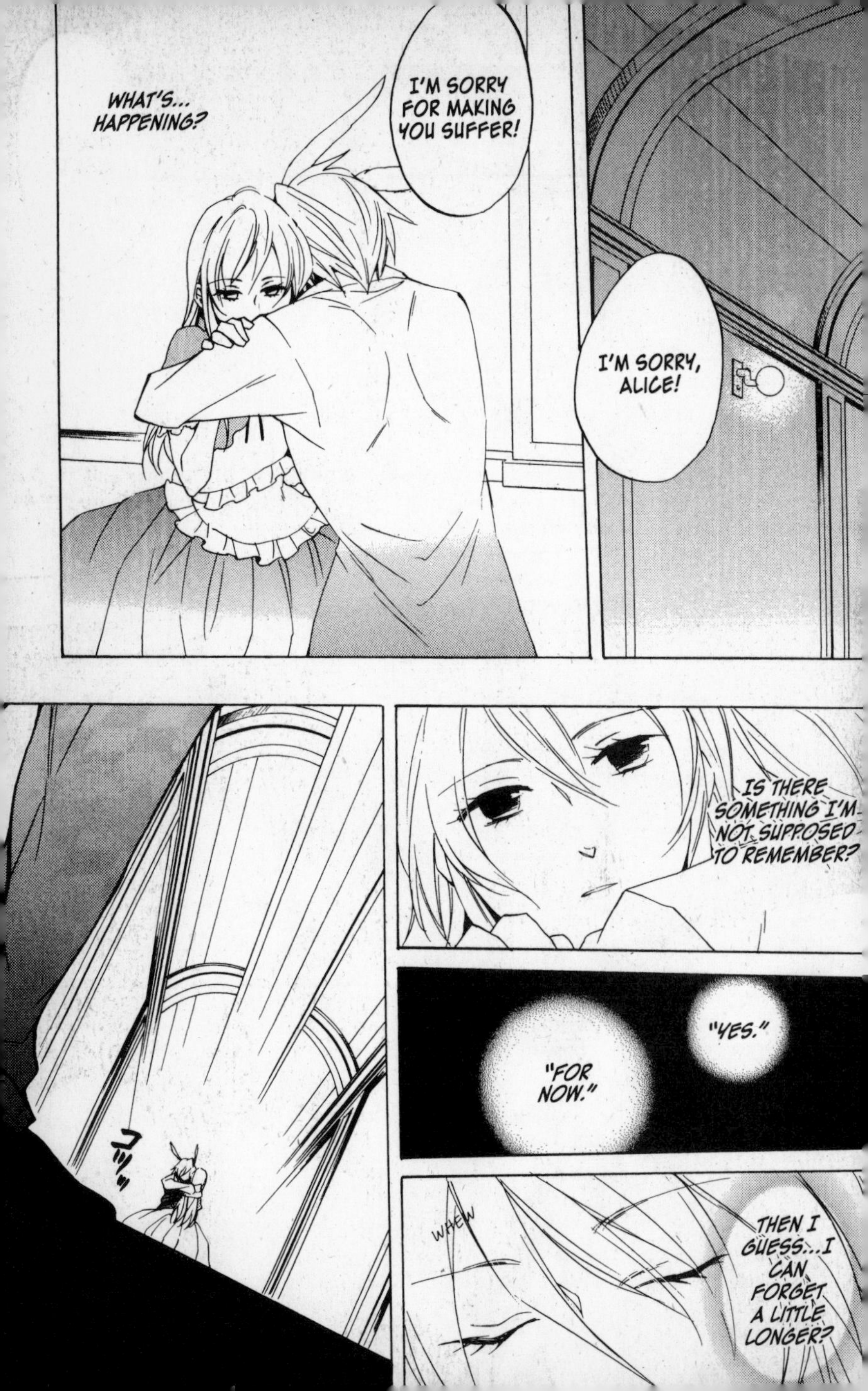
I'M SORRY, ALICE!
I'M SORRY FOR MAKING YOU SUFFER!
WHAT'S... HAPPENING?
IS THERE SOMETHING I'M NOT SUPPOSED TO REMEMBER?
"YES."
"FOR NOW."
THEN I GUESS...I CAN FORGET A LITTLE LONGER?
WHEW

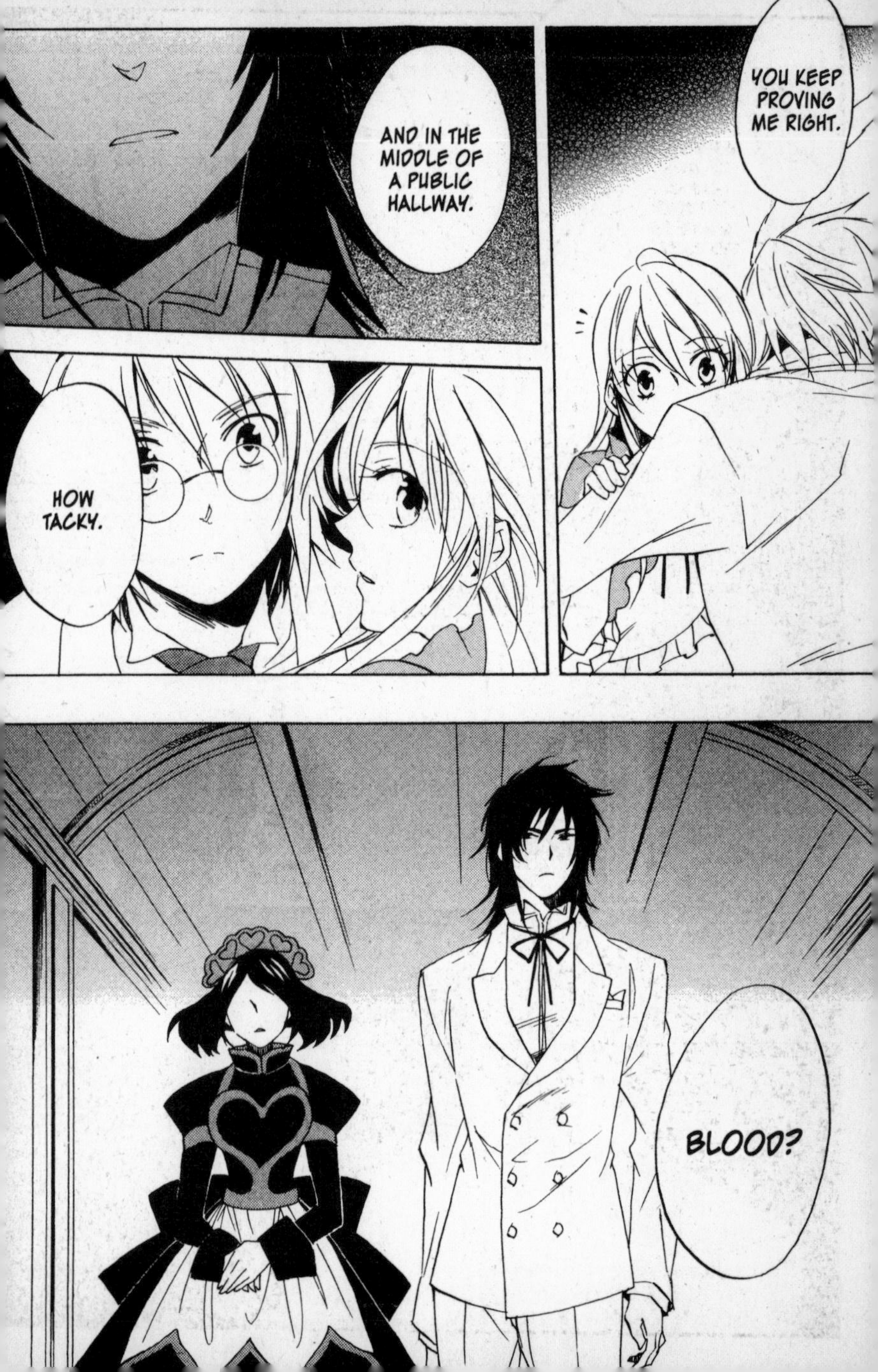
YOU KEEP PROVING ME RIGHT.
AND IN THE MIDDLE OF A PUBLIC HALLWAY.
HOW TACKY.
BLOOD?

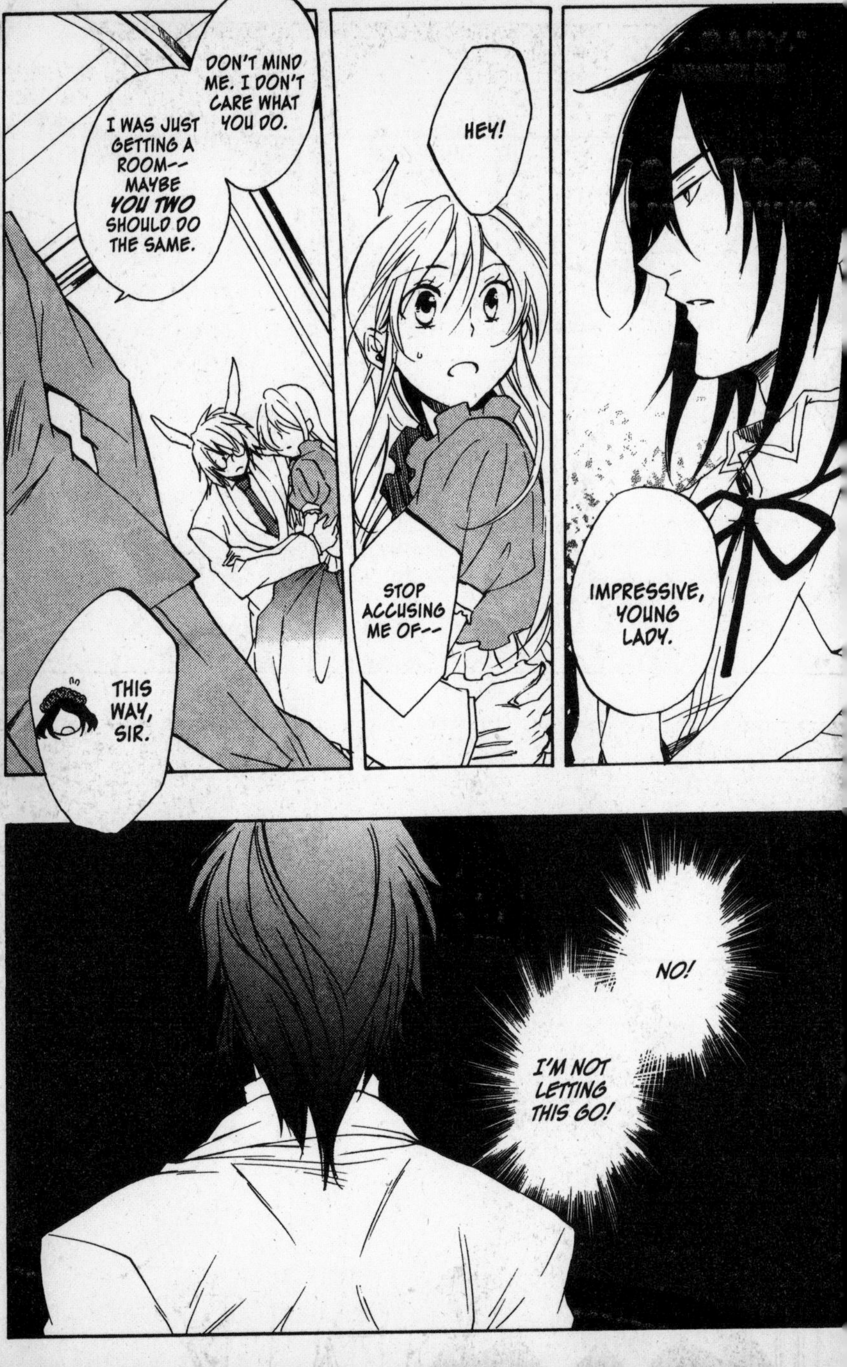
IMPRESSIVE, YOUNG LADY.
HEY!
STOP ACCUSING ME OF--
DON'T MIND ME. I DON'T CARE WHAT YOU DO.
I WAS JUST GETTING A ROOM-- MAYBE *YOU TWO* SHOULD DO THE SAME.
THIS WAY, SIR.
NO!
I'M NOT LETTING THIS GO!

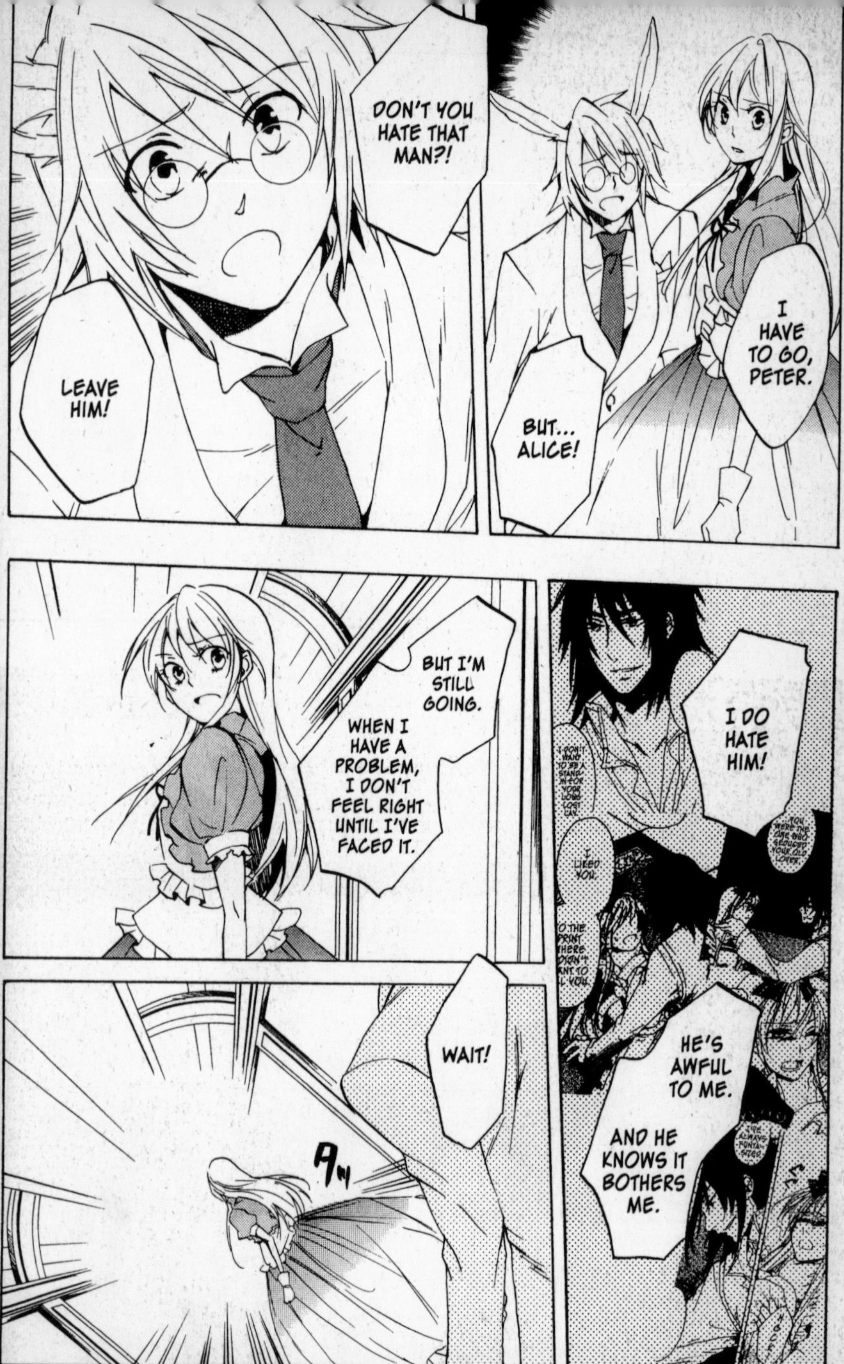
I HAVE TO GO, PETER.
BUT... ALICE!
DON'T YOU HATE THAT MAN?!
LEAVE HIM!
I DO HATE HIM!
I LIKED YOU.
HE'S AWFUL TO ME.
AND HE KNOWS IT BOTHERS ME.
BUT I'M STILL GOING.
WHEN I HAVE A PROBLEM, I DON'T FEEL RIGHT UNTIL I'VE FACED IT.
WAIT!

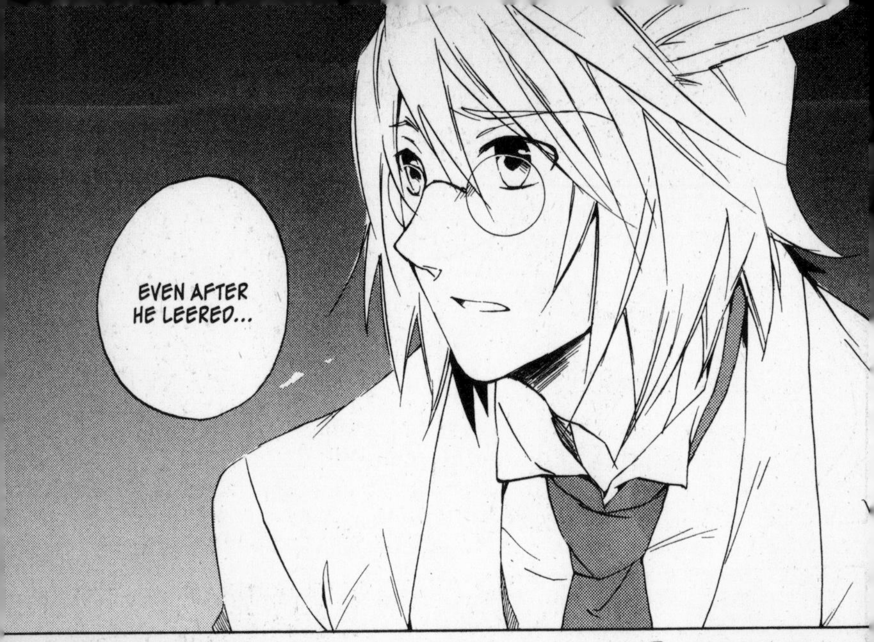
EVEN AFTER HE LEERED...
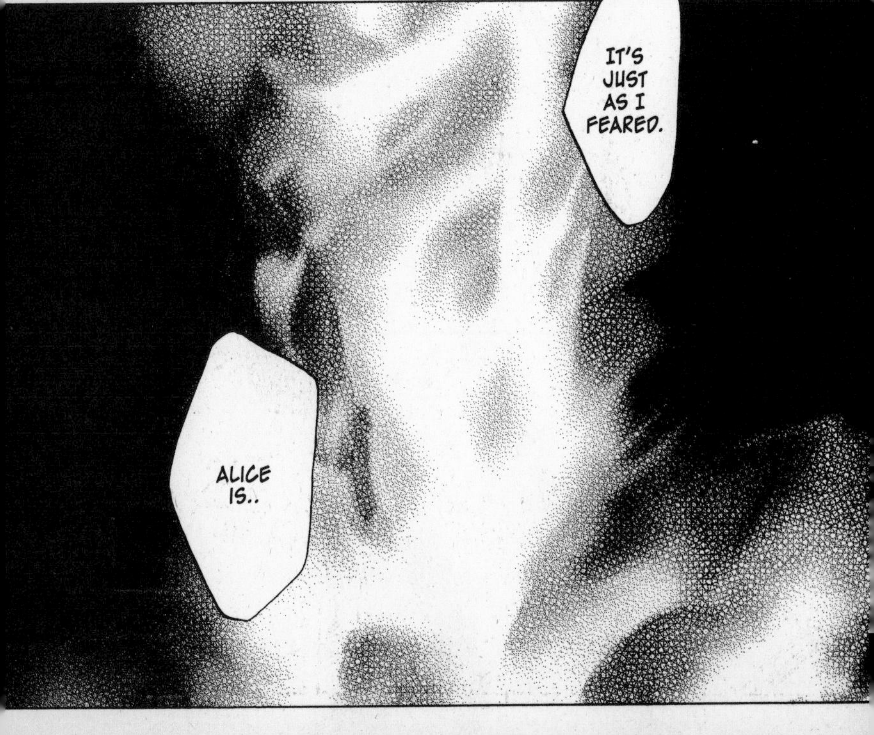
IT'S JUST AS I FEARED.
ALICE IS..

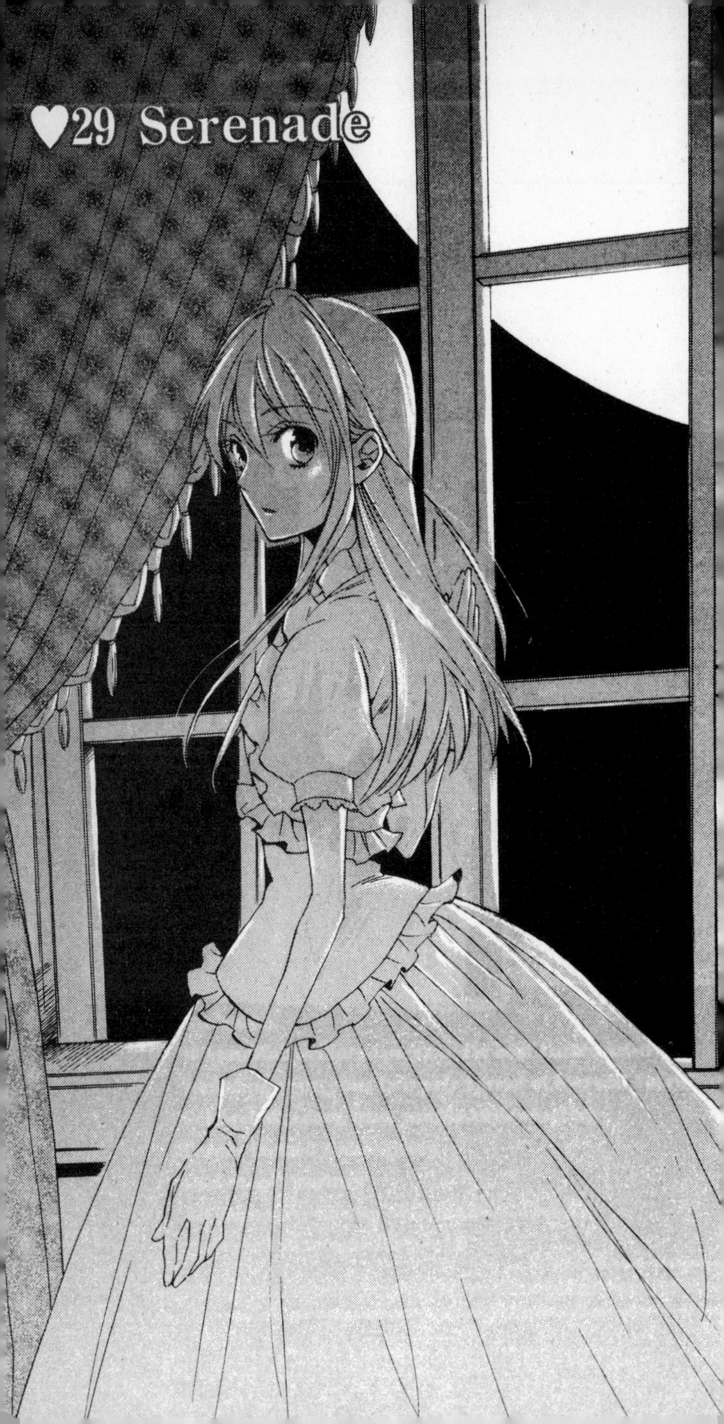
♥29 Serenade

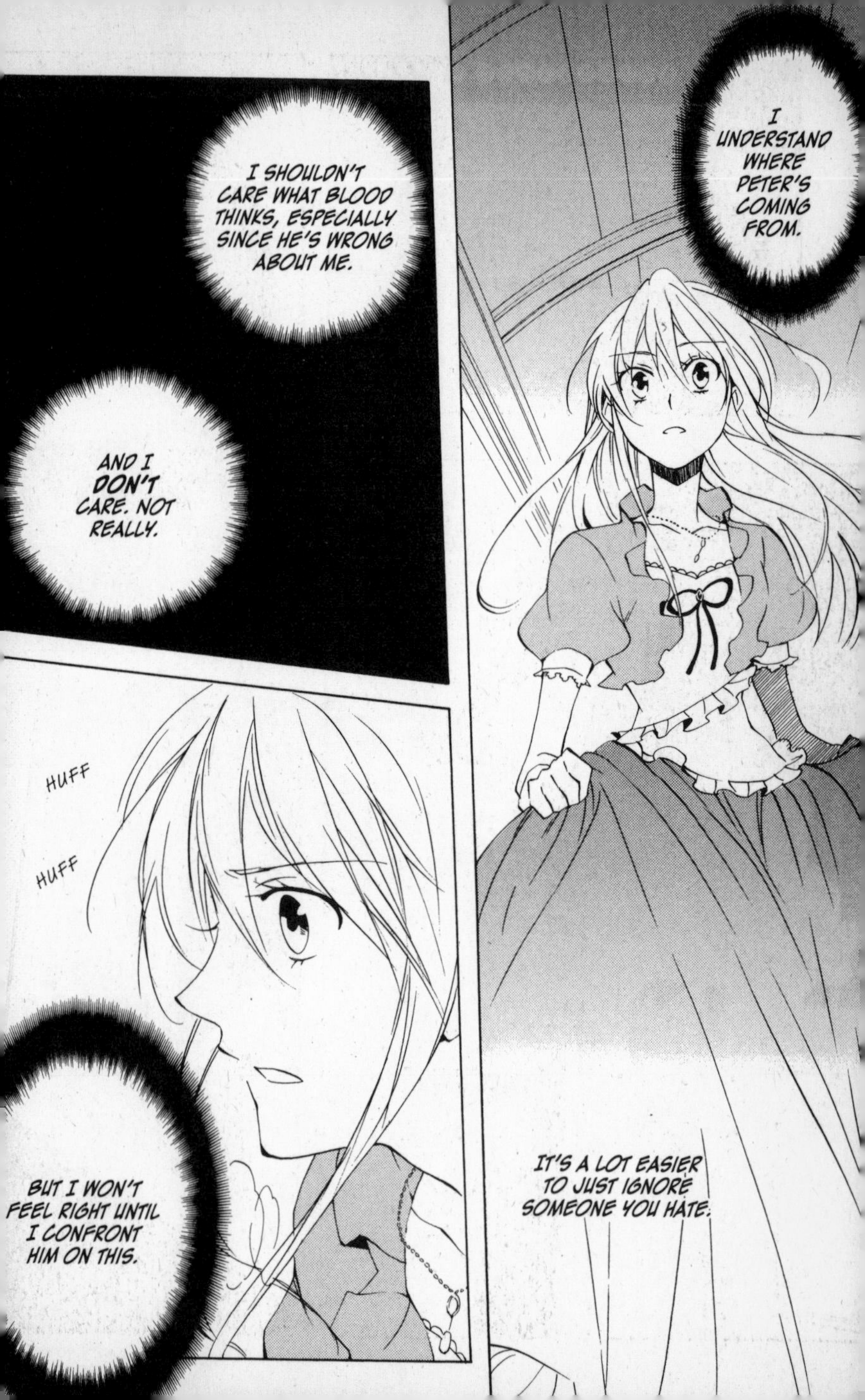
I UNDERSTAND WHERE PETER'S COMING FROM.
IT'S A LOT EASIER TO JUST IGNORE SOMEONE YOU HATE.
I SHOULDN'T CARE WHAT BLOOD THINKS, ESPECIALLY SINCE HE'S WRONG ABOUT ME.
AND I **DON'T** CARE. NOT REALLY.
HUFF
HUFF
BUT I WON'T FEEL RIGHT UNTIL I CONFRONT HIM ON THIS.

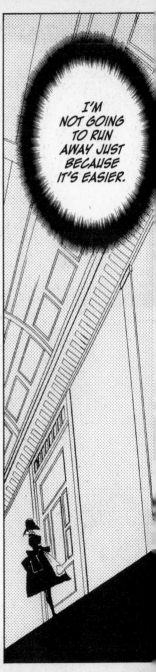

I'M NOT GOING TO RUN AWAY JUST BECAUSE IT'S EASIER.

IS THIS BLOOD'S ROOM?

HUFF

ER, YES.

?

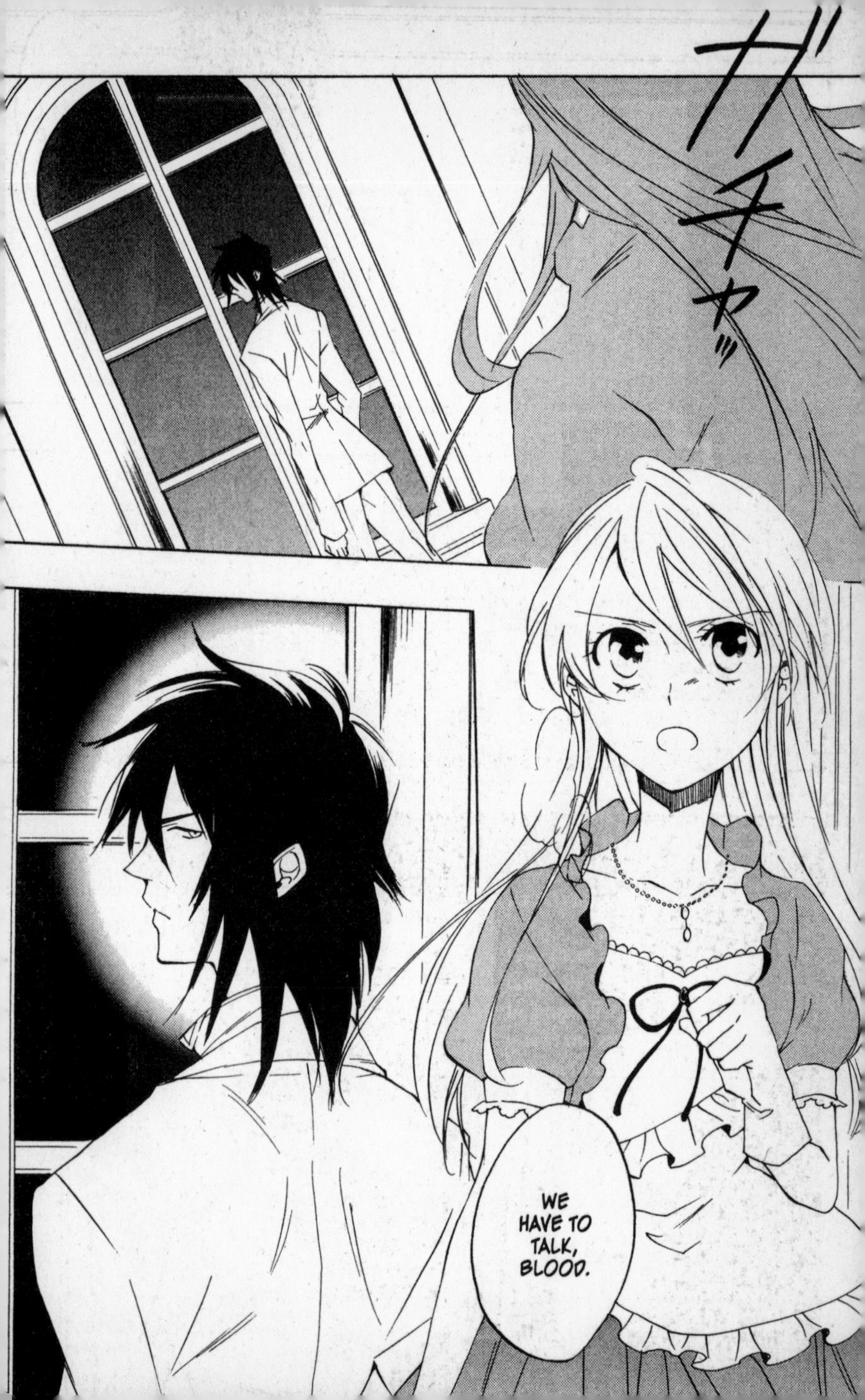

ガチャッ
WE HAVE TO TALK, BLOOD.

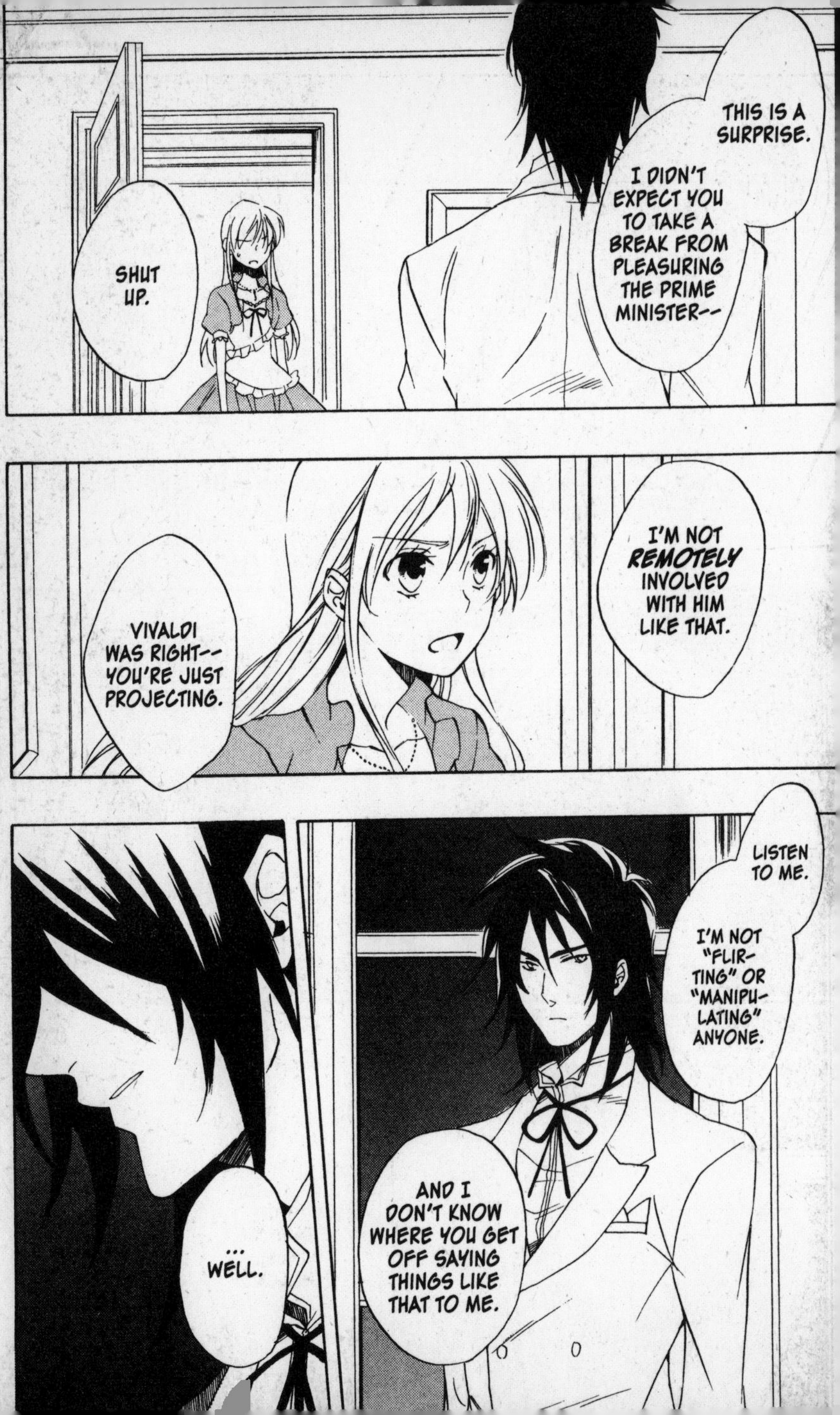
THIS IS A SURPRISE.
I DIDN'T EXPECT YOU TO TAKE A BREAK FROM PLEASURING THE PRIME MINISTER--
SHUT UP.
I'M NOT *REMOTELY* INVOLVED WITH HIM LIKE THAT.
VIVALDI WAS RIGHT--YOU'RE JUST PROJECTING.
LISTEN TO ME.
I'M NOT "FLIRTING" OR "MANIPULATING" ANYONE.
AND I DON'T KNOW WHERE YOU GET OFF SAYING THINGS LIKE THAT TO ME.
... WELL.

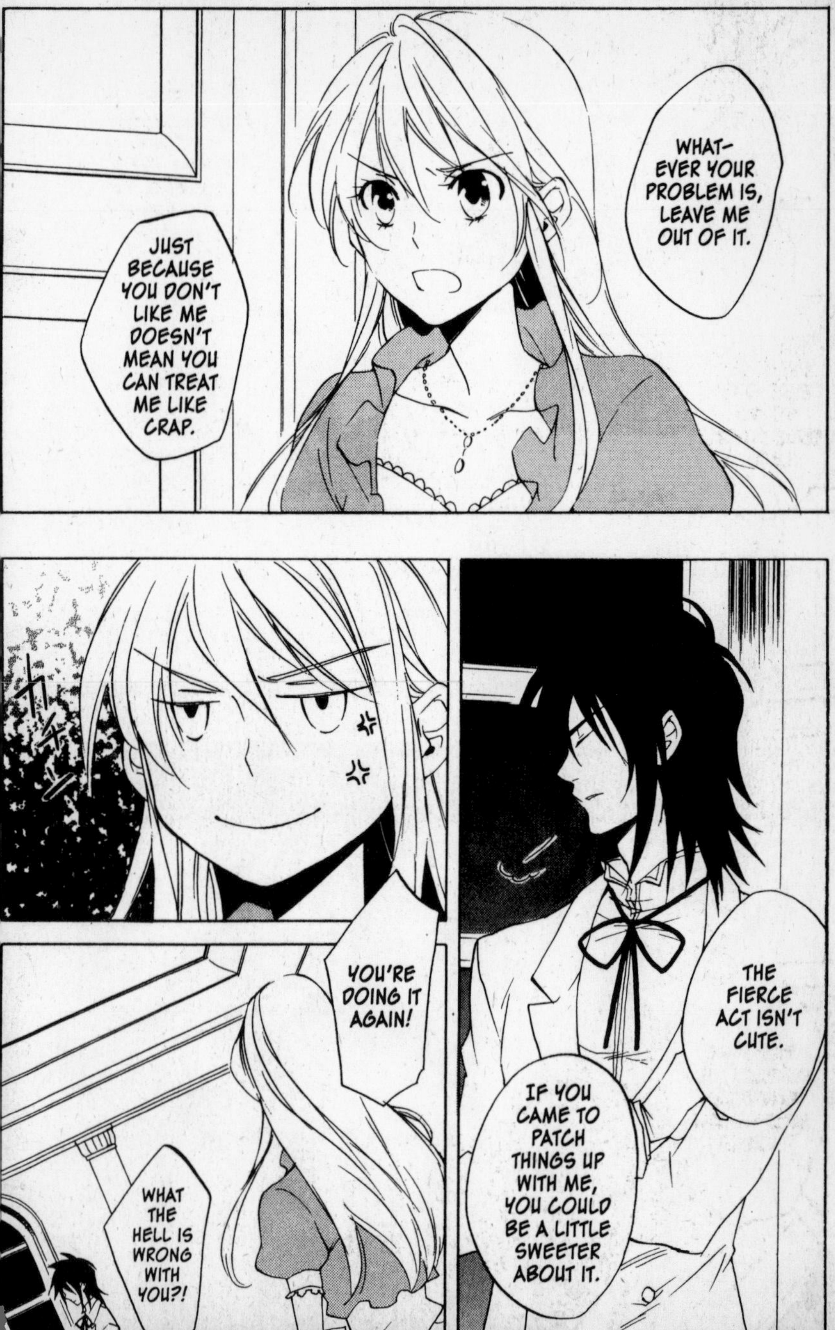
WHAT-EVER YOUR PROBLEM IS, LEAVE ME OUT OF IT.
JUST BECAUSE YOU DON'T LIKE ME DOESN'T MEAN YOU CAN TREAT ME LIKE CRAP.
THE FIERCE ACT ISN'T CUTE.
IF YOU CAME TO PATCH THINGS UP WITH ME, YOU COULD BE A LITTLE SWEETER ABOUT IT.
YOU'RE DOING IT AGAIN!
WHAT THE HELL IS WRONG WITH YOU?!

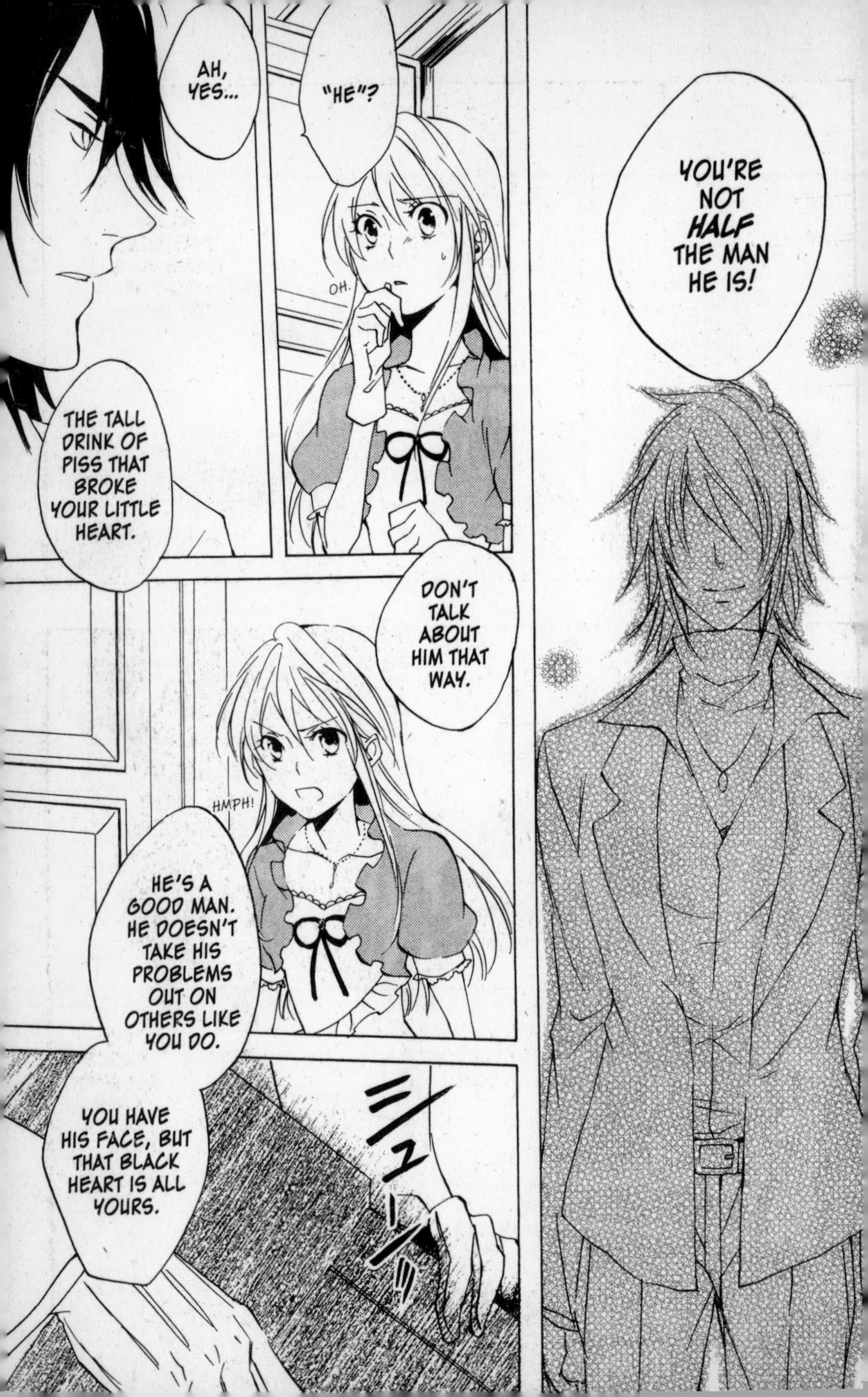
YOU'RE NOT HALF THE MAN HE IS!
"HE"?
OH.
AH, YES...
THE TALL DRINK OF PISS THAT BROKE YOUR LITTLE HEART.
DON'T TALK ABOUT HIM THAT WAY.
HMPH!
HE'S A GOOD MAN. HE DOESN'T TAKE HIS PROBLEMS OUT ON OTHERS LIKE YOU DO.
YOU HAVE HIS FACE, BUT THAT BLACK HEART IS ALL YOURS.

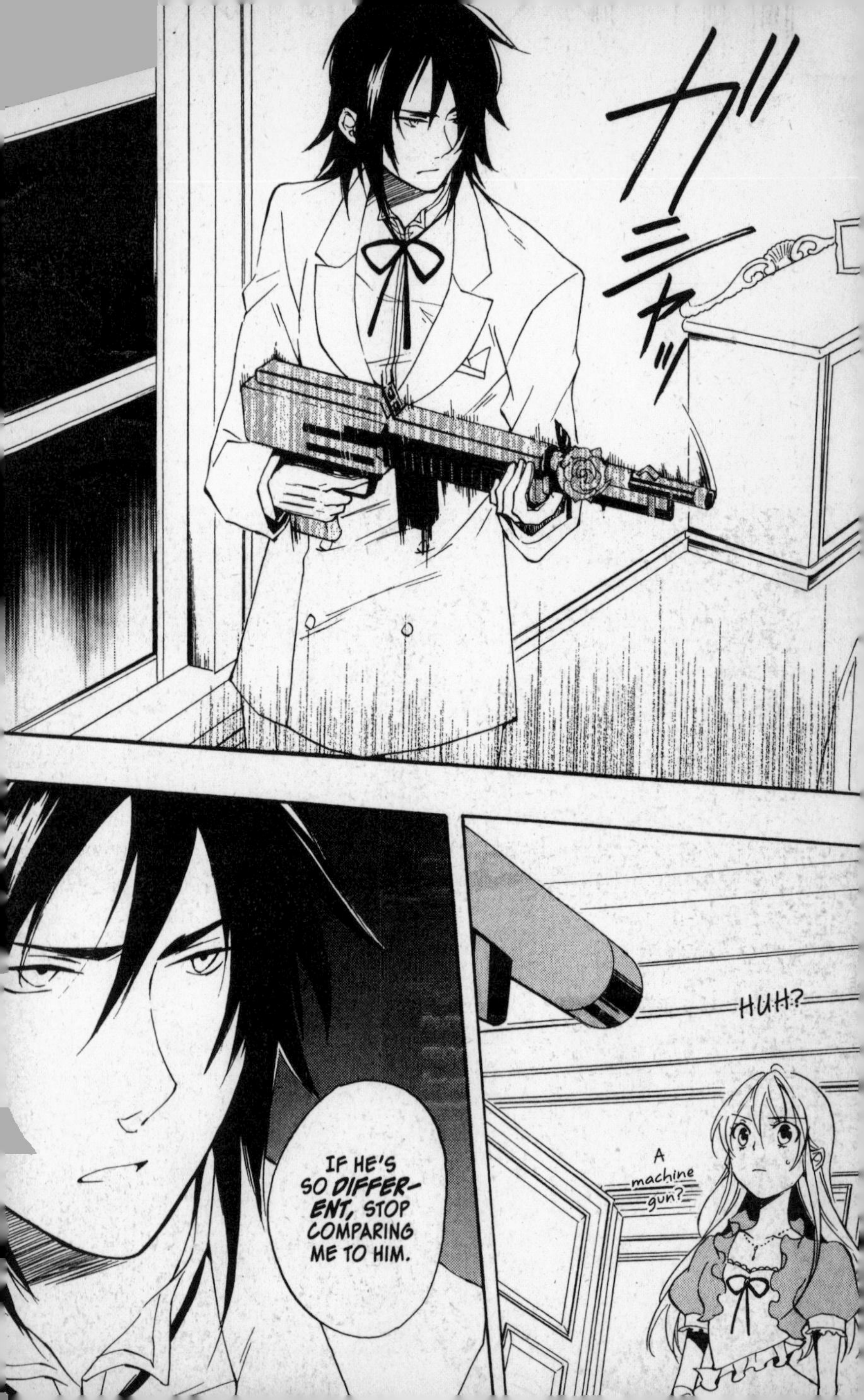
ガシャッ
HUH?
A machine gun?
IF HE'S SO DIFFERENT, STOP COMPARING ME TO HIM.

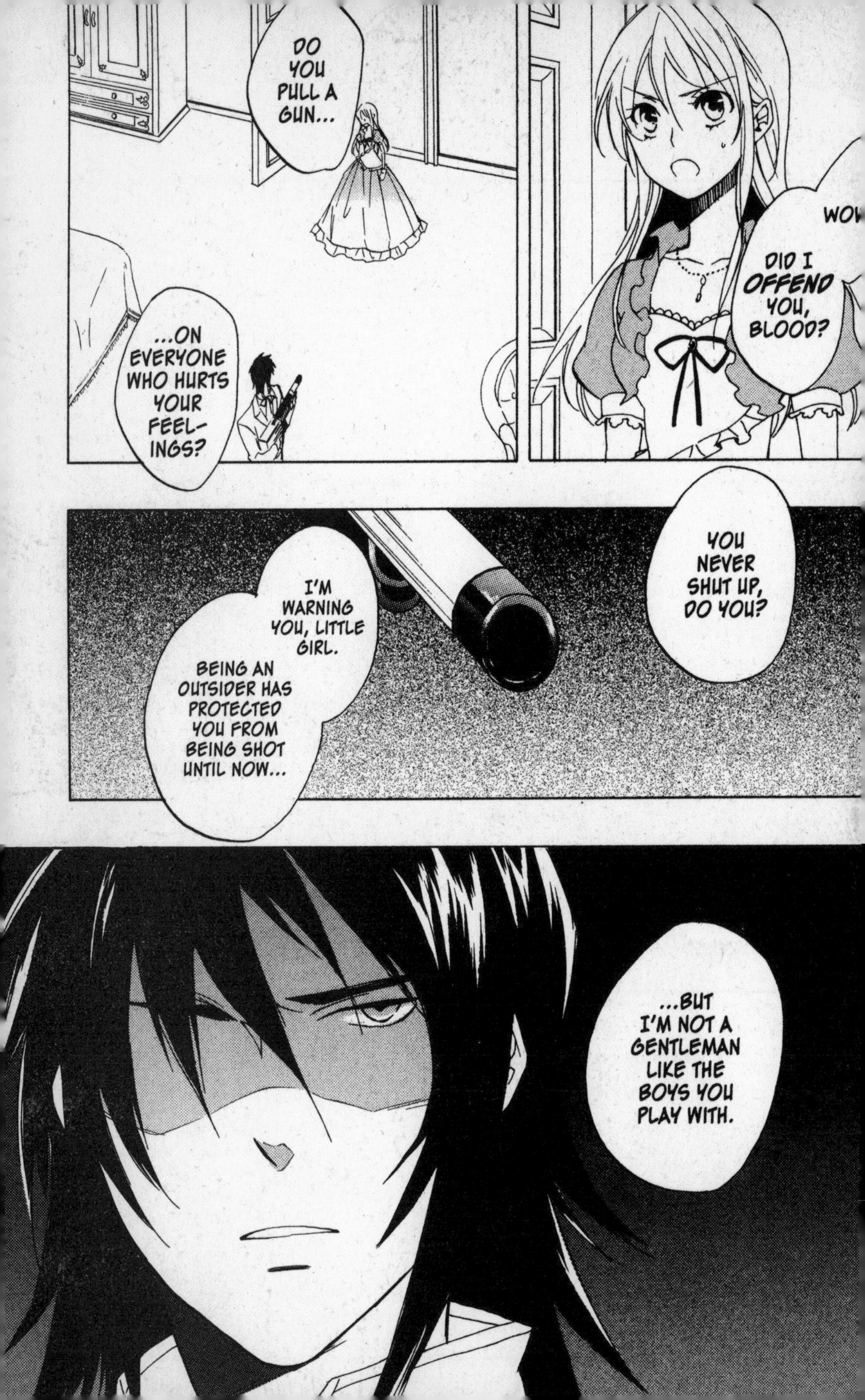
DID I OFFEND YOU, BLOOD?
DO YOU PULL A GUN...
...ON EVERYONE WHO HURTS YOUR FEELINGS?
YOU NEVER SHUT UP, DO YOU?
I'M WARNING YOU, LITTLE GIRL.
BEING AN OUTSIDER HAS PROTECTED YOU FROM BEING SHOT UNTIL NOW...
...BUT I'M NOT A GENTLEMAN LIKE THE BOYS YOU PLAY WITH.

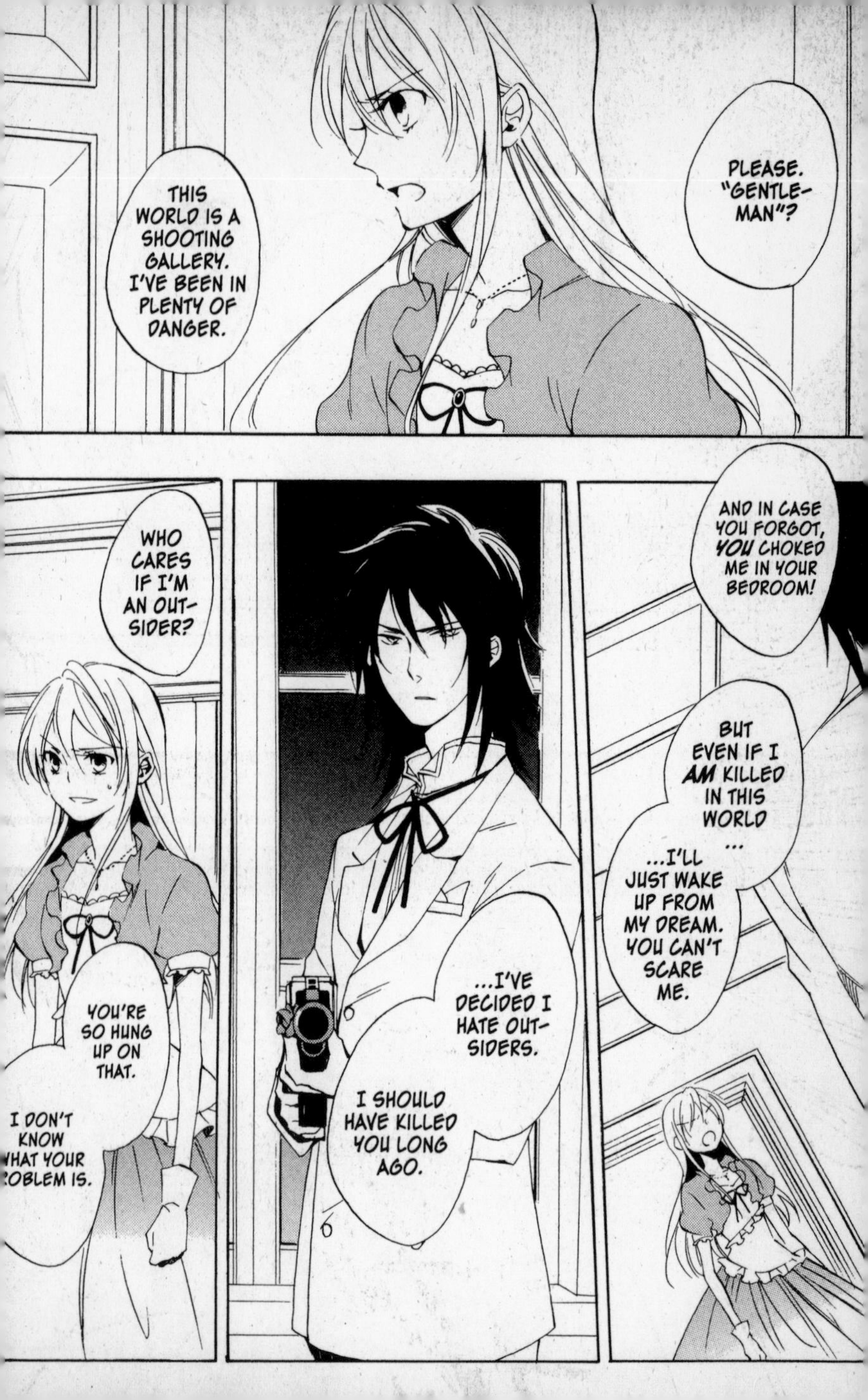
PLEASE. "GENTLEMAN"?
THIS WORLD IS A SHOOTING GALLERY. I'VE BEEN IN PLENTY OF DANGER.
AND IN CASE YOU FORGOT, YOU CHOKED ME IN YOUR BEDROOM!
BUT EVEN IF I AM KILLED IN THIS WORLD ...
...I'LL JUST WAKE UP FROM MY DREAM. YOU CAN'T SCARE ME.
...I'VE DECIDED I HATE OUTSIDERS.
I SHOULD HAVE KILLED YOU LONG AGO.
WHO CARES IF I'M AN OUTSIDER?
YOU'RE SO HUNG UP ON THAT.
I DON'T KNOW HAT YOUR ROBLEM IS.

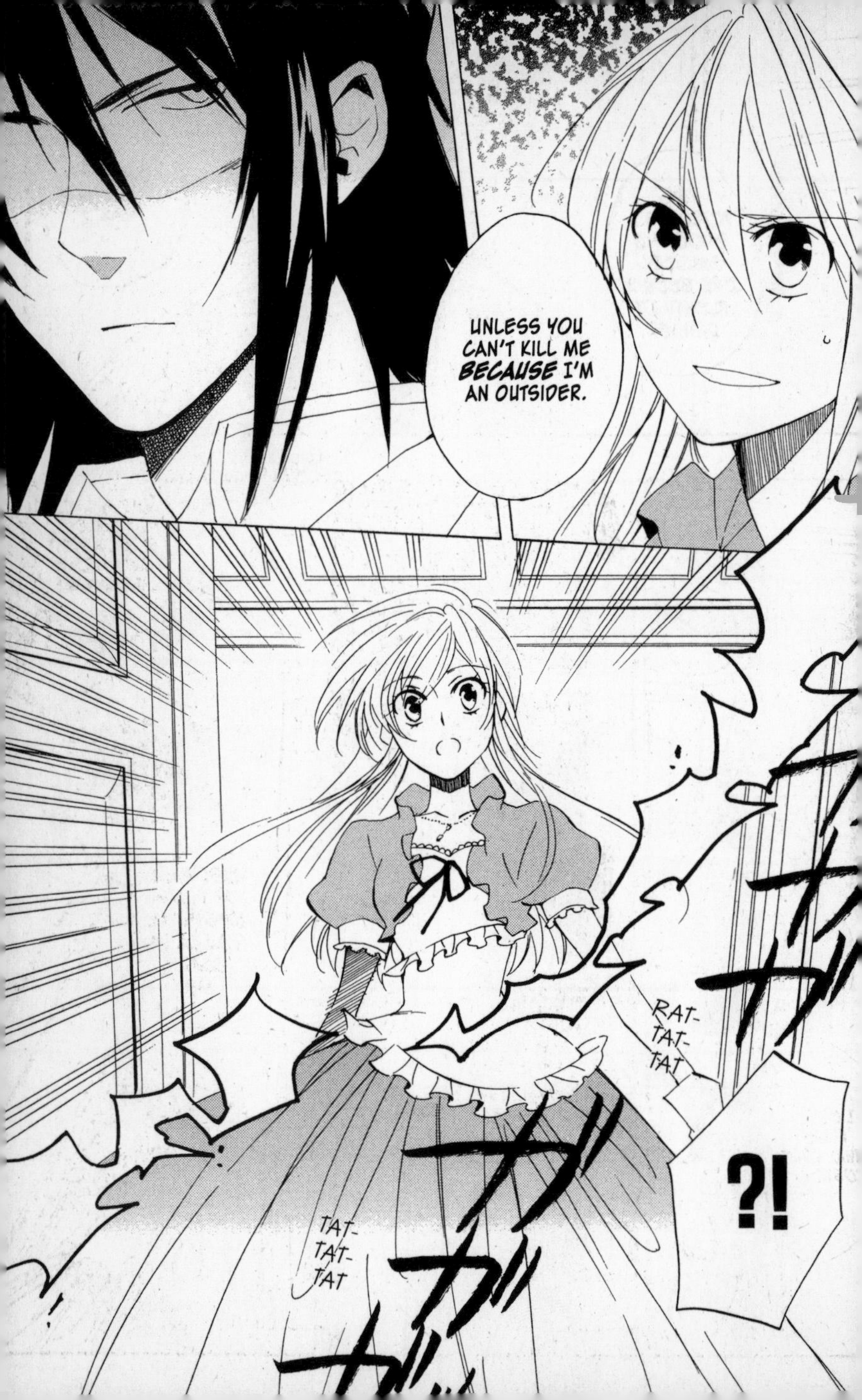

UNLESS YOU CAN'T KILL ME *BECAUSE* I'M AN OUTSIDER.
RAT-TAT-TAT
?!
TAT-TAT-TAT

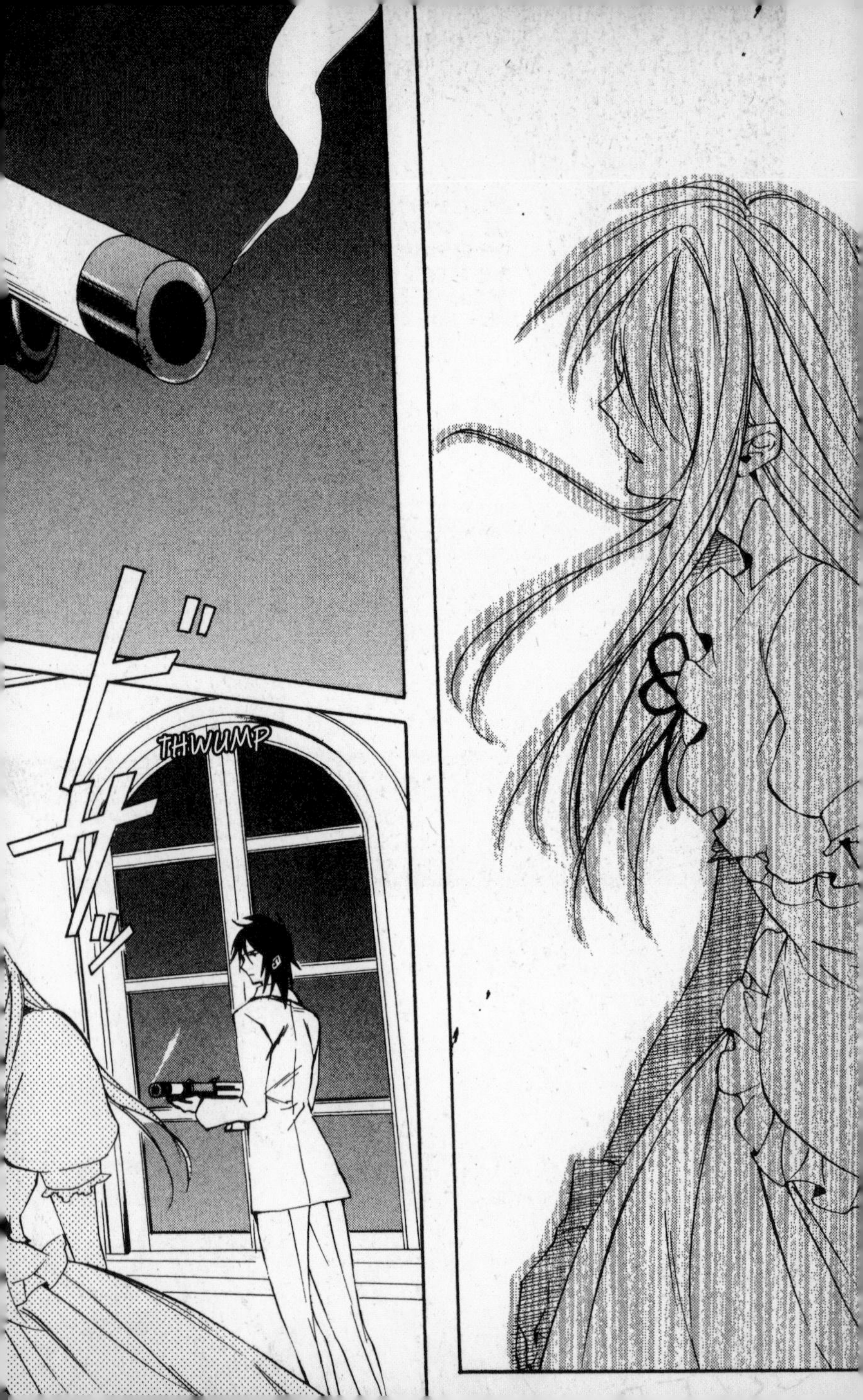
THWUMP

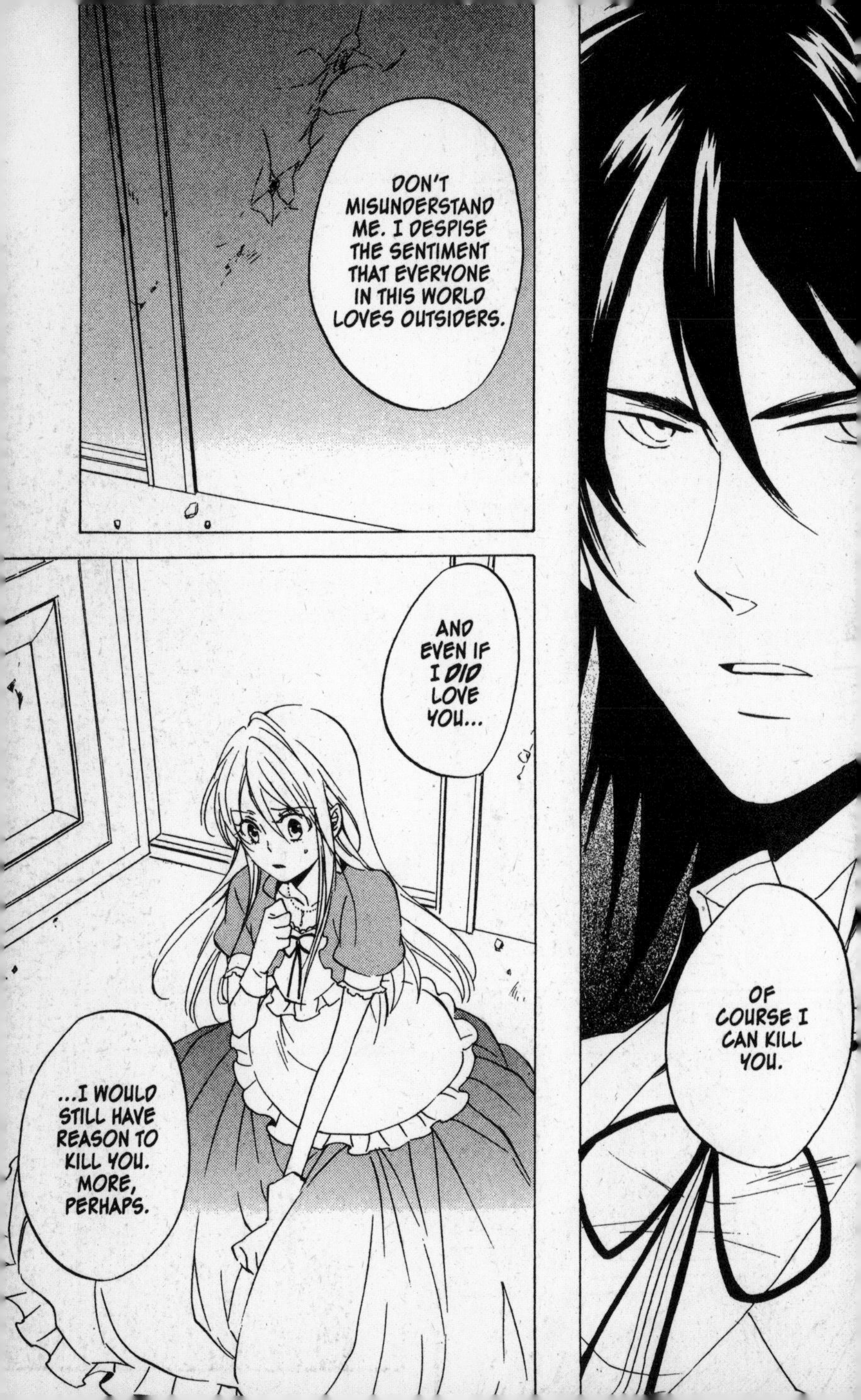
OF COURSE I CAN KILL YOU.
DON'T MISUNDERSTAND ME. I DESPISE THE SENTIMENT THAT EVERYONE IN THIS WORLD LOVES OUTSIDERS.
AND EVEN IF I *DID* LOVE YOU...
...I WOULD STILL HAVE REASON TO KILL YOU. MORE, PERHAPS.

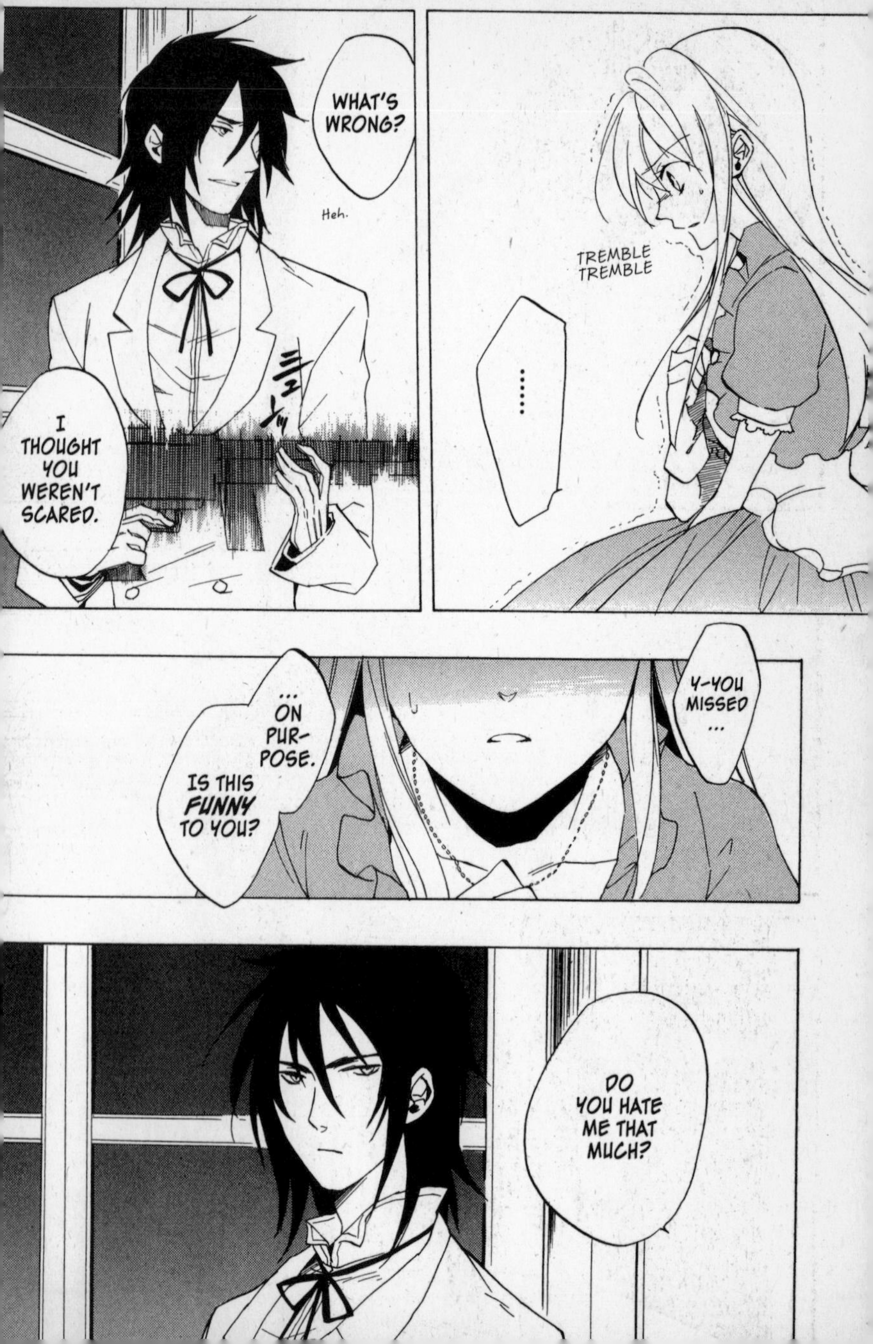
TREMBLE TREMBLE
……
WHAT'S WRONG?
Heh.
I THOUGHT YOU WEREN'T SCARED.
Y-YOU MISSED ...
... ON PURPOSE.
IS THIS *FUNNY* TO YOU?
DO YOU HATE ME THAT MUCH?

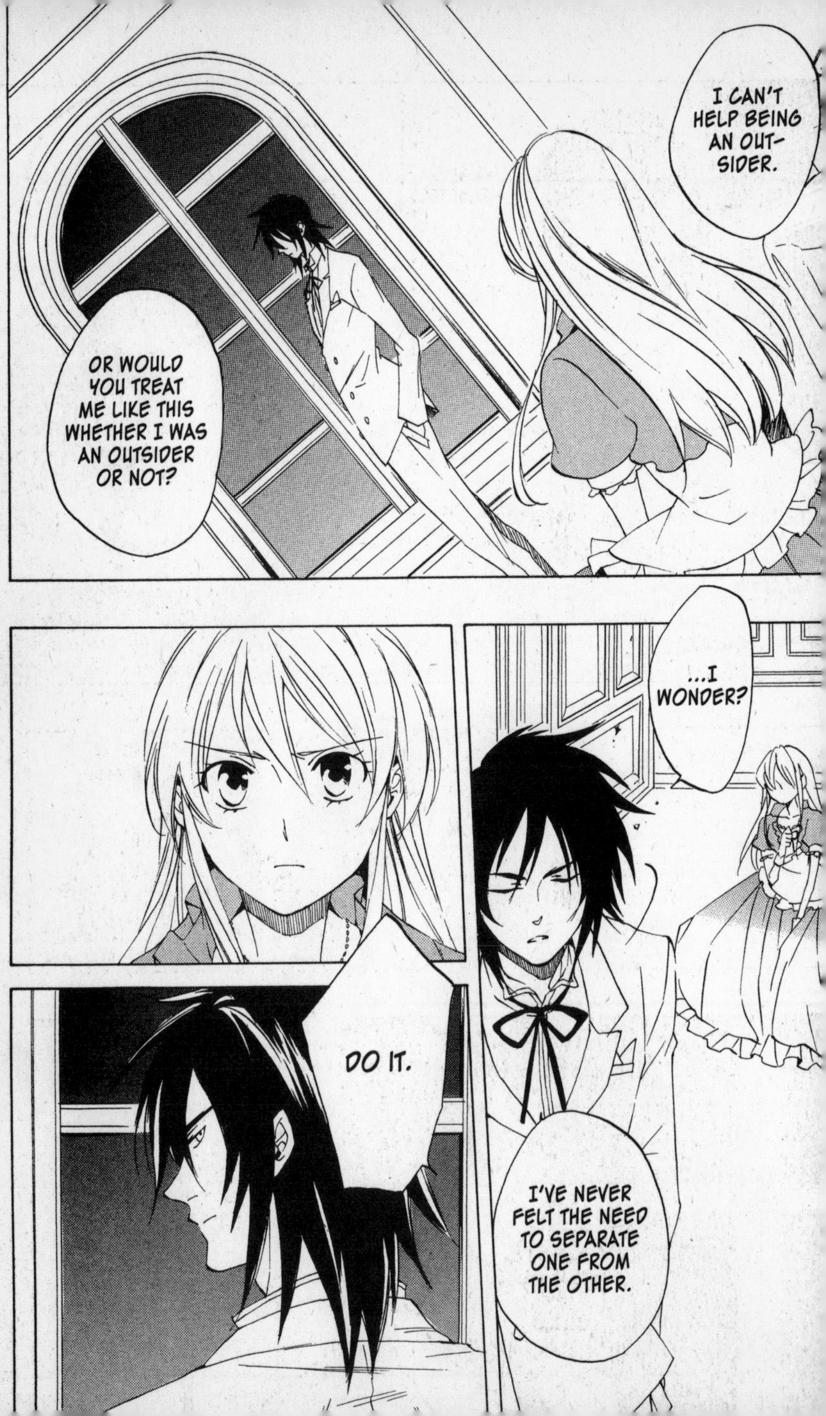
I CAN'T HELP BEING AN OUT-SIDER.
OR WOULD YOU TREAT ME LIKE THIS WHETHER I WAS AN OUTSIDER OR NOT?
...I WONDER?
I'VE NEVER FELT THE NEED TO SEPARATE ONE FROM THE OTHER.
DO IT.

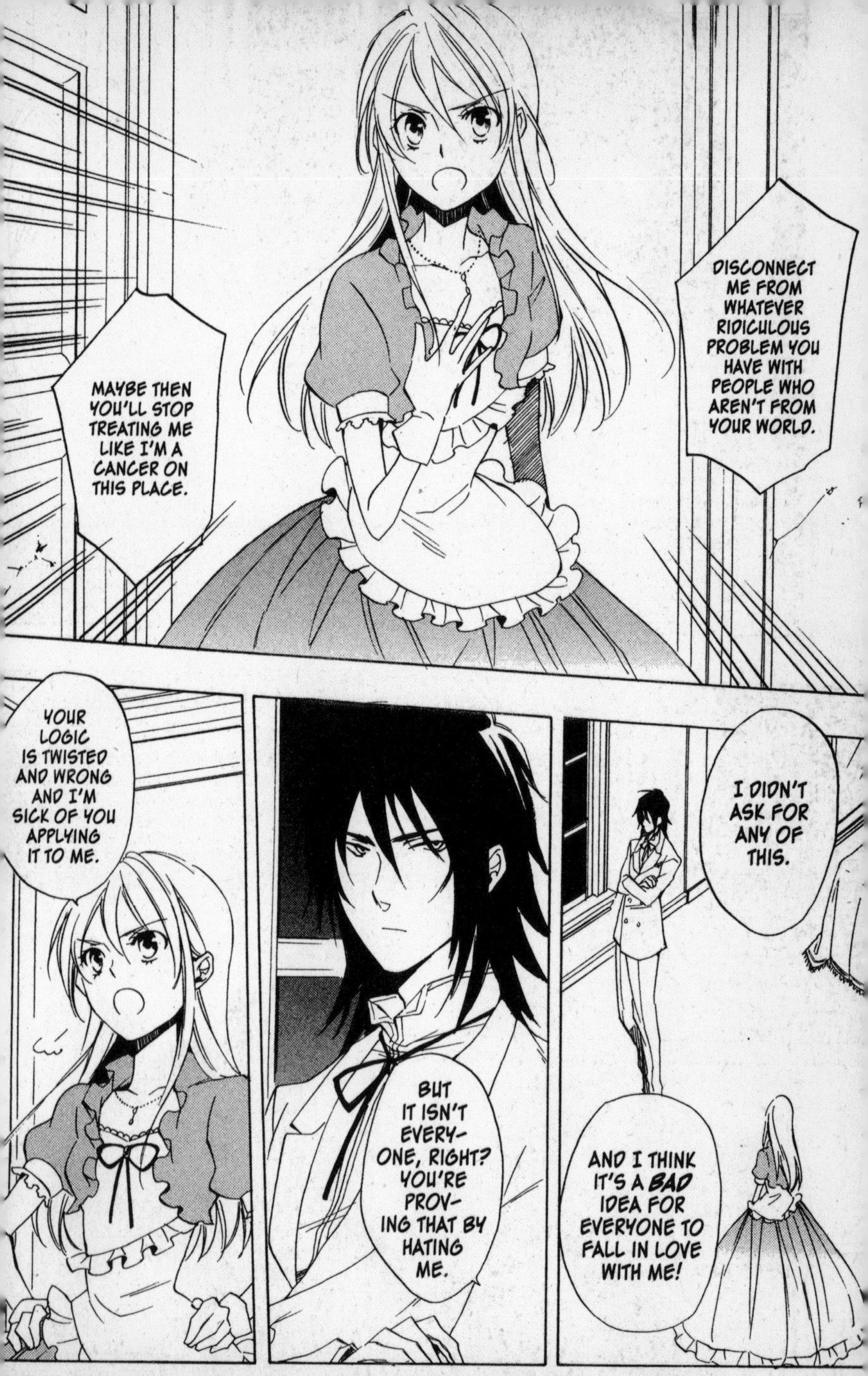
DISCONNECT ME FROM WHATEVER RIDICULOUS PROBLEM YOU HAVE WITH PEOPLE WHO AREN'T FROM YOUR WORLD.
MAYBE THEN YOU'LL STOP TREATING ME LIKE I'M A CANCER ON THIS PLACE.
I DIDN'T ASK FOR ANY OF THIS.
AND I THINK IT'S A *BAD* IDEA FOR EVERYONE TO FALL IN LOVE WITH ME!
BUT IT ISN'T EVERY-ONE, RIGHT? YOU'RE PROV-ING THAT BY HATING ME.
YOUR LOGIC IS TWISTED AND WRONG AND I'M SICK OF YOU APPLYING IT TO ME.

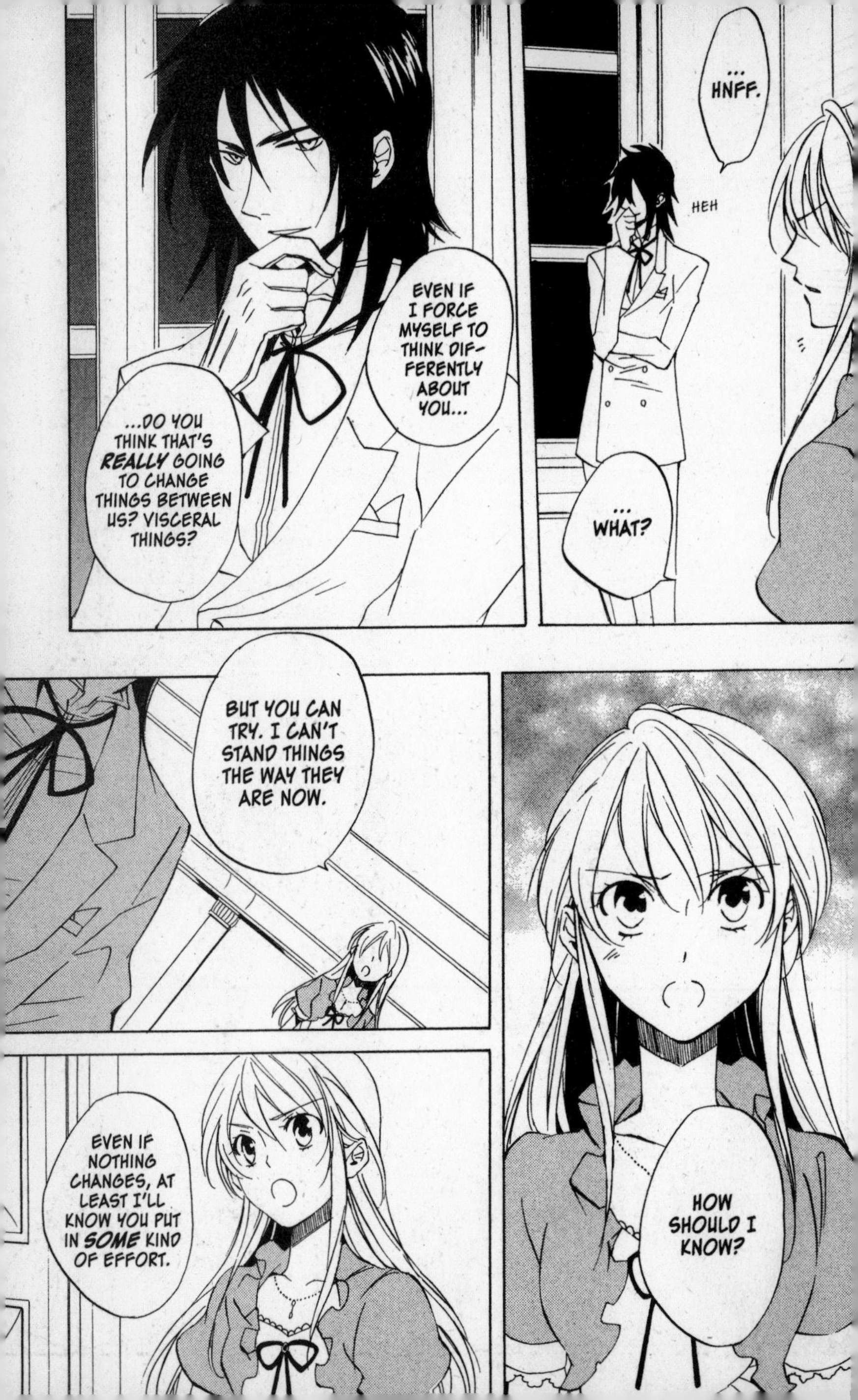
...HNFF.
HEH
...WHAT?
EVEN IF I FORCE MYSELF TO THINK DIF-FERENTLY ABOUT YOU...
...DO YOU THINK THAT'S *REALLY* GOING TO CHANGE THINGS BETWEEN US? VISCERAL THINGS?
HOW SHOULD I KNOW?
BUT YOU CAN TRY. I CAN'T STAND THINGS THE WAY THEY ARE NOW.
EVEN IF NOTHING CHANGES, AT LEAST I'LL KNOW YOU PUT IN *SOME* KIND OF EFFORT.

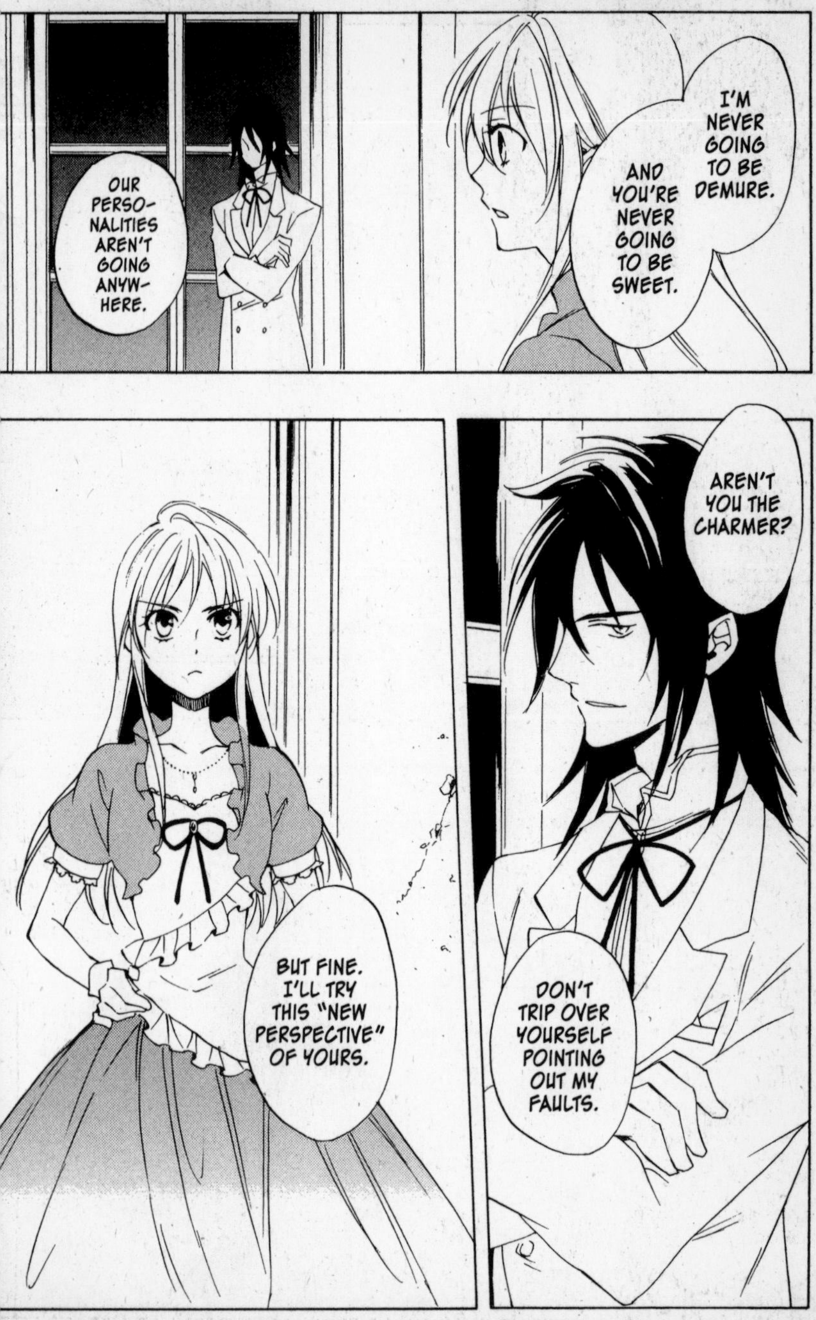
I'M NEVER GOING TO BE DEMURE.
AND YOU'RE NEVER GOING TO BE SWEET.
OUR PERSONALITIES AREN'T GOING ANYWHERE.
AREN'T YOU THE CHARMER?
DON'T TRIP OVER YOURSELF POINTING OUT MY FAULTS.
BUT FINE. I'LL TRY THIS "NEW PERSPECTIVE" OF YOURS.

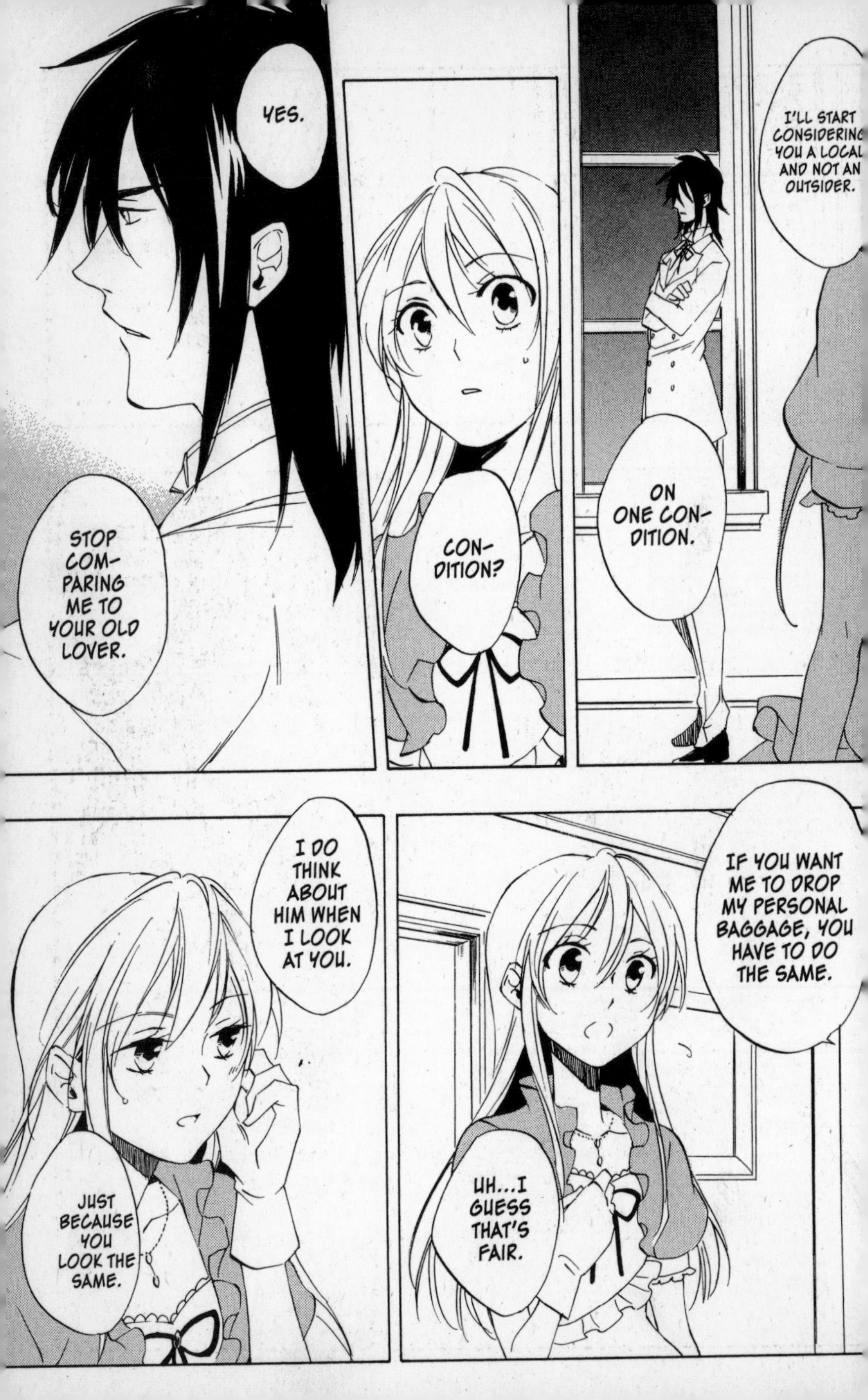
I'LL START CONSIDERING YOU A LOCAL AND NOT AN OUTSIDER.
ON ONE CON-DITION.
CON-DITION?
YES.
STOP COM-PARING ME TO YOUR OLD LOVER.
IF YOU WANT ME TO DROP MY PERSONAL BAGGAGE, YOU HAVE TO DO THE SAME.
UH...I GUESS THAT'S FAIR.
I DO THINK ABOUT HIM WHEN I LOOK AT YOU.
JUST BECAUSE YOU LOOK THE SAME.

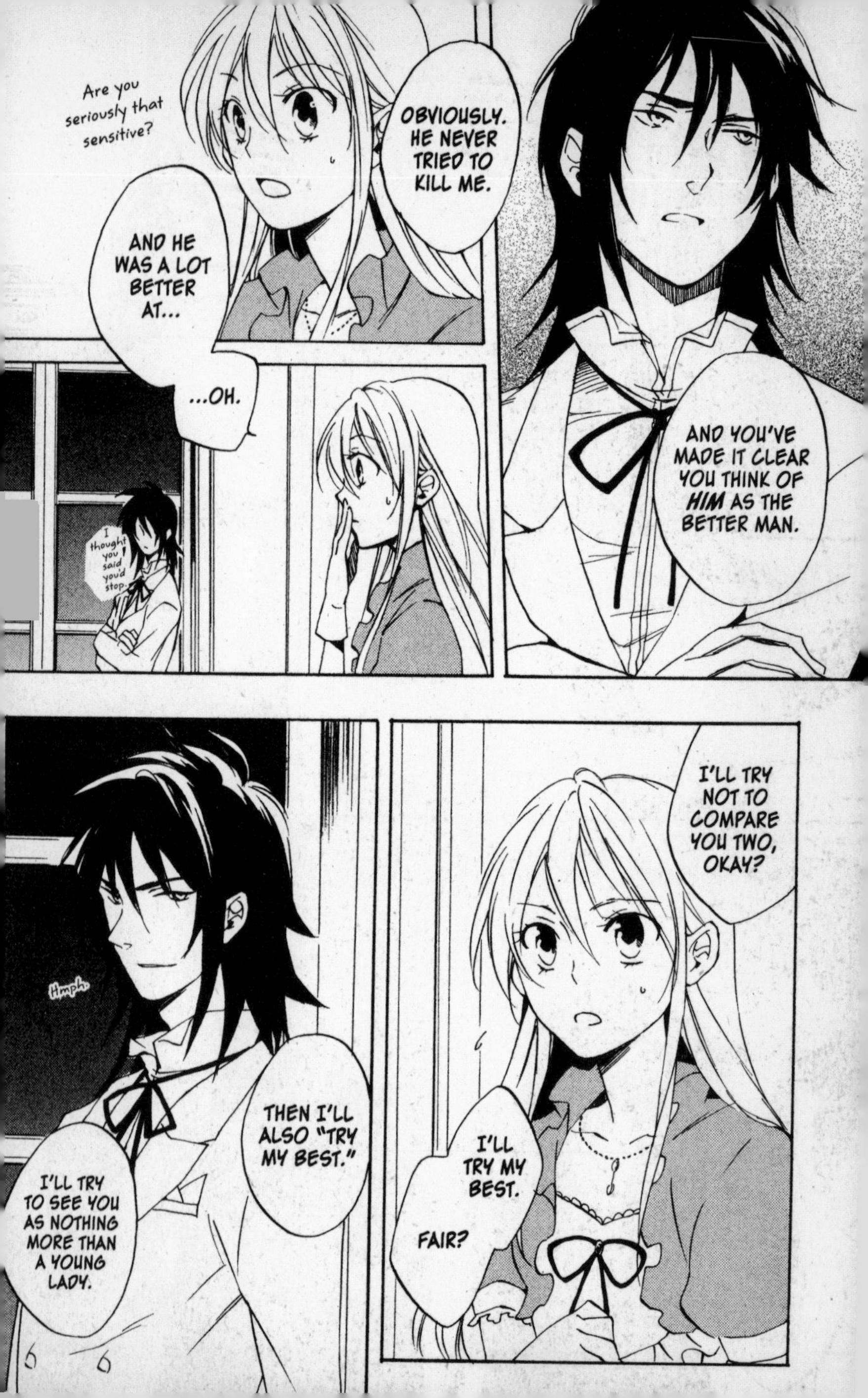
AND YOU'VE MADE IT CLEAR YOU THINK OF *HIM* AS THE BETTER MAN.
OBVIOUSLY. HE NEVER TRIED TO KILL ME.
Are you seriously that sensitive?
AND HE WAS A LOT BETTER AT...
...OH.
I thought you said you'd stop.
I'LL TRY NOT TO COMPARE YOU TWO, OKAY?
I'LL TRY MY BEST.
FAIR?
THEN I'LL ALSO "TRY MY BEST."
Hmph
I'LL TRY TO SEE YOU AS NOTHING MORE THAN A YOUNG LADY.

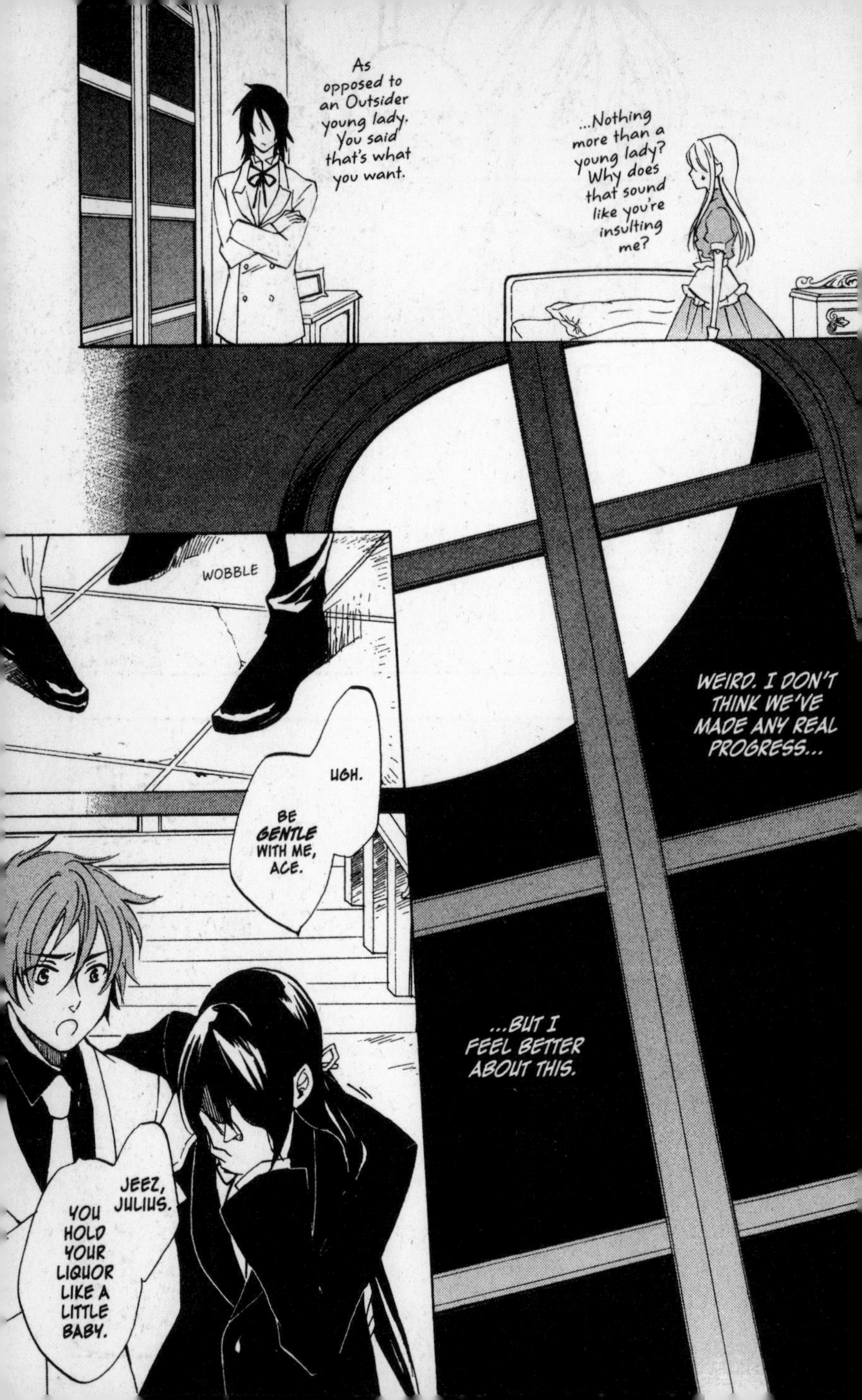
...Nothing more than a young lady? Why does that sound like you're insulting me?
As opposed to an Outsider young lady. You said that's what you want.
WEIRD. I DON'T THINK WE'VE MADE ANY REAL PROGRESS...
...BUT I FEEL BETTER ABOUT THIS.
WOBBLE
UGH.
BE GENTLE WITH ME, ACE.
JEEZ, JULIUS.
YOU HOLD YOUR LIQUOR LIKE A LITTLE BABY.

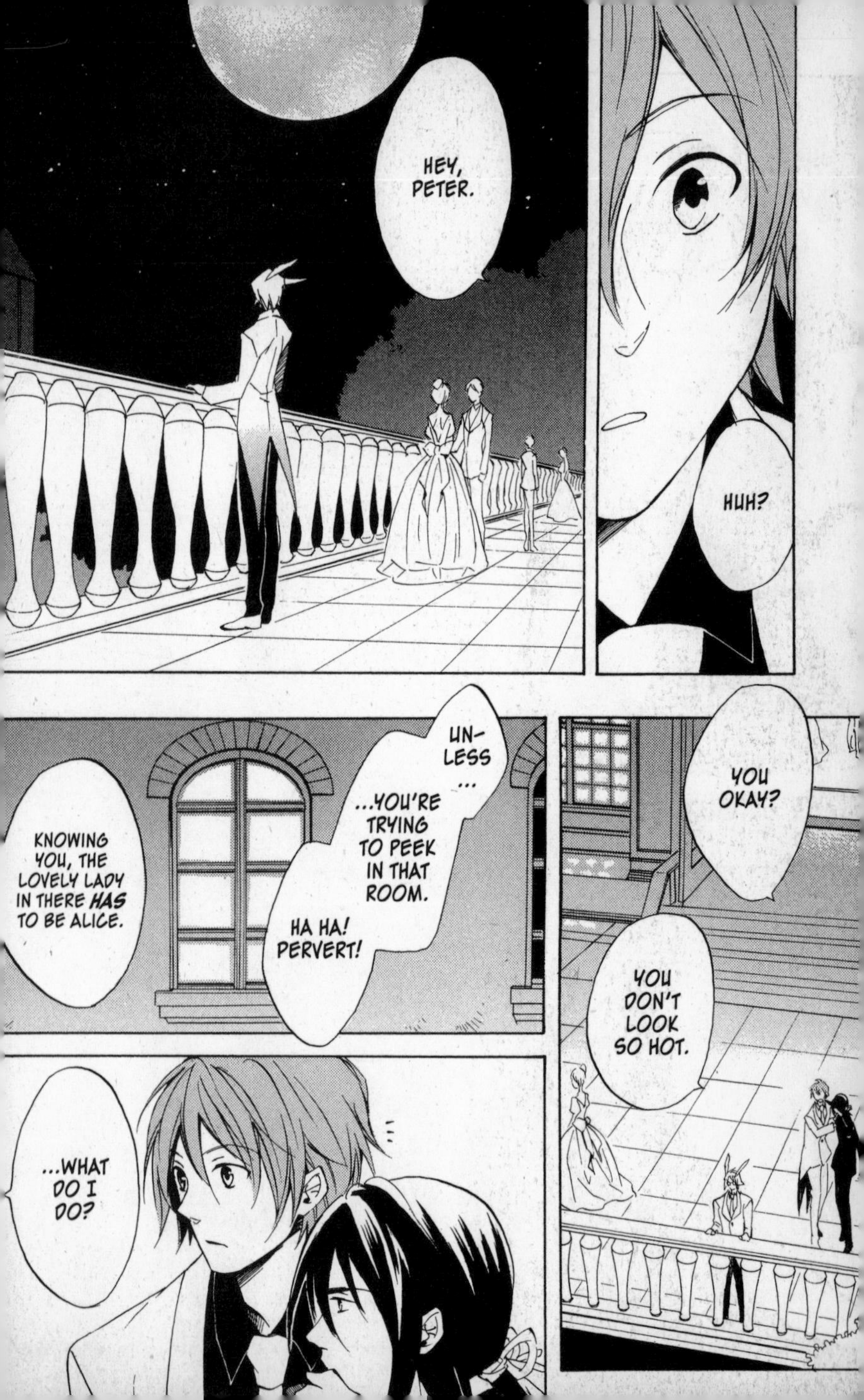
HUH?
HEY, PETER.
YOU OKAY?
YOU DON'T LOOK SO HOT.
UN-LESS...
...YOU'RE TRYING TO PEEK IN THAT ROOM.
HA HA! PERVERT!
KNOWING YOU, THE LOVELY LADY IN THERE HAS TO BE ALICE.
...WHAT DO I DO?

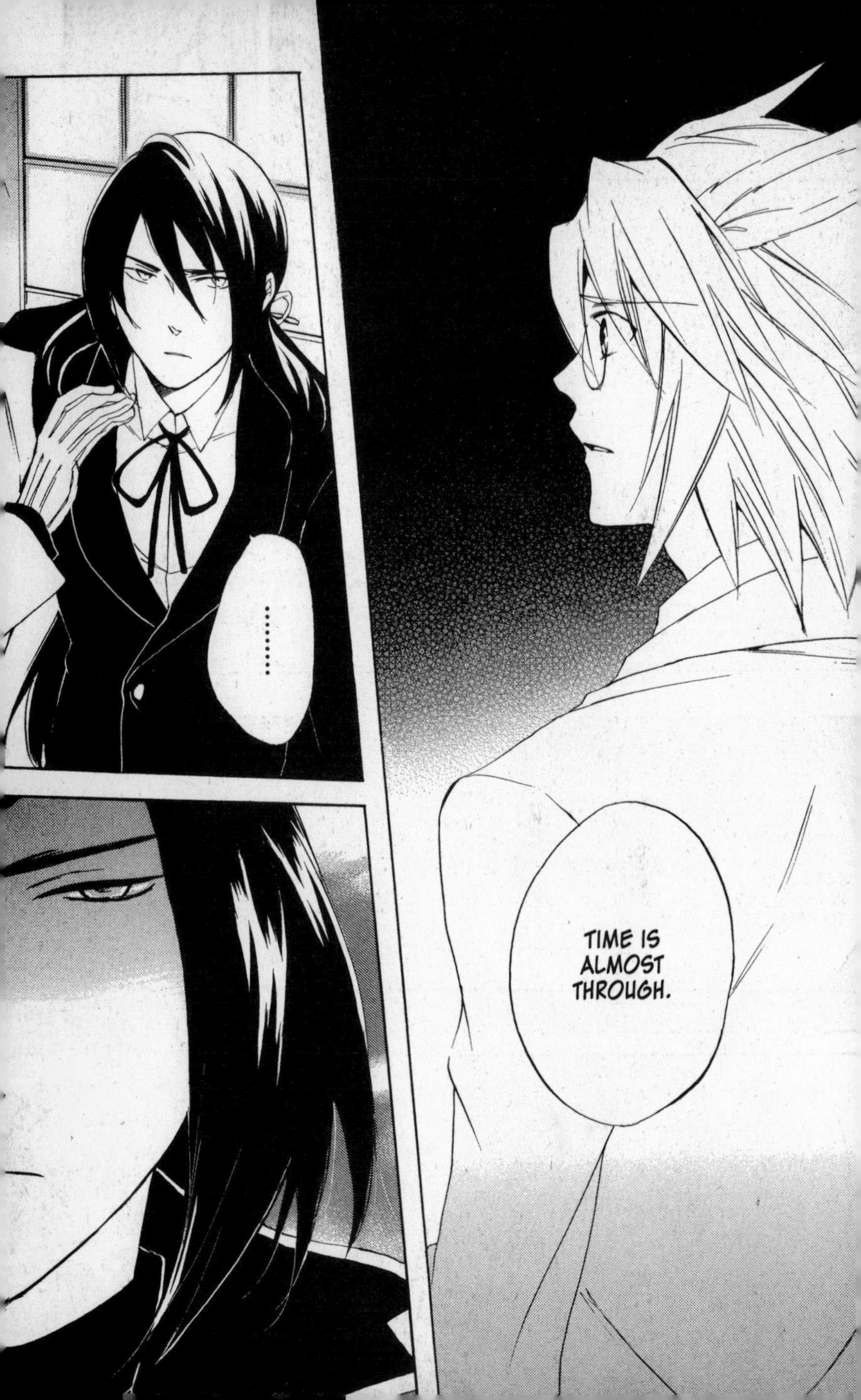
TIME IS ALMOST THROUGH.
……

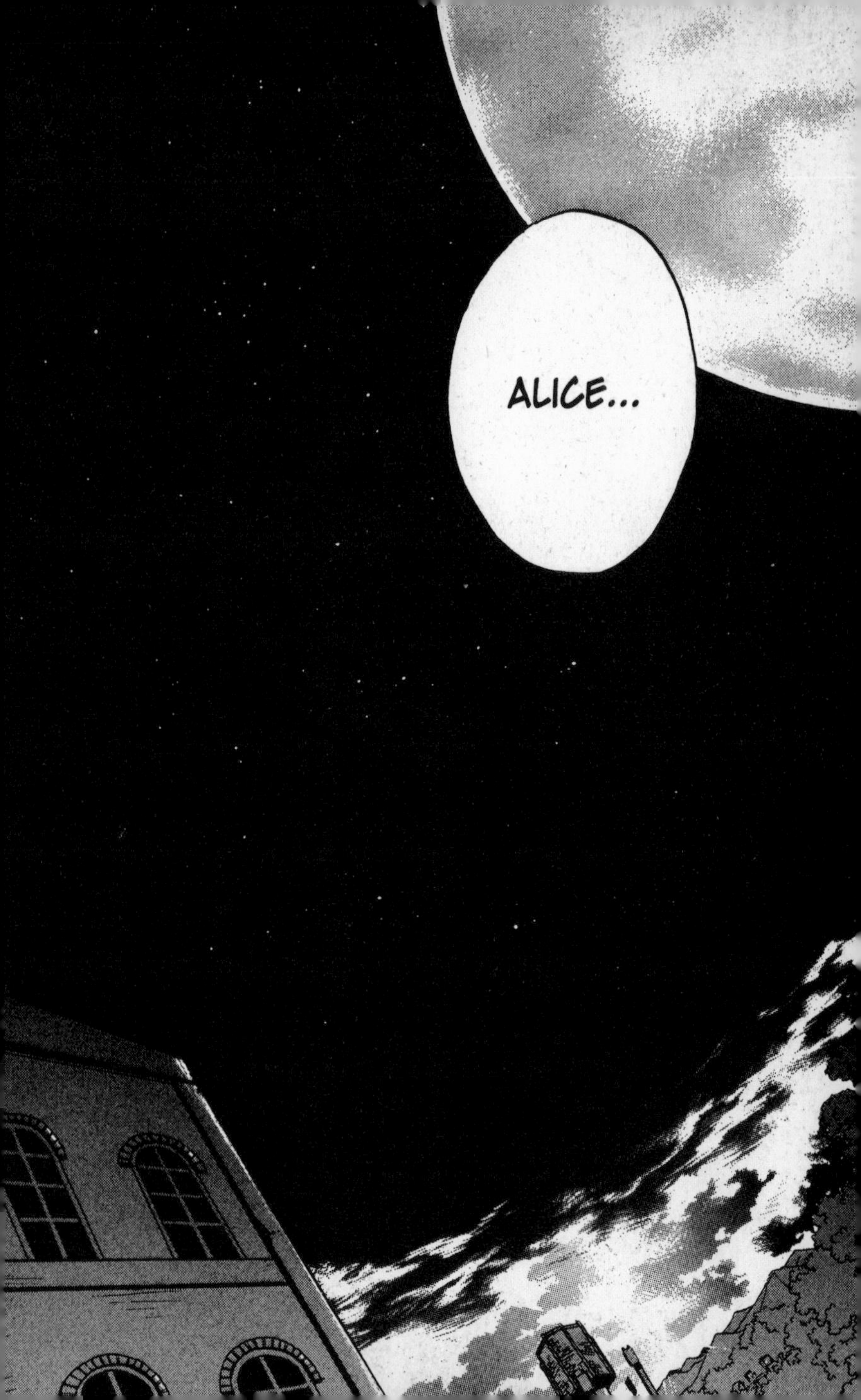
ALICE...

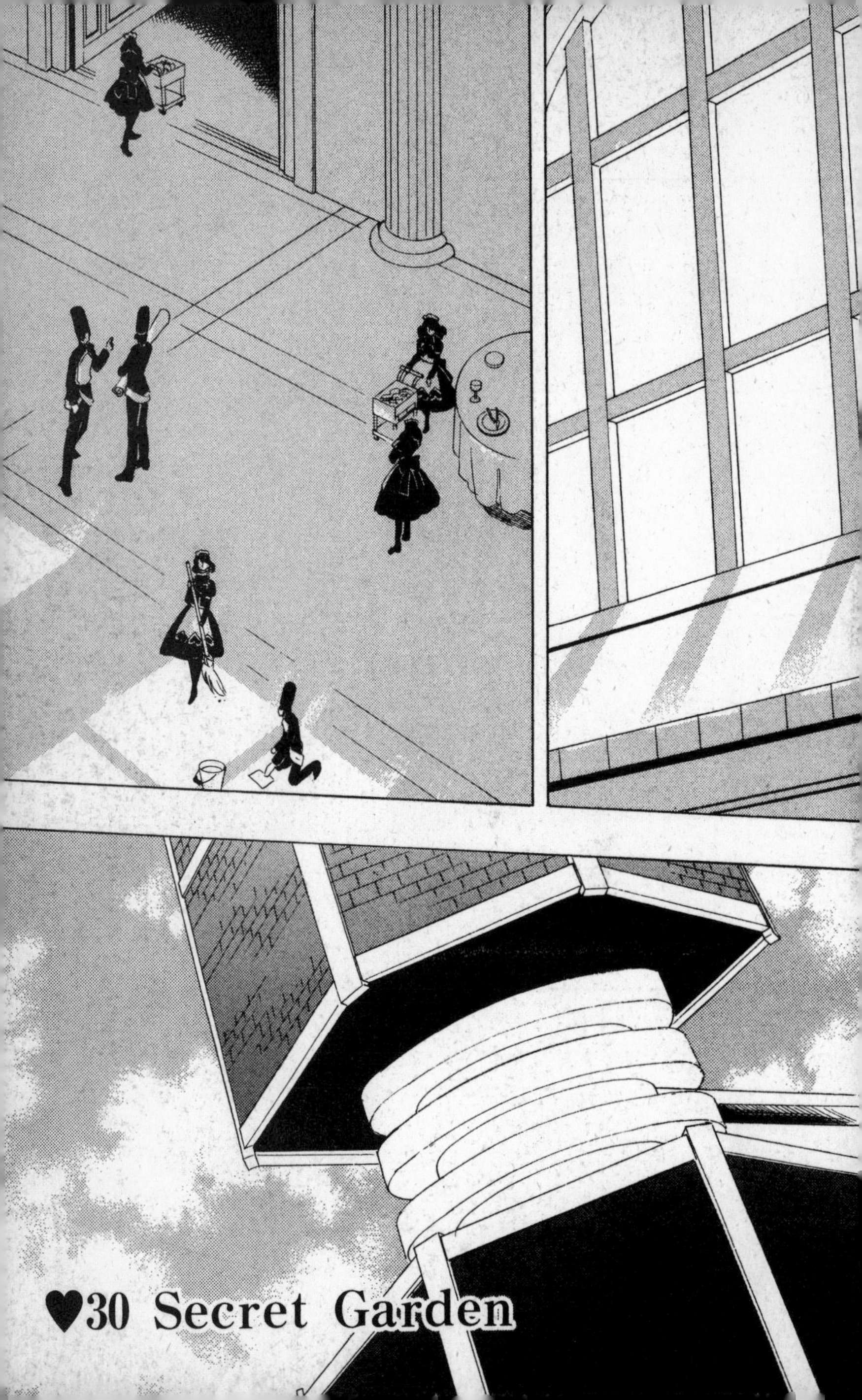
♥30 Secret Garden

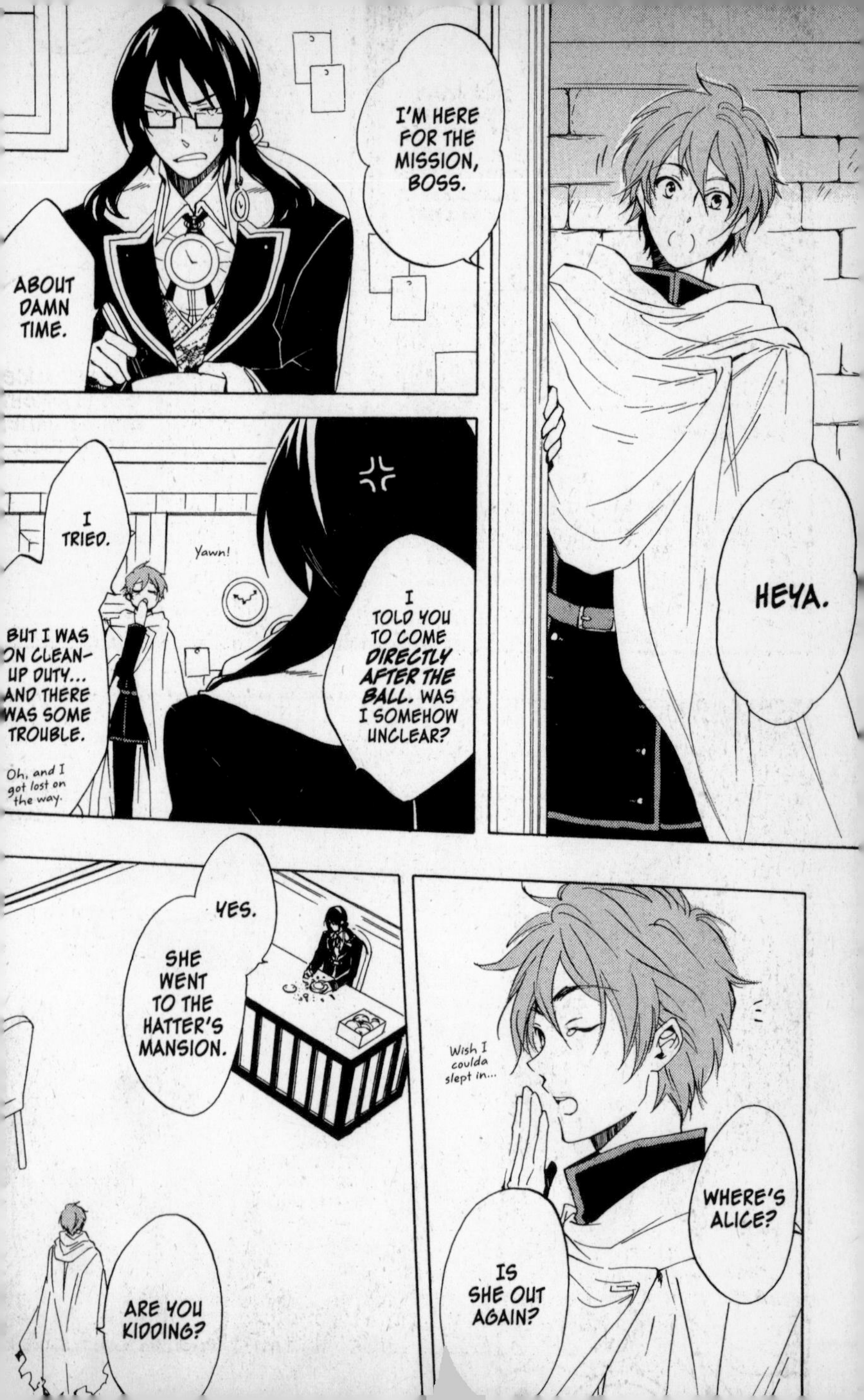
HEYA.
I'M HERE FOR THE MISSION, BOSS.
ABOUT DAMN TIME.
I TOLD YOU TO COME *DIRECTLY AFTER THE BALL*. WAS I SOMEHOW UNCLEAR?
I TRIED.
Yawn!
BUT I WAS ON CLEAN-UP DUTY... AND THERE WAS SOME TROUBLE.
Oh, and I got lost on the way.
WHERE'S ALICE?
IS SHE OUT AGAIN?
Wish I coulda slept in...
YES.
SHE WENT TO THE HATTER'S MANSION.
ARE YOU KIDDING?

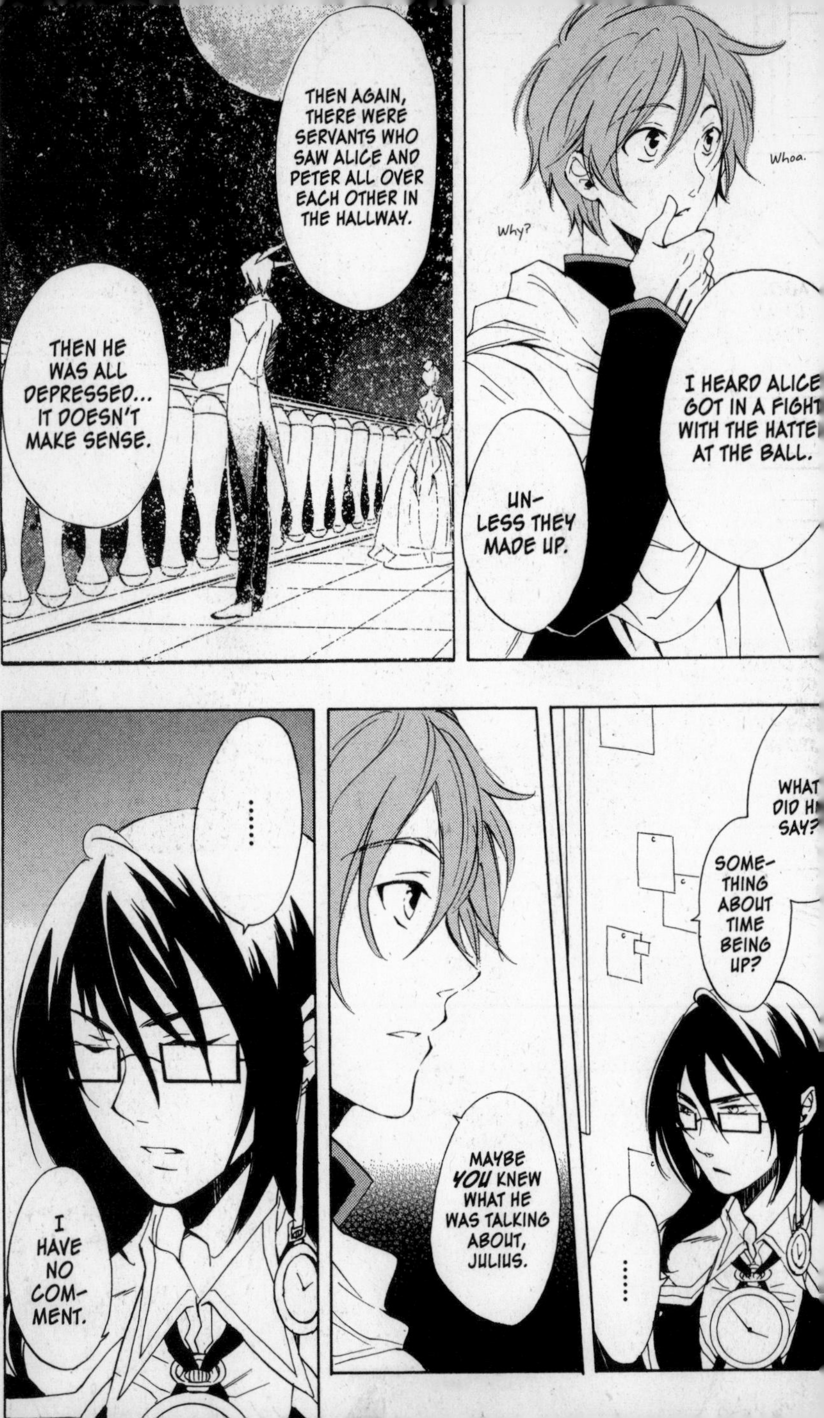
Whoa.
Why?
I HEARD ALICE GOT IN A FIGHT WITH THE HATTE AT THE BALL.
UN-LESS THEY MADE UP.
THEN AGAIN, THERE WERE SERVANTS WHO SAW ALICE AND PETER ALL OVER EACH OTHER IN THE HALLWAY.
THEN HE WAS ALL DEPRESSED... IT DOESN'T MAKE SENSE.
WHAT DID H SAY?
SOME-THING ABOUT TIME BEING UP?
......
MAYBE *YOU* KNEW WHAT HE WAS TALKING ABOUT, JULIUS.
......
I HAVE NO COM-MENT.

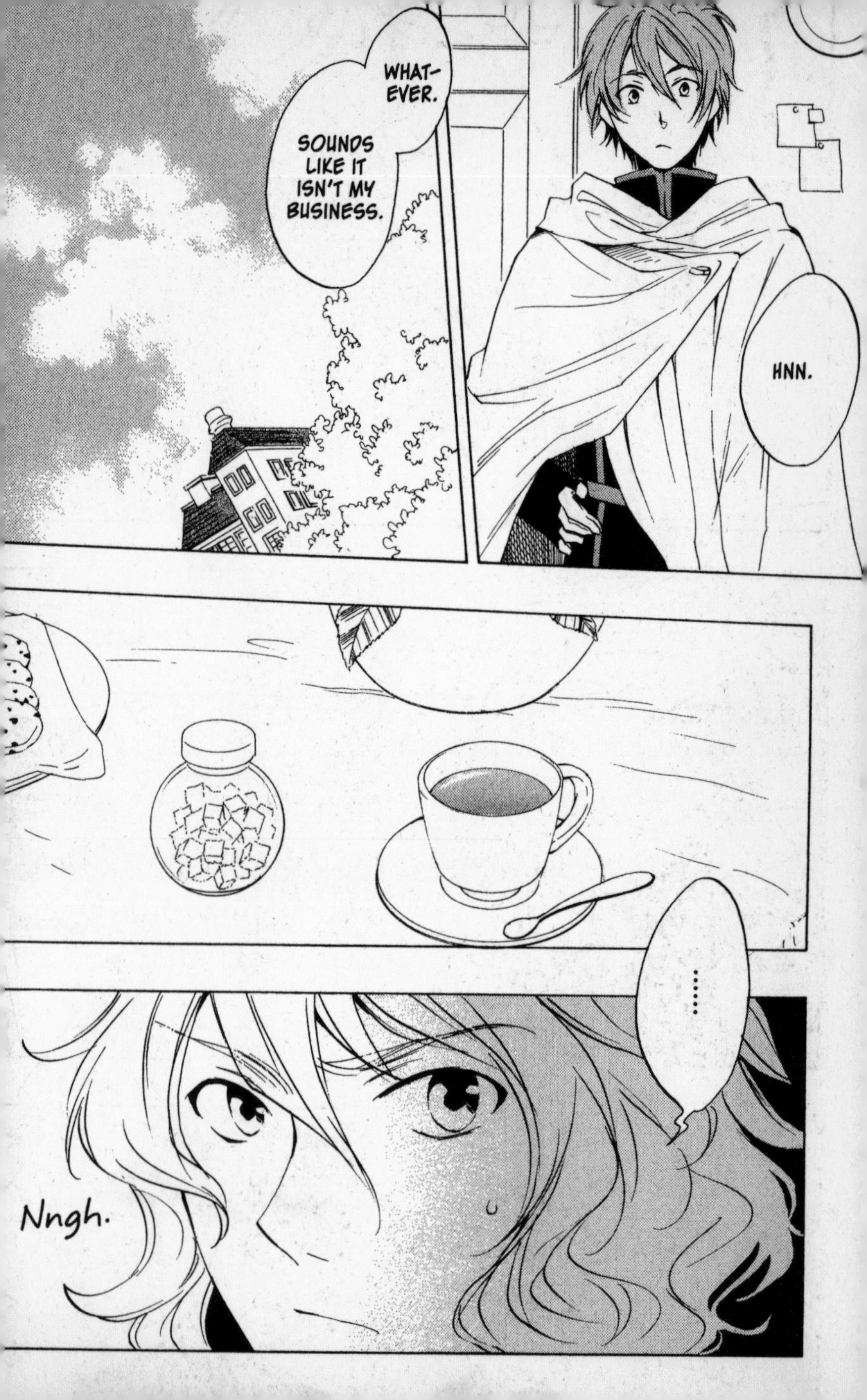
WHAT-EVER.
SOUNDS LIKE IT ISN'T MY BUSINESS.
HNN.
......
Nngh.

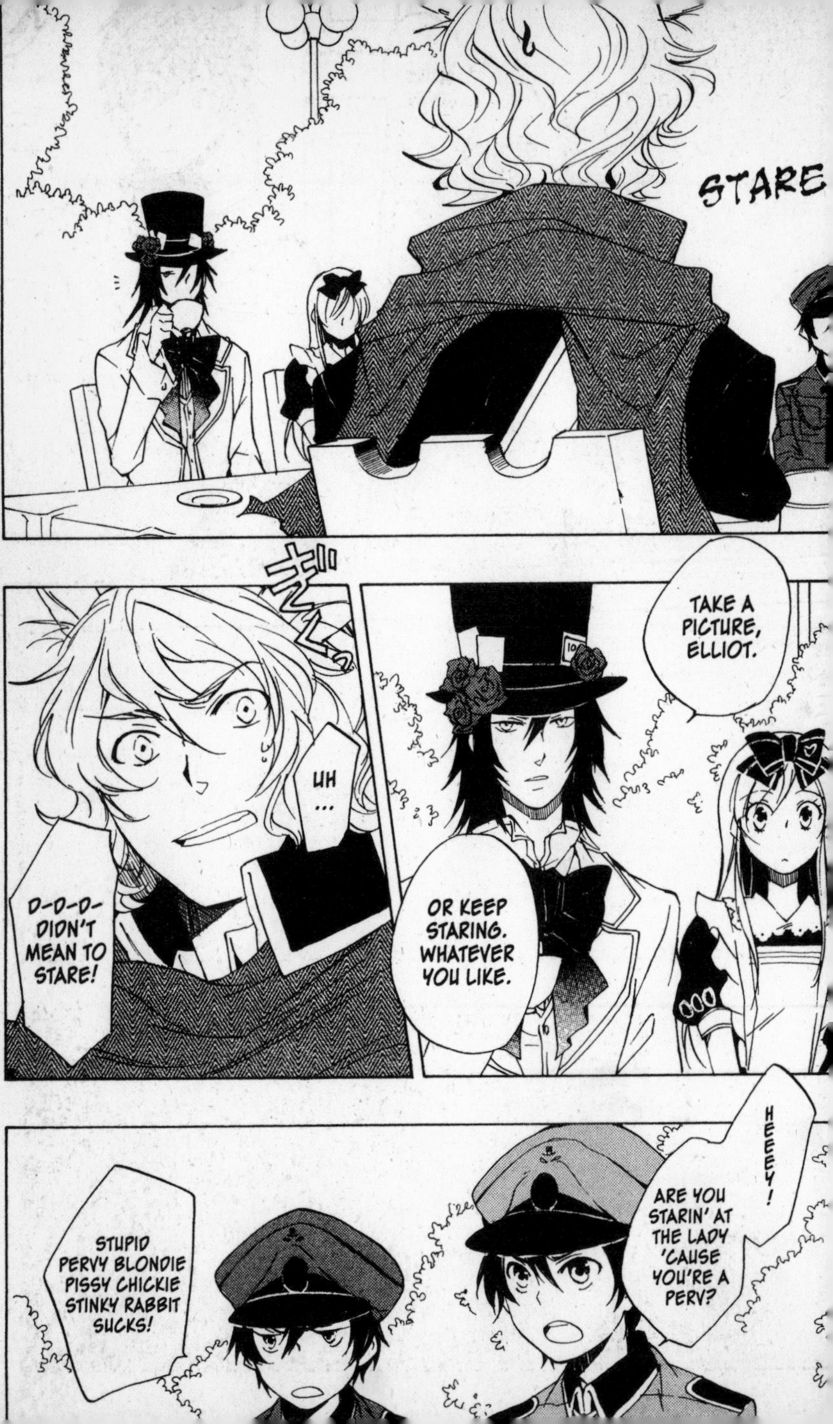
STARE
TAKE A PICTURE, ELLIOT.
OR KEEP STARING. WHATEVER YOU LIKE.
UH ...
D-D-D-DIDN'T MEAN TO STARE!
HEEEEY!
ARE YOU STARIN' AT THE LADY 'CAUSE YOU'RE A PERV?
STUPID PERVY BLONDIE PISSY CHICKIE STINKY RABBIT SUCKS!

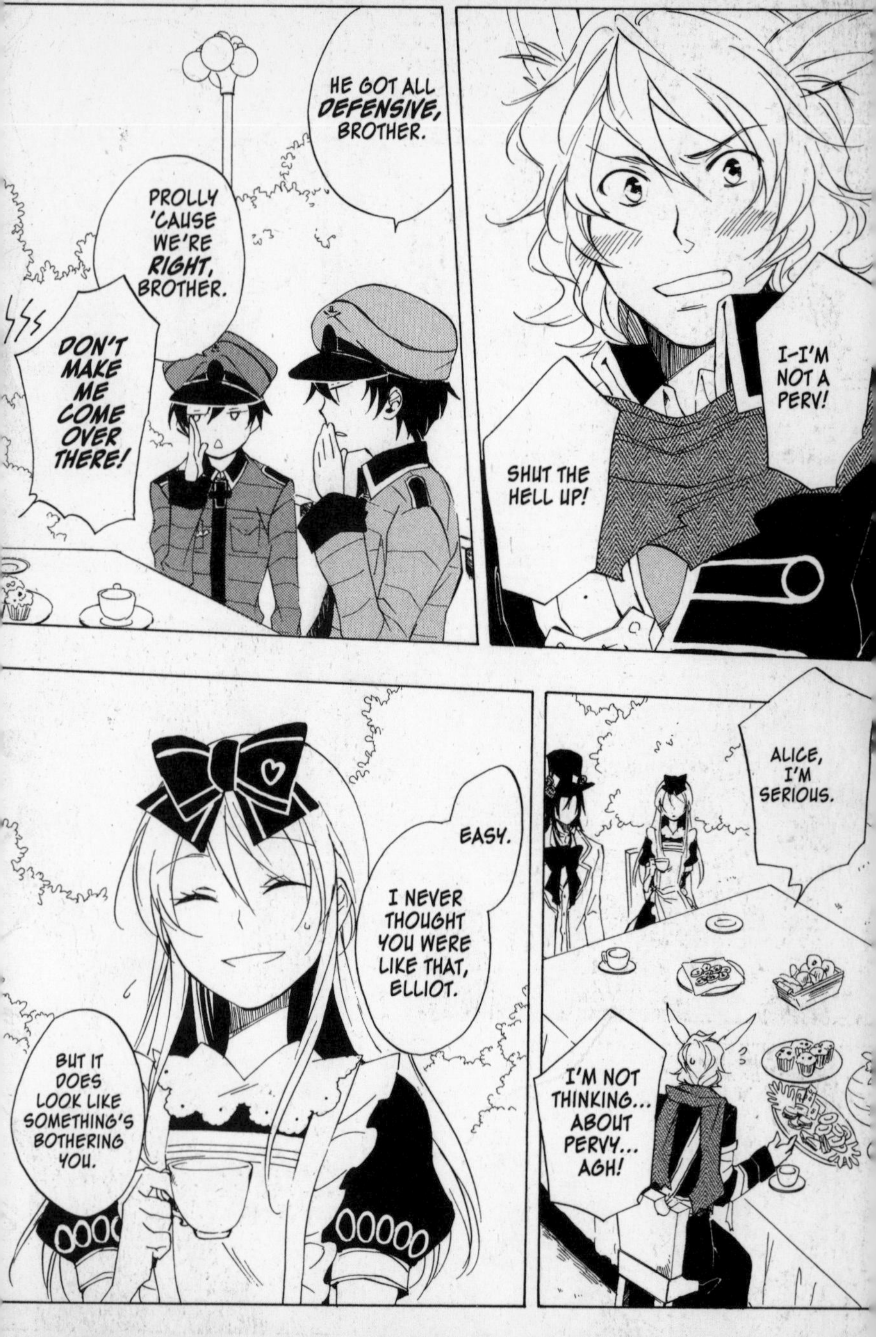

I-I'M NOT A PERV!
SHUT THE HELL UP!
HE GOT ALL DEFENSIVE, BROTHER.
PROLLY 'CAUSE WE'RE RIGHT, BROTHER.
DON'T MAKE ME COME OVER THERE!
ALICE, I'M SERIOUS.
I'M NOT THINKING... ABOUT PERVY... AGH!
EASY.
I NEVER THOUGHT YOU WERE LIKE THAT, ELLIOT.
BUT IT DOES LOOK LIKE SOMETHING'S BOTHERING YOU.

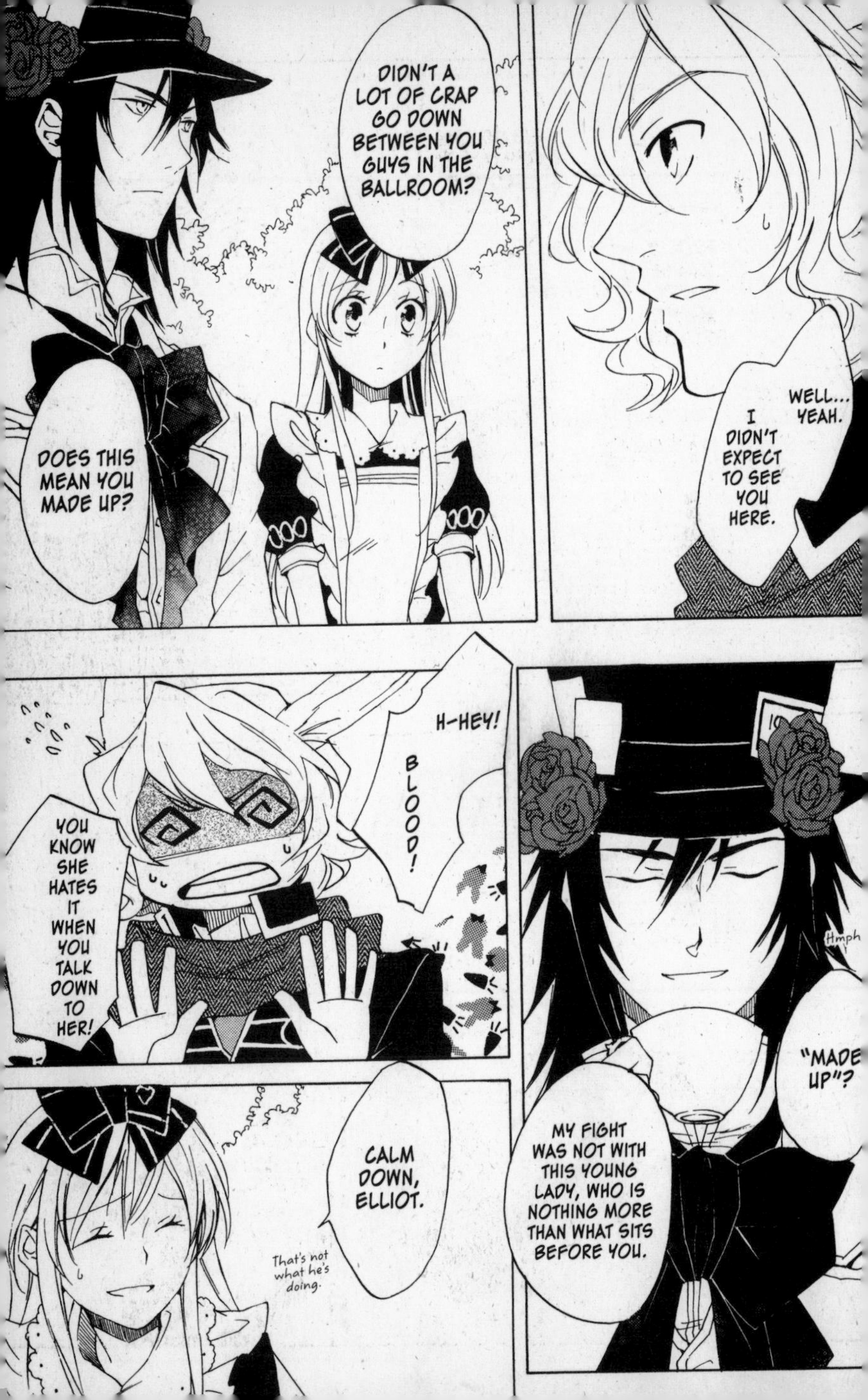
WELL... YEAH.
I DIDN'T EXPECT TO SEE YOU HERE.
DIDN'T A LOT OF CRAP GO DOWN BETWEEN YOU GUYS IN THE BALLROOM?
DOES THIS MEAN YOU MADE UP?
Hmph
"MADE UP"?
MY FIGHT WAS NOT WITH THIS YOUNG LADY, WHO IS NOTHING MORE THAN WHAT SITS BEFORE YOU.
H-HEY!
BLOOOD!
YOU KNOW SHE HATES IT WHEN YOU TALK DOWN TO HER!
CALM DOWN, ELLIOT.
That's not what he's doing.

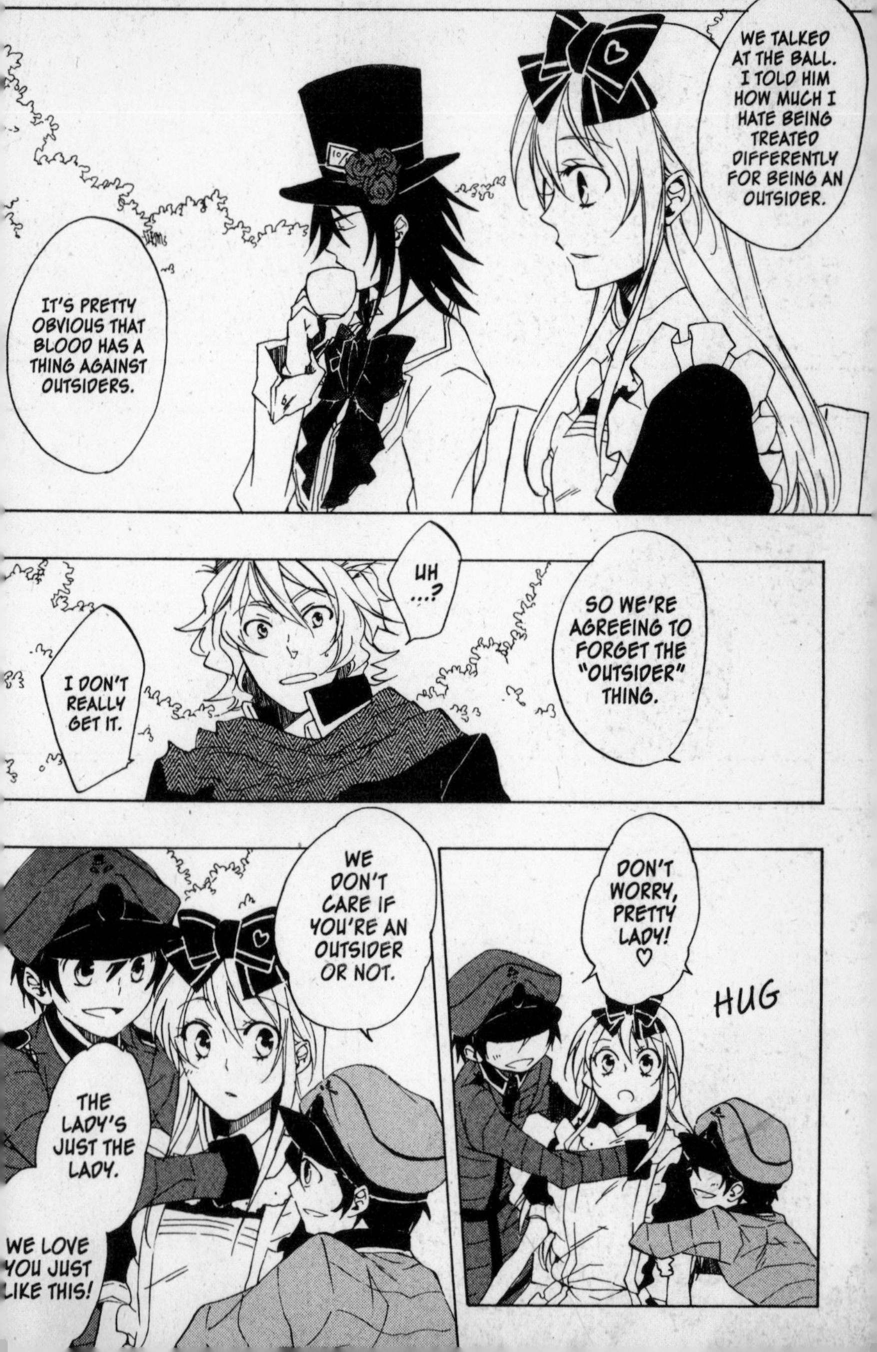
WE TALKED AT THE BALL. I TOLD HIM HOW MUCH I HATE BEING TREATED DIFFERENTLY FOR BEING AN OUTSIDER.
IT'S PRETTY OBVIOUS THAT BLOOD HAS A THING AGAINST OUTSIDERS.
SO WE'RE AGREEING TO FORGET THE "OUTSIDER" THING.
UH ...?
I DON'T REALLY GET IT.
DON'T WORRY, PRETTY LADY! ♡
HUG
WE DON'T CARE IF YOU'RE AN OUTSIDER OR NOT.
THE LADY'S JUST THE LADY.
WE LOVE YOU JUST LIKE THIS!

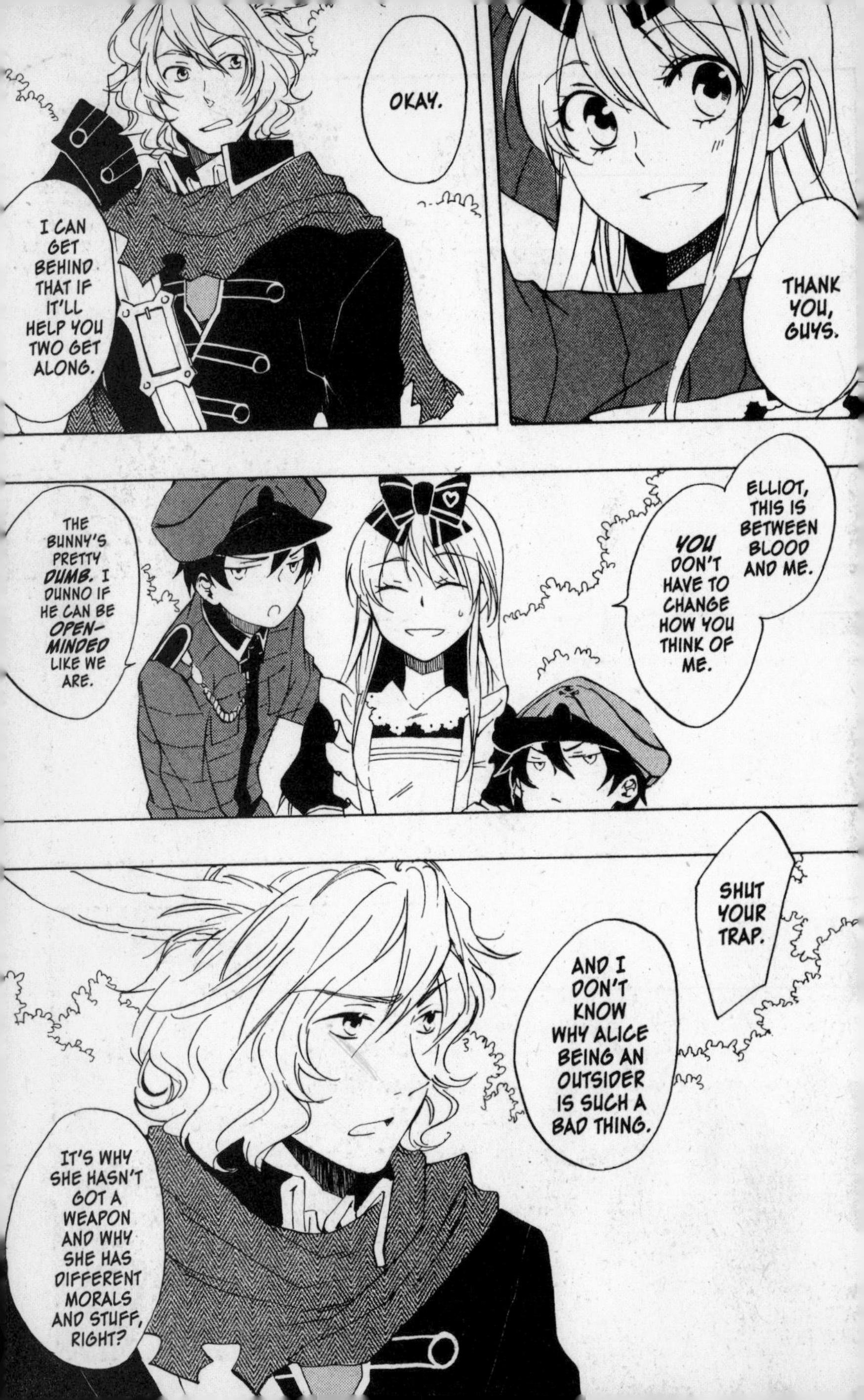
THANK YOU, GUYS.
OKAY.
I CAN GET BEHIND THAT IF IT'LL HELP YOU TWO GET ALONG.
ELLIOT, THIS IS BETWEEN BLOOD AND ME.
YOU DON'T HAVE TO CHANGE HOW YOU THINK OF ME.
THE BUNNY'S PRETTY DUMB. I DUNNO IF HE CAN BE OPEN-MINDED LIKE WE ARE.
SHUT YOUR TRAP.
AND I DON'T KNOW WHY ALICE BEING AN OUTSIDER IS SUCH A BAD THING.
IT'S WHY SHE HASN'T GOT A WEAPON AND WHY SHE HAS DIFFERENT MORALS AND STUFF, RIGHT?

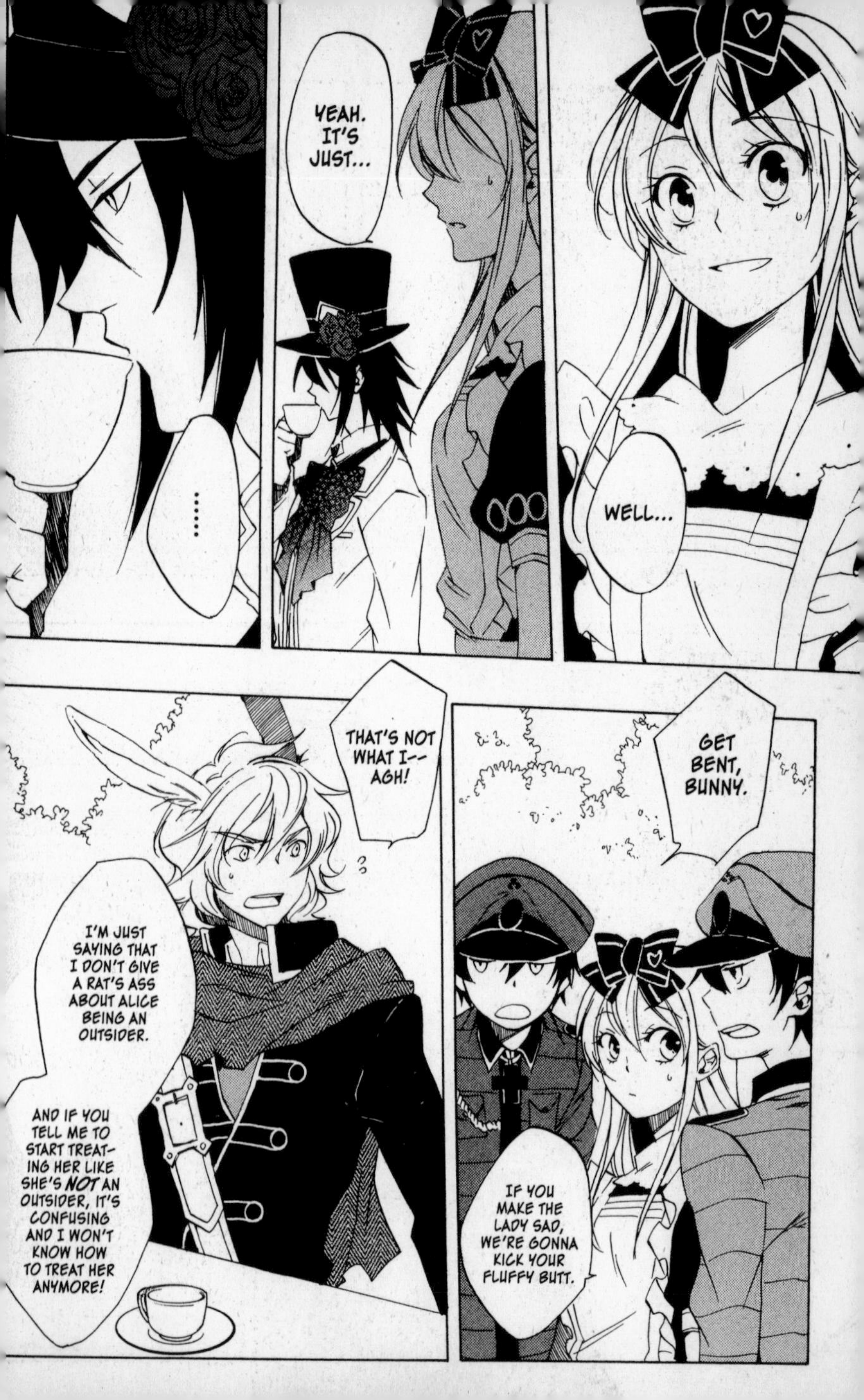
WELL...
YEAH. IT'S JUST...
......
GET BENT, BUNNY.
IF YOU MAKE THE LADY SAD, WE'RE GONNA KICK YOUR FLUFFY BUTT.
THAT'S NOT WHAT I-- AGH!
I'M JUST SAYING THAT I DON'T GIVE A RAT'S ASS ABOUT ALICE BEING AN OUTSIDER.
AND IF YOU TELL ME TO START TREATING HER LIKE SHE'S *NOT* AN OUTSIDER, IT'S CONFUSING AND I WON'T KNOW HOW TO TREAT HER ANYMORE!

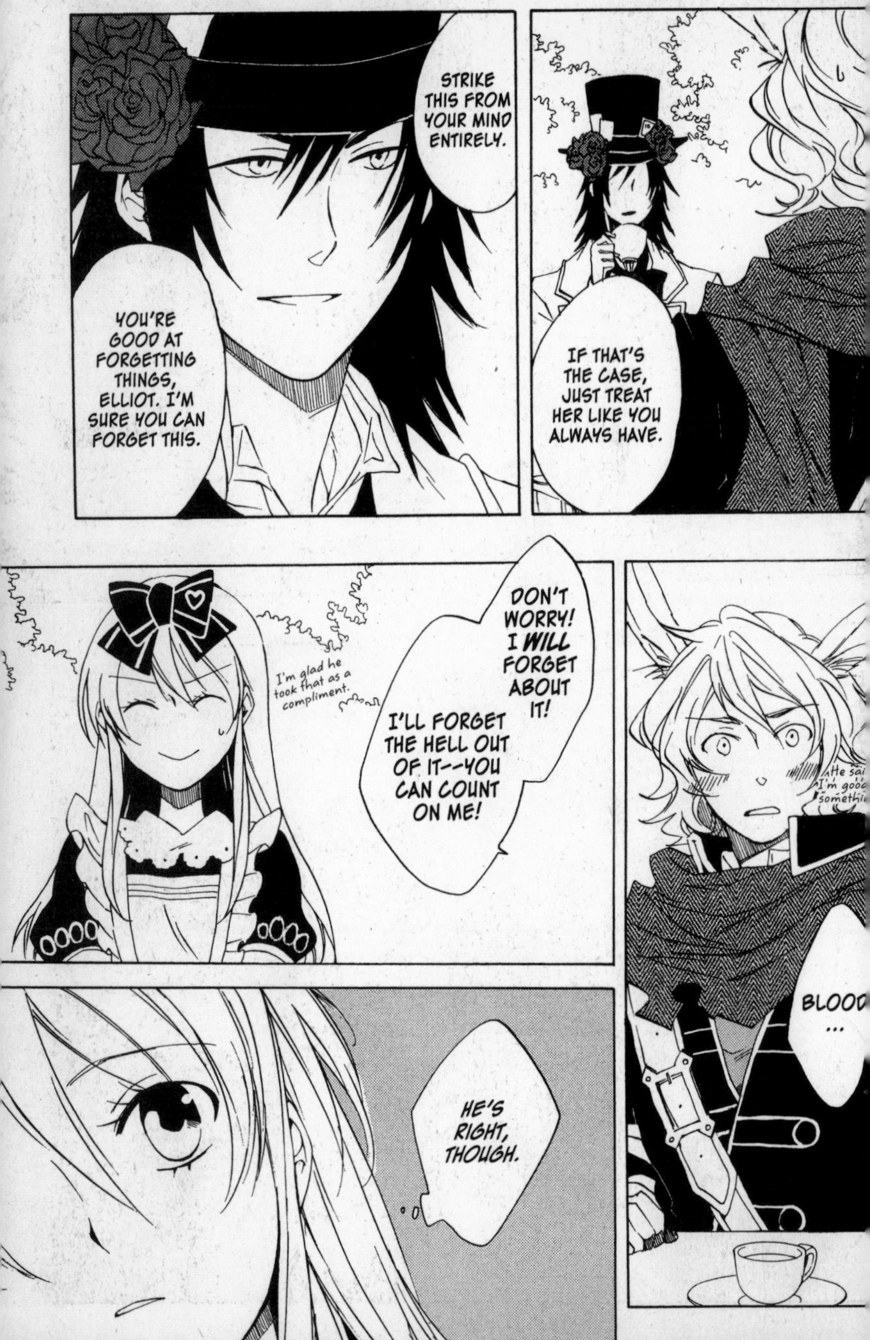
IF THAT'S THE CASE, JUST TREAT HER LIKE YOU ALWAYS HAVE.
STRIKE THIS FROM YOUR MIND ENTIRELY.
YOU'RE GOOD AT FORGETTING THINGS, ELLIOT. I'M SURE YOU CAN FORGET THIS.
BLOOD...
DON'T WORRY! I *WILL* FORGET ABOUT IT!
I'LL FORGET THE HELL OUT OF IT--YOU CAN COUNT ON ME!
I'm glad he took that as a compliment.
HE'S RIGHT, THOUGH.

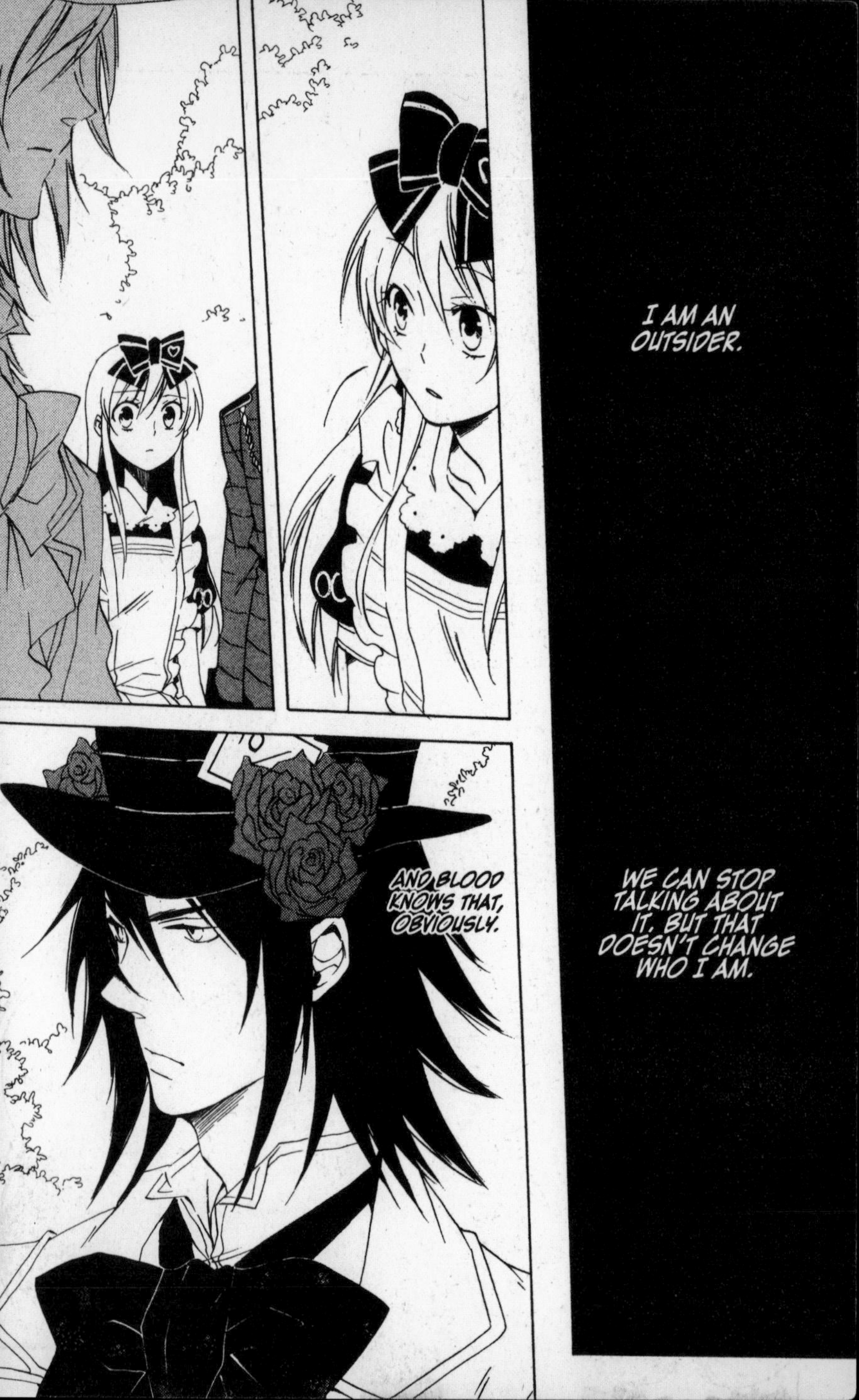
I AM AN OUTSIDER.
WE CAN STOP TALKING ABOUT IT, BUT THAT DOESN'T CHANGE WHO I AM.
AND BLOOD KNOWS THAT, OBVIOUSLY.

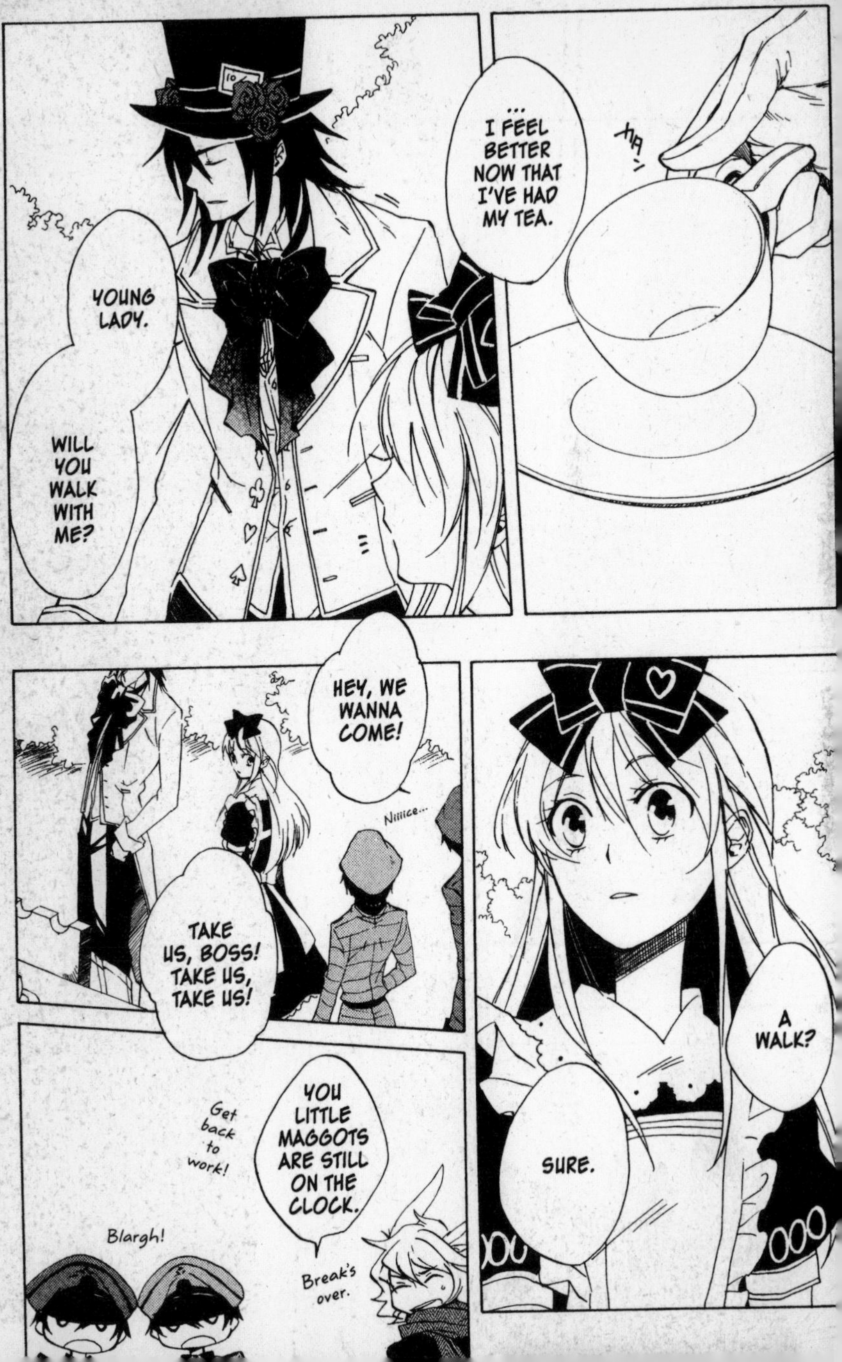
... I FEEL BETTER NOW THAT I'VE HAD MY TEA.
YOUNG LADY.
WILL YOU WALK WITH ME?
A WALK?
SURE.
HEY, WE WANNA COME!
Niiiice...
TAKE US, BOSS! TAKE US, TAKE US!
YOU LITTLE MAGGOTS ARE STILL ON THE CLOCK.
Get back to work!
Break's over.
Blargh!

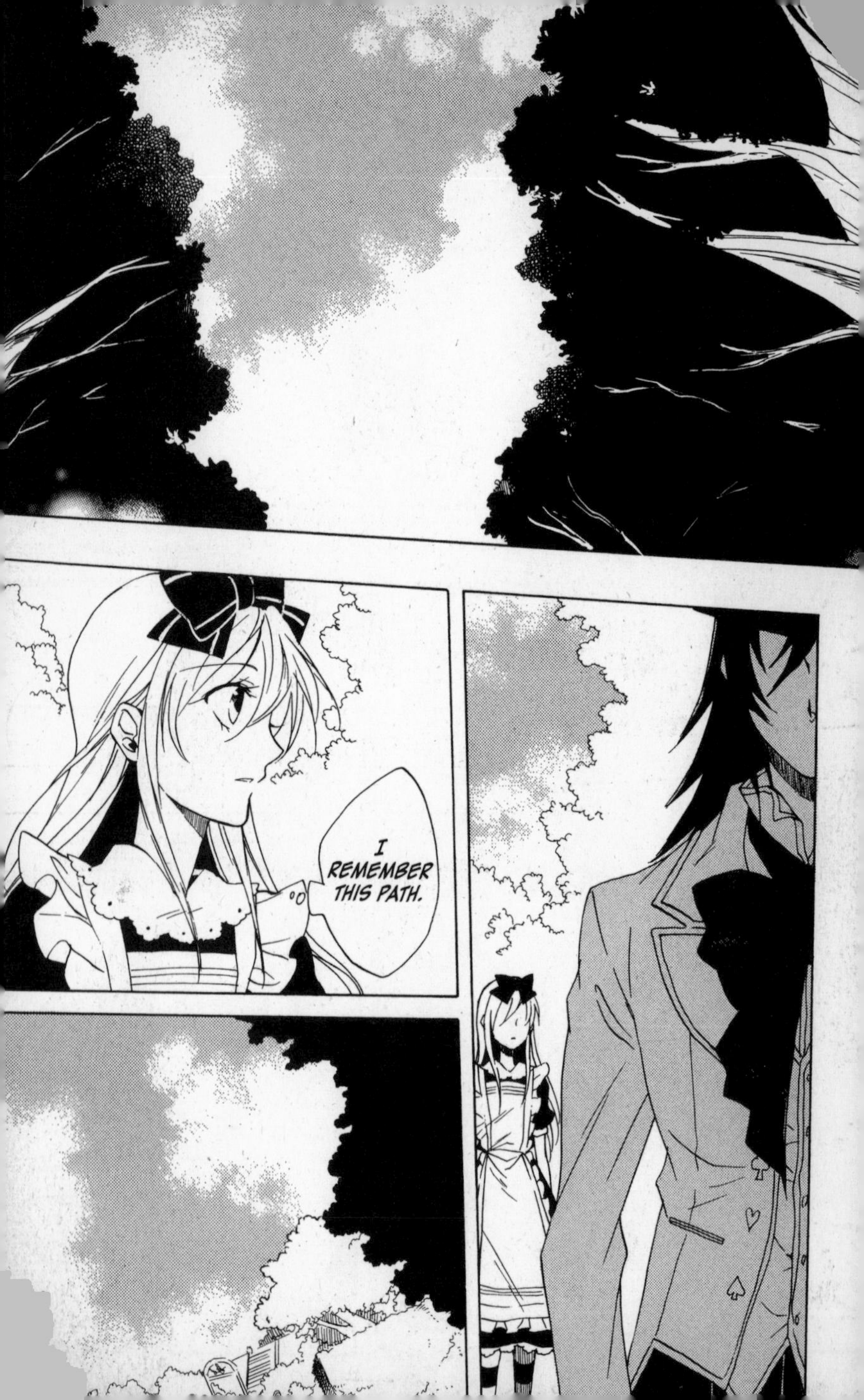
I REMEMBER THIS PATH.

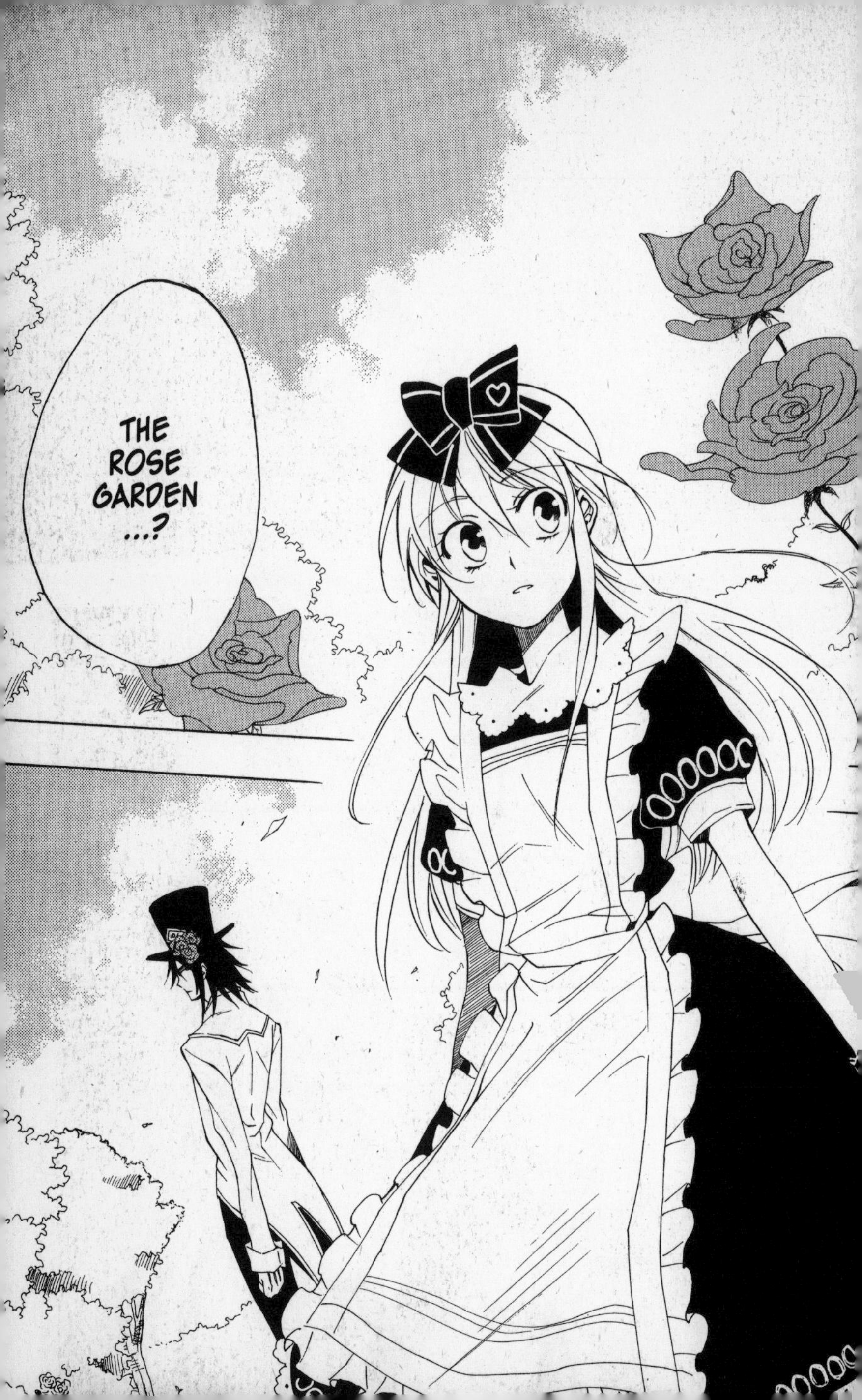
THE ROSE GARDEN ...?

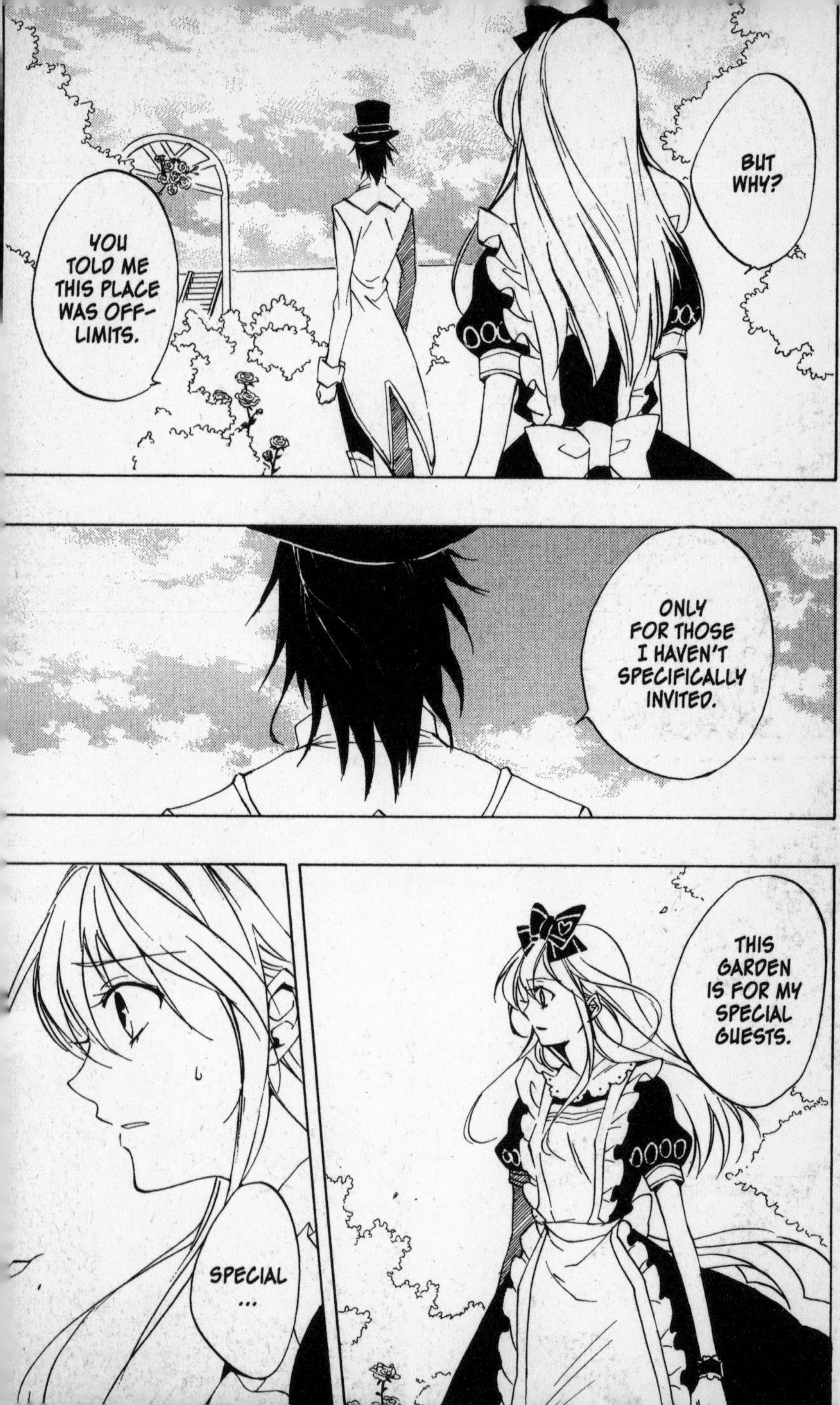
BUT WHY?
YOU TOLD ME THIS PLACE WAS OFF-LIMITS.
ONLY FOR THOSE I HAVEN'T SPECIFICALLY INVITED.
THIS GARDEN IS FOR MY SPECIAL GUESTS.
SPECIAL ...

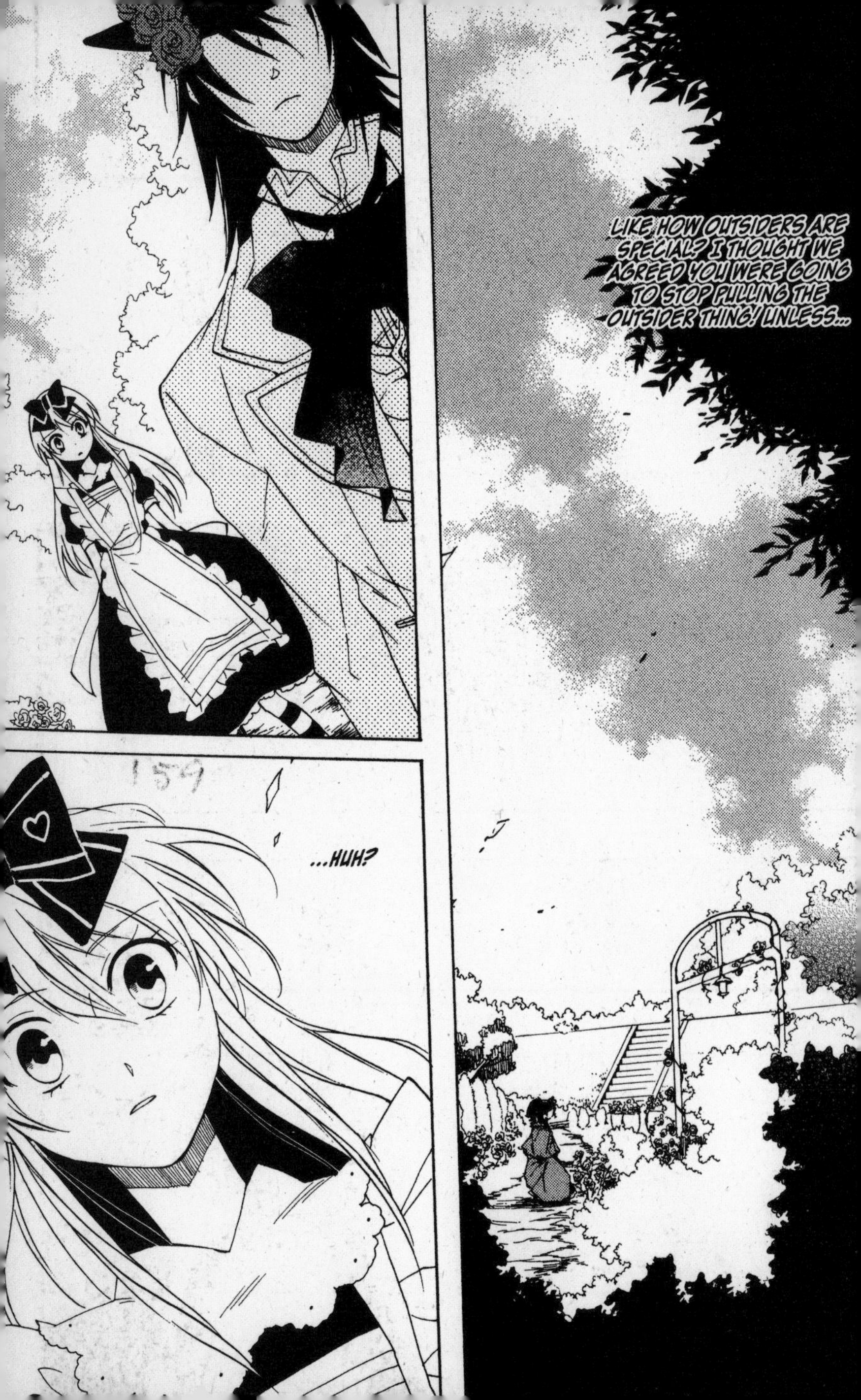
LIKE HOW OUTSIDERS ARE SPECIAL? I THOUGHT WE AGREED YOU WERE GOING TO STOP PULLING THE OUTSIDER THING! UNLESS...
...HUH?

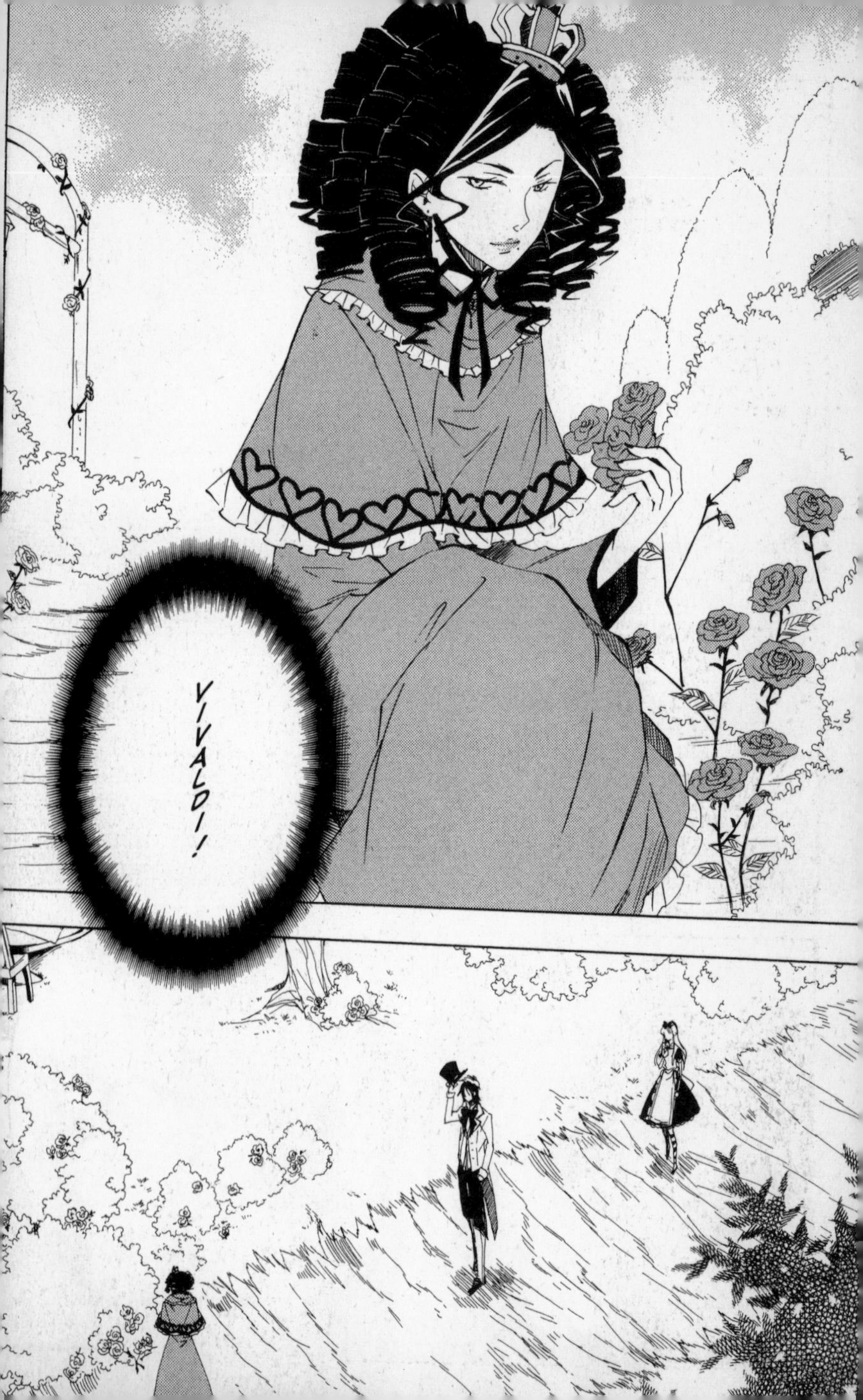
VIVALDI!

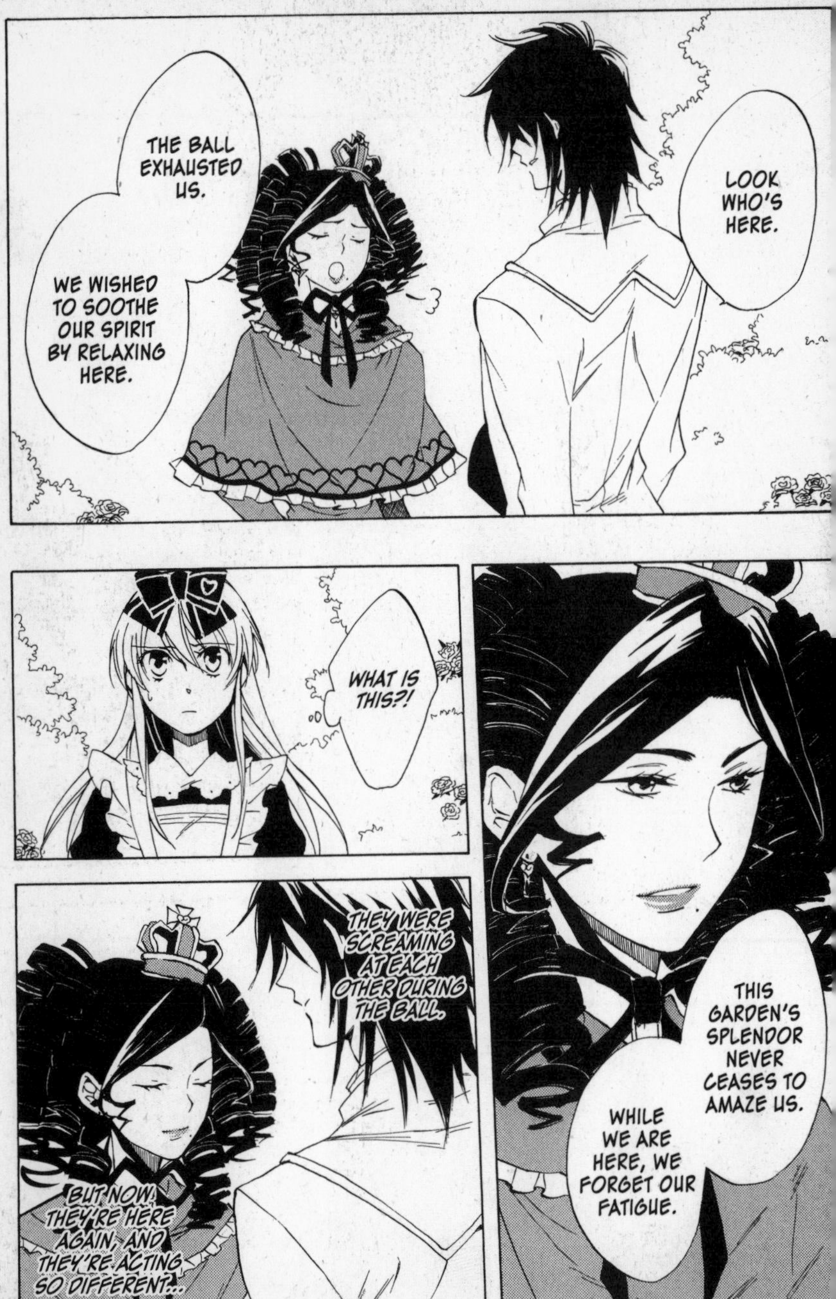
LOOK WHO'S HERE.
THE BALL EXHAUSTED US.
WE WISHED TO SOOTHE OUR SPIRIT BY RELAXING HERE.
THIS GARDEN'S SPLENDOR NEVER CEASES TO AMAZE US.
WHILE WE ARE HERE, WE FORGET OUR FATIGUE.
WHAT IS THIS?!
THEY WERE SCREAMING AT EACH OTHER DURING THE BALL.
BUT NOW THEY'RE HERE AGAIN, AND THEY'RE ACTING SO DIFFERENT...

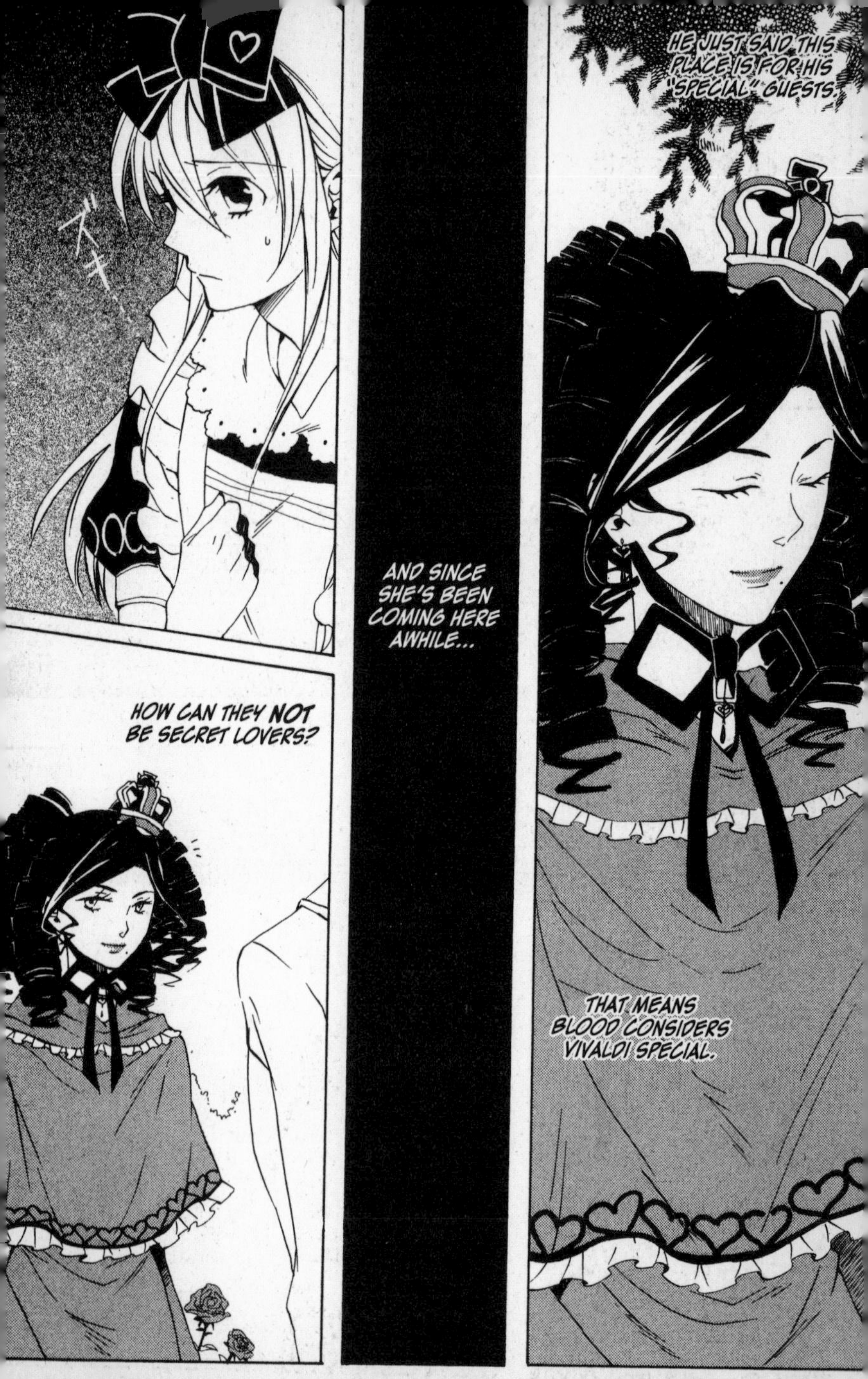

HE JUST SAID THIS PLACE IS FOR HIS "SPECIAL" GUESTS.
THAT MEANS BLOOD CONSIDERS VIVALDI SPECIAL.
AND SINCE SHE'S BEEN COMING HERE AWHILE...
ズキ
HOW CAN THEY NOT BE SECRET LOVERS?

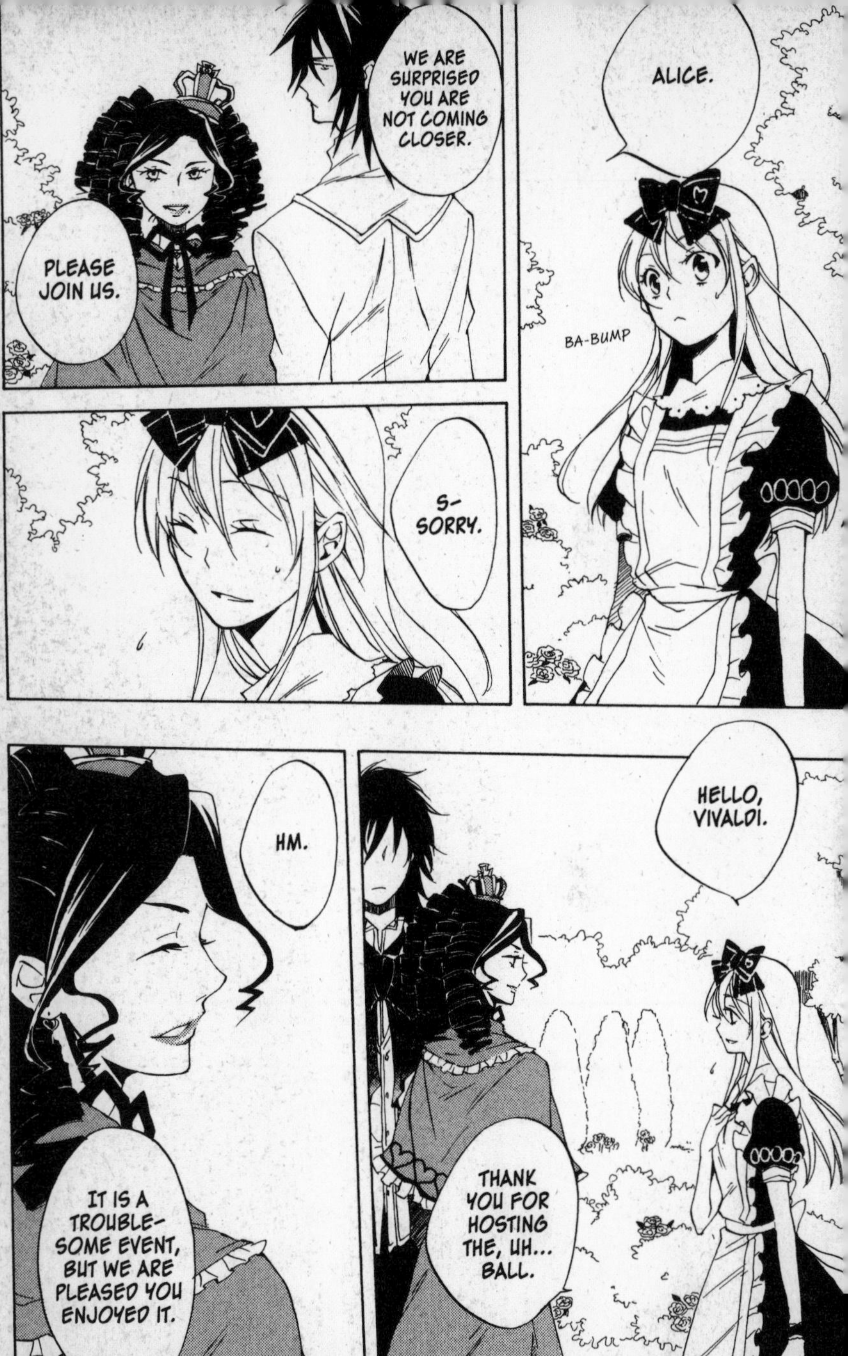
ALICE.
BA-BUMP
WE ARE SURPRISED YOU ARE NOT COMING CLOSER.
PLEASE JOIN US.
S- SORRY.
HELLO, VIVALDI.
THANK YOU FOR HOSTING THE, UH... BALL.
HM.
IT IS A TROUBLE-SOME EVENT, BUT WE ARE PLEASED YOU ENJOYED IT.

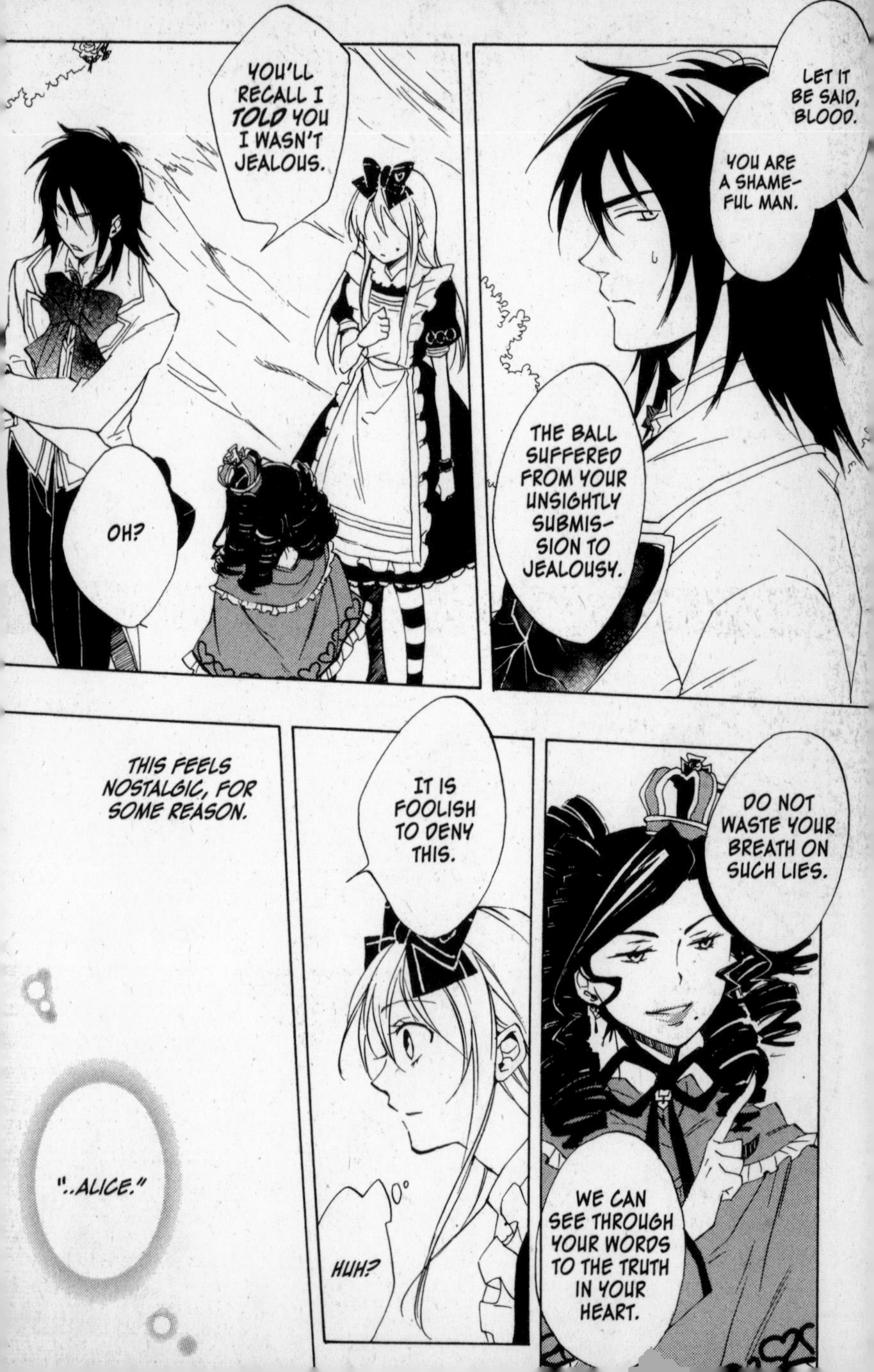
LET IT BE SAID, BLOOD.
YOU ARE A SHAME-FUL MAN.
THE BALL SUFFERED FROM YOUR UNSIGHTLY SUBMIS-SION TO JEALOUSY.
YOU'LL RECALL I TOLD YOU I WASN'T JEALOUS.
OH?
DO NOT WASTE YOUR BREATH ON SUCH LIES.
WE CAN SEE THROUGH YOUR WORDS TO THE TRUTH IN YOUR HEART.
IT IS FOOLISH TO DENY THIS.
HUH?
THIS FEELS NOSTALGIC, FOR SOME REASON.
"..ALICE."

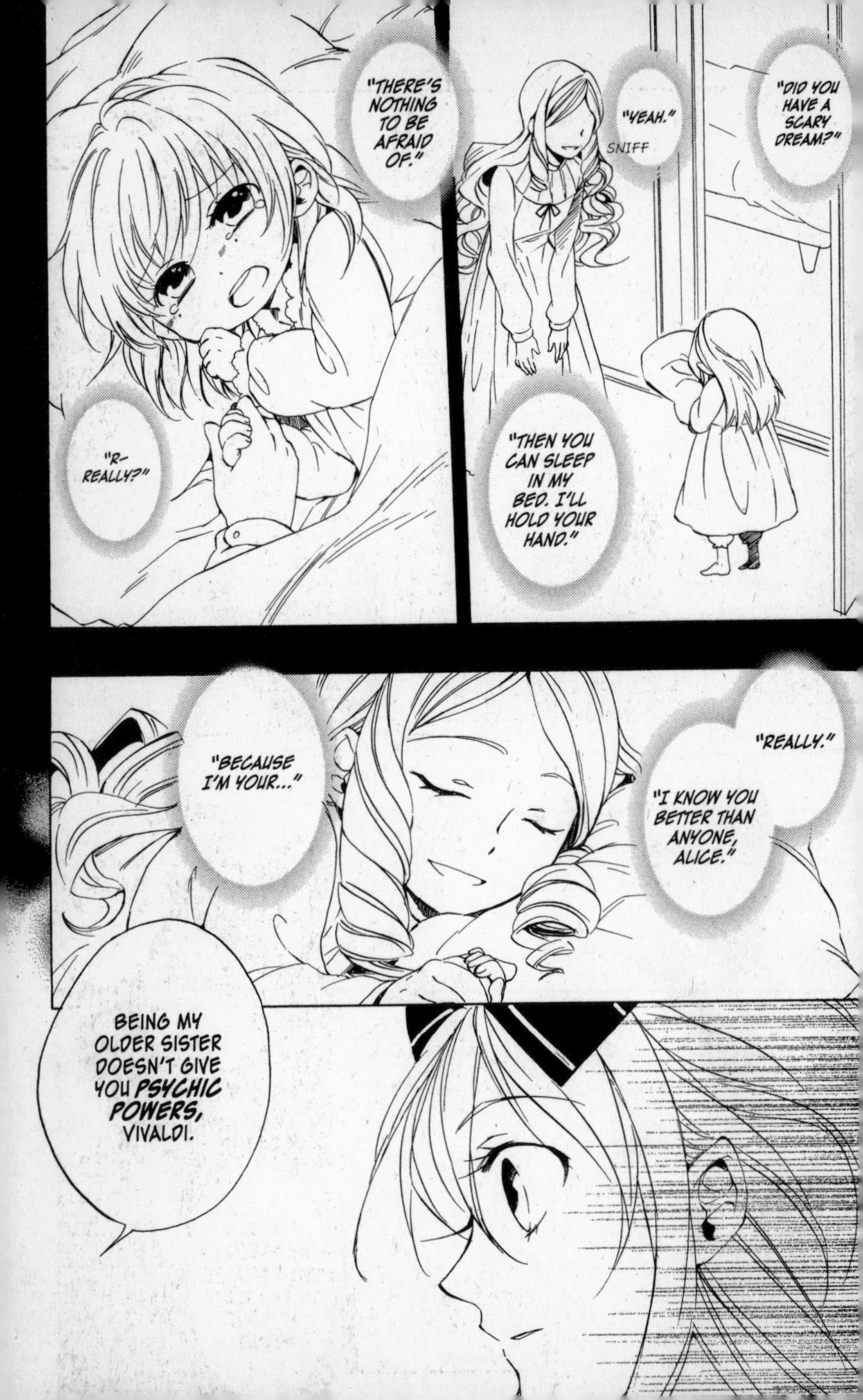
"DID YOU HAVE A SCARY DREAM?"
"YEAH."
SNIFF
"THEN YOU CAN SLEEP IN MY BED. I'LL HOLD YOUR HAND."
"THERE'S NOTHING TO BE AFRAID OF."
"R-REALLY?"
"REALLY."
"I KNOW YOU BETTER THAN ANYONE, ALICE."
"BECAUSE I'M YOUR..."
BEING MY OLDER SISTER DOESN'T GIVE YOU **PSYCHIC POWERS**, VIVALDI.

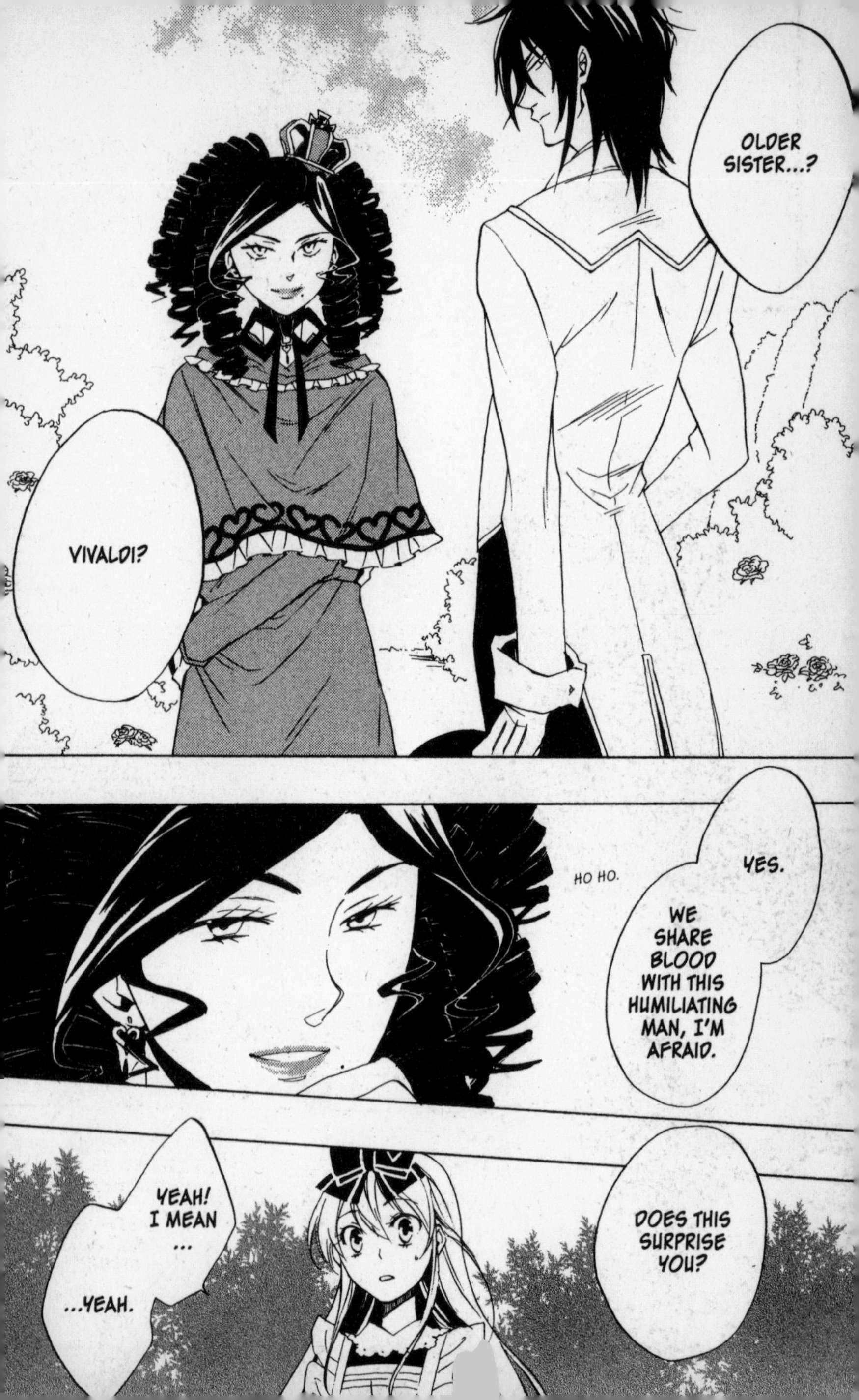
OLDER SISTER...?
VIVALDI?
YES.
HO HO.
WE SHARE BLOOD WITH THIS HUMILIATING MAN, I'M AFRAID.
DOES THIS SURPRISE YOU?
YEAH! I MEAN ...
...YEAH.

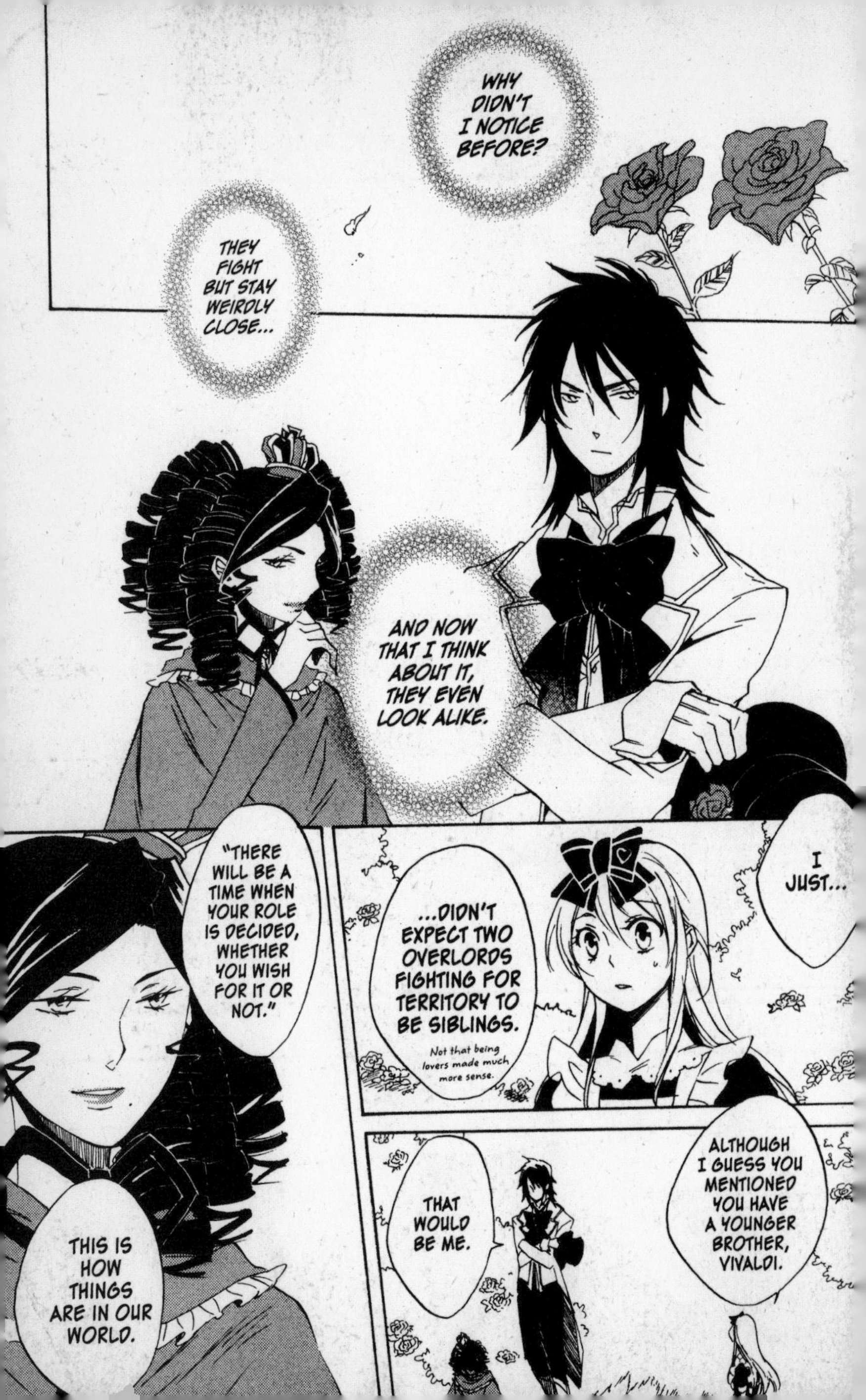
WHY DIDN'T I NOTICE BEFORE?
THEY FIGHT BUT STAY WEIRDLY CLOSE...
AND NOW THAT I THINK ABOUT IT, THEY EVEN LOOK ALIKE.
I JUST...
...DIDN'T EXPECT TWO OVERLORDS FIGHTING FOR TERRITORY TO BE SIBLINGS.
Not that being lovers made much more sense.
ALTHOUGH I GUESS YOU MENTIONED YOU HAVE A YOUNGER BROTHER, VIVALDI.
THAT WOULD BE ME.
"THERE WILL BE A TIME WHEN YOUR ROLE IS DECIDED, WHETHER YOU WISH FOR IT OR NOT."
THIS IS HOW THINGS ARE IN OUR WORLD.

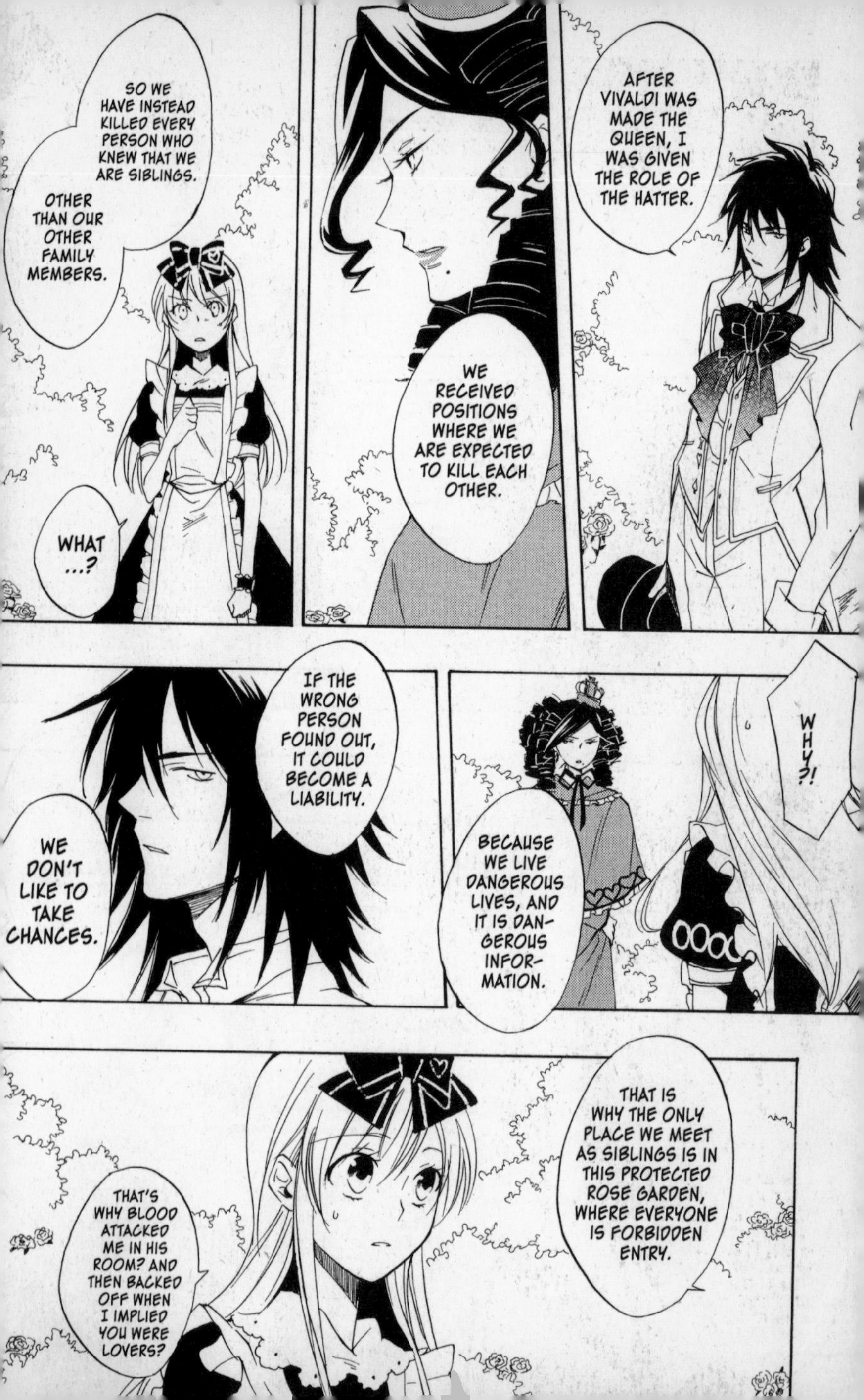
AFTER VIVALDI WAS MADE THE QUEEN, I WAS GIVEN THE ROLE OF THE HATTER.
WE RECEIVED POSITIONS WHERE WE ARE EXPECTED TO KILL EACH OTHER.
SO WE HAVE INSTEAD KILLED EVERY PERSON WHO KNEW THAT WE ARE SIBLINGS.
OTHER THAN OUR OTHER FAMILY MEMBERS.
WHAT ...?
WHY?!
BECAUSE WE LIVE DANGEROUS LIVES, AND IT IS DAN-GEROUS INFOR-MATION.
IF THE WRONG PERSON FOUND OUT, IT COULD BECOME A LIABILITY.
WE DON'T LIKE TO TAKE CHANCES.
THAT IS WHY THE ONLY PLACE WE MEET AS SIBLINGS IS IN THIS PROTECTED ROSE GARDEN, WHERE EVERYONE IS FORBIDDEN ENTRY.
THAT'S WHY BLOOD ATTACKED ME IN HIS ROOM? AND THEN BACKED OFF WHEN I IMPLIED YOU WERE LOVERS?

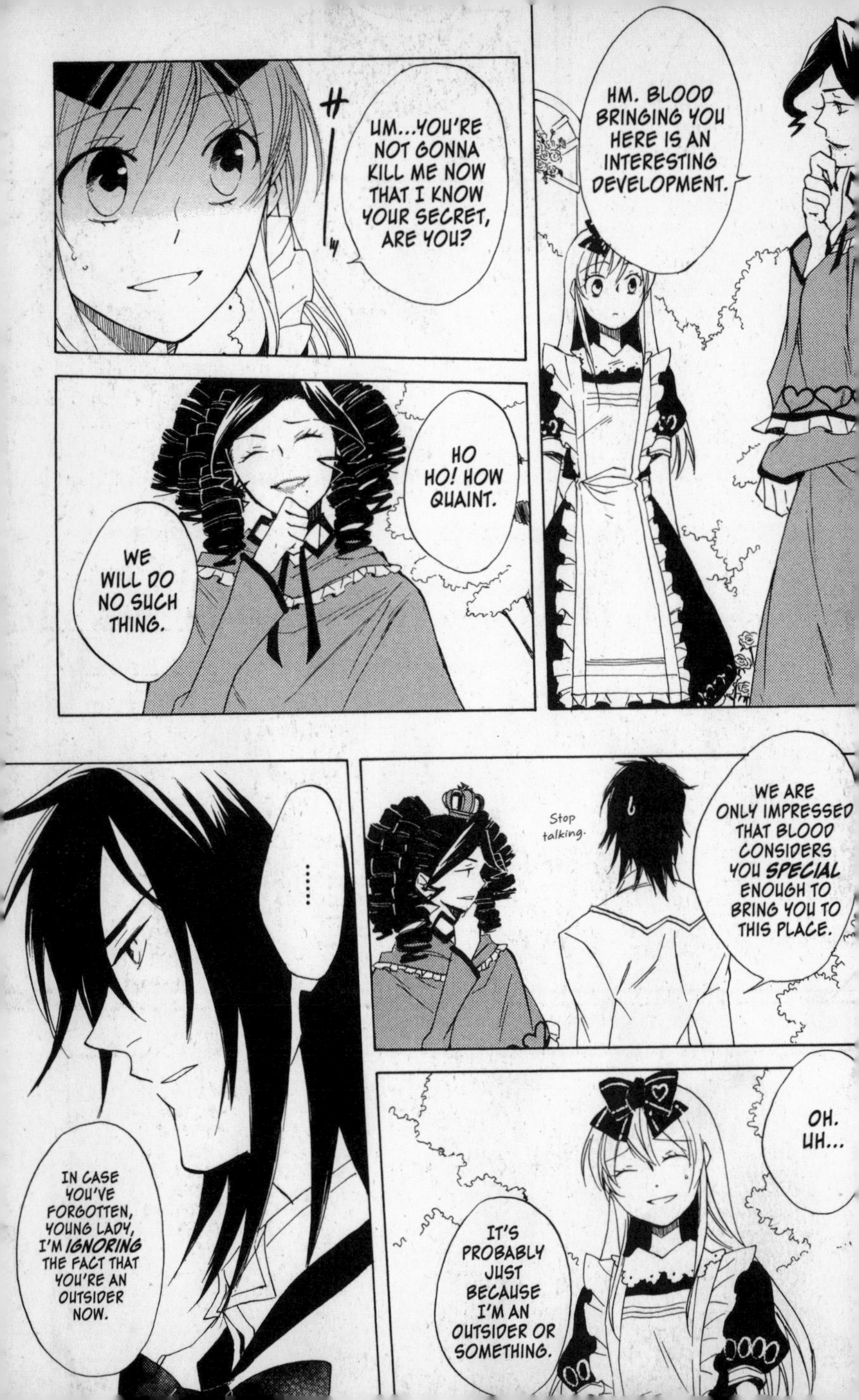
HM. BLOOD BRINGING YOU HERE IS AN INTERESTING DEVELOPMENT.
UM...YOU'RE NOT GONNA KILL ME NOW THAT I KNOW YOUR SECRET, ARE YOU?
HO HO! HOW QUAINT.
WE WILL DO NO SUCH THING.
WE ARE ONLY IMPRESSED THAT BLOOD CONSIDERS YOU *SPECIAL* ENOUGH TO BRING YOU TO THIS PLACE.
Stop talking.
OH. UH...
IT'S PROBABLY JUST BECAUSE I'M AN OUTSIDER OR SOMETHING.
......
IN CASE YOU'VE FORGOTTEN, YOUNG LADY, I'M *IGNORING* THE FACT THAT YOU'RE AN OUTSIDER NOW.

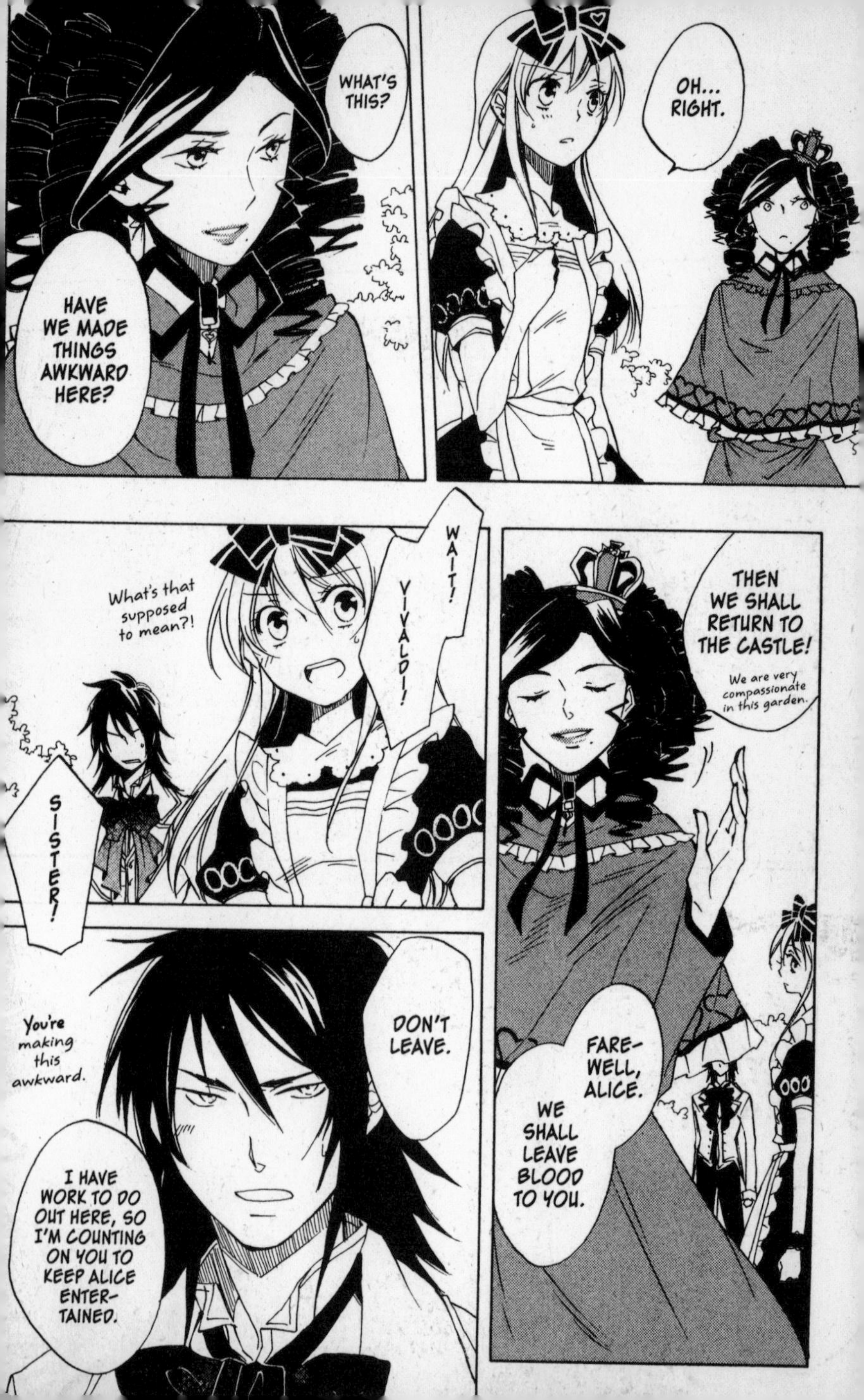
OH... RIGHT.
WHAT'S THIS?
HAVE WE MADE THINGS AWKWARD HERE?
THEN WE SHALL RETURN TO THE CASTLE!
We are very compassionate in this garden.
FARE-WELL, ALICE.
WE SHALL LEAVE BLOOD TO YOU.
WAIT! VIVALDI!
What's that supposed to mean?!
SISTER!
DON'T LEAVE.
You're making this awkward.
I HAVE WORK TO DO OUT HERE, SO I'M COUNTING ON YOU TO KEEP ALICE ENTER-TAINED.

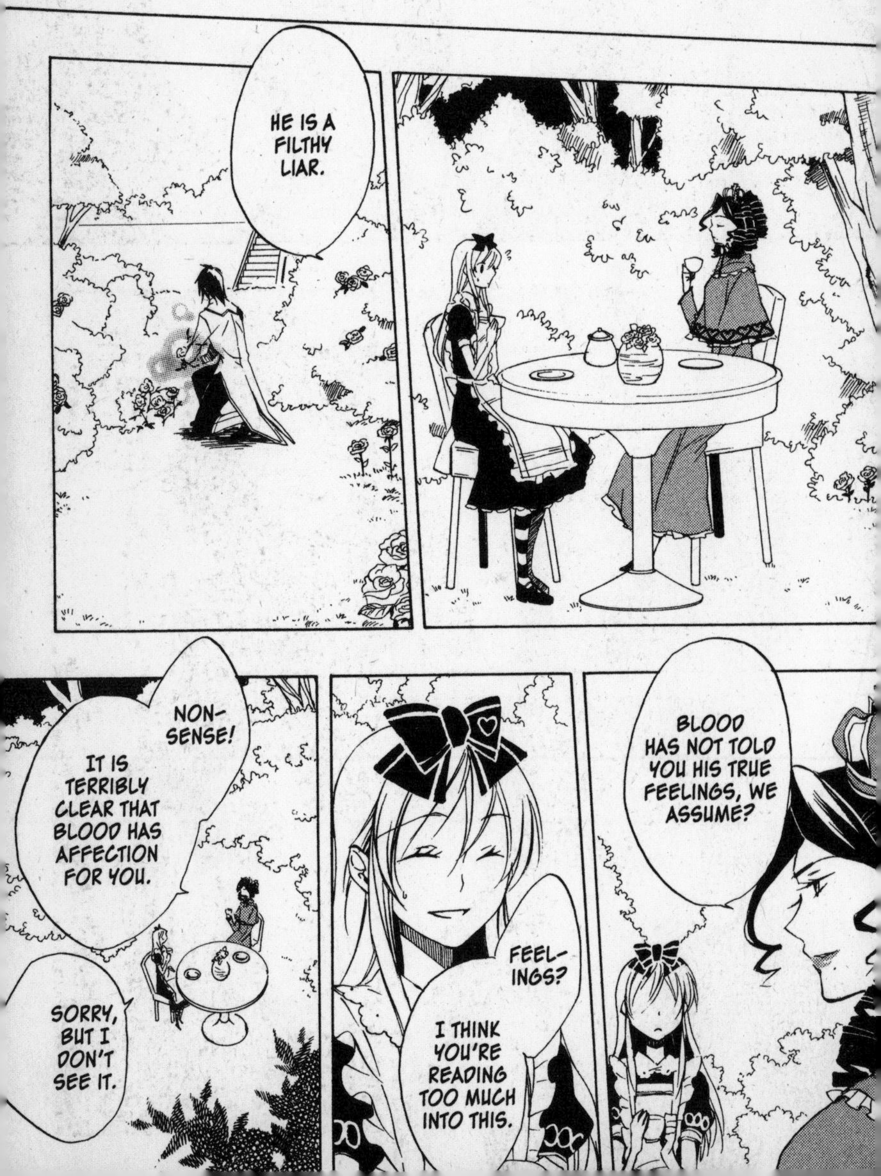
HE IS A FILTHY LIAR.
BLOOD HAS NOT TOLD YOU HIS TRUE FEELINGS, WE ASSUME?
FEEL-INGS?
I THINK YOU'RE READING TOO MUCH INTO THIS.
NON-SENSE! IT IS TERRIBLY CLEAR THAT BLOOD HAS AFFECTION FOR YOU.
SORRY, BUT I DON'T SEE IT.

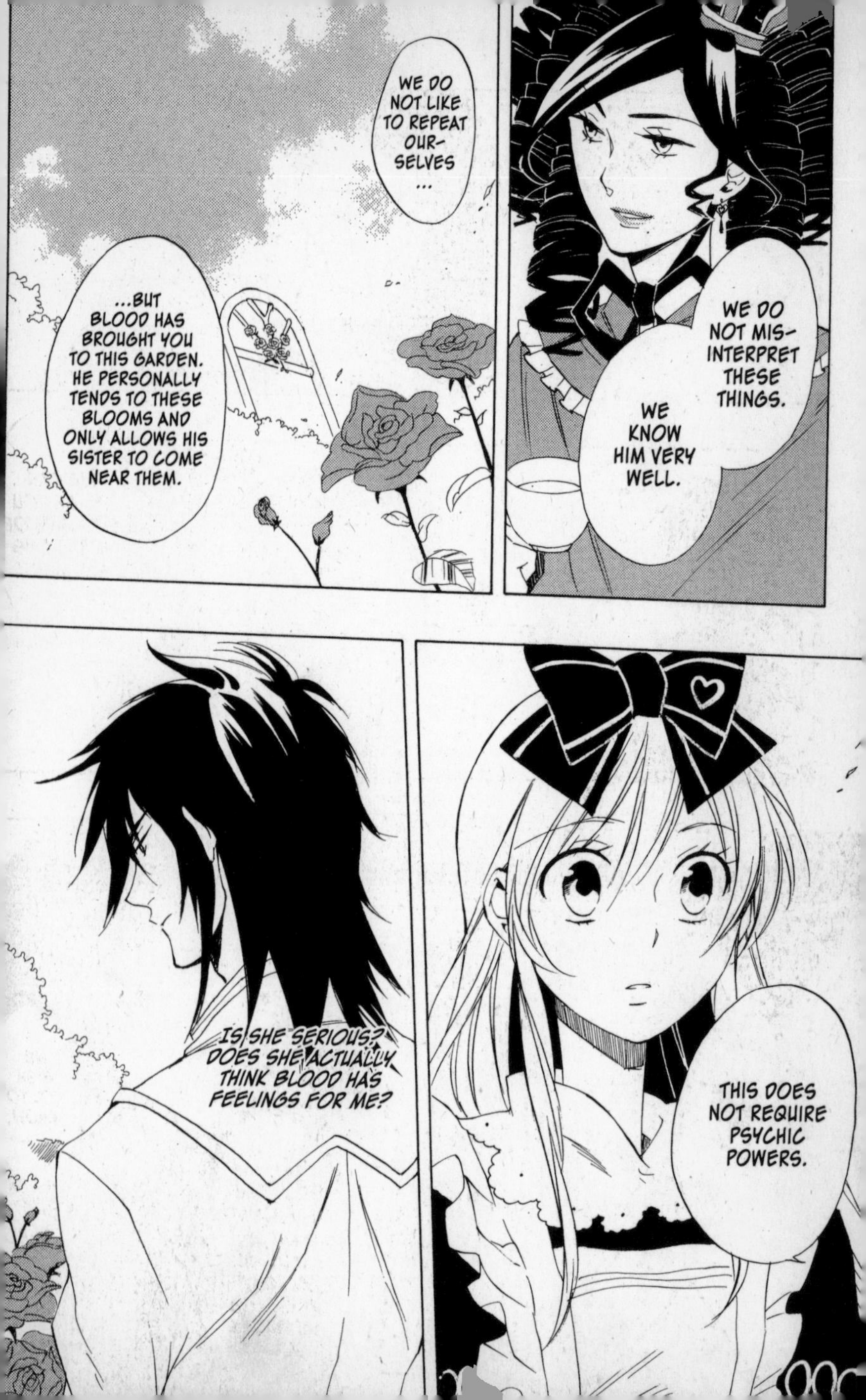
WE DO NOT MIS-INTERPRET THESE THINGS.
WE KNOW HIM VERY WELL.
WE DO NOT LIKE TO REPEAT OUR-SELVES ...
...BUT BLOOD HAS BROUGHT YOU TO THIS GARDEN. HE PERSONALLY TENDS TO THESE BLOOMS AND ONLY ALLOWS HIS SISTER TO COME NEAR THEM.
THIS DOES NOT REQUIRE PSYCHIC POWERS.
IS SHE SERIOUS? DOES SHE ACTUALLY THINK BLOOD HAS FEELINGS FOR ME?

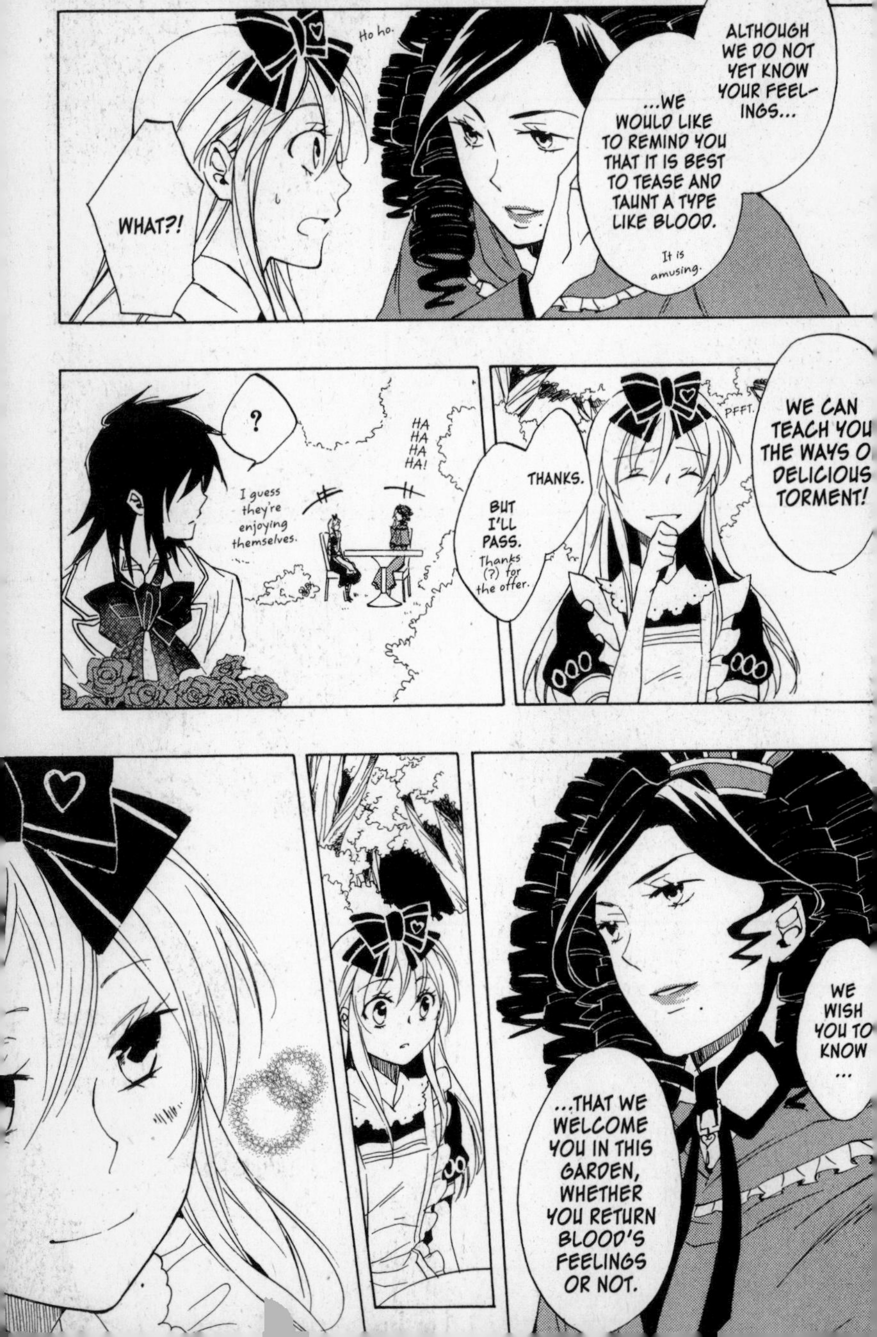
ALTHOUGH WE DO NOT YET KNOW YOUR FEEL- INGS...
...WE WOULD LIKE TO REMIND YOU THAT IT IS BEST TO TEASE AND TAUNT A TYPE LIKE BLOOD.
It is amusing.
Ho ho.
WHAT?!
WE CAN TEACH YOU THE WAYS O DELICIOUS TORMENT!
PFFT.
THANKS.
BUT I'LL PASS.
Thanks (?) for the offer.
HA HA HA HA!
?
I guess they're enjoying themselves.
WE WISH YOU TO KNOW ...
...THAT WE WELCOME YOU IN THIS GARDEN, WHETHER YOU RETURN BLOOD'S FEELINGS OR NOT.

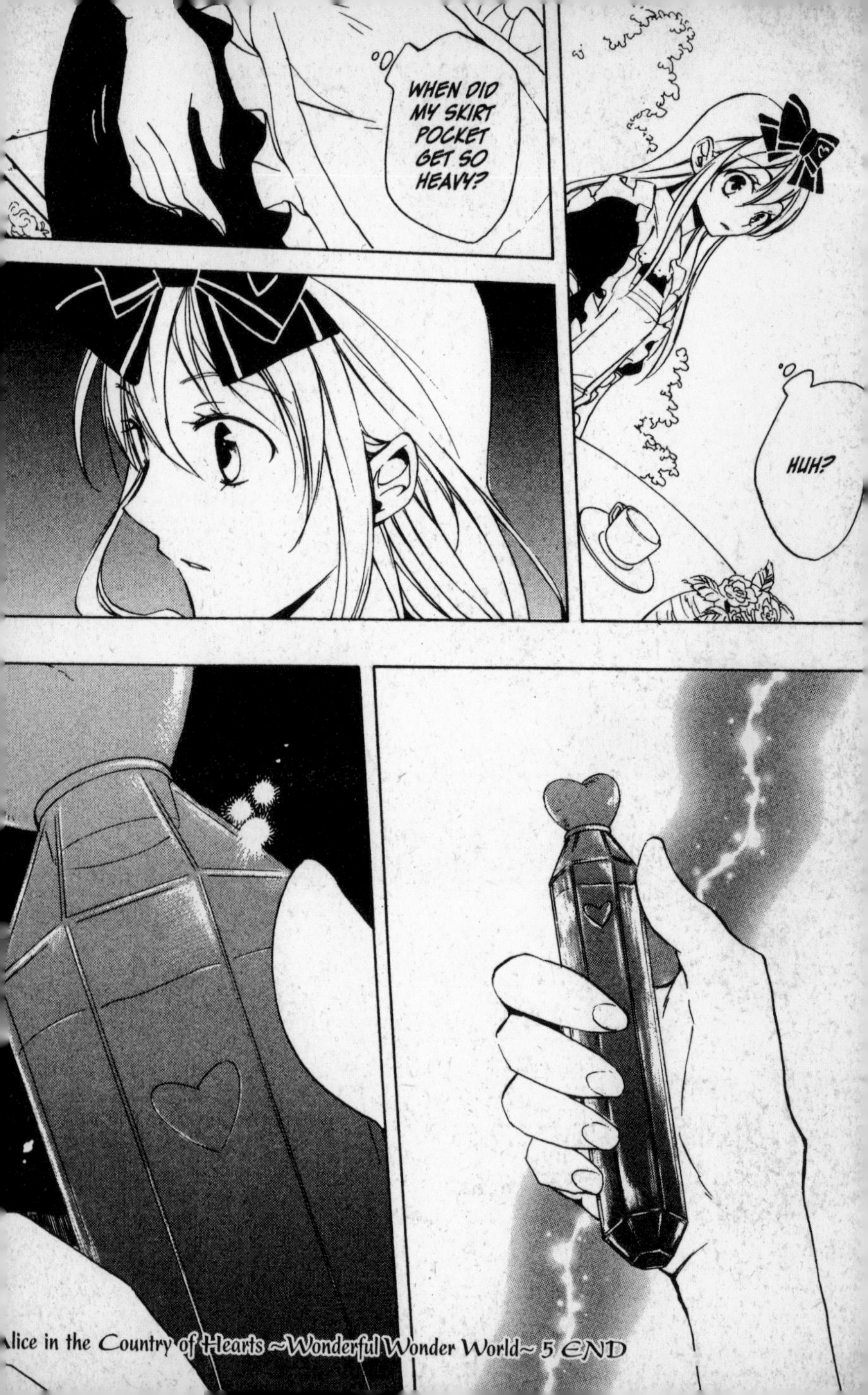
HUH?
WHEN DID MY SKIRT POCKET GET SO HEAVY?
Alice in the Country of Hearts ~Wonderful Wonder World~ 5 END

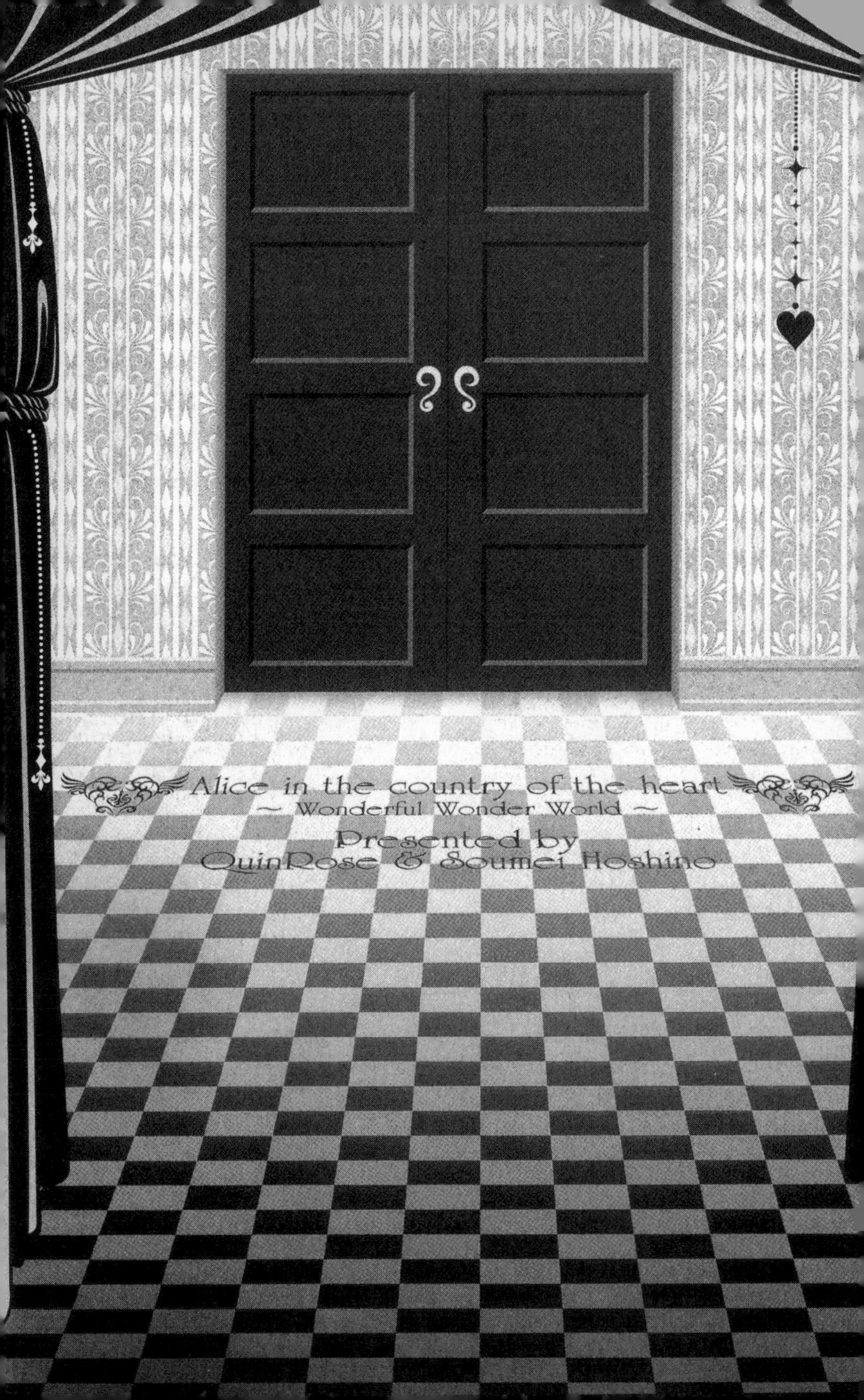
Alice in the country of the heart
~ Wonderful Wonder World ~
Presented by
QuinRose & Soumei Hoshino

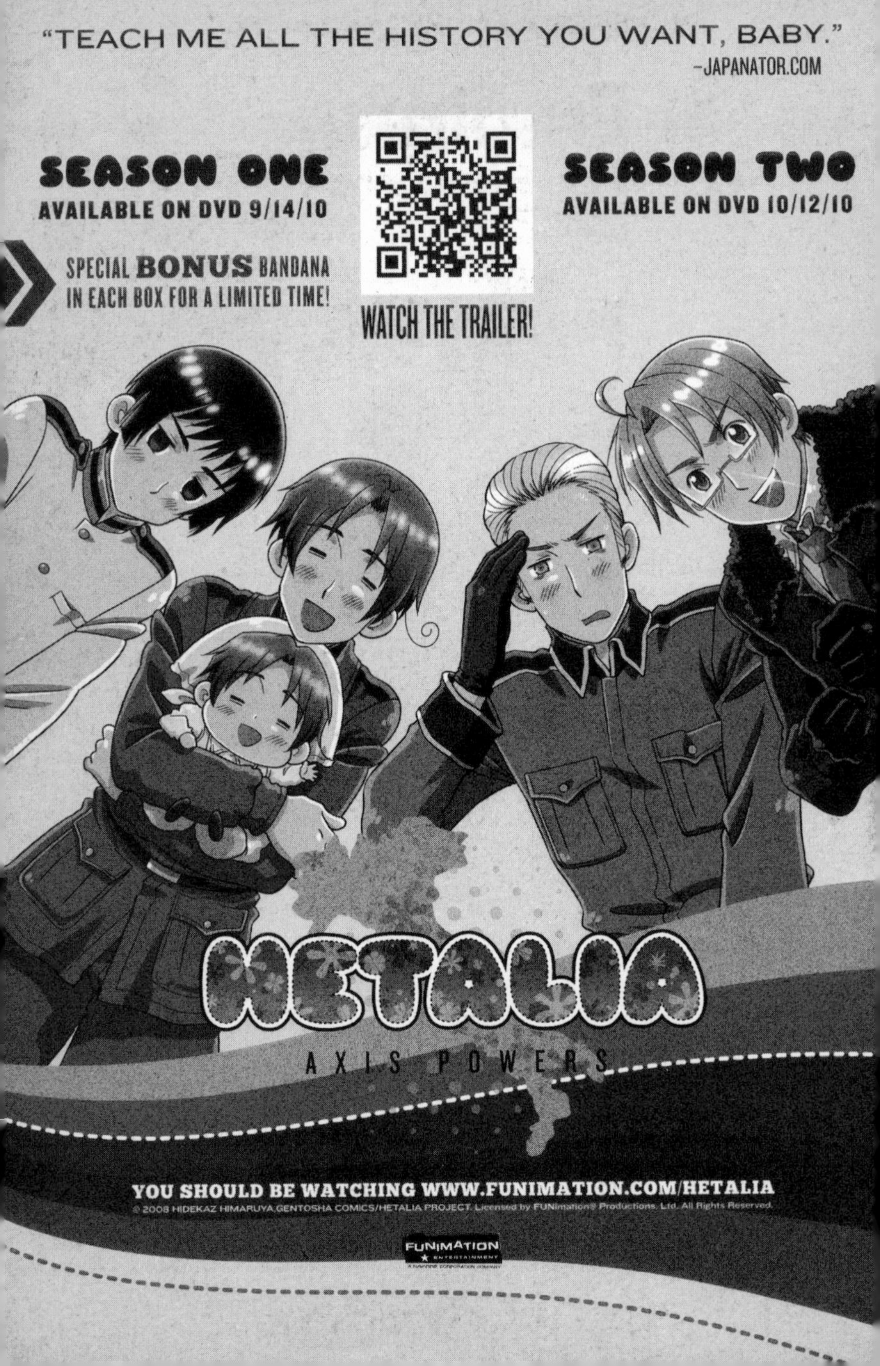
"TEACH ME ALL THE HISTORY YOU WANT, BABY."
–JAPANATOR.COM
SEASON ONE
AVAILABLE ON DVD 9/14/10
SPECIAL BONUS BANDANA IN EACH BOX FOR A LIMITED TIME!
WATCH THE TRAILER!
SEASON TWO
AVAILABLE ON DVD 10/12/10
HETALIA
AXIS POWERS
YOU SHOULD BE WATCHING WWW.FUNIMATION.COM/HETALIA
© 2008 HIDEKAZ HIMARUYA,GENTOSHA COMICS/HETALIA PROJECT. Licensed by FUNimation® Productions, Ltd. All Rights Reserved.
FUNIMATION ENTERTAINMENT

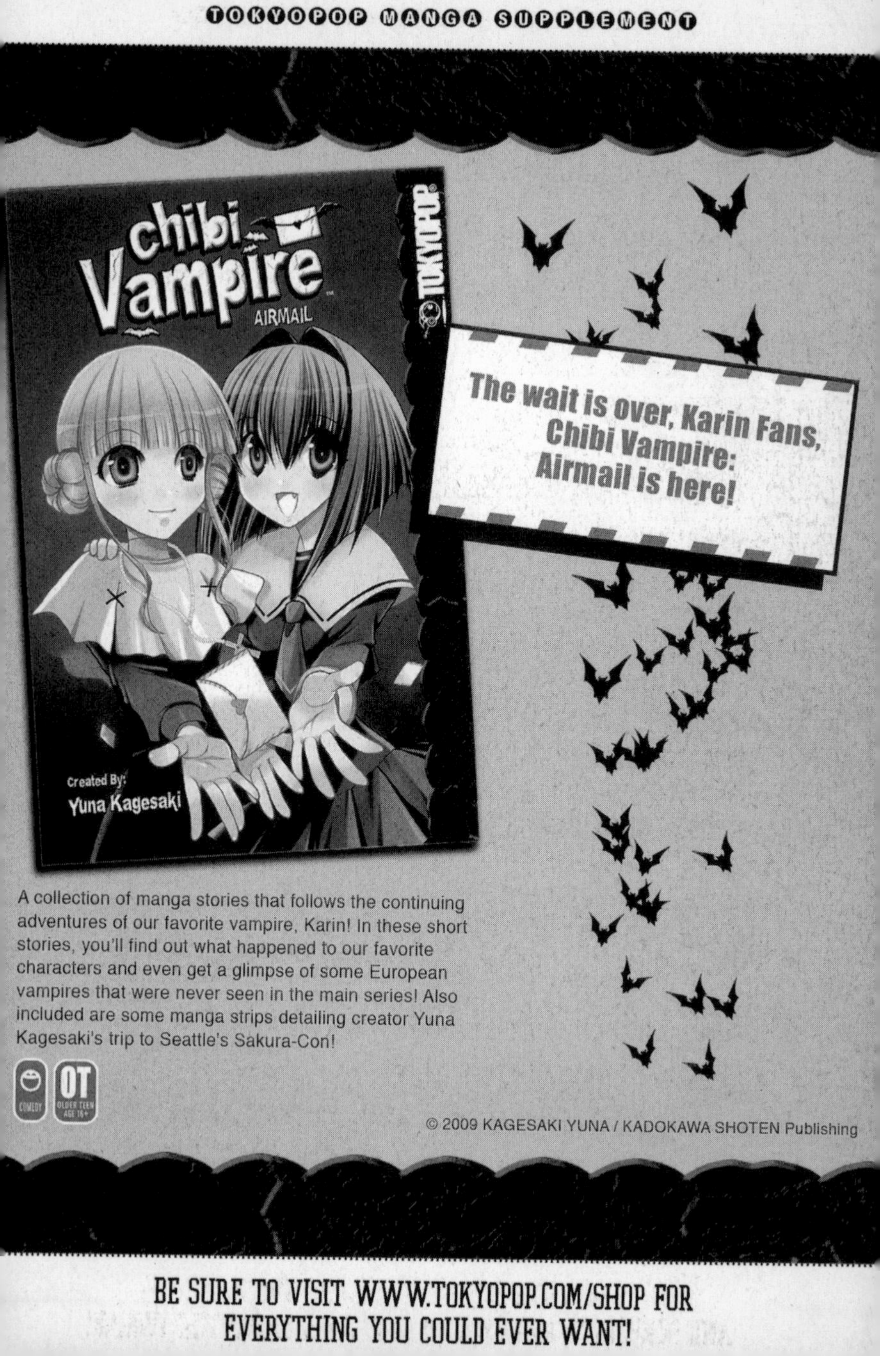
chibi Vampire
AIRMAIL
TOKYOPOP
Created By:
Yuna Kagesaki

The wait is over, Karin Fans, Chibi Vampire: Airmail is here!

A collection of manga stories that follows the continuing adventures of our favorite vampire, Karin! In these short stories, you'll find out what happened to our favorite characters and even get a glimpse of some European vampires that were never seen in the main series! Also included are some manga strips detailing creator Yuna Kagesaki's trip to Seattle's Sakura-Con!

COMEDY OT OLDER TEEN AGE 16+

BE SURE TO VISIT WWW.TOKYOPOP.COM/SHOP FOR EVERYTHING YOU COULD EVER WANT!

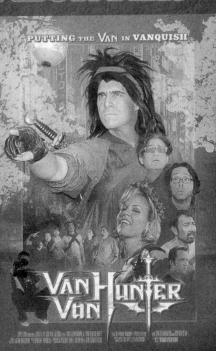

The second epic trilogy continues!

Ai fights to escape the clutches of her mysterious and malevolent captors, not knowing whether Kent, left behind on the Other Side, is even still alive. A frantic rescue mission commences, and in the end, even Ai's magical voice may not be enough to protect her from the trials of the Black Forest.

Dark secrets are revealed, and Ai must use all her strength and courage to face off against the new threat to Ai-Land. But will she ever see Kent again...?

"A very intriguing read that will satisfy old fans and create new fans, too."
– Bookloons

Maid Sama!

The class president has a little secret she's keeping from the sexy bad boy in school...

"It's hard to deny this guilty pleasure when it looks like it's having so much fun."
—About.com

The rogue hypnotist strikes again, this time planting the suggestion in Misaki that if she falls asleep, she'll wake up hating Usui! Well, hating him more than usual... So it's up to Usui to preserve their relationship (such as it is) by keeping Misaki awake as long as possible!

© 2005 Hiro Fujiwara / HAKUSENSHA, INC

JAN 03

STOP!

This is the back of the book.
You wouldn't want to spoil a great ending!

This book is printed "manga-style," in the authentic Japanese right-to-left format. Since none of the artwork has been flipped or altered, readers get to experience the story just as the creator intended. You've been asking for it, so TOKYOPOP® delivered: authentic, hot-off-the-press, and far more fun!

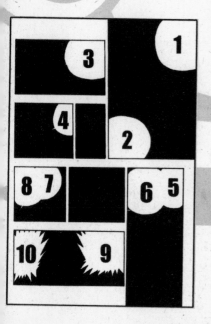

DIRECTIONS

If this is your first time reading manga-style, here's a quick guide to help you understand how it works.

It's easy... just start in the top right panel and follow the numbers. Have fun, and look for more 100% authentic manga from TOKYOPOP®!